Estimating and F
ARCH Models Using

G@RCH™ 6

Estimating and Forecasting ARCH Models Using

G@RCH™ 6

Sébastien Laurent

Published by Timberlake Consultants Ltd
www.timberlake.co.uk
www.timberlake-consultancy.com
www.oxmetrics.net

Estimating and Forecasting ARCH Models Using G@RCH™ 6
Copyright © 2009 Sébastien Laurent
First published by Timberlake Consultants in 2001.
Revised in 2006, 2009

British Library Cataloguing-in-Publication Data
A catalogue record of this book is available from the British Library

Library of Congress Cataloguing-in-Publication Data
A catalogue record of this book is available from the Library of Congress
Sébastien Laurent.
p. cm. – (Estimating and Forecasting ARCH Models Using G@RCH™6)

ISBN 978-0-9557076-0-5

Published by
Timberlake Consultants Ltd
Unit B3, Broomsleigh Business Park
London SE26 5BN, UK
http://www.timberlake.co.uk

842 Greenwich Lane,
Union, NJ 07083-7905, U.S.A.
http://www.timberlake-consultancy.com

Contents

Preface

A lot of energy is devoted to developing econometric models that are as accurate as possible. Researchers and practitioners are working hard to improve their predictions and reduce the uncertainty surrounding their analysis. That was one of the reason why the G@RCH project started at the end of 1999.

Besides one thing that makes our life worth living is its unpredictability. Isn't it ironic? And G@RCH is no exception.

Originally G@RCH was by no means intended to become a publicly released program: the initial objective of the project was to write some piece of code with a promising and well-suited language called Ox. The expected use of the program was limited to a couple of empirical studies. At that time none of us could have predicted that about five years later G@RCH would be sufficiently developed to write a manual!

The first publicly available version of G@RCH was released online in September 2000. This little piece of code was in fact more of a testimony of our research activities to our colleagues than something to be shared with the academic community. The real "kick-off" came with Version 2 in April 2001. Quite unexpectedly the package was heavily downloaded from various parts of the world. Even more gratifying was the positive feedback received from G@RCH users. All this gave us a strong motivation to improve the program. A year later, Version 3 was released while we were both at an important crossing road in our professional lives: Sébastien just graduated from his Ph.D. program at University Maastricht while Jean-Philippe left his research position at University of Liège after two enriching years to take a position at a consulting company.

Version 3 should have been the last one. But the idea of developing a stand-alone version of G@RCH emerged from discussions with Timberlake Consultants. Both of us felt still very excited about the G@RCH project and thus decided that we were far from being done with it and six years after its inception, G@RCH 4 was part of the OxMetrics modules family and has been integrated in OxMetrics Enterprise 4.

G@RCH 5.1 was an important upgrade. First it has been integrated in OxMetrics Enterprise. Among other things, G@RCH 5.1 allowed the estimation of some of the most widespread multivariate GARCH models. Furthermore, the slowest parts of the code have been translated in C which means that the estimation of EGARCH-type models and ARCH-in-mean model has been considerably improved. Two additional new features of G@RCH since version 5.1 are that Ox code can be generated after the estimation of a model via the rolling menus and that G@RCH is now available for Mac

OSX and Linux.

G@RCH 5.5 is the latest version. Special attention has been devoted to the creation of a new module, called RE@LIZED, dedicated to the implementation of univariate and multivariate non-parametric estimators of the quadratic variation and integrated volatility. Furthermore, daily and intradaily tests for jumps and (robust to jumps) intraday periodicity filters have also been included.

Feedback from G@RCH users have been for us a tremendous source of motivation throughout the years. It helped us increase the robustness and the accuracy of the program and enlarge the range of its features. Of course there are still a lot of possible improvements: suggestions, comments and/or remarks are thus more than welcome (to Sebastien.Laurent@fundp.ac.be).

Over the years a lot of people have contributed in some way to the development of our package. Special thanks should go to Luc Bauwens (CORE, Université Catholique de Louvain), Charles Bos (Vrije Universiteit Amsterdam), Kris Boudt (Lessius University College, Belgium), Jurgen Doornik (Nuffield College, University of Oxford), Valrie Goffin (FUNDP, Namur), Jose Fiuza (Timberlake Consultants), Pierre Giot (FUNDP and CORE), Jérome Lahaye (FUNDP, Namur), Michael McAleer (University of Western Australia), Les Oxley (University of Canterbury), Jeroen Rombouts (HEC Montreal), Ana Timberlake (Timberlake Consultants), Jean-Pierre Urbain (Maastricht University), Francesco Violante (FUNDP, Namur), Robert Yaffee (NYU) and Roy van der Weide (Poverty Research Group, The World Bank, Washington DC).

Coming back to "predictability", it is quite common to find a "last but not least" section in prefaces. This book makes no exception. I take this opportunity to dedicate this work to my family (Christelle, Mathis and Valentin) and to gratefully thank them for their support, encouragement, patience and love.

Sébastien LAURENT, *April 2009*.

I WISH YOU A PRODUCTIVE USE OF G@RCH !

Authors and Contributors

About the Author

Dr. Sébastien Laurent, the copyright owner of G@RCH, holds a Ph.D. (2002) in Financial Econometrics from University Maastricht (Netherlands). In 2002-2003 he worked as post-doc researcher at the CREST (Laboratory of Finance-Insurance) in Paris (France). He is currently associate professor in Econometrics and research director of the Economics Department at the Université Notre-Dame de la Paix in Namur (Belgium) and fellow of the CORE in Louvain-la-Neuve (Belgium). In 2008 and 2009 he has been invited professor at the London School of Economics (Finance Department). Sébastien has published in *Journal of Business and Economic Statistics, Journal of Applied Econometrics, Journal of Financial Econometrics, European Economic Review* and *Journal of Empirical Finance* among others.
Web Site: http://www.core.ucl.ac.be/~laurent/
Email: Sebastien.Laurent@fundp.ac.be

Contributors

Dr. Kris Boudt holds a Ph.D. (2008) in Applied Economics at K.U.Leuven, Belgium. He is afliated researcher at K.U.Leuven and since 2008 assistant professor of Finance at Lessius University College. His main research interests are empirical nance, risk management and robust statistics. His research has been published in the Journal of Risk and RISK magazine, among others.
Web Site: http://www.econ.kuleuven.be/public/N06054/
Email: Kris.Boudt@econ.kuleuven.be

Jerome Lahaye graduated from the HEC Management School of the University of Liège (Belgium) where he subsequently worked as teaching and research assistant (2000-2003). He holds a master of advanced studies in economics from the University of Leuven (2004) and is Ph.D. candidate of the Louvain Academy, at the University of Namur (2005 - expected 2009). His research interests are at the crossroads of applied econometrics and international finance. In particular, his research has focused on the link between economic information disclosure and discontinuities on financial time

series. In 2007, he was visiting scholar at the Saint-Louis Federal Reserve Bank.
Email: jerome.lahaye@fundp.ac.be

Jean-Philippe Peters has been involved in the G@RCH project until version 4.2. He
graduated from the HEC Management School of the University of Liège (Belgium) in
2000 with a M.Sc. in Management Sciences. His final dissertation, entitled "Development of a Package in the Ox Environment for GARCH Models and Two Empirical
Applications" was the founding ground of the current package. From 2000 to 2002, he
has worked as researcher in the Operations Research and Production Management unit
of the University of Liège. In October 2002 he joined the Advisory and Consulting
department of Deloitte Luxembourg where he is involved in consulting activities on risk
management for the financial industry. In parallel, he has started pursuing a Ph.D. in
September 2005 at the HEC Management School of the University of Liege (Belgium).

Dr. Jeroen VK Rombouts holds a Ph.D. (2004) in Econometrics from the Catholic
University of Louvain and is since 2004 assistant professor HEC Montreal. He
is elected member of the International Statistical Institute, reseacher at CIRANO
(Canada) and research associate at CORE (Belgium). Jeroen has published in *Econo-
metric Theory, Journal of Applied Econometrics, Econometric Reviews* and *The
Econometrics Journal* among others.
Web Site: http://neumann.hec.ca/pages/jeroen.rombouts/
Email: Jeroen.Rombouts@hec.ca

Francesco Violante graduated from the Bocconi University, Milan (Italy) where he
worked as teaching and research assistant in 2004 at Centre of Research on Innovation
and Internationalization (CESPRI). He holds a master of arts in economics from the
Universitè Catholique de Louvain (Belgium) and is currently Ph.D. candidate of the
Louvain Academy, at the University of Namur (2006). His research interests are
focused on applied econometrics and finance and in particular realized volatility and
forecast, multivariate GARCH models, volatility models comparison and selection. In
2007, he was visiting scholar at the HEC Management School of the University of
Montreal (Canada).
Email: francesco.violante@fundp.ac.be

Chapter 1

Introduction

This book documents G@RCH 6.0, an OxMetrics module (see Doornik, 2009) dedicated to the estimation and forecasting of univariate and multivariate ARCH-type models (Engle, 1982), including some of the most recent contributions in this field. Univariate GARCH (Bollerslev, 1986), EGARCH (Nelson, 1991), GJR (Glosten, Jagannathan, and Runkle, 1993), APARCH (Ding, Granger, and Engle, 1993), IGARCH (Engle and Bollerslev, 1986), RiskMetrics (J.P.Morgan, 1996), FIGARCH (Baillie, Bollerslev, and Mikkelsen, 1996a and Chung, 1999), FIEGARCH (Bollerslev and Mikkelsen, 1996), FIAPARCH (Tse, 1998) and HYGARCH (Davidson, 2001) specifications are available for the conditional variance. Moreover an AR(FI)MA process can be specified in the conditional mean (see Baillie, Chung, and Tieslau, 1996b, Tschernig, 1995, Teyssière, 1997, or Lecourt, 2000, for further details about ARFIMA models). All these models can be adapted to add an "ARCH-in-mean" term in the conditional mean as suggested by Engle, Lilien, and Robbins (1987).

G@RCH 6.0 allows the estimation of some of the most widespread multivariate GARCH models, including the scalar BEKK, diagonal BEKK(Engle and Kroner, 1995), RiskMetrics (J.P.Morgan, 1996), CCC (Bollerslev, 1990), DCC (Engle, 2002 and Tse and Tsui, 2002), DECO (Engle and Kelly, 2007), OGARCH (Kariya, 1988 and Alexander and Chibumba, 1997) and GOGARCH models (van der Weide, 2002 and Boswijk and van der Weide, 2006).

G@RCH 6.0 also allows the estimation of univariate and multivariate non-parametric estimators of the quadratic variation and the integrated volatility. These estimators include the realized volatility, bi-power-variation and realized outlyingness weighted variance. Several tests for daily and intradaily tests for jumps and intraday periodicity filters are also provided.

This software has been developed with Ox 6.0, a matrix programming language described in Doornik (2007b).[1] G@RCH 6.0 should be compatible with a lot of platforms, including Windows, Mac OsX, Linux, Unix and Solaris when it is used in combination with the Ox Console. Furthermore, G@RCH 6.0 provides a menu-driven graphical interface for Microsoft Windows, Mac OsX and Linux users as well as a comprehensive

---

[1] For a review of this language, see Cribari-Neto and Zarkos (2003).

HTML documentation. For most of the specifications, it is generally very fast and one of its main characteristic is its ease of use.

This book is structured as follows:

- This chapter introduces the G@RCH software.
- Chapter 2 explains how to get started with G@RCH.
- Chapter 3 presents the simple univariate ARCH model. Comments over estimation procedures (parameters constraints, distributions, standard deviation estimation methods, tests, forecasting procedures and accuracy of the package) are also reviewed.
- Chapter 4 presents more sophisticated ARCH-type models as well as more advanced estimation techniques.
- Then, Chapter 5 explains how to estimate these models using both the Batch editor of OxMetrics and the Ox programming language. Several illustrations are also provided.
- After a brief summary of the concept of Value-at-Risk (VaR), Chapter 6 shows how the package can be used to forecast the VaR and to test the adequacy of the selected models.
- Chapter 7 (written in collaboration with Kris Boudt and Jerome Lahaye) presents the concepts of realized volatility, some of its (robust to jumps) univariate and multivariate extensions and (robust to jumps) intraday periodicity filters.
- Chapter 8 explains how to use G@RCH (and in particular RE@LIZED) to apply the concepts presented in the previous chapter.
- Chapter 9 reviews the multivariate GARCH models available in G@RCH and gives several illustrations on how to estimate these models with the rolling menus, Batch language and finally the Ox language combined with the MGarch class.
- Finally, the structure and the functions of the Garch, MGarch and Realized classes are detailed in Chapter 10.

1.1 G@RCH

1.1.1 Definition

G@RCH 6.0 is a software dedicated to the estimation and the forecasting of univariate and multivariate (G)ARCH models and many of its extensions. It can be used within OxMetrics or via the classic programming way (using OxEdit for instance) for those who have access to the Ox programming language.

The available univariate models are all ARCH-type models. These include ARCH, GARCH, EGARCH, GJR, APARCH, IGARCH, RiskMetrics, FIGARCH , FIEGARCH , FIAPARCH and HYGARCH. They can be estimated by approximate (Quasi-) Maximum Likelihood under one of the four proposed distributions for the errors (Normal, Student-t, GED or skewed-Student). Moreover, ARCH-in-mean models are also available and explanatory variables can enter the conditional mean and/or the conditional variance equations.

G@RCH 6.0 also propose the some multivariate GARCH specifications including the scalar BEKK, diagonal BEKK, full BEKK, RiskMetrics, CCC, DCC, DECO, OG-ARCH and GOGARCH models.

Finally, h-steps-ahead forecasts of both equations are available as well as many univariate and multivariate miss-specification tests (Nyblom, Sign Bias Tests, Pearson goodness-of-fit, Box-Pierce, Residual-Based Diagnostic for conditional heteroscedasticity, Hosking's portmanteau test, Li and McLead test, constant correlation test, . . .).

1.1.2 Program Versions

This documentation refers to version 6.0 of G@RCH, which can be used in three different ways. The first one is through the menu-driven environment of OxMetrics, similarly to PcGive, PcGets or STAMP.

Second, one can estimate the models via the "Batch Editor" of OxMetrics.

Finally, Ox users can write Ox codes based on the Garch, MGarch and Realized classes. This solution is found to be particularly interesting when non-standard operations are considered (like a whole catalogue of estimations). A set of examples is provided with the G@RCH package. Please note however that this solution requires a registered version of Ox Professional or its console version. Check the Ox web site (http://www.doornik.com) for details.

The first method is illustrated in Chapters 3 and 4 while the next two are presented in Chapter 5.

1.1.3 What's new in G@RCH 6.0 ?

- Bug fixed: G@RCH experienced convergence problems when returns were not expressed in %. This is now fixed.
- G@RCH proposes a new module called RE@LIZED whose aim is to provide a full set of procedures to compute non-parametric estimates of the quadratic variation, integrated volatility and jumps using intraday data. The methods implemented in G@RCH 6.0 are based on the recent papers of Andersen, Bollerslev, Diebold and coauthors, Barndorff-Nielsen and Shephard and Boudt, Croux and Laurent. They include univariate and multivariate versions of the realized volatility, bi-power-variation and realized outlyingness weighted variance. Daily and intradaily tests for jumps are also implemented. The 'Realized' class allows to apply these estimators and tests on real data using the Ox programming language. Importantly, they are also accessible through the rolling menus of G@RCH. Interestingly, like for the other modules, an Ox code can be generated after the use of the rolling menus. The Model/Ox Batch Code command (or Alt+O) activates a new dialog box called 'Generate Ox Code' that allows the user to select an item

for which to generate Ox code. Here is an example of code generated after the
computation of Lee and Mykland (2008)'s test for intraday jumps detection.

```
#include <oxstd.h>
#import <packages/Garch5/garch>
#include <oxdraw.h>

main()
{
//--- Ox code for RE@LIZED
decl model = new Realized();

model.Load("C:\\Data\\Simulated_cont_GARCH_jumps_FFF_K_0.2_M_0.3.in7");
model.Deterministic(-1);

model.Select(Y_VAR, {"Ret_1", 0, 0});
...
model.Select(Y_VAR, {"Ret_288", 0, 0});

model.SetModelClass(MC_RV);
model.RV(1);
model.IV(1);
model.OPTIONS_JUMPS_TEST_BV(1,0,2,0.999);

model.SetSelSampleByDates(dayofcalendar(1987, 1, 5), dayofcalendar(1998, 7, 3));
model.Estimate();
model.Graphs_RV(0,0,1,0,0,0,0,1,1,0,0,10,0,0.999);
model.Append_in(model.m_vIV,"BV");
model.Append_in(model.m_vRJ,"RJ_BV");
model.Save("C:\\Data\\Simulated_cont_GARCH_jumps_FFF_K_0.2_M_0.3.in7");

delete model;
}
```

- Non-parametric and parametric (robust to jumps) intraday periodicity filters are
  also provided.

- The DCC-DECO model of Engle and Kelly (2008) is now documented in this
  manual.

- Conditional means, variances, covariances and correlations of MGARCH models
  can now be edited in a basic matrix or array editor.

- Bug fixed (thanks to Charles Bos). Several functions of the MGarch class had not
  been included in the oxo file, e.g. GetVarf_vec, Append_in, Append_out, etc.

- Bug fixed. DCC models: the empirical correlation matrix used when applying
  "Correlation Targeting" was computed on the residuals and not the devolatilized
  residuals as it should be.

1.1.4 What's new in G@RCH 5.1 ?

- The Mac OSX and Linux versions of G@RCH 6.0 are now available.

- Several tests have been added to the menu 'Descriptive Statistics', i.e. the Vari-
  ance Ratio test of Lo and MacKinlay (1988), the Runs test originally used by
  Fama (1965) and the Rescaled Range Tests of Mandelbrot (1972) and Lo (1991).
  These tests are described in Section 3.12. The size and power of these tests are

studied through some Monte Carlo experiments. The Ox codes used for these simulations is available in the folder `packages/Garch5/samples/`

- Bug fixed (thanks to Stefan De Wachter): Time-axis did not show the right time period when selecting a subsample. The time-axis started from the beginning of the dataset, regardless of what the selected estimation sample was.

- Problem fixed: annoying Internet Explorer 7 warning about running ActiveX controls when running the OxMetrics help.

- Thanks to Robert A. Yaffee, failure rates for short position in the output of the Kupiec LR test are now labelled success rates.

- Thanks to Christian Conrad, non-negativity conditions for FIGARCH and HYGARCH models are implemented in the following examples: `Stat_Constr_FIGARCH_Conrad_Haag_Check.ox` and `Stat_Constr_HYGARCH_Conrad_Check.ox` for a FIGARCH and HYGARCH $(1, d, 1)$ respectively. While the conditions are tested on the estimated parameters in the previous two example files, the conditions are imposed during the estimation in the next two, i.e. `Stat_Constr_FIGARCH_Conrad_Haag_Impose.ox` and `Stat_Constr_HYGARCH_Conrad_Impose.ox`.

- Bug fixed: Explanatory variables in the intraday seasonality FFF filter, i.e. procedure FFF_filter(), were not taken into account. The example file `FFF.ox` has been extended and can now be run using the simulated dataset `FX_USD_1990_1994.in7`. Furthermore, the normalizing constant N_2 in equation (7.37) has been changed. Indeed, the analytic solution for a sum of squares of integers $\sum_{k=1}^{M} k^2 = (2M^3 + 3M^2 + M)/6$ which leads the value $N_2 = (2M^2 + 3M + 1)/6$ and not $N_2 = (M + 1)(M + 2)/6$ as in Andersen and Bollerslev (1997) when computing the mean instead of the sum. Note that this change has only minor effects in practice on the results.

- The DECO (Dynamic EquiCOrrelation) model of Engle and Kelly (2007) has been added to MG@RCH (but is not yet documented).

- New function in MG@RCH: GetParEst(). The version without argument returns a $K \times 3$ matrix with respectively the estimated parameters, standard errors and t-statistics. The the example with one argument equal to 1, i.e. GetParEst(1) returns the names of the estimated parameters and the $K \times 3$ matrix explained above. An example is provided in the file `MGarchEstim_GetParEst.ox`. The relevant lines of code are

```
mgarchobj.DoEstimation();
```

```
decl names,out;
[names,out]=mgarchobj.GetParEst(1);
println("%r",names,"%c", {"MLE","Std-error","t-stat"},out);
delete mgarchobj;
```

This will produce the following output:

	MLE	Std-error	t-stat
Cst(M)	0.044056	0.018751	2.3495
AR(1)	0.026688	0.030135	0.88560
Cst(V)	0.0013516	0.0017330	0.77995
ARCH(Alpha1)	0.011494	0.0076399	1.5045
GARCH(Beta1)	0.98520	0.010640	92.590
Cst(M)	0.067069	0.025062	2.6761
AR(1)	0.23581	0.028032	8.4121
Cst(V)	0.069550	0.047670	1.4590
ARCH(Alpha1)	0.10320	0.043605	2.3667
GARCH(Beta1)	0.79178	0.10844	7.3015
rho_21	0.67544	0.091076	7.4162
alpha	0.011016	0.0055463	1.9862
beta	0.98470	0.011019	89.360

1.1.5 What's new in G@RCH 5.0 ?

This manual has been revised to account for the following new features:

- The estimation of EGARCH-type models and ARCH-in-mean model has been considerably improved.
- G@RCH now provides some simulation capabilities through the menu **Monte-Carlo**. GARCH, GJR, APARCH and EGARCH models are available with an ARMA in the conditional mean and normal, student, GED or skewed student errors. The simulated data can be plotted and stored in a separated dataset.
- Three unit root tests (ADF, KPSS and SP) and two long-memory tests (GPH and GSP) have been added (available through the 'descriptive statistics' menu).
- In- and out-of-sample VaR forecasts can be stored.
- Out-of-sample VaR forecasts can be plotted via the menu **Test/Forecast**.
- A new function is provided to compute the statistics of Lee and Mykland (2008) to detect jumps at ultra-high frequency.

- Several multivariate GARCH models are available including the scalar BEKK, diagonal BEKK, RiskMetrics, CCC, DCC, OGARCH and GOGARCH models.
- G@RCH also provides some specific multivariate miss-specification tests like a multivariate normality test, Hosking's portmanteau test, Li and McLead test, two constant correlation tests, etc.
- G@RCH also provides some functions to simulate BEKK, CCC and DCC models.
- A new feature of G@RCH 5.0 is that Ox code can be generated. The Model/Ox Batch Code command (or Alt+O) activates a new dialog box called 'Generate Ox Code' that allows the user to select an item for which to generate Ox code.

1.2 General Information

1.2.1 Queries about G@RCH

Suggestions, mistakes, typos and possible improvements can be reported to the first author via e-mail: Sebastien.Laurent@fundp.ac.be

The most appropriate way to discuss about problems and issues of the G@RCH package is the Ox-users discussion list. The ox-users discussion group is an email-based forum to discuss any problems related to Ox programming, and share code and programming solutions. Consult the online help of OxMetrics for information on joining the list.

1.2.2 Availability and Citation

The full independent version of G@RCH is exclusively distributed by Timberlake Consultants.

Contact information for the UK:

Phone: +44 (0)20 8697 3377 or

Internet: http://www.timberlake.co.uk

For the US:

Phone: +1 908 686 1251 or

Internet: http://www.timberlake-consultancy.com

For other countries, please go to the Timberlake web sites for contact information.

There are different versions of G@RCH. A console version of G@RCH is available on G@RCH web site http://www.garch.org.

This (and only this) version of G@RCH may be used freely for academic research and teaching purposes <u>only</u>. The Professional version (i.e. using OxRun, OxDebug, OxMetrics or oxli) is not free.

Commercial users and others who do not qualify for the free version must purchase the Professional version of G@RCH with documentation, regardless of which version they use (i.e., even with Linux or Unix). Redistribution of G@RCH in any form is not permitted.

Moreover, for easier validation and replication of empirical findings, please cite this documentation (or Laurent and Peters, 2002) in all reports and publications involving the use of G@RCH. Failure to cite the use of Ox in published work may result in loss of the right to use the free version, and an invoice at the full commercial price.

All company and product names referred to in this documentation are either trademarks or registered trademarks of their associated companies.

1.2.3 World Wide Web

Check `www.garch.org` for information on releases, online help and other relevant information on G@RCH.

1.3 Installing and Running G@RCH 6.0

To install the Professional version of G@RCH 6.0, run the installation file and follow the instructions.

To install the Console version of G@RCH, unzip the file available on our web page http://www.garch.org in the `ox/packages` directory (using folders names).

For OxMetrics enterprise users, not that the Console version of G@RCH 6.0 comes along with OxMetrics enterprise and is directly installed in the `ox/packages` directory.

THIS PACKAGE IS FUNCTIONAL BUT NO WARRANTY IS GIVEN
WHATSOEVER. YOU USE IT AT YOUR OWN RISK!

Chapter 2

Getting Started

We now discuss some of the basic skills required to get started with G@RCH. We will give a brief introduction to the functionalities provided by OxMetrics. The aim of this section is to explain how to load data and make graphs: for instructions on how to transform data using the calculator or algebra, consult the OxMetrics manuals.

We assume that you have the basic skills to operate programs under the Windows operating system (the OxMetrics books provides some hints). G@RCH runs on several versions of Windows, i.e. Windows Vista/XP/NT/2000 but also on Mac OsX and Linux.[1] The screen appearance of the program and dialogs will reflect the operating system you are using. The screen captures of this manual reflect the Windows XP operating system but should not be very different from the other systems.

2.1 Starting G@RCH

When launching OxMetrics, all the available modules (PcGive, G@RCH and Stamp) are automatically loaded and appear in the Modules group in the workspace window on the left-hand side of OxMetrics. This process is displayed in the following capture.

2.2 Loading and Viewing the Tutorial Data Set

G@RCH cannot operate without data. Once OxMetrics is activated, the very first step is to load data. Let us illustrate this with an example, loading `nasdaq.in7`. These are daily returns of the Nasdaq stock index. The covered period is 10/11/1984 - 12/21/2000, which represents 4093 daily observations. Daily returns (in %) are defined as

$$y_t = 100\left[log(p_t) - log(p_{t-1})\right], \qquad (2.1)$$

where p_t is the price series at time t.

---

[1] Note that Ox Console 4 still works on older versions of Windows.

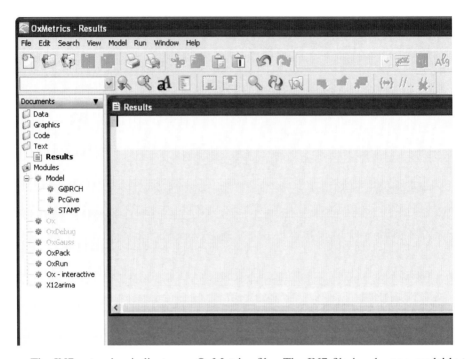

The IN7 extension indicates an OxMetrics file. The IN7 file is a human-readable file, describing the data. There is a companion BN7 file, which holds the actual numbers (in binary format, so this file cannot be edited). OxMetrics can handle a wide range of data files, among them Excel and Lotus files and, of course, plain human-readable (ASCII) files. You can also cut and paste data between Excel and OxMetrics. More details are available in OxMetrics handbooks.

To load this dataset, click File then Open in the main menu of OxMetrics, then select the data file. The default datasets provided by G@RCH are stored in the subdirectory \G@RCH\data of OxMetrics's main directory. Locate that directory and select nasdaq.in7.

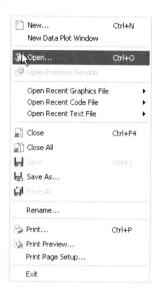

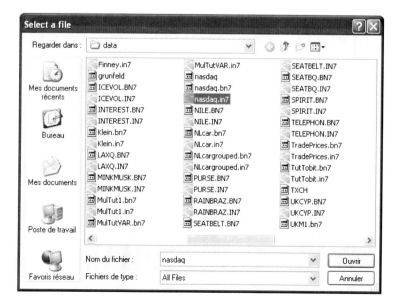

nasdaq.in7 - C:\OxMetrics5\data\nasdaq.in7

	Date	Nasdaq
1984-10-12	1984-10-12	.611124
1984-10-15	1984-10-15	.607412
1984-10-16	1984-10-16	-.161616
1984-10-17	1984-10-17	-.0809062
1984-10-18	1984-10-18	1.08675
1984-10-19	1984-10-19	.558884
1984-10-22	1984-10-22	-.239139
1984-10-23	1984-10-23	0
1984-10-24	1984-10-24	.0797766
1984-10-25	1984-10-25	-.720291
1984-10-26	1984-10-26	-.644644
1984-10-29	1984-10-29	-.364447
1984-10-30	1984-10-30	.404859
1984-10-31	1984-10-31	-.202225
1984-11-01	1984-11-01	.404041
1984-11-02	1984-11-02	0
1984-11-05	1984-11-05	.16116
1984-11-06	1984-11-06	.841857
1984-11-07	1984-11-07	-.279832
1984-11-08	1984-11-08	-.120168
1984-11-09	1984-11-09	0
1984-11-12	1984-11-12	-.0801925
1984-11-13	1984-11-13	-.603502
1984-11-14	1984-11-14	-.323363
1984-11-15	1984-11-15	-.40568
1984-11-16	1984-11-16	-.366525
1984-11-19	1984-11-19	-.901645
1984-11-20	1984-11-20	.123431
1984-11-21	1984-11-21	-.0822707

Double clicking on the variable name shows the documentation of the variable.

The data can be manipulated, much like in a spreadsheet program. Here we shall not need these facilities, so minimize the database window again: click on the first button in the right-hand side of the window. Do not click on the cross: this closes the database, thus removing it from OxMetrics and hence from G@RCH.

2.3 OxMetrics Graphics

The graphics facilities of OxMetrics are powerful yet easy to use. This section will show you how to make time-plots of variables in the database. OxMetrics offers automatic selections of scaling etc., but you will be able to edit these graphs, and change the default layout such as line colors and line types. Graphs can also be saved in a variety of formats for later use in a word processor or for reloading to OxMetrics.

2.3.1 A First Graph

Graphics is the first entry on the Model menu. Activate the command to see the following dialog box (or click on the cross-plot graphics icon on the toolbar).

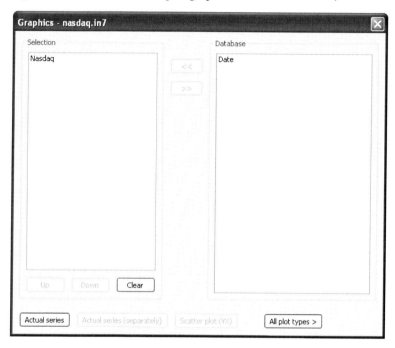

In this example we select Nasdaq and then press the $<<$ button to move the database variables to the selection listbox, as shown above. Then press the button labelled Actual series. Figure 2.1 should appear on the screen. OxMetrics can also draw multiple graphs simultaneously on-screen. For other types of graphs, select All plot types to open the related menu, as seen hereunder (additional details on graphics are available in Doornik, 2009).

2.3.2 Graph Saving and Printing

To print a graph directly to the printer, click on the printer icon in OxMetrics. You can preview the result first using the Print Preview command from the File menu.

Graphs can be saved in various formats. See Doornik (2009) for more details.

2.3.3 Including Graphs in LATEX Documents

Saving graphs in the .EPS format is useful to include them in a LATEX document. The example given below is the Latex code used to include Figure 2.1 in the current document. Note that the command \includegraphics requires the use of the package graphicx. This can be done using the \usepackage{graphicx} command in the preamble of the LaTeX document.

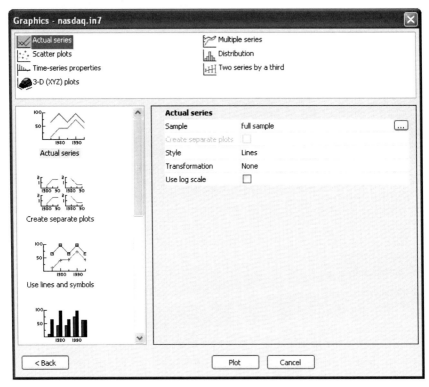

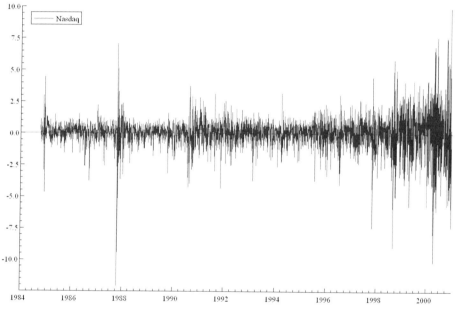

Figure 2.1 Daily returns (in %) of the NASDAQ.

Chapter 3

Introduction to the Univariate ARCH Model

In this chapter, our attention is first devoted to review the specifications of the conditional mean equation. Then, the most simple univariate ARCH specification will be presented as well as the estimation and testing issues with G@RCH. More recent developments about ARCH-type models are discussed in the next chapter.

3.1 Visual Inspection

Panel 1 of Figure 3.1 indicates that the NASDAQ exhibits volatility clustering as periods of low volatility mingle with periods of high volatility. This is a clear sign of presence of ARCH effect in the series.

Panel 2 also shows that the unconditional distribution of the NASDAQ returns (full line) is not normal. Indeed, it is more peaked than the normal density (dashed line) and it has fatter tails as indicated by panels 3 and 4 (this visual indication is validated by the computation of the kurtosis, which is is equal to 9.34). While not obvious on a visual basis, the skewness parameter (-0.627) indicates a negatively skewed behavior.

Recall that the skewness coefficient (SK) equals 0 for a symmetric distribution while the kurtosis coefficient (KU) equals 3 for the normal distribution. The excess kurtosis equals $KU - 3$. Formally these coefficients are expressed as

$$SK = \frac{E[(y - \mu)^3]}{\sigma^3} \text{ and } KU = \frac{E[(y - \mu)^4]}{\sigma^4} \tag{3.1}$$

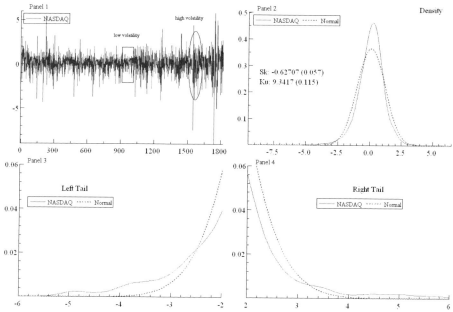

Figure 3.1 Daily Returns of the NASDAQ and Unconditional Density Estimation using OxMetrics.

3.2 Preliminary Graphics

When the error term is not independent of previous errors, it is said to be autocorrelated. Autocorrelation of order h is computed as follows

$$r_h = \frac{cov(y_t, y_{t-h})}{\sigma_{y,t}\sigma_{y,t-h}} \tag{3.2}$$

Plotting the autocorrelation function against the lag gives a first visual impression of the magnitude of the autocorrelation problem. This plot is called "autocorrelogram" and it provides information about simple correlation coefficients. When the errors are strongly time dependent, the autocorrelations tend to be fairly large even for large values of h. The next screen shot shows how to obtain an autocorrelogram in OxMetrics.

The obtained graphic is displayed in Figure 3.2. It suggests that the daily return series of the NASDAQ is a short memory process (in the level) and an AR(1) term might be needed in the conditional mean equation.

We have previously seen from the visual inspection that the NASDAQ exhibits volatility clustering as periods of low volatility mingle with periods of high volatility. In addition to this inspection, one can plot the autocorrelogram of the squared (or absolute) returns to highlight the presence of ARCH effects in the data. This can be done using the calculator of OxMetrics. We can compute squared returns of the NASDAQ, as shown in the screen shot below.

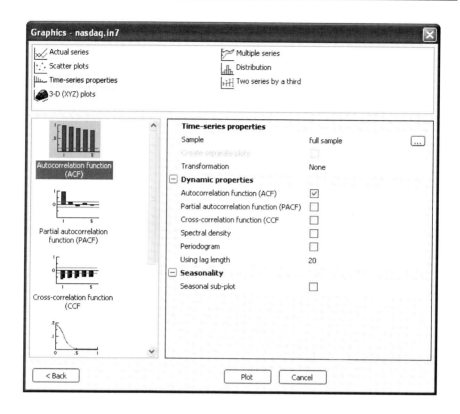

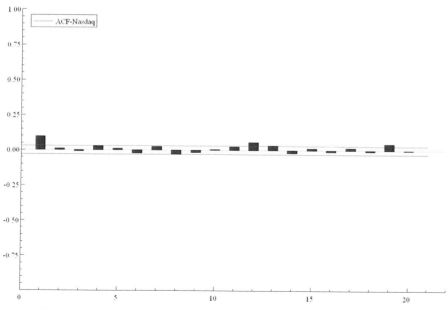

Figure 3.2 Autocorrelogram on daily returns (in %) of the NASDAQ.

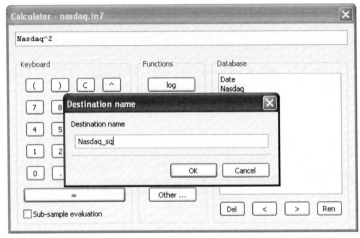

Figure 3.3 shows the autocorrelogram (with 100 lags) of the squared returns. It suggests that squared returns are strongly autocorrelated, exhibiting volatility clustering.

3.3 Preliminary Tests

G@RCH 6.0 provides several tests on the raw data (in addition to the possibilities offered by OxMetrics: ACF, PACF, QQ-plots,...):

- Basic Statistics: number of (missing) observations, minimum, maximum, mean
  and standard deviation.
- The value of the skewness and the kurtosis of the series, their t-tests and p-
  values. Moreover, the Jarque-Bera normality test (Jarque and Bera, 1987) is also
  reported.
- The Box-Pierce statistics at lag l^* for both series, i.e. $BP(l^*)$, and squared series, i.e. $BP^2(l^*)$. Under the null hypothesis of no autocorrelation, the statistics

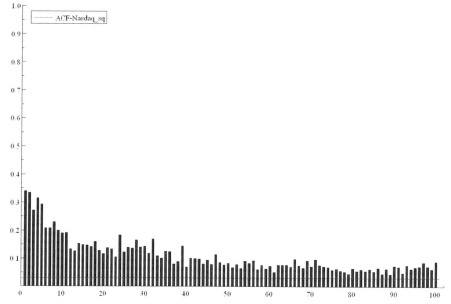

Figure 3.3 Autocorrelogram on daily squared returns (in %) of the NASDAQ.

$BP(l^*)$ and $BP^2(l^*)$ should be evaluated against the $\chi^2(l^*)$ and $\chi^2(l^*)$, respectively. A Monte Carlo study of the size and power of this this is given in example file `Simulation_Q.ox`.

- Engle's LM ARCH test (Engle, 1982) to test the presence of ARCH effects in a series. For each specified order, the squared series is regressed on p of its own lags. The test statistic is distributed $\chi^2(p)$ under the null hypothesis of no ARCH effects.

- Unit root tests on y_t.

  1. The Augmented Dickey-Fuller test $H_0 : y_t$ is $I(1)$ against $H_1 : y_t$ is $I(0)$ (see Dickey and Fuller, 1981) is provided by the t-statistic on $\hat{\theta}$ in:

$$\Delta y_t = \beta_0 + \beta_1 t + \theta y_{t-1} + \sum_{i=1}^{q} \gamma_i \Delta y_{t-i} + e_t, \tag{3.3}$$

where q is the number of lagged first differences included in the ADF regression. The constant and the trend are optional and can be excluded if needed. Note that e_t is assumed to be a white noise. Critical values are taken from MacKinnon (1991).

  2. The KPSS test of Kwiatkowski, Phillips, Schmidt, and Shin (1992) tests $H_0 : y_t$ is $I(0)$ against $H_1 : y_t$ is $I(1)$. The regression model with a time trend has the

form

$$y_t = \beta_0 + \beta_1 t + \gamma \sum_{i=1}^{t} x_i + e_t, \tag{3.4}$$

where e_t is assumed to be stationary with mean 0 and variance σ_e^2 and x_i an $i.i.d.$ process with $E(x_i) = 0$ and $V(x_i) = 1$. When $\gamma \neq 0, y_t$ is integrated while when $k = 0$ it is trend-stationary (or stationary if $\beta_1 = 0$). As a consequence, H_0 implies $k = 0$ while H_1 implies $k \neq 0$. After the estimation of the above model under H_0 by OLS (including or not a time-trend), the KPSS test rejects H_0 in favor of H_1 for large values of the statistic

$$KPSS_l = \frac{\sum_{t=1}^{T} (\sum_{i=1}^{t} \hat{e}_t)^2}{T^2 \hat{\omega}_T^2}, \tag{3.5}$$

where $\hat{\omega}_T^2$ is an estimator of the spectral density at a frequency of zero (non-parametric estimator of the so-called long-run variance). This estimator is based on a weighted sum of the autocovariances, where the weights are defined by a kernel function. We thus need to specify a truncation lag in the covariance or bandwidth, denoted l. G@RCH 6.0 provides a Bartlett kernel. The bandwidth can be specified by the user. In their original work, Kwiatkowski, Phillips, Schmidt, and Shin (1992) considered three values of l as a function of T: $l_0 = 0, l_4 = integer[4(T/100)1/4]$, and $l_{12} = integer[12(T/100)1/4]$.

3. Schmidt and Phillips (1992) have proposed a test for the null hypothesis of a unit root when a deterministic linear trend is present. These authors end-up with two statistics, denoted $Z(rho)$ and $Z(tau)$ based on a nonparametric estimator of the so-called long-run variance (see above) that involves a truncation lag in the covariance or bandwidth (l). Critical values for these two statistics are reported in Schmidt and Phillips (1992).

- Long-memory tests

    1. GPH: implements the log-periodogram regression method for estimating the long-memory parameter as discussed in Geweke and Porter-Hudak (1983). Periodogram points are evaluated at Fourier frequencies $\frac{2\pi j}{T}, j = 1, \ldots, l$, where l is the number of low frequency periodogram points used in estimation (bandwidth).

    2. GSP: implements the Gaussian semi-parametric method for estimating the long-memory parameter as discussed in Robinson and Henry (1998).

- Other Long-memory tests: Rescaled Range Tests of Mandelbrot (1972) and Lo

(1991). See Section 3.12.

- Variance-ratio test of Lo and MacKinlay (1988). See Section 3.12.
- Runs tests. See Section 3.12.

To launch the descriptive statistics, click on G@RCH in the Modules group in the workspace window on the left-hand side of OxMetrics. Then change the **Category** to Other models and **Model Class** to Descriptive Statistics using G@RCH and click on Formulate.

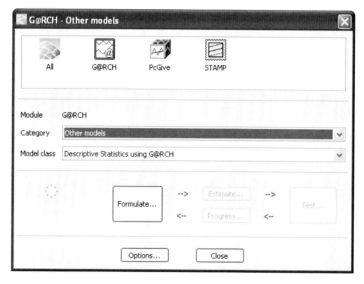

A new dialog box Formulate is launched and the user is asked to select the series to be tested. Selected series are labelled 'T'.

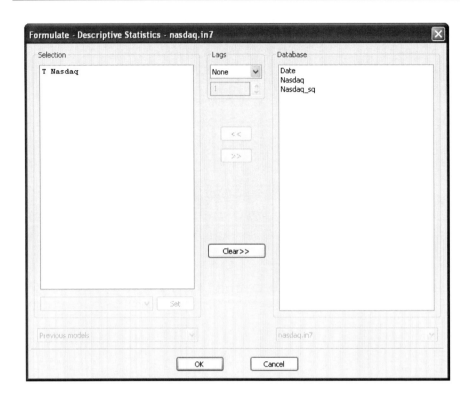

Next, the user select the tests to be run. Lag values of the ARCH LM and Box-Pierce tests can be changed by the user. The subsequent window displays options related to the sample period. As can be seen, if the date variable is well formatted in the database, the sample selection is made easier by allowing selecting a starting date and an ending date. See Chapter 9 of Doornik (2007a) for details on OxMetrics file formats.

Once the OK button of the Estimate - Descriptive Statistics dialog box is pressed, tests are launched and results are printed out in OxMetrics. Note that if a unit root test has been selected, an additional dialog box is launched and the user is asked to select some options related to the test (to include a constant or a trend for instance and the lag length for differences or bandwidth). They should be similar to the output of "Box 1 - Descriptive Statistics". Results confirm that NASDAQ returns exhibit ARCH-type effects (see the ARCH LM tests and the Q-Statistics on squared data). Looking at the Q-Statistics on raw data, one concludes that an ARMA-type model seems justified. Finally, the Jarque-Bera statistic clearly rejects the normality assumption for the unconditional distribution of the NASDAQ while the KPSS Statistics indicated that the series is likely to be I(0).

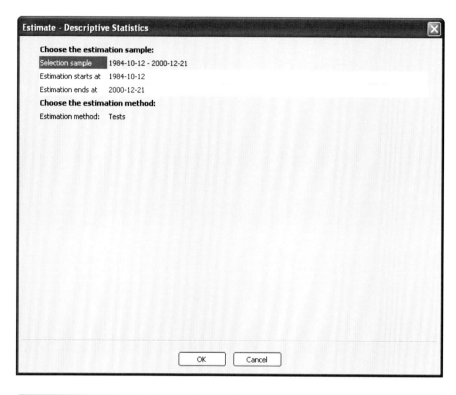

```
                        Box 1 - Descriptive Statistics for the NASDAQ
---- Database information ----
Sample:    1984-10-12 - 2000-12-21 (4093 observations)
Frequency: 1
Variables: 4

Variable      #obs  #miss    type        min       mean         max    std.dev
Date          4093      0    date   1984-10-12              2000-12-21
Nasdaq        4093      0  double    -12.043   0.055166      9.9636     1.2617
Constant      4093      0  double          1          1           1          0
Trend         4093      0  double          1       2047        4093     1181.5


Series #1/1: Nasdaq
---------
Normality Test

                    Statistic     t-Test      P-Value
Skewness             -0.74128     19.368   1.4336e-083
Excess Kurtosis        11.255     147.07      0.00000
Jarque-Bera            21979.        .NaN     0.00000
----------------
ARCH 1-2 test:    F(2,4088)=    420.80 [0.0000]**
ARCH 1-5 test:    F(5,4082)=    228.90 [0.0000]**
ARCH 1-10 test:   F(10,4072)=   118.16 [0.0000]**
----------------
```

```
Q-Statistics on Raw data
   Q( 5) =   41.8697   [0.0000001]
   Q( 10) =  50.9695   [0.0000002]
   Q( 20) =  83.6251   [0.0000000]
   Q( 50) = 167.368    [0.0000000]
H0 : No serial correlation ==> Accept H0 when prob. is High [Q < Chisq(lag)]
---------------
Q-Statistics on Squared data
   Q( 5) =  1988.77    [0.0000000]
   Q( 10) = 2874.40    [0.0000000]
   Q( 20) = 3748.75    [0.0000000]
   Q( 50) = 5491.27    [0.0000000]
H0 : No serial correlation ==> Accept H0 when prob. is High [Q < Chisq(lag)]
---------------------------------------------

KPSS Test without trend and 2 lags
H0: Nasdaq is I(0)

KPSS Statistics: 0.0743478
Asymptotic critical values of Kwiatkowski et al. (1992), JoE, 54,1, p. 159-178

    1%    5%   10%
  0.739 0.463 0.347

---- Log Periodogram Regression ----
d parameter         0.0691465 (0.015793) [0.0000]
No of observations: 4093; no of periodogram points: 2046
```

3.4 Conditional Mean Specification

Let us consider a univariate time series y_t. If Ω_{t-1} is the information set at time $t-1$, we can define its functional form as:

$$y_t = E(y_t|\Omega_{t-1}) + \varepsilon_t, \tag{3.6}$$

where $E(.|.)$ denotes the conditional expectation operator and ε_t is the disturbance term (or unpredictable part), with $E(\varepsilon_t) = 0$ and $E(\varepsilon_t\varepsilon_s) = 0, \forall\, t \neq s$.

Equation (3.6) is the conditional mean equation which has been studied and modelled in many ways. Two of the most famous specifications are the Autoregressive (AR) and Moving Average (MA) models. Combining these two processes and introducing n_1

explanatory variables in the equation, we obtain the ARMAX(n, s) process

$$\Psi\left(L\right)\left(y_t - \mu_t\right) = \Theta\left(L\right)\varepsilon_t$$
$$\mu_t = \mu + \sum_{i=1}^{n_1} \delta_i x_{i,t}, \qquad (3.7)$$

where L is the lag operator[1], $\Psi\left(L\right) = 1 - \sum_{i=1}^{n} \psi_i L^i$ and $\Theta\left(L\right) = 1 + \sum_{j=1}^{s} \theta_j L^j$. The ARMA residuals are obtained using the `arma0` function of Ox on the demeaned series $(y_t - \mu_t)$. See the Ox manual for more details about `arma0`.

Several studies have shown that the dependent variables (interest rate returns, exchange rate returns, etc.) may exhibit significant autocorrelation between observations widely separated in time. In such a case, y_t is said to display long memory (or long-term dependence) and is best modelled by a fractionally integrated ARMA process. This ARFIMA process was initially developed in Granger (1980) and Granger and Joyeux (1980) among others.[2] The ARFIMA(n, ζ, s) is given by:

$$\Psi\left(L\right)\left(1 - L\right)^\zeta \left(y_t - \mu_t\right) = \Theta\left(L\right)\varepsilon_t, \qquad (3.8)$$

where the operator $(1 - L)^\zeta$ accounts for the long memory of the process and is defined as:

$$
\begin{aligned}
(1 - L)^\zeta &= \sum_{k=0}^{\infty} \frac{\Gamma(\zeta + 1)}{\Gamma(k + 1)\,\Gamma(\zeta - k + 1)} L^k \\
&= 1 - \zeta L - \frac{1}{2}\zeta(1 - \zeta)L^2 - \frac{1}{6}\zeta(1 - \zeta)(2 - \zeta)L^3 - \dots \\
&= 1 - \sum_{k=1}^{\infty} c_k(\zeta)L^k, \qquad (3.9)
\end{aligned}
$$

with $0 < \zeta < 1$, $c_1(\zeta) = \zeta$, $c_2(\zeta) = \frac{1}{2}\zeta(1 - \zeta)$, $\dots$ and $\Gamma(.)$ denoting the Gamma function (see Baillie, 1996, for a survey on this topic). The truncation order of the infinite summation is set to $t - 1$. Note that The ARFIMA residuals are obtained using `diffpow` function on the ARMA residuals. See the Ox manual for more details about `diffpow`.

It is worth noting that Doornik and Ooms (1999) provided an Ox package for estimating, forecasting and simulating ARFIMA models. However, contrary to G@RCH, the conditional variance is assumed to be constant over time.[3]

---

[1]Recall that $L^k y_t = y_{t-k}$.

[2]ARFIMA models have been combined with an ARCH-type specification by Baillie, Chung, and Tieslau (1996), Tschernig (1995), Teyssière (1997), Lecourt (2000) and Beine, Laurent, and Lecourt (2002).

[3]Note that the ARFIMA package provides exact and modified profile likelihood methods.

A feature of G@RCH 6.0 is the availability of ARCH "in-mean" models. If we introduce the conditional variance (or the conditional standard error) as additional explanatory variables in Equation (9.6), we get the ARCH-in-Mean model of Engle, Lilien, and Robbins (1987), i.e.

$$\mu_t = \mu + \sum_{i=1}^{n_1} \delta_i x_{i,t} + \vartheta \sigma_t^k, \tag{3.10}$$

with $k = 1$ to include the conditional standard deviation and $k = 2$ for the conditional variance.

The ARCH-M model is often used in financial applications where the expected return on an asset is related to the expected asset risk. The estimated coefficient of the expected risk is a measure of the risk-return tradeoff.

3.5 Conditional Variance Specification: the ARCH Model

The ε_t term in Equations (3.6)-(3.8) is the innovation of the process. More than two decades ago, Engle (1982) defined as an Autoregressive Conditional Heteroscedastic (ARCH) process, all ε_t of the form:

$$\varepsilon_t = z_t \sigma_t, \tag{3.11}$$

where z_t is an independently and identically distributed (*i.i.d.*) process with $E(z_t) = 0$ and $Var(z_t) = 1$. By assumption, ε_t is serially uncorrelated with a mean equal to zero but its conditional variance equals σ_t^2. Therefore, it may change over time, contrary to what is assumed in the standard regression model.

The models provided by our program are all ARCH-type.[4] They differ on the functional form of σ_t^2 but the basic principles are the same (see the next chapter for details). Besides the traditional ARCH and GARCH models, we focus mainly on two kinds of models: the asymmetric models and the fractionally integrated models. The former are defined to account for the so-called "leverage effect" observed in many stock returns, while the latter allows for long-memory in the variance. Early evidence of the "leverage effect" can be found in Black (1976), while persistence in volatility is a common finding of many empirical studies; see for instance the excellent surveys on ARCH models proposed in Bollerslev, Chou, and Kroner (1992), Bera and Higgins (1993) or Palm (1996).

---

[4]For stochastic volatility models, see Koopman, Shepard, and Doornik (1998).

The ARCH (q) model can be expressed as:

$$\varepsilon_t = z_t \sigma_t$$

$$z_t \sim i.i.d.\ D(0,1)$$

$$\sigma_t^2 = \omega + \sum_{i=1}^{q} \alpha_i \varepsilon_{t-i}^2, \tag{3.12}$$

where $D(.)$ is a probability density function with mean 0 and unit variance (see Section 3.6.2).

The ARCH model can describe volatility clustering. The conditional variance of ε_t is indeed an increasing function of the square of the shock that occurred in $t-1$. Consequently, if ε_{t-1} was large in absolute value, σ_t^2 and thus ε_t is expected to be large (in absolute value) as well. Notice that even if the conditional variance of an ARCH model is time-varying, i.e. $\sigma_t^2 = E(\varepsilon_t^2|\psi_{t-1})$, the unconditional variance of ε_t is constant and, provided that $\omega > 0$ and $\sum_{i=1}^{q} \alpha_i < 1$, we have:

$$\sigma^2 \equiv E[E(\varepsilon_t^2|\psi_{t-1})] = \frac{\omega}{1 - \sum_{i=1}^{q} \alpha_i}. \tag{3.13}$$

If z_t is normally distributed, $E(z_t^3) = 0$ and $E(z_t^4) = 3$. Consequently, $E(\varepsilon_t^3) = 0$ and the skewness of y is zero. The kurtosis coefficient for the ARCH(1) is $3\frac{1-\alpha_1^2}{1-3\alpha_1^2}$ if $\alpha_1 < \sqrt{1/3} \approx 0.577$. In this case, the unconditional distribution of the returns features fat tails whenever $\alpha_1 > 0$.

In most applications, the excess kurtosis implied by the ARCH model (coupled with a normal density) is not enough to mimic what we observe on real data. Other distributions are possible. For example we could assume that z_t follows a Student distribution with unit variance and v degrees of freedom, i.e. z_t is $ST(0, 1, v)$. In that case, the unconditional kurtosis of the ARCH(1) is $\lambda\frac{1-\alpha_1^2}{1-\lambda\alpha_1^2}$ with $\lambda = 3(v-2)/(v-4)$. Because of the additional coefficient v, the ARCH(1) model based on the Student distribution does feature fatter tails than the corresponding model based on the Normal distribution. See Section 3.6.2 for more details.

The computation of σ_t^2 in Equation (3.12) depends on past (squared) residuals (ε_t^2), that are not observed for $t = 0, -1, \ldots, -q+1$. To initialize the process, the unobserved squared residuals are set to their sample mean.

3.5.1 Explanatory Variables

Explanatory variables can be introduced in the conditional variance as follows:

$$\omega_t = \omega + \sum_{i=1}^{n_2} \omega_i x_{i,t} \tag{3.14}$$

For the ease of presentation, we will use the notation ω for both ω and ω_t in all subsequent equations.[5]

3.5.2 Positivity Constraints

σ_t^2 has obviously to be positive for all t. Sufficient conditions to ensure that the conditional variance in Equation (3.12) is positive are given by $\omega > 0$ and $\alpha_i \geq 0$.[6] Furthermore, when explanatory variables enter the ARCH equation, these positivity constraints are not valid anymore (but the conditional variance is still required to be non-negative).

3.5.3 Variance Targeting

A simple trick to reduce the number of parameters to be estimated is referred to as variance targeting by Engle and Mezrich (1996).

The conditional variance matrix of the ARCH model (and most of its generalizations), may be expressed in terms of the unconditional variance and other parameters. Doing so one can reparametrize the model using the unconditional variance and replace it by a consistent estimator (before maximizing the likelihood).

Applying variance targeting to the ARCH model implies replacing ω by $\sigma^2 \left(1 - \sum_{i=1}^{q} \alpha_i \right)$, where σ^2 is the unconditional variance of ε_t, which can be consistently estimated by its sample counterpart.

If explanatory variables appear in the ARCH equation, ω is then replaced by $\sigma^2 \left(1 - \sum_{i=1}^{q} \alpha_i \right) - \sum_{i=1}^{n_2} \omega_i \bar{x}_i$, where $\bar{x}_i$ is the sample average of variable $x_{i,t}$ (assuming the stationarity of the n_2 explanatory variables). In other words, the explanatory variables are centered.

---

[5]Note that in earlier versions of G@RCH 6.0, explanatory variables of EGARCH-type models where included as follows: $\omega_t = \omega + \log \left(1 + \sum_{i=1}^{n_2} \omega_i x_{i,t} \right)$.

[6]However, these conditions are not necessary as shown by Nelson and Cao (1992).

3.6 Estimation

3.6.1 G@RCH menus

Estimating (3.12) with G@RCH is intended to be very simple.

Note that in the example we will use a Monday dummy and a Friday dummy. These dummies are easily created with the Calculator (recall that the dataset is dated). First, use the function dayofweek() to created a variable DAY with $DAY = 2$ on Mondays, 3 on Wednesdays, etc. Then, create the Monday and Friday dummy as follows: $Monday = Day == 2$ and $Friday = Day == 6$.

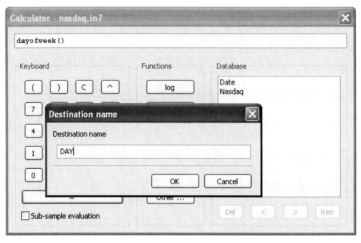

To specify the model, first click on G@RCH in the Modules group in the workspace window on the left-hand side of OxMetrics. Next change the **Category** to Models for financial data and the **Model class** to Univariate GARCH models using G@RCH, then click on Formulate.

A list with all the variables of the database appears in the Database frame. To select variables that will enter your model, click on the variable name and then click on the $<<$ button. There are three possible statuses for each variable (see the list of statuses under the Selection frame): dependent variable (Y variable), regressor in the conditional mean (Mean), or regressor in the conditional variance (Variance). In the univariate module, only one Y variable per model is accepted. However one can include several regressors in the conditional mean and the conditional variance equations and the same variable can be a regressor in both equations. In the example a Monday dummy is included in the conditional mean and a Friday dummy in the conditional variance equation.

Once the OK button is pressed, the Model Settings box automatically appears. This box allows to select the specification of the model: AR(FI)MA orders for the mean equation, GARCH orders, type of GARCH model for the variance equation and the distribution. The default specification is an ARMA(0,0)-GARCH(1,1) with normal errors. In our application, we select an ARMA(1,0)-GARCH(0,1) specification or equivalently an ARMA(1,0)-ARCH(1).[7]

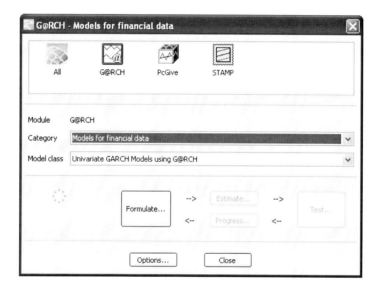

---

[7]Notice that the dialog boxes are resizable.

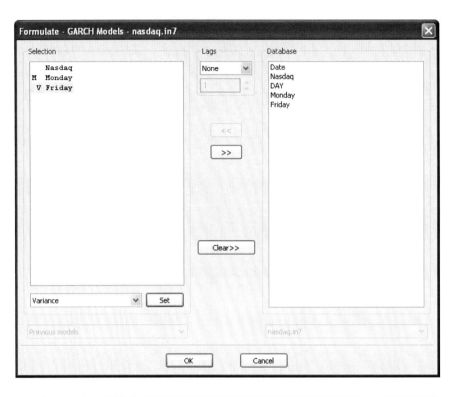

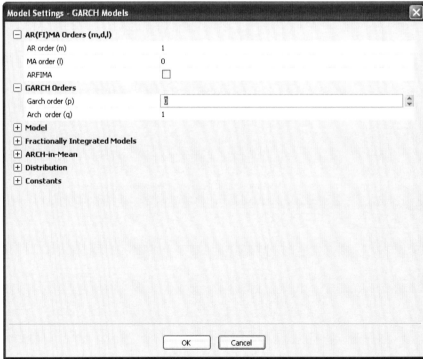

3.6.2 Distributions

Estimation of ARCH-type models is commonly done by maximum likelihood so that one has to make an additional assumption about the innovation process z_t, i.e. choosing a density function $D(0, 1)$ with a mean 0 and a unit variance.

Weiss (1986) and Bollerslev and Wooldridge (1992) show that under the normality assumption, the quasi-maximum likelihood (QML) estimator is consistent if the conditional mean and the conditional variance are correctly specified. This estimator is, however, inefficient with the degree of inefficiency increasing with the degree of departure from normality (Engle and González-Rivera, 1991).

As reported by Palm (1996), Pagan (1996) and Bollerslev, Chou, and Kroner (1992), the use of a fat-tailed distributions is widespread in the literature. In particular, Bollerslev (1987), Hsieh (1989), Baillie and Bollerslev (1989) and Palm and Vlaar (1997) among others show that these distributions perform better in order to capture the higher observed kurtosis.

As shown below, four distributions are available in G@RCH 6.0 : the usual Gaussian (normal) distribution, the Student-t distribution, the Generalized Error distribution (GED) and the skewed-Student distribution.

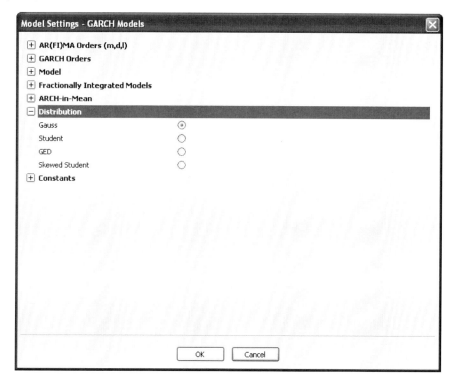

The logic of ML is to interpret the density as a function of the parameter set, conditional on a set of sample outcomes. This function is called the *likelihood function*. It is quite evident from Equation (3.12) (and all the following equations of Section 3) that the recursive evaluation of this function is conditional on unobserved values. The ML estimation is therefore not perfectly exact. To solve the problem of unobserved values, we have set these quantities to their unconditional expected values. For this reason we talk about approximate (or conditional) ML and not exact ML.

If we express the mean equation as in Equation (3.6) and $\varepsilon_t = z_t \sigma_t$, the log-likelihood function of the standard normal distribution is given by:

$$L_{norm} = -\frac{1}{2} \sum_{t=1}^{T} \left[\log (2\pi) + \log \left(\sigma_t^2 \right) + z_t^2 \right], \tag{3.15}$$

where T is the number of observations.

For a Student-t distribution, the log-likelihood is:

$$
\begin{aligned}
L_{Stud} = {} & T \left\{ \log \Gamma \left(\frac{v+1}{2} \right) - \log \Gamma \left(\frac{v}{2} \right) - \frac{1}{2} \log \left[\pi (v-2) \right] \right\} \\
& - \frac{1}{2} \sum_{t=1}^{T} \left[\log(\sigma_t^2) + (1+v) \log \left(1 + \frac{z_t^2}{v-2} \right) \right],
\end{aligned}
\tag{3.16}
$$

where v is the degrees of freedom, $2 < v \le \infty$ and $\Gamma(.)$ is the gamma function.

The GED log-likelihood function of a normalized random variable is given by:

$$L_{GED} = \sum_{t=1}^{T} \left[\log \left(\frac{v}{\lambda_v} \right) - 0.5 \left| \frac{z_t}{\lambda_v} \right|^v - (1 + v^{-1}) \log(2) - \log \Gamma \left(\frac{1}{v} \right) - 0.5 \log(\sigma_t^2) \right], \tag{3.17}$$

where $0 < v < \infty$ and

$$\lambda_v \equiv \sqrt{ \frac{\Gamma (1/v) \, 2^{(-2/v)}}{\Gamma (3/v)} }.$$

The main drawback of the last two densities is that even if they may account for fat tails, they are symmetric. Skewness and kurtosis are important in financial applications in many respects (in asset pricing models, portfolio selection, option pricing theory or Value-at-Risk among others). Quite recently, Lambert and Laurent (2000, 2001) applied and extended the skewed-Student density proposed by Fernández and Steel (1998) to the GARCH framework.

The log-likelihood of a standardized (zero mean and unit variance) skewed-Student is:

$$L_{SkSt} = T\left\{\log\Gamma\left(\frac{\upsilon+1}{2}\right) - \log\Gamma\left(\frac{\upsilon}{2}\right) - 0.5\log\left[\pi\left(\upsilon-2\right)\right] + \log\left(\frac{2}{\xi+\frac{1}{\xi}}\right) + \log\left(s\right)\right\}$$
$$- 0.5\sum_{t=1}^{T}\left\{\log\sigma_t^2 + (1+\upsilon)\log\left[1 + \frac{(sz_t+m)^2}{\upsilon-2}\xi^{-2I_t}\right]\right\}, \tag{3.18}$$

where

$$I_t = \left\{\begin{array}{l} 1 \text{ if } z_t \geq -\frac{m}{s} \\ -1 \text{ if } z_t < -\frac{m}{s} \end{array}\right.,$$

ξ is the asymmetry parameter, υ is the degree of freedom of the distribution,

$$m = \frac{\Gamma\left(\frac{\upsilon+1}{2}\right)\sqrt{\upsilon-2}}{\sqrt{\pi}\Gamma\left(\frac{\upsilon}{2}\right)}\left(\xi - \frac{1}{\xi}\right),$$

and

$$s = \sqrt{\left(\xi^2 + \frac{1}{\xi^2} - 1\right) - m^2}.$$

Note that G@RCH does not estimate ξ but $\log(\xi)$ to facilitate inference about the null hypothesis of symmetry (since the skewed-Student equals the symmetric Student distribution when $\xi = 1$ or $\log(\xi) = 0$). The estimated value of $\log(\xi)$ is reported in the output under the label "Asymmetry". See Lambert and Laurent (2001) and Bauwens and Laurent (2005) for more details.

The gradient vector and the hessian matrix can be obtained numerically or by evaluating their analytical expression. Due to the high number of possible models and distributions available, G@RCH uses numerical techniques to approximate the derivatives of the log-likelihood function with respect to the parameter vector.

The next window is (Starting Values). The user is asked to make a choice regarding the starting values of the parameters to be estimated: (1) let the program choose the starting values, (2) enter them manually, element by element (the one selected here), or (3) enter the starting values in a vector form (one value per row) and potentially fix some parameters at their starting value.

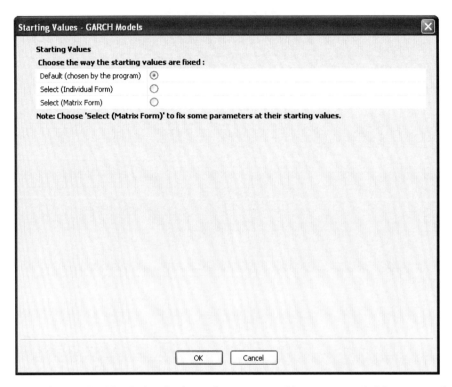

The first method is obviously the easiest to use and is recommended for unexperienced users since it prevents from entering aberrant values. The last two methods are useful if the user wants specific starting values for the estimation. The third method is particularly useful when one wants to fix some parameters.

Next, the Estimate window proposes options on two important characteristics of the model: the sample size and the estimation method.

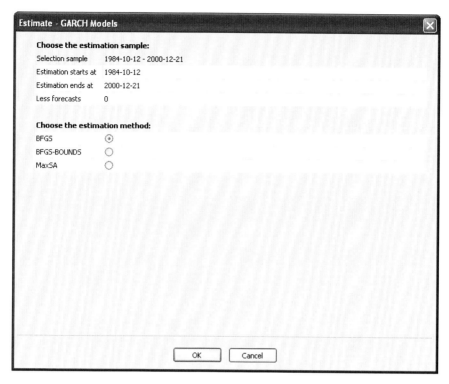

When the variable corresponding to the date is correctly formatted, the sample can conveniently be fixed based on starting and ending date (see Chapter 9 of Doornik, 2007, for details). The number of forecasts can be also subtracted when out-of-sample forecasting is to be performed.

The models are estimated using a maximum likelihood (ML) approach. Basically, three methods are proposed to estimate these models (see the option Optimization Methods in the Model Settings window).

(1) By default, a standard ML approach is selected. This method uses the quasi-Newton method of Broyden, Fletcher, Goldfarb and Shanno (BFGS). This function is the well-known MaxBFGS function provided by Ox. See the Ox documentation for details.

(2) A constraint optimization technique that uses the MaxSQPF algorithm. MaxSQPF implements a sequential quadratic programming technique to maximize a non-linear function subject to non-linear constraints, similar to Algorithm 18.7 in Nocedal and Wright (1999). MaxSQPF is particularly useful to impose the stationarity and/or positivity constraints like $\alpha_1 \geq 0$ in the ARCH(1) model (see Sections 3.9 and 5.3.2).

(3) And finally, a simulated annealing algorithm for optimizing non-smooth functions with possible multiple local maxima, ported to Ox by Charles Bos and called MaxSA. See *http://www.tinbergen.nl/~cbos/software/maxsa.html* for more details.

G@RCH provides three methods to compute the covariance matrix of the estimates: Second Derivatives (based on the inverse of the hessian), Outer-Product of Gradients and Robust standard errors, also known as Quasi-Maximum Likelihood (QML) or 'Sandwich formula'. This choice is accessible by clicking on the button 'Options...'. By default, Robust standard errors are reported.

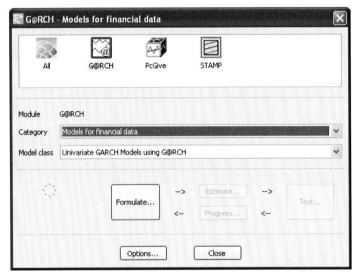

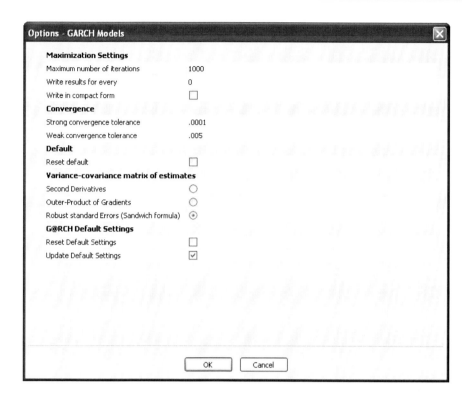

Note that a new feature of G@RCH 5.0 is that the default settings are updated after each estimation (the default model is thus the previously estimated one). To disable this option, disable 'Update Default Settings'. Option 'Reset default Settings' is self-explanatory.

Once all the options have been selected, the estimation procedure is launched if the default starting values are used. Otherwise, a new dialog box appears. Let us assume that second method has been selected for the starting values, i.e. 'Select (Individual Form)'. This new window contains an exhaustive list of parameters used in the different models. Depending on the specification, some parameters have a value, others have not.

The user should replace only the former since they correspond to the parameters to be estimated for the specified model. Note that it is crucially important to respect the format of these initial values. More specifically, when two values are associated with a single parameter (say, both ARCH coefficients in a ARCH(2) model), the mandatory format is "value1 ; value2". Here is an example:

```
0.1;0.1
```

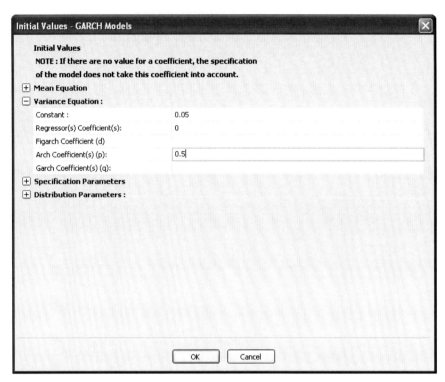

If the third method is selected for the starting values, i.e. 'Select (Matrix Form)', the corresponding window contains a column with the default starting values of the parameter vector (Column 'Value') and a Column 'FIX' that allows to fix some parameters to their starting value.

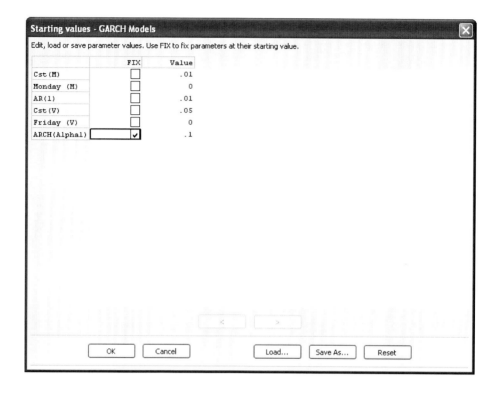

Note that estimating the same model with different values starting values is interesting to check the robustness of the maximum likelihood procedure.

Once this step is completed, the program starts the iteration process. Depending on the options selected[8], G@RCH prints intermediate iteration results or not. The final output is divided in two main parts: first, the model specification reminder; second, the estimated values and other useful statistics of the parameters.[9] The outputs "Box 2 - Output of the ARMA(1,0)-GARCH(1,1)" and "Box 3 - Output of the ARMA(1,0)-GARCH(1,1) by QMLE" correspond respectively to the estimation results of the ARMA$(1,0)$-GARCH$(1,1)$ model by ML and QMLE.

---

[8]These options can be edited by clicking on the Options... button in the main G@RCH box.

[9]Recall that the estimations are based on the numerical evaluation of the gradients.

```
                              Box 2 - Output of the ARMA(1,0)-GARCH(0,1)
 ******************************
 ** G@RCH( 1) SPECIFICATIONS **
 ******************************
Dependent variable : Nasdaq
Mean Equation : ARMA (1, 0) model.
1 regressor(s) in the mean.
Variance Equation : GARCH (0, 1) model.
1 regressor(s) in the variance.
The distribution is a Gauss distribution.

Strong convergence using numerical derivatives
Log-likelihood = -6106.36
Please wait : Computing the Std Errors ...

  Maximum Likelihood Estimation (Std.Errors based on Second derivatives)
                   Coefficient  Std.Error  t-value  t-prob
Cst(M)                0.188314   0.016176    11.64  0.0000
Monday (M)           -0.143636   0.033629    -4.271 0.0000
AR(1)                -0.021047   0.017378    -1.211 0.2259
Cst(V)                0.737026   0.028148    26.18  0.0000
Friday (V)           -0.289467   0.040311    -7.181 0.0000
ARCH(Alpha1)          0.746336   0.046922    15.91  0.0000

No. Observations :      4093  No. Parameters  :        6
Mean (Y)         :   0.05517  Variance (Y)    :  1.59189
Skewness (Y)     :  -0.74128  Kurtosis (Y)    : 14.25531
Log Likelihood   : -6106.357  Alpha[1]+Beta[1]:  0.74614

The sample mean of squared residuals was used to start recursion.
Positivity & stationarity constraints are not computed because
there are explanatory variables in the conditional variance equation.

Estimated Parameters Vector :
  0.188314;-0.143636;-0.021047; 0.737026;-0.289467; 0.746341

Elapsed Time : 1.542 seconds (or 0.0257 minutes).
```

Parameters labelled '(M)' relate to the conditional mean while those labelled '(V)' relate to the conditional variance equation. AR(1) and ARCH(Alpha1) correspond to ψ_1 and α_1, respectively.

Surprisingly, the AR(1) coefficient is not significantly different from 0 (we will come back to this issue latter) while it was expected to be significantly negative. Interestingly, the returns and volatility are, on average, found to be lower on Monday and on Friday, respectively. Furthermore, the ARCH coefficient α_1 is highly significant (rejecting the null of no ARCH effects) and incompatible with the existence of the kurtosis (since it is above 0.577). The log-likelihood value is -6106.357.

```
                    Box 3 - Output of the ARMA(1,0)-GARCH(0,1) by QMLE
********************************
 ** G@RCH( 2) SPECIFICATIONS **
********************************
Dependent variable : Nasdaq
Mean Equation : ARMA (1, 0) model.
1 regressor(s) in the mean.
Variance Equation : GARCH (0, 1) model.
1 regressor(s) in the variance.
The distribution is a Gauss distribution.

Strong convergence using numerical derivatives
Log-likelihood = -6106.36
Please wait : Computing the Std Errors ...

 Robust Standard Errors (Sandwich formula)
               Coefficient  Std.Error  t-value  t-prob
Cst(M)            0.188314   0.025747    7.314   0.0000
Monday (M)       -0.143636   0.049195   -2.920   0.0035
AR(1)            -0.021047   0.055644   -0.3782  0.7053
Cst(V)            0.737026   0.062300   11.83    0.0000
Friday (V)       -0.289467   0.081034   -3.572   0.0004
ARCH(Alpha1)      0.746336   0.10484     7.119   0.0000

No. Observations :     4093  No. Parameters  :        6
Mean (Y)         :  0.05517  Variance (Y)    :  1.59189
Skewness (Y)     : -0.74128  Kurtosis (Y)    : 14.25531
Log Likelihood   : -6106.357 Alpha[1]+Beta[1]:  0.74634

The sample mean of squared residuals was used to start recursion.
Positivity & stationarity constraints are not be computed because
there are explanatory variables in the conditional variance equation.

Estimated Parameters Vector :
 0.188314;-0.143636;-0.021047; 0.737026;-0.289467; 0.746341

Elapsed Time : 1.522 seconds (or 0.0253667 minutes).
```

Ex-post, it is desirable to test the adequacy of the ARCH model. New options are thus available after the estimation of the model when clicking on the Test... button of the main G@RCH box: Tests, Graphic Analysis, Forecasts, Exclusion Restrictions, Linear Restrictions and Store.

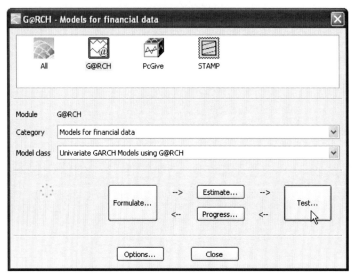

3.7 Graphics

The Graphic Analysis... option allows to plot different graphics.

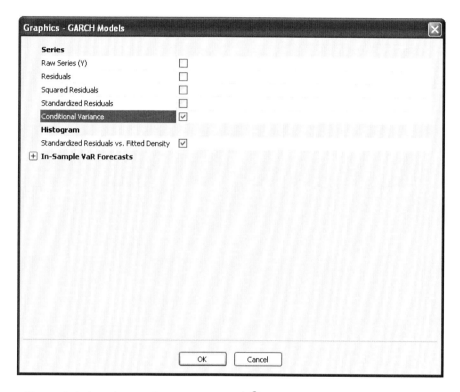

Figure 3.4 plots the conditional variance $(\hat{\sigma}_t^2)$ as well as the histogram of the standardized residuals $\left(\hat{z}_t = \frac{\hat{\varepsilon}_t}{\hat{\sigma}_t}\right)$ obtained with the AR(1)-ARCH(1) model, together with a kernel estimation of its unconditional distribution (solid line) and the $N(0,1)$ (dotted line).

Just as any other graphs in the OxMetrics environment, all graphs plotted from G@RCH can be easily edited (color, size,...) and exported in many formats (.eps, .ps, .wmf, .emf and .gwg).

3.8 Misspecification Tests

The Tests... option allows the user to run different tests but also to print the variance-covariance matrix of the estimated parameters.

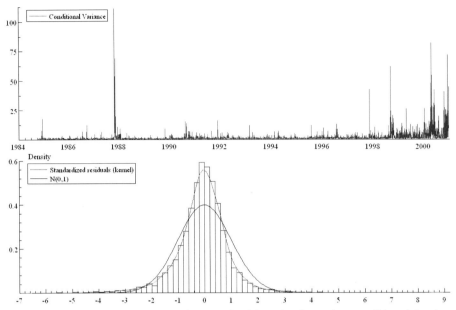

Figure 3.4   Conditional variance of the NASDAQ and estimated unconditional density of the standardized residuals.

Once again, in addition to the possibilities offered by OxMetrics (ACF, PACF, QQ-plots,...), several misspecification tests are indeed provided in G@RCH:

- Four Information Criteria (divided by the number of observations):[10]

$$
\begin{aligned}
Akaike &= -2\frac{LogL}{n} + 2\frac{k}{n}; \\
Hannan - Quinn &= -2\frac{LogL}{n} + 2\frac{k \log\left[\log(n)\right]}{n}; \\
Schwartz &= -2\frac{LogL}{n} + 2\frac{\log(k)}{n}; \\
Shibata &= -2\frac{LogL}{n} + \log\left(\frac{n + 2k}{n}\right).
\end{aligned}
$$

- The value of the skewness and the kurtosis of the standardized residuals of the estimated model ($\hat{z}_t$), their t-tests and p-values. Moreover, the Jarque-Bera normality test (Jarque and Bera, 1987) is also reported.
- The Box-Pierce statistics at lag l^* for both standardized, i.e. $BP(l^*)$, and squared standardized, i.e. $BP^2(l^*)$, residuals. Under the null hypothesis of no auto-correlation, the statistics $BP(l^*)$ and $BP^2(l^*)$ should be evaluated against the $\chi^2(l^* - m - l)$ and $\chi^2(l^* - p - q)$, respectively (see McLeod and Li, 1983).
- Engle's LM ARCH test (Engle, 1982) to test the presence of ARCH effects in a series. For each specified order, the squared residual series is regressed on p of its own lags. The test statistic is distributed $\chi^2(p)$ under the null hypothesis of no ARCH effects.
- The diagnostic test of Engle and Ng (1993) that investigates possible misspecification of the conditional variance equation. Let S_t^- denotes a dummy variable which takes the value 1 when $\hat{\varepsilon}_t < 0$, and 0 otherwise (and $S_t^+ \equiv 1 - S_t^-$). The Sign Bias Test (SBT) examines whether $\hat{\varepsilon}_t^2$ can be predicted by $S_{t-1}^-, S_{t-1}^-\hat{\varepsilon}_{t-1}$, and/or $S_{t-1}^+\hat{\varepsilon}_{t-1}$. To test the presence of leverage effects, Engle and Ng (1993) propose to run the following regressions:

$$
\begin{aligned}
\hat{\varepsilon}_t^2 &= a_0 + a_1 S_{t-1}^- + u_t : \text{SBT} \\
\hat{\varepsilon}_t^2 &= b_0 + b_1 S_{t-1}^-\hat{\varepsilon}_{t-1} + u_t : \text{NSBT} \\
\hat{\varepsilon}_t^2 &= c_0 + c_1 S_{t-1}^+\hat{\varepsilon}_{t-1} + u_t : \text{PSBT},
\end{aligned}
$$

---

[10]$LogL$ is the log-likelihood value, n is the number of observations and k the number of estimated parameters.

and test the significance of a_1, b_1 and c_1 through a t-test. The tests are called respectively, Sign Bias Test (SBT), Negative Sign Bias Test (NSBT) and Positive Sign Bias Test (PSBT). The NSBT and PSBT also test whether the effect of negative and positive shocks on the conditional variance depend on their size. Instead of running three different regressions, G@RCH follows Engle and Ng (1993) in estimating jointly the three effect, i.e.

$$\hat{\varepsilon}_t^2 = d_0 + d_1 S_{t-1}^- + d_2 S_{t-1}^- \hat{\varepsilon}_{t-1} + d_3 S_{t-1}^+ \hat{\varepsilon}_{t-1} + u_t. \tag{3.19}$$

T-stats corresponding to $H_0 : d_i = 0$ ($H_1 : d_i \neq 0$), $\forall i = 1, 2$ and 3 are reported, as well as their p-value. Finally, a joint test for $H_0 : d_1 = d_2 = d_3 = 0$ is also provided.

- The adjusted Pearson goodness-of-fit test that compares the empirical distribution of the innovations with the theoretical one. In order to carry out this testing procedure, it is necessary to first classify the residuals in cells according to their magnitude.[11] Let n be the number of observations, r the number of categories we consider, p_i ($i = 1,...,r$) the observed proportion of observations being in the ith category and p_i^t ($i = 1,...,r$) the theoretical probability for an observation to be in the ith category. The Pearson goodness-of-fit test has the null H_0: $p_1 = p_1^t$, $p_2 = p_2^t, \ldots, p_r = p_r^t$. The statistic is computed as

$$P(g) = \sum_{i=1}^{r} \frac{(n_i - En_i)^2}{En_i}, \tag{3.20}$$

where n_i is the observed number in the sample that fall into the ith category and En_i is the number of observations expected to be in this i^{th} category when Ho is true. The Pearson statistic is therefore "small" when all of the observed counts (proportions) are close to the expected counts (proportions) and it is "large" when one or more observed counts (proportions) differs noticeably from what is expected when H_0 is true.[12] For $i.i.d.$ observations, Palm and Vlaar (1997) show that under the null of a correct distribution the asymptotic distribution of $P(g)$ is bounded between a $\chi^2(r - 1)$ and a $\chi^2(r - k - 1)$ where k is the number of estimated parameters. As explained by Palm and Vlaar (1997), the choice of r is far from being obvious.[13] According to König and Gaab (1982), the number of cells must increase at a rate equal to $T^{0.4}$.

---

[11] See Palm and Vlaar (1997) for more details.
[12] Large values of *GoF* suggest therefore that H_0 is false.
[13] For $T = 2252$, these authors set r equal to 50.

- The Nyblom test (Nyblom, 1989 and Lee and Hansen, 1994) can be used to check the constancy of parameters over time. See also Hansen (1994) for an overview of this test.

- The Residual-Based Diagnostic (RBD) for Conditional Heteroscedasticity of Tse (2002). The BoxPierce portmanteau statistic is perhaps the most widely used diagnostic for conditional heteroscedasticity models. Although it has been noted that the portmanteau statistics do not have an asymptotic χ^2 distribution, many authors, nonetheless, apply the χ^2 distribution as an approximation (the problem lies in the fact that estimated residuals are used to calculate the portmanteau statistics). To overcome this problem, Tse (2002) proposes a Residual-Based Diagnostic for conditional heteroscedasticity. The diagnostic involves running artificial regressions and testing for the statistical significance of the regression parameters. The key problem is that since the regressors are estimated, the usual ordinary least squares (OLS) result does not apply.

  The idea of the test is the following: after estimating the model, the standardized residuals $\hat{z}_t = \hat{\varepsilon}_t/\hat{\sigma}_t$ can be computed. It is obvious that $\hat{z}_t$ depends on the set of estimated parameters. $E(\hat{z}_t^2) = 1$ by construction, so we can run a regression of $E(\hat{z}_t^2) - 1$ on some information variables and examine the statistical significance of the regression parameters. Tse (2002) proposes to run the following OLS regression to test the presence of remaining heteroscedasticity in the standardized residuals:

  $E(\hat{z}_t^2) - 1 = d_1 \hat{z}_{t-1}^2 + \ldots + d_M \hat{z}_{t-M}^2 + u_t$. Since the regressors are not observed (but estimated), standard inference procedures of OLS is invalid. Tse (2002) derives the asymptotic distribution of the estimated parameters and shows that a joint test of significance of the $d_1, \ldots, d_M$ is now $\chi^2(M)$ distributed. Notice that in G@RCH the maximum lag values M of the test are set by default to 2, 5 and 10 but can be changed by the user.

Monte Carlo experiment

To study the performance of this test, let us consider a first simulation study (see `Simulation_RBD_TSE.ox`). We simulate 1000 series of $T = 2000$ observations following a N-AR(0)-GARCH(1,1) model with $\mu = 0.1$, i.e. $(y_t - \mu) = \varepsilon_t$, where $\varepsilon_t \sim N(0, \sigma_t^2)$ and $\sigma_t^2 = 0.2 + 0.1\varepsilon_{t-1}^2 + 0.8\sigma_{t-1}^2$. We than estimate a N-AR(0)-GARCH(1,1) and the simulated data and apply Tse (2002)'s test on $\hat{z}_t^2 \equiv \frac{\varepsilon_t^2}{\sigma_t}$ with $M = 1, 2, 3$ and 4. We report both the test with and without the RBD correction.

The number of times that the null is rejected at the $\alpha\%$ nominal size (called the empirical size of the test) is reported below.

```
RBD TEST OF TSE (2002)
Empirical size with alpha=0.10 and M=1: 9.7
Empirical size with alpha=0.05 and M=1: 5.4
Empirical size with alpha=0.01 and M=1: 2.2


Empirical size with alpha=0.10 and M=2: 8.5
Empirical size with alpha=0.05 and M=2: 4.5
Empirical size with alpha=0.01 and M=2: 2.9


Empirical size with alpha=0.10 and M=3: 8.4
Empirical size with alpha=0.05 and M=3: 5.7
Empirical size with alpha=0.01 and M=3: 3


Empirical size with alpha=0.10 and M=4: 8.3
Empirical size with alpha=0.05 and M=4: 6.1
Empirical size with alpha=0.01 and M=4: 3.4


RBD TEST OF TSE (2002) without the correction
Empirical size with alpha=0.10 and M=1: 0.9
Empirical size with alpha=0.05 and M=1: 0.3
Empirical size with alpha=0.01 and M=1: 0.1


Empirical size with alpha=0.10 and M=2: 3
Empirical size with alpha=0.05 and M=2: 1.1
Empirical size with alpha=0.01 and M=2: 0.3


Empirical size with alpha=0.10 and M=3: 4.7
Empirical size with alpha=0.05 and M=3: 2.1
Empirical size with alpha=0.01 and M=3: 0.4


Empirical size with alpha=0.10 and M=4: 4.1
Empirical size with alpha=0.05 and M=4: 2.5
Empirical size with alpha=0.01 and M=4: 0.4
```

These results suggest that the version of the test that implements the RBD correction has a reasonable size for $\alpha = 10$ and 5% and suffers from a positive size distortion for $\alpha = 1\%$. However, the 'OLS' version of the test (that does not take into account the uncertainty of the estimation of the GARCH model) is clearly inadequate because it has a tendency to under-reject the null whatever the value of M and α. For instance, for $M = 1$ and $\alpha = 10\%$, the empirical size is 0.9%, which suggests a strong size distortion.

In the example, 6 tests have been selected. The output is reported in "Box 4 - Misspecification Tests".

```
                                              Box 4 - Misspecification Tests
TESTS :
------------
Information Criterium (to be minimized)
Akaike          2.986737  Shibata        2.986733
Schwarz         2.995997  Hannan-Quinn   2.990016
---------------

                  Statistic      t-Test      P-Value
Skewness          -0.28941      7.5616       0.00000
Excess Kurtosis    5.9872      78.235        0.00000
Jarque-Bera        6170.5       .NaN         0.00000
---------------


Q-Statistics on Standardized Residuals
  --> P-values adjusted by 1 degree(s) of freedom
  Q(  5) =  62.3925   [0.0000000]
  Q( 10) =  68.3636   [0.0000000]
  Q( 20) =  84.2257   [0.0000000]
  Q( 50) = 125.350    [0.0000000]
HO : No serial correlation ==> Accept HO when prob. is High [Q < Chisq(lag)]
---------------


Q-Statistics on Squared Standardized Residuals
  --> P-values adjusted by 1 degree(s) of freedom
  Q(  5) =  323.697   [0.0000000]
  Q( 10) =  628.454   [0.0000000]
  Q( 20) = 1035.75    [0.0000000]
  Q( 50) = 1695.16    [0.0000000]
HO : No serial correlation ==> Accept HO when prob. is High [Q < Chisq(lag)]
---------------


Adjusted Pearson Chi-square Goodness-of-fit test

# Cells(g)  Statistic    P-Value(g-1)    P-Value(g-k-1)
     40     526.9756      0.000000         0.000000
     50     540.9238      0.000000         0.000000
     60     565.9641      0.000000         0.000000
Rem.: k = 6 = # estimated parameters
---------------


Residual-Based Diagnostic for Conditional Heteroskedasticity of Tse (2001)

  RBD( 2) = 104.753   [0.0000000]
  RBD( 5) = 246.916   [0.0000000]
  RBD(10) = 303.489   [0.0000000]
-------------------------------------------------
P-values in brackets
```

Without going too deeply into the analysis of these results, we can briefly argue that the model does not capture the dynamics of the the the NASDAQ.

The Q-statistics on standardized and squared standardized residuals, and RBD test with various lag values as well as the adjusted Pearson Chi-square goodness-of-fit test (with different cell numbers) reject the null hypothesis of a correct specification. This result is not very surprising. Early empirical evidence has indeed shown that a high ARCH order has to be selected to catch the dynamics of the conditional variance (thus involving the estimation of numerous parameters).

3.9 Parameter Constraints

When numerical optimization is used to maximize the log-likelihood function with respect to the vector of parameters Ψ, the inspected range of the parameter space is $(-\infty; \infty)$. The problem is that some parameters might have to be constrained in a smaller interval. For instance, it is convenient to constrain the α_i parameters of an ARCH(q) to be positive. Constraining parameters to lie between given lower and upper bounds is easily done by selecting the 'BFGS-BOUNDS' option in the Estimate - GARCH Models dialog box in G@RCH.

If the user fixes bounds on parameters, the program uses `MaxSQPF` instead of `MaxBFGS` (Broyden, Fletcher, Goldfarb and Shanno quasi-Newton method) to optimize the likelihood function. `MaxSQPF` enforces all iterates to be feasible, using the algorithm by Lawrence and Tits (2001). If a starting point is infeasible, `MaxSQPF` will try to minimize the squared constraint violations to find a feasible point. See Doornik (2007b) for more details on these two optimization functions.

To change the values of the bounds, select option 'Select (Matrix Form)' in the 'Starting Value' dialog box together with option 'BFGS-BOUNDS' in the Estimate - GARCH Models dialog box. In addition to columns 'FIX' and 'Value', two new columns appear with the default lower and upper bounds.

Furthermore, nonlinear constraints (like the stationarity constraint of the GARCH $(1,1)$ model, $\alpha_1 + \beta_1 < 1$) can be imposed during the estimation with the Console version. For more details, see 5.3.2.

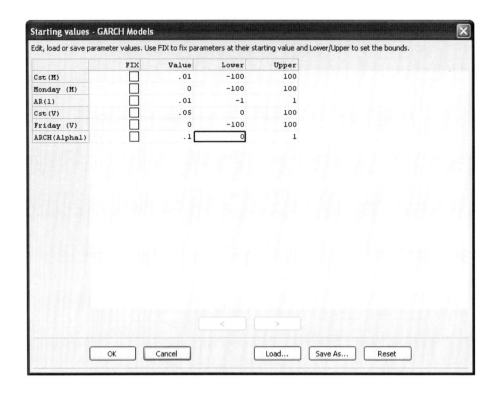

3.10 Forecasts

The main purpose of building and estimating a model with financial data is probably to produce a forecast. With the Forecast... option, G@RCH 6.0 also provides forecasting tools: forecasts of both the conditional mean and the conditional variance are available as well as several forecast error measures.

The first parameter to specify is the horizon h of the h-step-ahead forecasts. The default value is 10. Three options are available to:

(1) print several forecasts error measures;

(2) print the forecasts;

(3) and make a graph of the forecasts.

Finally, graphical options are available for the standard error bands (error bands, bars or fans).

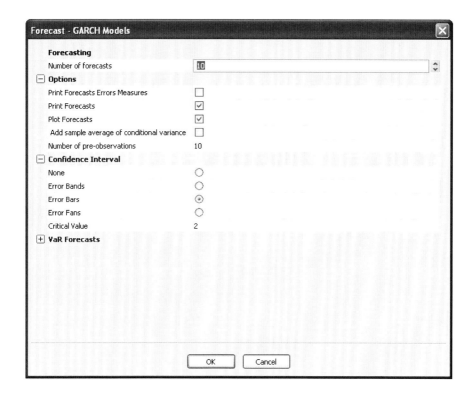

3.10.1 Forecasting the Conditional Mean

Our first goal is to give the optimal h-step-ahead predictor of y_{t+h} given the information we have up to time t.

For instance, in an AR(1) process such as

$$y_t = \mu + \psi_1(y_{t-1} - \mu) + \varepsilon_t,$$

the optimal[14] h-step-ahead predictor of y_{t+h} (i.e. $\hat{y}_{t+h|t}$) is its conditional expectation at time t (given the estimated parameters $\hat{\mu}$ and $\hat{\psi}_1$):

$$\hat{y}_{t+h|t} = \hat{\mu} + \hat{\psi}_1(\hat{y}_{t+h-1|t} - \hat{\mu}), \tag{3.21}$$

where $\hat{y}_{t+i|t} = y_{t+i}$ for $i \leq 0$.

For the AR(1), the optimal 1-step-ahead forecast equals $\hat{\mu} + \hat{\psi}_1(\hat{y}_t - \hat{\mu})$. For $h > 1$, the optimal forecast can be obtained recursively or directly as $\hat{y}_{t+h|t} = \hat{\mu} + \hat{\psi}_1^h(\hat{y}_t - \hat{\mu})$.

More generally, for the ARFIMA(n, ζ, s) model described Equation (3.8), the opti-

---

[14]By optimal, we mean optimal under expected quadratic loss, or in a mean square error sense.

mal h-step-ahead predictor of y_{t+h} is:

$$
\hat{y}_{t+h|t} = \left[\hat{\mu}_{t+h|t} + \sum_{k=1}^{\infty} \hat{c}_k (\hat{y}_{t+h-k} - \hat{\mu}_{t+h|t}) \right]
$$
$$
+ \sum_{i=1}^{n} \hat{\psi}_i \left\{ \hat{y}_{t+h-i} - \left[\hat{\mu}_{t+h|t} + \sum_{k=1}^{\infty} \hat{c}_k (\hat{y}_{t+h-i-k} - \hat{\mu}_{t+h|t}) \right] \right\}
$$
$$
+ \sum_{j=1}^{s} \hat{\theta}_j (\hat{y}_{t+h-j} - \hat{y}_{t+h-j|t}). \tag{3.22}
$$

Recall that when exogenous variables enter the conditional mean equation, μ becomes $\mu_t = \mu + \sum_{i=1}^{n_1} \delta_i x_{i,t}$ and consequently, provided that the information $x_{i,t+h}$ is available at time t (which is the case for instance if $x_{i,t}$ is a "day-of-the-week" dummy variable), $\hat{\mu}_{t+h|t}$ is also available at time t. When there is no exogenous variable in the ARFIMA model and $n = 1, s = 0$ and $\zeta = 0$ ($c_k = 0$), the forecast of the AR(1) process given in Equation (3.21) can be recovered.

Note that for ARCH-in-mean models, $\hat{\mu}_{t+h|t} = \mu + \sum_{i=1}^{n_1} \delta_i x_{i,t+h|t} + \vartheta \sigma_{t+h|t}^k$ (with $k = 1$ or 2).

3.10.2 Forecasting the Conditional Variance

Independently from the conditional mean, one can forecast the conditional variance. In the simple ARCH(q) case, the optimal h-step-ahead forecast of the conditional variance, i.e. $\hat{\sigma}_{t+h|t}^2$ is given by:

$$
\sigma_{t+h|t}^2 = \hat{\omega} + \sum_{i=1}^{q} \hat{\alpha}_i \varepsilon_{t+h-i|t}^2, \tag{3.23}
$$

where $\varepsilon_{t+i|t}^2 = \sigma_{t+i|t}^2$ for $i > 0$ while $\varepsilon_{t+i|t}^2 = \varepsilon_{t+i}^2$ for $i \leq 0$. Equation (3.23) is usually computed recursively, even if a closed form solution of $\sigma_{t+h|t}^2$ can be obtained by recursive substitution in Equation (3.23).

Leaving out the last 10 observation for the forecasting experiment (as shown in the Estimate Model windows here below) and performing a 10-step-ahead forecasts of the Nasdaq based on the AR(1)-ARCH(1) produces Figure 3.5.

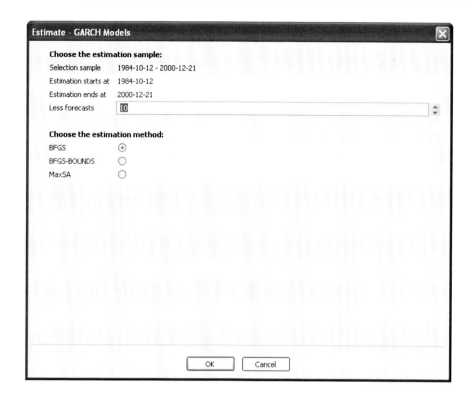

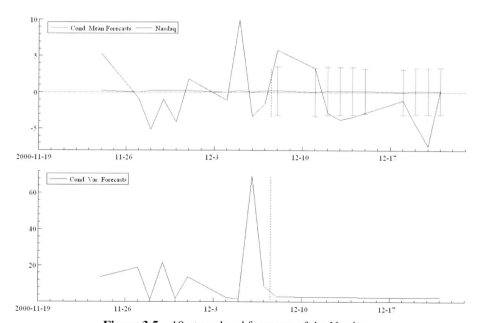

Figure 3.5   10-step-ahead forecasts of the Nasdaq.

The forecasted bands are $\pm 2\hat{\sigma}_{t+h|t}$ which gives a 95 % confidence interval (note that the critical value 2 can be changed).

Furthermore, if we leave enough observations for the out-of-sample period, G@RCH can report some standard measures of forecasting performance derived from the forecasts errors (see Box 5). Note that certain criteria are not computed on both the mean and the variance (because they are not relevant, e.g. Percentage Correct Sign(PCS) for the variance). In such a case, G@RCH reports a .NaN.

```
                               Box 5 - Forecast Evaluation Measures
                                              Mean      Variance
Mean Squared Error(MSE)                      16.81        438.5
Median Squared Error(MedSE)                  11.71         72.5
Mean Error(ME)                              -1.781        13.72
Mean Absolute Error(MAE)                      3.58        14.45
Root Mean Squared Error(RMSE)                  4.1        20.94
Mean Absolute Percentage Error(MAPE)          .NaN        4.602
Adjusted Mean Absolute Percentage Error(AMAPE) .NaN       0.674
Percentage Correct Sign(PCS)                   0.3         .NaN
Theil Inequality Coefficient(TIC)           0.9795       0.8254
Logarithmic Loss Function(LL)                 .NaN        4.344
```

3.11 Further Options

Finally, three options are also available in the Test menu: an Exclusion Restrictions dialog box, a Linear Restrictions dialog box and a Store in database dialog.

3.11.1 Exclusion Restrictions Dialog Box

The Exclusion Restrictions dialog box option allows you to select explanatory variables and test whether they are jointly significant. A more general form is the test for linear restrictions.

Mark all the variables you wish to include in the test in this Multiple-Selection List box. G@RCH tests whether the selected variables can be deleted from the model.

3.11.2 Linear Restrictions Dialog Box

Tests for linear restrictions are specified in the form of a matrix R, and a vector r. These are entered as one matrix $[R : r]$ in the dialog. (This is more general than testing for exclusion restrictions).

The first four columns are the columns of R, specifying two restrictions. The last column is r, which specifies what the restrictions should add up to.

The dimensions of the matrix must be specified in the rows and columns fields. It is your responsibility to specify the right values, G@RCH will not try to work it out (because elements of a row may be spread over several lines).

- **Rows** : The number of rows in the matrix.
- **Columns** : The number of columns in the matrix.
- **Matrix** : This window is a basic text editor in which you can edit a matrix file. Here you can enter the R:r matrix as in the above example.
- **Set to zero** : This could be useful to create an initial matrix. Select variables in the model box (this is a this multiple-selection list box) and press this button to specify the $R : r$ matrix which corresponds to the restriction that each selected variable has coefficient zero (so one row for each selected variable).
- **Load** : Enables you to load an existing matrix file into the editor. Any existing matrix in the editor will be lost.
- **Save** : Enables you to save the contents of the editor in an matrix file, so that it can be used again.

3.11.3 Store in Database Dialog

Finally, the residuals, the squared residuals, the standardized residuals, the conditional variance and the h-step-ahead forecasts (of the conditional mean and the conditional variance) can be stored in the database as new variables. When selecting this option, a first window appears and the user selects the series to be stored. A default name is then proposed for this series.

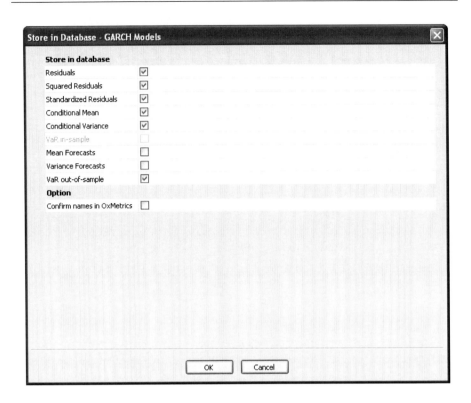

3.12 The random walk hypothesis (RWH)

This section has been largely inspired by Taylor (1995).

Are prices (or returns) of financial assets forecastable? According to the random walk hypothesis (RWH) not. The steps of a random walk are unpredictable. The RWH associates steps with returns, so that returns can not be predicted from past values. In G@RCH, the RWH is here defined by two statements about the stochastic process $\{r_t\}$ that provides observed returns: The mean is stationary, $E[r_t] = \mu$, and returns are uncorrelated, $\text{corr}(r_t, r_{t+\tau}) = 0, \tau \neq 0$.

When RWH is true, the latest return and all past returns are irrelevant if we attempt to predict future returns using linear predictors. In this case, the variables can be assumed to be a martingale difference and thus expected returns do not depend on the history of time series information.[15]

---

[15]Tests of the RWH can provide insights into issues of market efficiency. However, rejection of the RWH is not sufficient to reject the weak-form of the efficient market hypothesis. See Taylor (1995) for an excellent discussion about the implications of a rejection of the RWH on the weak-form of the efficient market hypothesis.

3.12.1 The Variance-ratio test

The Variance-ratio test of Lo and MacKinlay (1988) is designed to detect either mean reversion or price trend behaviour. Let $x_t = \log(p_t)$ be the price logarithm (with any dividends reinvested). Then one-period returns are $r_t = x_t - x_{t-1}$. N-period returns are $r_t + ... + r_{t+N-1} = x_{t+N-1} - x_{t-1}$. Also, assuming the returns process is stationary, let $V(N) = \text{var}(r_t + ... + r_{t+N-1})$. When RWH is true, $V(N) = NV(1)$. The test attempts to decide if this property is true. N is any integer, ≥ 2.

For any stationary process, the variance-ratio is

$$\frac{V(N)}{NV(1)} = 1 + 2 \sum_{\tau=1}^{N-1} \frac{N-\tau}{N} \rho_\tau,$$

by using the formula for the variance of a linear combination. Consequently, the variance-ratio test is appropriate when any dependence occurs for at least $N-1$ lags and when the autocorrelations all have the same sign. It is a good test when the alternative to RWH is an ARMA(1,1) process that have a positive autoregressive parameter for returns.

Implementation of the test requires:

(1) Estimates of $V(1), V(N)$.
(2) An estimate of the standard error of the variance-ratio estimate.
(3) Five steps to implement the tests.

Assume there are n returns.

<u>Step 1</u> : Calculate the average return and unbiased variance estimates, thus:

$$\hat{V}(1) = \frac{1}{n-1} \sum_{t=1}^{n} (r_t - \bar{r})^2$$

$$\hat{V}(N) = \frac{n}{(n-N)(n-N+1)} \sum_{t=1}^{n-N+1} (r_t + ... + r_{t+N-1} - N\bar{r})^2.$$

<u>Step 2</u> : Calculate the sample variance ratio as

$$V\hat{R}(N) = \frac{\hat{V}(N)}{N\hat{V}(1)}.$$

Reject RWH if $V\hat{R}(N)$ is far from 1.

Recall that

$$VR(N) \equiv \frac{V(N)}{NV(1)} = 1 + 2 \sum_{\tau=1}^{N-1} \frac{N-\tau}{N} \rho_\tau,$$

and

$$V\hat{R}(N) \equiv \frac{V(N)}{NV(1)} \cong 1 + 2 \sum_{\tau=1}^{N-1} \frac{N-\tau}{N} \hat{\rho}_\tau.$$

Under H_0, $E(V\hat{R}(N)) = 1$ and thus $Var(V\hat{R}(N)) = Var\left(2 \sum_{\tau=1}^{N-1} \frac{N-\tau}{N} \hat{\rho}_\tau\right)$. An appropriate estimate of $nVar(\rho_\tau)$ is provided by b_τ.

Step 3 : Estimate variances for the sample autocorrelations, $\hat{\rho}_\tau$, of the n returns, for $1 \le \tau \le N-1$, under the assumption that RWH is true.

$$b_\tau = \frac{n \sum_{t=1}^{n-\tau} s_t s_{t+\tau}}{(\sum_{t=1}^n s_t)^2} = \frac{n \sum_{t=1}^{n-\tau} (r_t - \bar{r})^2 (r_{t+\tau} - \bar{r})^2}{[\sum_{t=1}^n (r_t - \bar{r})^2]^2},$$

where $s_t = (r_t - \bar{r})^2$.

A very good approximation is given by $b_\tau \cong 1 + (ku - 1)\hat{\rho}_{\tau,s}$, where ku is the sample kurtosis of the returns r_t and $\hat{\rho}_{\tau,s}$ is the sample autocorrelation at lag τ of the time series $\{s_1, ..., s_n\}$ defined by $s_t = (r_t - \bar{r})^2$.

Step 4 : Estimate a variance for the variance-ratio $V\hat{R}(N)$, under the assumption that RWH is true.

This is denoted by $\frac{v_N}{n}$. Then

$$v_N = \sum_{\tau=1}^{N-1} \left[\frac{2(N-\tau)}{N}\right]^2 b_\tau = nVar(V\hat{R}).$$

Equivalently,

$$v_N = \frac{4}{N^2} \sum_{\tau=1}^{N-1} (N-\tau)^2 b_\tau.$$

Step 5 : Calculate the test statistic,

$$z_N = \frac{V\hat{R}(N) - 1}{\sqrt{v_N/n}}.$$

The asymptotic distribution of this statistic is $N(0,1)$ when RWH is true.

Monte Carlo experiment

To study the performance of this test, let us consider a first simulation study (see Simulation_VR.ox). We simulate 1000 series of $T = 2000$ observations following a N-AR(0) model with $\mu = 0.1$, i.e. $(y_t - \mu) = \varepsilon_t$, where $\varepsilon_t \sim N(0, \sigma^2)$ and $\sigma = 0.2$. We than apply the Variance-ratio test with $N = 2, 3$ and 10. The 1000 realisations of the VR statistics are plotted in Figure 3.6 while the empirical distribution of the VR statistics is plotted in Figure 3.7 (together with a N(0,1)).

   We see from Figure 3.6 that the VR statistics varies between -3 and 3. Furthermore, Figure 3.7 suggests that the VR statistics is close to be standard normal distributed.

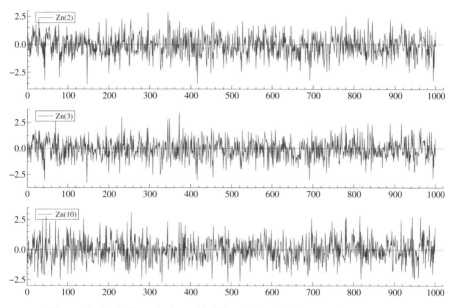

Figure 3.6   VR statistics with $N = 2, 3$ and 10. DGP is a N-AR(0).

   The number of times that the null is rejected at the $\alpha\%$ nominal size (called the empirical size of the test) is reported below.

```
Empirical size with alpha=0.10 and M=2:8.1
Empirical size with alpha=0.05 and M=2:3.3
Empirical size with alpha=0.01 and M=2:0.4
Empirical size with alpha=0.10 and M=3:7.5
Empirical size with alpha=0.05 and M=3:3.7
Empirical size with alpha=0.01 and M=3:0.8
Empirical size with alpha=0.10 and M=10:8.2
Empirical size with alpha=0.05 and M=10:4.7
Empirical size with alpha=0.01 and M=10:1.4
```

   These results suggest that the test suffers from a minor size distortion for the three considered values of M.

   To study the power of the test, we now simulate $T = 2000$ observations of a N-

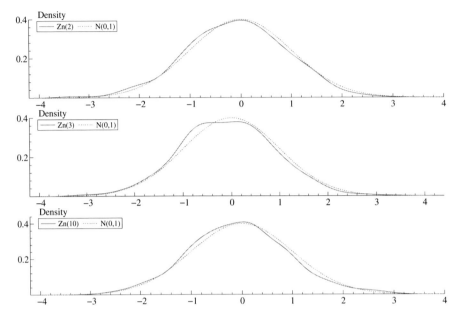

Figure 3.7   SIZE: Empirical distribution of the VR test with $N = 2, 3$ and 10. DGP is a N-AR(0).

AR(1) model with $\mu = 0.1$ and $\rho = 0.1$, i.e. $(1 - \rho L)(y_t - \mu) = \varepsilon_t$, where $\varepsilon_t \sim N(0, \sigma^2)$ and $\sigma = 0.2$. To obtain this configuration of the model, chose the following options:

```
decl m_vAR=<0.05>;
decl m_cAR=1;
```

The empirical distribution of the VR statistics (under the alternative) is plotted in Figure 3.8 (together with a N(0,1)).

Both Figure 3.8 and the output here below suggest that the VR test has good power to detect the presence of serial correlation in the series.

```
Empirical power with alpha=0.10 and M=2:69.5
Empirical power with alpha=0.05 and M=2:58.4
Empirical power with alpha=0.01 and M=2:33.3
Empirical power with alpha=0.10 and M=3:61.5
Empirical power with alpha=0.05 and M=3:50.4
Empirical power with alpha=0.01 and M=3:28
Empirical power with alpha=0.10 and M=10:32.1
Empirical power with alpha=0.05 and M=10:22.9
```

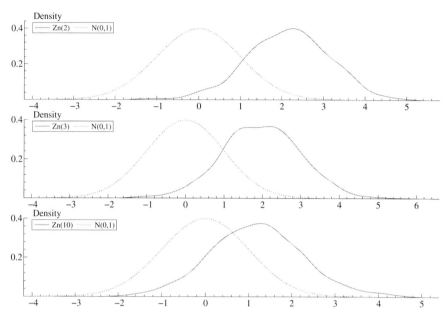

Figure 3.8 POWER: Empirical distribution of the VR test with $N = 2, 3$ and 10. DGP is a N-AR(1).

```
Empirical power with alpha=0.01 and M=10:8.9
```

A potential weakness of the VR test is that it assumes a constant variance while it is clear that most financial time series do not have constant conditional variance. To study the impact of the presence of GARCH effects on the VR test, let us now simulate $T = 2000$ observations of a N-AR(0)-GARCH(1,1) model with $\mu = 0.1$, i.e. $(y_t - \mu) = \varepsilon_t$, where $\varepsilon_t \sim N(0, \sigma_t^2)$, $\sigma_t^2 = \omega + \alpha_1 \varepsilon_{t-1}^2 + \beta_1 \sigma_{t-1}^2$ with $\omega = 0.2, \alpha_1 = 0.1$ and $\beta_1 = 0.8$.

Again, we simulate 1000 series following this DGP and apply the VR test with the same values for M.

Chose now the following options in `Simulation_VR.ox`:

```
decl m_cModel=1;
decl m_cAR=0;

Empirical size with alpha=0.10 and M=2:12.1
Empirical size with alpha=0.05 and M=2:6.2
Empirical size with alpha=0.01 and M=2:0.9
Empirical size with alpha=0.10 and M=3:10.4
Empirical size with alpha=0.05 and M=3:5
```

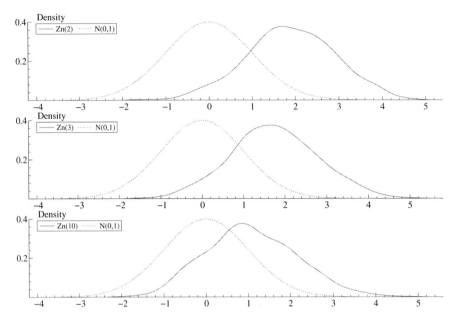

Figure 3.9   Empirical size of the VR test with $N = 2, 3$ and 10. DGP is a N-AR(0)-GARCH(1,1).

```
Empirical size with alpha=0.01 and M=3:0.7
Empirical size with alpha=0.10 and M=10:8.5
Empirical size with alpha=0.05 and M=10:3.5
Empirical size with alpha=0.01 and M=10:0.7
```

The empirical distribution of the VR statistics is plotted in Figure 3.9 and the empirical size in the output just below. The main conclusion is that the presence of GARCH effects has a negligible impact on the size of the test.

However, the power of the test is slightly affected by the presence of GARCH effects. Indeed, adding an AR(1) component to this GARCH model (with $\rho = 0.05$) substantially reduces the power of the test as suggested below.

To obtain these results, chose the following options in `Simulation_VR.ox`:

```
decl m_cModel=1;
decl m_vAR=<0.05>;
decl m_cAR=1;
```

```
Empirical power with alpha=0.10 and M=2:59.2
Empirical power with alpha=0.05 and M=2:47.4
Empirical power with alpha=0.01 and M=2:25.4
```

```
Empirical power with alpha=0.10 and M=3:53.1
Empirical power with alpha=0.05 and M=3:40.6
Empirical power with alpha=0.01 and M=3:21.4
Empirical power with alpha=0.10 and M=10:29.9
Empirical power with alpha=0.05 and M=10:19.7
Empirical power with alpha=0.01 and M=10:8.4
```

To overcome this problem some authors have proposed to apply the VR test on the rescaled or standardized residuals of a GARCH-type model.

This is illustrated in `Simulation_VR_GARCH.ox`.

As suggested by the next output, applying the VR test on the rescaled returns restores its original power to the test (i.e. case AR(1) without GARCH effects).

```
Empirical power with alpha=0.10 and M=2:69.5
Empirical power with alpha=0.05 and M=2:58.4
Empirical power with alpha=0.01 and M=2:33.3
Empirical power with alpha=0.10 and M=3:61.5
Empirical power with alpha=0.05 and M=3:50.4
Empirical power with alpha=0.01 and M=3:28
Empirical power with alpha=0.10 and M=10:32.1
Empirical power with alpha=0.05 and M=10:22.9
Empirical power with alpha=0.01 and M=10:8.9
```

See Taylor (1995) for more details about the VR tests as well as some applications on real data.

3.12.2 Runs test

Another popular test of the RMH is the Runs test, first used by Fama (1965). The runs test (also called Wald-Wolfowitz test) is a non-parametric test that checks the randomness hypothesis of a two- or three-valued data sequence. Similar to a first-autocorrelation test but is non-parametric and does not require any assumption of normality and stationary distribution. A run' is a sequence of adjacent equal elements. For example, the sequence "1111000111001111110000" is divided in six runs, three of which consist of 1's and the others of 0's. If the 1's and 0's alternate randomly, the number of runs is a random variable whose asymptotic distribution is N.

Let q_t be the sign of the return r_t, q_t is $1, 0, -1$, respectively for positive, zero, negative values of r_t. Let c_t be 1 if $q_t \neq q_{t+1}$ and 0 otherwise. The total number of runs of all types is

$$C = 1 + \sum_{t=1}^{n-1} c_t.$$

Suppose there are n_1 positive returns, n_2 zero returns, and n_3 negative returns in a series of n returns (with 0 mean $\rightarrow$ apply the test on $r_t - \bar{r}$). Then the mean and variance of the random variable generating C, conditional upon n_1, n_2, and n_3, are

$$E(C) = n + 1 - 1/n \sum_{j=1}^{3} n_j^2$$
$$\text{Var}(C) = \frac{\sum_{j=1}^{3} n_j^2 \left(n + n^2 + \sum_{j=1}^{3} n_j^2\right) - n^3 - 2n \sum_{j=1}^{3} n_j^3}{n^3 - n},$$

when the signs q_t are generated by i.i.d. variables (Mood, 1940).

The statistic C has an approximate normal distribution, for large n. Tests can then be decided by evaluating

$$K = (C - E(C))/\sqrt{\text{Var}(C)},$$

with RWH rejected at the 5% level if $|K| > 1.96$. The Runs test avoids all the problems created by conditional heteroskedasticity. Note that trends in prices (vs. no trend) would give fewer runs than expected.

To study the performance of the Runs test, let us consider a first simulation study (see `Simulation_VR.ox`). We simulate 1000 series of $T = 2000$ observations following a N-AR(0) model with $\mu = 0.1$, i.e. $(y_t - \mu) = \varepsilon_t$, where $\varepsilon_t \sim N(0, \sigma^2)$ and $\sigma = 0.2$. We than apply the Variance-ratio test with $N = 2, 3$ and 10. The empirical distribution of the K statistics is plotted in Figure 3.10 (together with a N(0,1)).

The output reported here below also suggests that the test has a correct size at the three chosen significance levels. Results not reported here suggest (as expected) that the test is not affected by the presence of GARCH effects.

```
Empirical size with alpha=0.10:11.1
Empirical size with alpha=0.05:5.1
Empirical size with alpha=0.01:0.9
```

Let us now study the power of the Runs test by considering a N-AR(1) model. The results suggest that this tests suffers from a reduction in power (compared to the VR test on the same DGP) due to the loss of information in the transformation form returns to their signs.

```
Empirical power with alpha=0.10:41.8
Empirical power with alpha=0.05:30.7
Empirical power with alpha=0.01:12.5
```

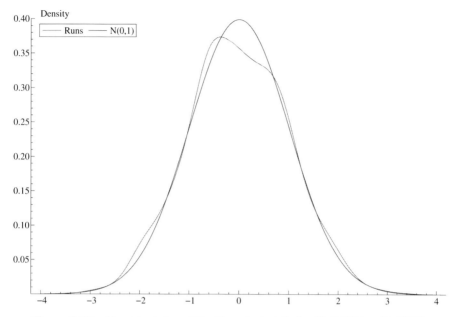

Figure 3.10 Empirical size of the Runs test statistics K. DGP is a N-AR(0).

3.12.3 Rescaled Range Tests

Range statistics that have power to detect long-term dependence were first developed for hydrological data by Hurst (1951) and later applied to financial returns.

Lo (1991) provides many references and a rigorous description of appropriate tests when the preferred alternative to randomness is long-term dependence. The range defined by a set of returns $\{r_1, ..., r_n\}$:

$$M_n = \left[\max_{1 \leq T \leq n} \sum_{t=1}^{T} (r_t - \bar{r}) \right] - \left[\min_{1 \leq T \leq n} \sum_{t=1}^{T} (r_t - \bar{r}) \right].$$

R/S-test statistics are ranges divided by scaled standard deviations

$$\frac{R}{S} = \frac{1}{\sqrt{n}\hat{\sigma}} M_n.$$

Two special cases define Mandelbrot (1972)'s and Lo (1991)'s test statistics:

$$\hat{\sigma} = s \text{ defines } (R/S)_{Man}$$

and

$$\hat{\sigma}^2 = s^2 \left[1 + 2 \sum_{j=1}^{q} \left(1 - \frac{j}{q+1} \right) \hat{\rho}_j \right] \text{ defines } (R/S)_{Lo}$$

with s^2 the sample variance of returns.

Under certain assumptions, the distributions of these statistics converge, as n and q increase, to that of the range of a Brownian bridge on the unit interval. The rule is the

following: do not reject the null when

$$\frac{R}{S} \in \quad [0.861 ; 1.747] \quad \text{at the 10\% level}$$
$$\frac{R}{S} \in \quad [0.809 ; 1.862] \quad \text{at the 5\% level}$$
$$\frac{R}{S} \in \quad [0.721 ; 2.098] \quad \text{at the 1\% level}$$

The null hypothesis of an uncorrelated process can be tested using $(R/S)Man$, and Lo focuses on the null hypothesis of a short memory process and then the appropriate test statistic is $(R/S)LO$.

To study the performance of the R/S tests, let us consider the following simulation study (see Simulation_RS.ox). We simulate 1000 series of $T = 2000$ observations following a N-AR(0) model with $\mu = 0.1$, i.e. $(y_t - \mu) = \varepsilon_t$, where $\varepsilon_t \sim N(0, \sigma^2)$ and $\sigma = 0.2$. We than apply the $(R/S)Man$ test and the $(R/S)LO$ test with $q = 10$ and 20.

The empirical size of the tests is reported below. The results suggest that the test is perfectly sized.

```
(R/S)Man Test
Empirical size with alpha=0.10:10.6
Empirical size with alpha=0.05:5.3
Empirical size with alpha=0.01:1.4


(R/S)Lo Test
Empirical size with alpha=0.10 and q=10:9.5
Empirical size with alpha=0.05 and q=10:5.3
Empirical size with alpha=0.01 and q=10:1.5
Empirical size with alpha=0.10 and q=20:9.1
Empirical size with alpha=0.05 and q=20:5
Empirical size with alpha=0.01 and q=20:1.1
```

The next output corresponds to the AR(1) case with $\rho = 0.05$, obtained with the following options

```
decl m_vAR=<0.05>;
decl m_cAR=1;
```

It is clear that the tests have no power against short memory processes.

```
(R/S)Man Test
Empirical power with alpha=0.10:11
Empirical power with alpha=0.05:5.5
```

```
Empirical power with alpha=0.01:1.4
```

```
(R/S)Lo Test
Empirical power with alpha=0.10 and q=10:9.7
Empirical power with alpha=0.05 and q=10:5.4
Empirical power with alpha=0.01 and q=10:1.4
Empirical power with alpha=0.10 and q=20:8.9
Empirical power with alpha=0.05 and q=20:4.8
Empirical power with alpha=0.01 and q=20:1.1
```

With a much higher value of ρ, i.e. $\rho = 0.5$, we see that the statistics of Lo (1991) is close to its nominal size while the one of Mandelbrot (1972) has some power to detect short memory.

```
(R/S)Man Test
Empirical power with alpha=0.10:74.4
Empirical power with alpha=0.05:65.6
Empirical power with alpha=0.01:45.1
```

```
(R/S)Lo Test
Empirical power with alpha=0.10 and q=10:10.6
Empirical power with alpha=0.05 and q=10:6.2
Empirical power with alpha=0.01 and q=10:1.2
Empirical power with alpha=0.10 and q=20:9.4
Empirical power with alpha=0.05 and q=20:5.5
Empirical power with alpha=0.01 and q=20:1.2
```

Results not reported here suggest that theses two statistics are not affected by the presence of GARCH effects.

To study the ability of the $(R/S)LO$ statistics to detect long range dependance, we now use the ARFIMA package of Doornik and Ooms (1999) to simulate $T = 2000$ observations of a N-ARFIMA(0,0.2,0) model with $\mu = 0.1$, i.e. $(1-L)^{0.2}(y_t - \mu) = \varepsilon_t$, where $\varepsilon_t \sim N(0, \sigma^2)$ and $\sigma = 0.2$.

This results of this simulation have been obtained using example file Simulation_RS.ox with the following options:

```
decl m_cAR=0;
decl m_cD=1;
decl m_vD=0.2;
```

The next output suggests that the $(R/S)LO$ statistics indeed has power to detect long-memory.

```
(R/S)Man Test
Empirical size with alpha=0.10:96.1
Empirical size with alpha=0.05:94.6
Empirical size with alpha=0.01:87.2

(R/S)Lo Test
Empirical size with alpha=0.10 and q=10:64.4
Empirical size with alpha=0.05 and q=10:55.9
Empirical size with alpha=0.01 and q=10:37.6
Empirical size with alpha=0.10 and q=20:47.5
Empirical size with alpha=0.05 and q=20:37.9
Empirical size with alpha=0.01 and q=20:22
```

Chapter 4

Further Univariate GARCH Models

While Engle (1982) is certainly the most important contribution in financial econometrics, the ARCH model is rarely used in practice due to its simplicity.

A useful generalization of this model is the GARCH model introduced by Bollerslev
(1986). This model is also a weighted average of past squared residuals, but it has
declining weights that never go completely to zero. This model is more parsimonious
than the ARCH and, even in its simplest form, has proven surprisingly successful in
predicting conditional variances.

The GARCH model is not the only extension. Indeed, G@RCH 6.0 proposes no
less than 12 specifications. As shown below, choosing an alternative model is extremely
easy in G@RCH.

4.1 GARCH Model

The Generalized ARCH (GARCH) model of Bollerslev (1986) is based on an infinite
ARCH specification and it allows to reduce the number of estimated parameters by
imposing nonlinear restrictions on them. The GARCH (p, q) model can be expressed
as:

$$\sigma_t^2 = \omega + \sum_{i=1}^{q} \alpha_i \varepsilon_{t-i}^2 + \sum_{j=1}^{p} \beta_j \sigma_{t-j}^2. \tag{4.1}$$

Using the lag (or backshift) operator L, the GARCH (p, q) model becomes:

$$\sigma_t^2 = \omega + \alpha(L)\varepsilon_t^2 + \beta(L)\sigma_t^2,$$

with $\alpha(L) = \alpha_1 L + \alpha_2 L^2 + \ldots + \alpha_q L^q$ and $\beta(L) = \beta_1 L + \beta_2 L^2 + \ldots + \beta_p L^p$.

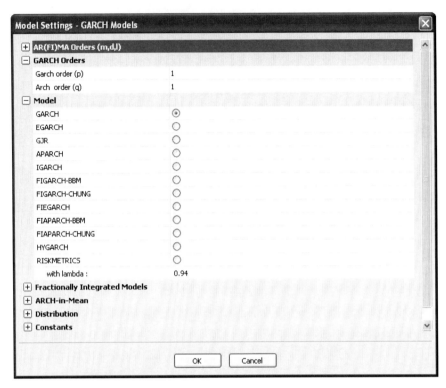

If all the roots of the polynomial $|1 - \beta(L)| = 0$ lie outside the unit circle, we have:

$$\sigma_t^2 = \omega \left[1 - \beta(L)\right]^{-1} + \alpha(L) \left[1 - \beta(L)\right]^{-1} \varepsilon_t^2, \tag{4.2}$$

which may be seen as an ARCH(∞) process since the conditional variance linearly depends on all previous squared residuals. In this case, the conditional variance of y_t can become larger than the unconditional variance given by

$$\sigma^2 \equiv E(\varepsilon_t^2) = \frac{\omega}{1 - \sum\limits_{i=1}^{q} \alpha_i - \sum\limits_{j=1}^{p} \beta_j},$$

if past realizations of ε_t^2 are larger than σ^2 (Palm, 1996).

Applying variance targeting to the GARCH model implies replacing ω by $\sigma^2 \left(1 - \sum\limits_{i=1}^{q} \alpha_i - \sum\limits_{j=1}^{p} \beta_j\right)$, where σ^2 is the unconditional variance of ε_t, which can be consistently estimated by its sample counterpart.[1]

---

[1] If explanatory variables appear in the GARCH equation, ω is then replaced by $\sigma^2 \left(1 - \sum\limits_{i=1}^{q} \alpha_i - \sum\limits_{j=1}^{p} \beta_j\right) - \sum\limits_{i=1}^{n_2} \omega_i \bar{x}_i$, where $\bar{x}_i$ is the sample average of variable $x_{i,t}$ (assuming the stationarity of the n_2 explanatory variables).

Bollerslev (1986) has shown that for a GARCH$(1, 1)$ with normal innovations, the kurtosis of y is $3[1 - (\alpha_1 + \beta_1)^2]/\left[1 - (\alpha_1 + \beta_1)^2 - 2\alpha_1^2\right] > 3$. The autocorrelations of ε_t^2 have been derived by Bollerslev (1986). For a stationary GARCH$(1,1)$, $\rho_1 = \alpha_1 + [\alpha_1^2\beta_1/(1 - 2\alpha_1\beta_1 - \beta_1^2)]$, and $\rho_k = (\alpha_1 + \beta_1)^{k-1}\rho_1$, $\forall k = 2, 3, \ldots$ In other words, the autocorrelations decline exponentially with a decay factor of $\alpha_1 + \beta_1$.

As in the ARCH case, some restrictions are needed to ensure σ_t^2 to be positive for all t. Bollerslev (1986) shows that imposing $\omega > 0$, $\alpha_i \geq 0$ (for $i = 1, \ldots, q$) and $\beta_j \geq 0$ (for $j = 1, \ldots, p$) is sufficient for the conditional variance to be positive. In practice, the GARCH parameters are often estimated without the positivity constraints. Nelson and Cao (1992) argue that imposing all coefficients to be nonnegative is too restrictive and that some of these coefficients are found to be negative in practice while the conditional variance remains positive (by checking on a case-by-case basis). Consequently, they relaxed this constraint and gave sufficient conditions for the GARCH$(1, q)$ and GARCH$(2, q)$ cases based on the infinite representation given in Equation (4.2). Indeed, the conditional variance is strictly positive provided $\omega\left[1 - \beta(1)\right]^{-1}$ is positive and all the coefficients of the infinite polynomial $\alpha(L)\left[1 - \beta(L)\right]^{-1}$ in Equation (4.2) are nonnegative. The positivity constraints proposed by Bollerslev (1986) can be imposed during the estimation (see Section 3.9). If not, these constraints, as well as the ones implied by the ARCH(∞) representation, will be tested a posteriori and reported in the output (if there is no explanatory variable in the conditional variance equation).

Estimation results of an ARMA(1,0)-GARCH(1,1) model by QML are reported in the next Output (labelled Box 6).

```
                   Box 6 - Output of the ARMA(1,0)-GARCH(1,1) by QMLE
********************************
** G@RCH( 3) SPECIFICATIONS **
********************************
Dependent variable : Nasdaq
Mean Equation : ARMA (1, 0) model.
1 regressor(s) in the mean.
Variance Equation : GARCH (1, 1) model.
1 regressor(s) in the variance.
The distribution is a Gauss distribution.

Strong convergence using numerical derivatives
Log-likelihood = -5370.86
Please wait : Computing the Std Errors ...

Robust Standard Errors (Sandwich formula)
                 Coefficient  Std.Error  t-value  t-prob
Cst(M)              0.116210   0.015919    7.300  0.0000
Monday (M)         -0.174801   0.028920   -6.044  0.0000
AR(1)               0.193905   0.017177   11.29   0.0000
Cst(V)              0.009292   0.012566    0.7394 0.4597
Friday (V)          0.067380   0.059745    1.128  0.2595
ARCH(Alpha1)        0.164808   0.028030    5.880  0.0000
GARCH(Beta1)        0.826238   0.026107   31.65   0.0000

No. Observations :     4093  No. Parameters  :        7
Mean (Y)          :  0.05517  Variance (Y)    :  1.59189
Skewness (Y)      : -0.74128  Kurtosis (Y)    : 14.25531
Log Likelihood    : -5370.858 Alpha[1]+Beta[1]:  0.99105

The sample mean of squared residuals was used to start recursion.

Estimated Parameters Vector :
  0.116210;-0.174801; 0.193905; 0.009292; 0.067380; 0.164808; 0.826243

Elapsed Time : 2.975 seconds (or 0.0495833 minutes).
```

Interestingly, the log-likelihood now equals -5370.858 against -6106.357 for the corresponding ARCH(1) model. Any likelihood ratio test (LRT), asymptotically $\sim \chi^2(1)$, would reject the ARCH(1) model in favour of the GARCH(1, 1).

Furthermore, we report below the same 6 misspecification tests as for the ARCH(1) model. The output is reported in Box 7 - Misspecification Tests.

```
                                        Box 7 - Misspecification Tests
TESTS :
------------
Information Criterium (to be minimized)
Akaike          2.627832  Shibata         2.627826
Schwarz         2.638636  Hannan-Quinn    2.631657
---------------

                 Statistic      t-Test      P-Value
Skewness         -0.65157      17.024    5.4349e-065
Excess Kurtosis   2.6513       34.645    5.2745e-263
Jarque-Bera       1488.4        .NaN       0.00000
---------------


Q-Statistics on Standardized Residuals
  --> P-values adjusted by 1 degree(s) of freedom
  Q(  5) =  4.57820    [0.3333749]
  Q( 10) =  5.22369    [0.8143890]
  Q( 20) = 18.7431     [0.4734248]
  Q( 50) = 58.5113     [0.1657199]
HO : No serial correlation ==> Accept HO when prob. is High [Q < Chisq(lag)]
---------------


Q-Statistics on Squared Standardized Residuals
  --> P-values adjusted by 2 degree(s) of freedom
  Q(  5) =  3.79989    [0.2838986]
  Q( 10) =  7.15170    [0.5203577]
  Q( 20) = 16.8830     [0.5311632]
  Q( 50) = 46.2948     [0.5429339]
HO : No serial correlation ==> Accept HO when prob. is High [Q < Chisq(lag)]
---------------


Adjusted Pearson Chi-square Goodness-of-fit test

# Cells(g)  Statistic    P-Value(g-1)    P-Value(g-k-1)
   40       201.6787       0.000000         0.000000
   50       221.5492       0.000000         0.000000
   60       230.5035       0.000000         0.000000
Rem.: k = 7 = # estimated parameters
---------------


Residual-Based Diagnostic for Conditional Heteroskedasticity of Tse(2001)

  RBD( 2) =  2.02370    [0.3635463]
  RBD( 5) =  3.62445    [0.6046453]
  RBD(10) =  6.84825    [0.7396890]
-------------------------------------------------
P-values in brackets
```

Unlike the ARCH(1) model, the Q-Statistics on standardized and squared standardized residuals, as well as the RBD test with various lag values suggest that the GARCH(1, 1) does a good job in modelling the dynamics of the first two conditional moments of the NASDAQ.

However, the adjusted Pearson Chi-square goodness-of-fit test (with different cell numbers) still points out some misspecification of the overall conditional distribution.

Several authors have proposed to use a Student-t or GED distribution in combination with a GARCH model to model the fat tails of the high-frequency financial time-series. Furthermore, since the NASDAQ seems to be skewed, a skewed-Student distributions might be justified (see Section 6 for a discussion about non-normal distributions).

4.2 EGARCH Model

The Exponential GARCH (EGARCH) model, originally introduced by Nelson (1991), is re-expressed in Bollerslev and Mikkelsen (1996) as follows:

$$\log \sigma_t^2 = \omega + [1 - \beta(L)]^{-1} [1 + \alpha(L)] g(z_{t-1}). \tag{4.3}$$

The value of $g(z_t)$ depends on several elements. Nelson (1991) notes that, *"to accommodate the asymmetric relation between stock returns and volatility changes (...) the value of $g(z_t)$ must be a function of both the magnitude and the sign of z_t"*.[2] That is why he suggests to express the function $g(.)$ as

$$g(z_t) \equiv \underbrace{\gamma_1 z_t}_{\text{sign effect}} + \underbrace{\gamma_2[|z_t| - E|z_t|]}_{\text{magnitude effect}} \tag{4.4}$$

$E|z_t|$ depends on the assumption made on the unconditional density of z_t. Indeed, for the normal distribution,

$$E(|z_t|) = \sqrt{2/\pi}. \tag{4.5}$$

For the skewed-Student distribution,

$$E(|z_t|) = \frac{4\xi^2}{\xi + 1/\xi} \frac{\Gamma\left(\frac{1+v}{2}\right) \sqrt{v - 2}}{\sqrt{\pi}\Gamma(v/2)} \tag{4.6}$$

where $\xi = 1$ for the symmetric Student.

For the GED, we have

$$E(|z_t|) = 2^{(1/v)} \lambda_v \frac{\Gamma(2/v)}{\Gamma(1/v)}. \tag{4.7}$$

ξ, v and λ_v concern the shape of the non-normal densities and was defined in Section 3.6.2.

Note that the use of a $\log$ transformation of the conditional variance ensures that σ_t^2 is always positive.

Applying variance targeting to the EGARCH model implies replacing ω by $log(\sigma^2)$, where σ^2 is the unconditional variance of ε_t, which can be consistently estimated by its sample counterpart.[3]

---

[2]Note that with the EGARCH parameterization of Bollerslev and Mikkelsen (1996), it is possible to estimate an EGARCH $(p, 0)$ since $\log \sigma_t^2$ depends on $g(z_{t-1})$, even when $q = 0$.

[3]If explanatory variables appear in the EGARCH equation, ω is then replaced by $log(\sigma^2) - \sum_{i=1}^{n_2} w_i \bar{x}_i$, where $\bar{x}_i$ is the sample average of variable $x_{i,t}$ (assuming the stationarity of the n_2 explanatory variables).

The output reported below corresponds to the ARMA(1,0)-EGARCH(1,1) with a GED distribution. Interestingly, both θ_1 and θ_2 are significant. Note that the degree of freedom of the GED distribution is significantly lower than 2, confirming that the standardized residuals are fat-tailed.

```
                                                      Box 8 - EGARCH
*******************************
** G@RCH( 4) SPECIFICATIONS **
*******************************
Dependent variable : Nasdaq
Mean Equation : ARMA (1, 0) model.
1 regressor(s) in the mean.
Variance Equation : EGARCH (1, 1) model.
1 regressor(s) in the variance.
The distribution is a GED distribution, with a tail coefficient of 1.31814.

Strong convergence using numerical derivatives
Log-likelihood = -5233.92
Please wait : Computing the Std Errors ...

 Robust Standard Errors (Sandwich formula)
                 Coefficient  Std.Error  t-value  t-prob
Cst(M)              0.133901   0.010949    12.23  0.0000
Monday (M)         -0.166042   0.026034    -6.378  0.0000
AR(1)               0.188276   0.014182    13.28  0.0000
Cst(V)             -0.342968    0.21183    -1.619  0.1055
Friday (V)         -0.203655   0.079556    -2.560  0.0105
ARCH(Alpha1)       -0.355466    0.14267    -2.491  0.0128
GARCH(Beta1)        0.987227  0.0058283    169.4  0.0000
EGARCH(Theta1)     -0.085730   0.020159    -4.253  0.0000
EGARCH(Theta2)      0.305338   0.037692    8.101  0.0000
G.E.D.(DF)          1.318137   0.052628    25.05  0.0000

No. Observations :     4093  No. Parameters   :        10
Mean (Y)          :  0.05517  Variance (Y)    :   1.59189
Skewness (Y)      : -0.74128  Kurtosis (Y)    :  14.25531
Log Likelihood    : -5233.919

The sample mean of squared residuals was used to start recursion.

Estimated Parameters Vector :
0.133901;-0.166042; 0.188276;-0.342968;-0.203655;-0.355466;
0.987227;-0.085730; 0.305338; 1.318142
```

4.3 GJR Model

This popular model is proposed by Glosten, Jagannathan, and Runkle (1993). Its generalized version is given by:

$$\sigma_t^2 = \omega + \sum_{i=1}^{q} \left(\alpha_i \varepsilon_{t-i}^2 + \gamma_i S_{t-i}^- \varepsilon_{t-i}^2 \right) + \sum_{j=1}^{p} \beta_j \sigma_{t-j}^2, \qquad (4.8)$$

where S_t^- is a dummy variable that take the value 1 when γ_i is negative and 0 when it is positive.

In this model, it is assumed that the impact of ε_t^2 on the conditional variance σ_t^2 is different when ε_t is positive or negative. The TGARCH model of Zakoian (1994) is very similar to the GJR but models the conditional standard deviation instead of the conditional variance. Ling and McAleer (2002) provide, among other stationarity conditions for various GARCH models, the conditions of existence of the second and fourth moment of the GJR.

Applying variance targeting to the GJR model implies replacing ω by

$$\sigma^2 \left[1 - \sum_{i=1}^{q} \left(\alpha_i - \gamma_i E(S_t^-) \right) - \sum_{j=1}^{p} \beta_j \right], \quad \text{where } \sigma^2 \text{ is the unconditional variance}$$

of ε_t, which can be consistently estimated by its sample counterpart and $E(S_t^-)$ is 0.5 for symmetric distributions (i.e. Normal, Student and GED) and $\frac{1}{1+\xi^2}$ for the SKST.[4]

A nice feature of the GJR model is that the null hypothesis of no leverage effect is easy to test. Indeed, $\gamma_1 = \ldots = \gamma_q = 0$ implies that the news impact curve is symmetric, i.e. past positive shocks have the same impact on today's volatility as past negative shocks.

The output reported below suggests the presence of such an effect on the NASDAQ since $\hat{\gamma}_1 = 0.107988$ with a robust t-value of 2.826.

---

[4]If explanatory variables appear in the GJR equation, ω is then replaced by

$$\sigma^2 \left[1 - \sum_{i=1}^{q} \left(\alpha_i - \gamma_i E(S_t^-) \right) - \sum_{j=1}^{p} \beta_j \right] - \sum_{i=1}^{n_2} \omega_i \bar{x}_i, \quad \text{where } \bar{x}_i \text{ is the sample average of vari-}$$

able $x_{i,t}$ (assuming the stationarity of the n_2 explanatory variables).

```
                                                              Box 9 - GJR
   ********************************
   ** G@RCH( 5) SPECIFICATIONS **
   ********************************
   Dependent variable : Nasdaq
   Mean Equation : ARMA (1, 0) model.
   1 regressor(s) in the mean.
   Variance Equation : GJR (1, 1) model.
   1 regressor(s) in the variance.
   The distribution is a Gauss distribution.

   Strong convergence using numerical derivatives
   Log-likelihood = -5354.08
   Please wait : Computing the Std Errors ...

    Robust Standard Errors (Sandwich formula)
                    Coefficient  Std.Error  t-value  t-prob
   Cst(M)             0.093388    0.015714    5.943  0.0000
   Monday (M)        -0.163882    0.028471   -5.756  0.0000
   AR(1)              0.203798    0.018417   11.07   0.0000
   Cst(V)             0.014065    0.013479    1.044  0.2968
   Friday (V)         0.053779    0.060397    0.8904 0.3733
   ARCH(Alpha1)       0.105963    0.018002    5.886  0.0000
   GARCH(Beta1)       0.825532    0.026830   30.77   0.0000
   GJR(Gamma1)        0.107988    0.038216    2.826  0.0047

   No. Observations :      4093  No. Parameters   :        8
   Mean (Y)          :   0.05517  Variance (Y)    :   1.59189
   Skewness (Y)      :  -0.74128  Kurtosis (Y)    :  14.25531
   Log Likelihood    : -5354.076

   The sample mean of squared residuals was used to start recursion.

   Estimated Parameters Vector :
   0.093388;-0.163882; 0.203798; 0.014065; 0.053779; 0.105963; 0.825532; 0.107993

   Elapsed Time : 4.086 seconds (or 0.0681 minutes).
```

4.4 APARCH Model

This model has been introduced by Ding, Granger, and Engle (1993). The APARCH (p, q) model can be expressed as:

$$\sigma_t^\delta = \omega + \sum_{i=1}^{q} \alpha_i \left(|\varepsilon_{t-i}| - \gamma_i \varepsilon_{t-i} \right)^\delta + \sum_{j=1}^{p} \beta_j \sigma_{t-j}^\delta, \tag{4.9}$$

where $\delta > 0$ and $-1 < \gamma_i < 1$ $(i = 1, ..., q)$.

The parameter δ plays the role of a Box-Cox transformation of σ_t while γ_i reflects the so-called leverage effect. Properties of the APARCH model are studied in He and Teräsvirta (1999a, 1999b).

The APARCH includes seven other ARCH extensions as special cases:[5]

---

[5]Complete developments leading to these conclusions are available in Ding, Granger, and Engle (1993).

- The ARCH of Engle (1982) when $\delta = 2$, $\gamma_i = 0$ $(i = 1, \ldots, p)$ and $\beta_j = 0$ $(j = 1, \ldots, p)$.
- The GARCH of Bollerslev (1986) when $\delta = 2$ and $\gamma_i = 0$ $(i = 1, \ldots, p)$.
- Taylor (1986)/Schwert (1990)'s GARCH when $\delta = 1$, and $\gamma_i = 0$ $(i = 1, \ldots, p)$.
- The GJR of Glosten, Jagannathan, and Runkle (1993) when $\delta = 2$.
- The TARCH of Zakoian (1994) when $\delta = 1$.
- The NARCH of Higgins and Bera (1992) when $\gamma_i = 0$ $(i = 1, \ldots, p)$ and $\beta_j = 0$ $(j = 1, \ldots, p)$.
- The Log-ARCH of Geweke (1986) and Pentula (1986), when $\delta \to 0$.

Following Ding, Granger, and Engle (1993), if $\omega > 0$ and $\sum_{i=1}^{q} \alpha_i E(|z| - \gamma_i z)^\delta + \sum_{j=1}^{p} \beta_j < 1$, a stationary solution for Equation (4.9) exists and is expressed as:

$$E\left(\sigma_t^\delta\right) = \frac{\alpha_0}{1 - \sum_{i=1}^{q} \alpha_i E(|z| - \gamma_i z)^\delta - \sum_{j=1}^{p} \beta_j}. \qquad (4.10)$$

Notice that if we set $\gamma = 0$, $\delta = 2$ and if z_t has zero mean and unit variance, we have the usual stationarity condition of the GARCH(1,1) model ($\alpha_1 + \beta_1 < 1$). However, if $\gamma \neq 0$ and/or $\delta \neq 2$, this condition depends on the assumption made on the innovation process.

Ding, Granger, and Engle (1993) derive a closed form solution to $\kappa_i = E(|z| - \gamma_i z)^\delta$ in the Gaussian case. Lambert and Laurent (2001) show that for the standardized skewed-Student:[6]

$$\kappa_i = \left\{ \xi^{-(1+\delta)} (1+\gamma_i)^\delta + \xi^{1+\delta} (1-\gamma_i)^\delta \right\} \frac{\Gamma\left(\frac{\delta+1}{2}\right)\Gamma\left(\frac{v-\delta}{2}\right)(v-2)^{\frac{1+\delta}{2}}}{\left(\xi + \frac{1}{\xi}\right)\sqrt{(v-2)\pi}\,\Gamma\left(\frac{v}{2}\right)}.$$

For the GED, we can show that:

$$\kappa_i = \frac{[(1+\gamma_i)^\delta + (1-\gamma_i)^\delta] 2^{\frac{\delta-v}{v}} \Gamma\left(\frac{\delta+1}{v}\right) \lambda_v^\delta}{\Gamma\left(\frac{1}{v}\right)}.$$

Note that ξ, v and λ_v concern the shape of the non-normal densities and was defined in Section 3.6.2.

Applying variance targeting to the APARCH model implies replacing ω by

$$\sigma^\delta \left(1 - \sum_{i=1}^{q} \kappa_i \alpha_i - \sum_{j=1}^{p} \beta_j\right), \text{ where } \sigma \text{ is the unconditional standard deviation of } \varepsilon_t,$$

---

[6] For the symmetric Student density, $\xi = 1$.

which can be consistently estimated by its sample counterpart.[7]

Once again, the APARCH model suggest the presence of a leverage effect on the NASDAQ (see Box 10). Importantly, δ is significantly different from 2 ($\hat{\delta} = 1.146366$) but not significantly different from 1. This suggests that, instead of modelling the conditional variance (GARCH), it is more relevant in this case to model the conditional standard deviation. This result is in line with those of Taylor (1986), Schwert (1990) and Ding, Granger, and Engle (1993) who indicate that there is substantially more correlation between absolute returns than squared returns, a stylized fact of high frequency financial returns (often called 'long memory').

```
                                                              Box 10 - APARCH
 ********************************
 ** G@RCH( 6) SPECIFICATIONS **
 ********************************
 Dependent variable : Nasdaq
 Mean Equation : ARMA (1, 0) model.
 1 regressor(s) in the mean.
 Variance Equation : APARCH (1, 1) model.
 1 regressor(s) in the variance.
 The distribution is a Gauss distribution.

 Strong convergence using numerical derivatives
 Log-likelihood = -5341.37
 Please wait : Computing the Std Errors ...

  Robust Standard Errors (Sandwich formula)
                   Coefficient  Std.Error  t-value  t-prob
 Cst(M)               0.088279   0.019660    4.490  0.0000
 Monday (M)          -0.167957   0.028627   -5.867  0.0000
 AR(1)                0.194576   0.018647    10.43  0.0000
 Cst(V)               0.020683   0.011917    1.736  0.0827
 Friday (V)           0.028304   0.050441   0.5611  0.5747
 ARCH(Alpha1)         0.154370   0.024000    6.432  0.0000
 GARCH(Beta1)         0.855355   0.024859    34.41  0.0000
 APARCH(Gamma1)       0.288072   0.076177    3.782  0.0002
 APARCH(Delta)        1.146366   0.20559     5.576  0.0000

 No. Observations :     4093  No. Parameters  :        9
 Mean (Y)         :  0.05517  Variance (Y)    :  1.59189
 Skewness (Y)     : -0.74128  Kurtosis (Y)    : 14.25531
 Log Likelihood   : -5341.369

 The sample mean of squared residuals was used to start recursion.

 Estimated Parameters Vector :
 0.088279;-0.167957; 0.194576; 0.020683; 0.028304; 0.154370; 0.855355;
 0.288072; 1.146371

 Elapsed Time : 7.941 seconds (or 0.13235 minutes).
```

---

[7]If explanatory variables appear in the APARCH equation, ω is then replaced by

$$\sigma^{\delta}\left(1 - \sum_{i=1}^{q}\kappa_i\alpha_i - \sum_{j=1}^{p}\beta_j\right) - \sum_{i=1}^{n_2}\omega_i\bar{x}_i,$$ where $\bar{x}_i$ is the sample average of variable $x_{i,t}$ (as-

suming the stationarity of the n_2 explanatory variables).

4.5 IGARCH Model

In many high-frequency time-series applications, the conditional variance estimated using a GARCH(p, q) process exhibits a strong persistence, that is:

$$\sum_{j=1}^{p} \beta_j + \sum_{i=1}^{q} \alpha_i \approx 1.$$

If $\sum_{j=1}^{p} \beta_j + \sum_{i=1}^{q} \alpha_i < 1$, the process (ε_t) is second order stationary, and a shock to the conditional variance σ_t^2 has a decaying impact on σ_{t+h}^2, when h increases, and is asymptotically negligible. Indeed, let us rewrite the ARCH(∞) representation of the GARCH(p, q), given in Equation (4.2), as follows:

$$\sigma_t^2 = \omega^* + \lambda(L)\varepsilon_t^2, \tag{4.11}$$

where $\omega^* = \omega \left[1 - \beta(L)\right]^{-1}$, $\lambda(L) = \alpha(L) \left[1 - \beta(L)\right]^{-1} = \sum_{i=1}^{\infty} \lambda_i L^i$ and λ_i are lag coefficients depending nonlinearly on α_i and β_j. For a GARCH(1,1), $\lambda_i = \alpha_1 \beta_1^{i-1}$. Recall that this model is said to be second order stationary provided that $\alpha_1 + \beta_1 < 1$ since it implies that the unconditional variance exists and equals $\omega/(1 - \alpha_1 - \beta_1)$. As shown by Davidson (2004), the amplitude of the GARCH(1,1) is measured by $S = \sum_{i=1}^{\infty} \lambda_i = \alpha_1/(1 - \beta_1)$, which determines "how large the variations in the conditional variance can be" (and hence the order of the existing moments). This concept is often confused with the memory of the model that determines "how long shocks to the volatility take to dissipate". In this respect, the GARCH(1,1) model has a geometric memory $\rho = 1/\beta_1$, where $\lambda_i = O\left(\rho^{-i}\right)$. In practice, we often find $\alpha_1 + \beta_1 = 1$. In this case, we are confronted with an Integrated GARCH (IGARCH) model.

The GARCH(p, q) model can be expressed as an ARMA process. Using the lag operator L, we can rearrange Equation (4.1) as:

$$[1 - \alpha(L) - \beta(L)]\varepsilon_t^2 = \omega + [1 - \beta(L)] \left(\varepsilon_t^2 - \sigma_t^2\right).$$

When the $[1 - \alpha(L) - \beta(L)]$ polynomial contains a unit root, i.e. the sum of all the α_i and the β_j is one, we have the IGARCH(p, q) model of Engle and Bollerslev (1986). It can then be written as:

$$\phi(L)(1 - L)\varepsilon_t^2 = \omega + [1 - \beta(L)](\varepsilon_t^2 - \sigma_t^2), \tag{4.12}$$

where $\phi(L) = [1 - \alpha(L) - \beta(L)](1 - L)^{-1}$ is of order $\max\{p, q\} - 1$.

We can rearrange Equation (4.12) to express the conditional variance as a function of the squared residuals. After some manipulations, we have its ARCH(∞) representation:

$$\sigma_t^2 = \frac{\omega}{[1 - \beta(L)]} + \left\{ 1 - \phi(L)(1 - L)[1 - \beta(L)]^{-1} \right\} \varepsilon_t^2. \qquad (4.13)$$

For this model, $S = 1$ and thus the second moment does not exist. However, this process is still short memory. To show this, Davidson (2004) considers an IGARCH(0,1) model defined as $\varepsilon_t = \sigma_t z_t$ and $\sigma_t^2 = \varepsilon_{t-1}^2$. This process is often wrongly compared to a random walk since the long-range forecast $\sigma_{t+h}^2 = \varepsilon_t^2$, for any h. However $\varepsilon_t = z_t \varepsilon_{t-1}$ which means that the memory of a large deviation persists for only one period.

4.6 RiskMetrics^{TM}

In October 1994, the risk management group at J.P. Morgan released a technical document describing its internal market risk management methodology (J.P.Morgan, 1996). This methodology, called RiskMetrics^{TM} soon became a standard in the market risk measurement due to its simplicity.

Basically, the RiskMetrics^{TM} model is an IGARCH(1,1) model where the ARCH and GARCH coefficients are fixed.

The model is given by:

$$\sigma_t^2 = \omega + (1 - \lambda)\varepsilon_{t-1}^2 + \lambda\sigma_{t-1}^2, \qquad (4.14)$$

where $\omega = 0$ and λ is generally set to 0.94 with daily data and to 0.97 with weekly data.[8] Note also that Equation 4.14 is the very basic conditional variance model of the RiskMetrics^{TM} methodology, but there exist many extensions of the original model. See the RiskMetrics Group website for details.

To illustrate the need for flexible ARCH-type models, here is the output of the Box-Pierce test on squared standardized residuals and the RBD test applied after the estimation of the RiskMetrics model (including an AR(1) term and the two dummy variables). There is no doubt that the RiskMetrics specification is not appropriate.

---

[8] In G@RCH, this value can obviously be changed by the user.

```
Q-Statistics on Squared Standardized Residuals
  --> P-values adjusted by 2 degree(s) of freedom
  Q(  5) =  82.0593   [0.0000]
  Q( 10) =  84.1246   [0.0000]
  Q( 20) =  93.3285   [0.0000]
  Q( 50) =  119.353   [0.0000]
HO : No serial correlation ==> Accept HO when prob. is High [Q < Chisq(lag)]
---------------

Residual-Based Diagnostic for Conditional Heteroskedasticity of Tse (2001)

  RBD( 2) =  54.0450   [0.0000]
  RBD( 5) =  54.6773   [0.0000]
  RBD(10) =  59.6488   [0.0000]
--------------------------------------------------
P-values in brackets
```

4.7 Fractionally Integrated Models

Volatility tends to change quite slowly over time, and, as shown in Ding, Granger, and Engle (1993) among others, the effects of a shock can take a considerable time to decay.[9] Therefore the distinction between stationary and unit root processes seems to be far too restrictive. Indeed, the propagation of shocks in a stationary process occurs at an exponential rate of decay (so that it only captures the short-memory), while for an unit root process the persistence of shocks is infinite. In the conditional mean, the ARFIMA specification has been proposed to fill the gap between short and complete persistence, so that the short-run behavior of the time-series is captured by the ARMA parameters, while the fractional differencing parameter allows for modelling the long-run dependence.[10]

To mimic the behavior of the correlogram of the observed volatility, Baillie, Bollerslev, and Mikkelsen (1996) (hereafter denoted BBM) introduce the Fractionally Integrated GARCH (FIGARCH) model by replacing the first difference operator of Equation (4.13) by $(1 - L)^d$.

The conditional variance of the FIGARCH (p, d, q) is given by:

$$\sigma_t^2 = \underbrace{\omega[1 - \beta(L)]^{-1}}_{\omega^*} + \underbrace{\left\{ 1 - [1 - \beta(L)]^{-1}\phi(L)(1 - L)^d \right\}}_{\lambda(L)}\varepsilon_t^2, \qquad (4.15)$$

---

[9]In their study of the daily S&P500 index, they find that the squared returns series has positive autocorrelations over more than 2,500 lags (or more than 10 years !).

[10]See Bollerslev and Mikkelsen (1996, p.158) for a discussion on the importance of non-integer values of integration when modelling long-run dependencies in the conditional mean of economic time series.

or $\sigma_t^2 = \omega^* + \sum_{i=1}^{\infty} \lambda_i L^i \varepsilon_t^2 = \omega^* + \lambda(L)\varepsilon_t^2$, with $0 \leq d \leq 1$. It is fairly easy to show that $\omega > 0, \beta_1 - d \leq \phi_1 \leq \frac{2-d}{3}$ and $d\left(\phi_1 - \frac{1-d}{2}\right) \leq \beta_1 \left(\phi_1 - \beta_1 + d\right)$ are sufficient to ensure that the conditional variance of the FIGARCH $(1, d, 1)$ is positive almost surely for all t. Setting $\phi_1 = 0$ gives the condition for the FIGARCH $(1, d, 0)$. See Section 3.9 to see how to impose these constraints.

When estimating a FIGARCH $(1, d, 1)$ model by QML on the NASDAQ dataset (see the next output, labelled Box 11), one sees that d is significantly different from 0 and 1 while ϕ_1 is barely significant. Importantly, comparing its log-likelihood with the one of the simple GARCH$(1,1)$, i.e. -5359.179 vs. -5370.858, justifies the use of a long-memory process in the conditional variance.

```
                                          Box 11 - FIGARCH-BBM
*******************************
** G@RCH( 7) SPECIFICATIONS **
*******************************
Dependent variable : Nasdaq
Mean Equation : ARMA (1, 0) model.
1 regressor(s) in the mean.
Variance Equation : FIGARCH (1, d, 1) model estimated with BBM's method
(Truncation order : 1000).
1 regressor(s) in the variance.
The distribution is a Gauss distribution.

Strong convergence using numerical derivatives
Log-likelihood = -5359.18
Please wait : Computing the Std Errors ...

 Robust Standard Errors (Sandwich formula)
                Coefficient  Std.Error  t-value  t-prob
Cst(M)             0.119253   0.016127    7.394  0.0000
Monday (M)        -0.174214   0.028834   -6.042  0.0000
AR(1)              0.195242   0.017134   11.40   0.0000
Cst(V)             0.023438   0.015515    1.511  0.1309
Friday (V)         0.074531   0.065791    1.133  0.2573
d-Figarch          0.581512   0.079626    7.303  0.0000
ARCH(Phi1)         0.144459   0.075900    1.903  0.0571
GARCH(Beta1)       0.536264   0.093287    5.749  0.0000

No. Observations :     4093  No. Parameters  :        8
Mean (Y)          :  0.05517  Variance (Y)    :  1.59189
Skewness (Y)      : -0.74128  Kurtosis (Y)    : 14.25531
Log Likelihood    : -5359.179

The sample mean of squared residuals was used to start recursion.

Estimated Parameters Vector :
0.119253;-0.174214; 0.195242; 0.023438; 0.074531; 0.581512; 0.144459; 0.536269

Elapsed Time : 45.115 seconds (or 0.751917 minutes).
```

Davidson (2004) notes the interesting and counterintuitive fact that the memory parameter of this process is $-d$, and is increasing as d approaches zero, while in the ARFIMA model the memory increases when ζ increases. According to Davidson (2004), the unexpected behavior of the FIGARCH model may be due less to any inherent paradoxes than to the fact that, embodying restrictions appropriate to a model in levels, it has been transplanted into a model of volatility. The main characteristic of this model is that it is not stationary when $d > 0$. Indeed,

$$
\begin{aligned}
(1 - L)^d &= \sum_{k=0}^{\infty} \frac{\Gamma(d+1)}{\Gamma(k+1)\,\Gamma(d-k+1)} L^k \\
&= 1 - dL - \frac{1}{2}d(1-d)L^2 - \frac{1}{6}d(1-d)(2-d)L^3 - \ldots \\
&= 1 - \sum_{k=1}^{\infty} c_k(d) L^k,
\end{aligned}
\tag{4.16}
$$

where $c_1(d) = d, c_2(d) = \frac{1}{2}d(1-d)$, etc. By construction, $\sum_{k=1}^{\infty} c_k(d) = 1$ for any value of d, and consequently, the FIGARCH belongs to the same "knife-edge-nonstationary" class represented by the IGARCH model. To test whether this non-stationarity feature holds, Davidson (2004) proposes a generalized version of the FI-GARCH and calls it the HYperbolic GARCH. The HYGARCH is given by Equation (4.15), when $\lambda(L)$ is replaced by $1 - [1 - \beta(L)]^{-1}\phi(L)\{1 + \alpha\left[(1-L)^d\right]\}$. Note that G@RCH reports $\log(\alpha)$ and not α. The $c_k(d)$ coefficients are thus weighted by α. Interestingly, the HYGARCH nests the FIGARCH when $\alpha = 1$ (or equivalently when $\log(\alpha) = 0$) and the process is stationary when $\alpha < 1$ (or equivalently when $\log(\alpha) < 0$) in which case the GARCH component observes the usual covariance stationarity restrictions (see Davidson, 2004 for more details).

Note that when estimating the HYGARCH model on the NASDAQ dataset (see the next output, labelled Box 12), one cannot reject the FIGARCH specification in favour of the HYGARCH since $\log(\hat{\alpha}) = -0.006962$ with a robust standard error of 0.029515.

```
                                                          Box 12 - HYGARCH
 ******************************
 ** G@RCH( 8) SPECIFICATIONS **
 ******************************
 Dependent variable : Nasdaq
 Mean Equation : ARMA (1, 0) model.
 1 regressor(s) in the mean.
 Variance Equation : HYGARCH (1, d, 1) model of Davidson
 (Truncation order : 1000).
 1 regressor(s) in the variance.
 The distribution is a Gauss distribution.

 Strong convergence using numerical derivatives
 Log-likelihood = -5359.13
 Please wait : Computing the Std Errors ...
```

```
Robust Standard Errors (Sandwich formula)
                   Coefficient  Std.Error  t-value  t-prob
Cst(M)                0.119324   0.016057    7.431   0.0000
Monday (M)           -0.174009   0.028839   -6.034   0.0000
AR(1)                 0.195311   0.017189   11.36    0.0000
Cst(V)                0.025119   0.017519    1.434   0.1517
Friday (V)            0.074334   0.065858    1.129   0.2591
d-Figarch             0.589652   0.081351    7.248   0.0000
ARCH(Phi1)            0.143596   0.075199    1.910   0.0563
GARCH(Beta1)          0.541468   0.091022    5.949   0.0000
Log Alpha (HY)       -0.006962   0.029515   -0.2359  0.8135

No. Observations :      4093  No. Parameters  :         9
Mean (Y)          :   0.05517  Variance (Y)    :   1.59189
Skewness (Y)      :  -0.74128  Kurtosis (Y)    :  14.25531
Log Likelihood    : -5359.126

The sample mean of squared residuals was used to start recursion.

Estimated Parameters Vector :
0.119324;-0.174009; 0.195311; 0.025119; 0.074334; 0.589652;
0.143596; 0.541468;-0.006957

Elapsed Time : 51.875 seconds (or 0.864583 minutes).
```

Chung (1999) underscores some additional drawbacks in the BBM model: there is a structural problem in the BBM specification since the parallel with the ARFIMA framework of the conditional mean equation is not perfect, leading to difficult interpretations of the estimated parameters. Indeed the fractional differencing operator applies to the constant term in the mean equation (ARFIMA) while it does not in the variance equation (FIGARCH). Chung (1999) proposes a slightly different process:

$$\phi(L)(1 - L)^d \left(\varepsilon_t^2 - \sigma^2 \right) = [1 - \beta(L)](\varepsilon_t^2 - \sigma_t^2), \qquad (4.17)$$

where σ^2 is the <u>unconditional</u> variance of ε_t .

Applying variance targeting to this model implies replacing σ^2 its sample counterpart.

If we keep the same definition of $\lambda(L)$ as in Equation (4.15), we can formulate the conditional variance as:

$$\sigma_t^2 = \sigma^2 + \left\{ 1 - [1 - \beta(L)]^{-1}\phi(L)(1 - L)^d \right\} \left(\varepsilon_t^2 - \sigma^2 \right)$$

or

$$\sigma_t^2 = \sigma^2 + \lambda(L) \left(\varepsilon_t^2 - \sigma^2 \right) . \qquad (4.18)$$

Chung (1999) shows that $\sigma^2 > 0$ and $0 \le \phi_1 \le \beta_1 \le d \le 1$ is sufficient to ensure the positivity of Equation (4.18) when $p = q = 1$.[11]

$\lambda(L)$ is an infinite summation which, in practice, has to be truncated. BBM propose to truncate $\lambda(L)$ at 1000 lags (this truncation order has been implemented as the default

---

[11]Setting $\phi_1 = 0$ gives the condition for a FIGARCH$(1, d, 0)$.

value in our package, but it may be changed by the user) and replace the unobserved ε_t^2's by the empirical counterpart of $E(\varepsilon_t^2)$, i.e. $1/T \sum_{t=1}^{T} \hat{\varepsilon}_t^2$. Contrary to BBM, Chung (1999) proposes to truncate $\lambda(L)$ at the size of the information set $(T-1)$ and to initialize the unobserved $(\varepsilon_t^2 - \sigma^2)$ at 0 (this quantity is small in absolute values and has a zero mean).[12]

Recently, Conrad and Haag (2006) and Conrad (2007) have derived non-negativity conditions for FIGARCH and HYGARCH models (respectively). Thanks to Christian Conrad, these conditions are implemented in the following examples: Stat_Constr_FIGARCH_Conrad_Haag_Check.ox and Stat_Constr_HYGARCH_Conrad_Check.ox for a FIGARCH and HYGARCH$(1, d, 1)$ respectively. While the conditions are tested on the estimated parameters in the previous two example files, the conditions are imposed during the estimation in the next two, i.e. Stat_Constr_FIGARCH_Conrad_Haag_Impose.ox and Stat_Constr_HYGARCH_Conrad_Impose.ox.

The idea of fractional integration has been extended to other GARCH types of models, including the Fractionally Integrated EGARCH (FIEGARCH) of Bollerslev and Mikkelsen (1996) and the Fractionally Integrated APARCH (FIAPARCH) of Tse (1998).[13]

Similarly to the GARCH(p, q) process, the EGARCH(p, q) of Equation (4.3) can be extended to account for long memory by factorizing the autoregressive polynomial $[1 - \beta(L)] = \phi(L)(1 - L)^d$ where all the roots of $\phi(z) = 0$ lie outside the unit circle. The FIEGARCH (p, d, q) is specified as follows:

$$\log\left(\sigma_t^2\right) = \omega + \phi(L)^{-1} (1 - L)^{-d} [1 + \alpha(L)] g(z_{t-1}). \tag{4.19}$$

Finally, the FIAPARCH (p, d, q) model can be written as:[14]

$$\sigma_t^\delta = \omega + \left\{1 - [1 - \beta(L)]^{-1} \phi(L)(1 - L)^d\right\} (|\varepsilon_t| - \gamma\varepsilon_t)^\delta. \tag{4.20}$$

To illustrate, the next outputs, labelled Box 13 and 14, report the estimation results of a FIAPARCH$(1, d, 1)$ and a FIEGARCH$(1, d, 1)$ respectively. Once again, long-memory is detected in the conditional variance equation.

---

[12]See Chung (1999) for more details.

[13]Notice that the GJR has not been extended to the long-memory framework. It is however nested in the FIAPARCH class of models.

[14]When using the BBM option in G@RCH for the FIEGARCH and FIAPARCH, $(1 - L)^d$ and $(1 - L)^{-d}$ are truncated at some predefined value (see above). It is also possible to truncate this polynomial at the information size at time t, i.e. $t - 1$.

```
                                                        Box 13 - FIAPARCH
   *******************************
   ** G@RCH( 9) SPECIFICATIONS **
   *******************************
   Dependent variable : Nasdaq
   Mean Equation : ARMA (1, 0) model.
   1 regressor(s) in the mean.
   Variance Equation : FIAPARCH (1, d, 1) model estimated with BBM's method
   (Truncation order : 1000).
   1 regressor(s) in the variance.
   The distribution is a Gauss distribution.

   Strong convergence using numerical derivatives
   Log-likelihood = -5319.06
   Please wait : Computing the Std Errors ...

   Robust Standard Errors (Sandwich formula)
                   Coefficient  Std.Error  t-value  t-prob
   Cst(M)             0.090488   0.016690    5.422   0.0000
   Monday (M)        -0.155500   0.027083   -5.742   0.0000
   AR(1)              0.206201   0.018850   10.94    0.0000
   Cst(V)             0.069862   0.027352    2.554   0.0107
   Friday (V)         0.032353   0.062970    0.5138  0.6074
   d-Figarch          0.442479   0.048626    9.100   0.0000
   ARCH(Alpha1)       0.175341   0.085768    2.044   0.0410
   GARCH(Beta1)       0.444875   0.10163     4.377   0.0000
   APARCH(Gamma1)     0.358940   0.080621    4.452   0.0000
   APARCH(Delta)      1.500260   0.12889    11.64    0.0000

   No. Observations :     4093  No. Parameters  :       10
   Mean (Y)          :  0.05517  Variance (Y)    :  1.59189
   Skewness (Y)      : -0.74128  Kurtosis (Y)    : 14.25531
   Log Likelihood    : -5319.060

   The sample mean of squared residuals was used to start recursion.

   Estimated Parameters Vector :
   0.090488;-0.155500; 0.206201; 0.069862; 0.032353; 0.442479; 0.175341;
   0.444875; 0.358940; 1.500265

   Elapsed Time : 173.209 seconds (or 2.88682 minutes).
```

```
                                                         Box 14 - FIEGARCH
********************************
** G@RCH(10) SPECIFICATIONS **
********************************
Dependent variable : Nasdaq
Mean Equation : ARMA (1, 0) model.
1 regressor(s) in the mean.
Variance Equation : FIEGARCH (1, d, 1) model
(Truncation order : 1000).
1 regressor(s) in the variance.
The distribution is a Gauss distribution.

Strong convergence using numerical derivatives
Log-likelihood = -5308.76
Please wait : Computing the Std Errors ...

Robust Standard Errors (Sandwich formula)
                  Coefficient  Std.Error  t-value  t-prob
Cst(M)               0.096537   0.015428    6.257  0.0000
Monday (M)          -0.172178   0.028035   -6.142  0.0000
AR(1)                0.192984   0.017946   10.75   0.0000
Cst(V)               0.588445   0.28539     2.062  0.0393
Friday (V)          -0.100769   0.096499   -1.044  0.2964
d-Figarch            0.493427   0.045323   10.89   0.0000
ARCH(Alpha1)        -0.246505   0.25960    -0.9496 0.3424
GARCH(Beta1)         0.603661   0.14050     4.297  0.0000
EGARCH(Theta1)      -0.119277   0.026220   -4.549  0.0000
EGARCH(Theta2)       0.302285   0.048533    6.228  0.0000

No. Observations :      4093  No. Parameters  :        10
Mean (Y)          :   0.05517  Variance (Y)    :   1.59189
Skewness (Y)      :  -0.74128  Kurtosis (Y)    :  14.25531
Log Likelihood    : -5308.762

The sample mean of squared residuals was used to start recursion.

Estimated Parameters Vector :
0.096537;-0.172178; 0.192984; 0.588445;-0.100769; 0.493427;
-0.246505; 0.603661;-0.119277; 0.302290

Elapsed Time : 242.118 seconds (or 4.0353 minutes).
```

4.8 Forecasting the Conditional Variance of GARCH-type models

Like for the simple ARCH(q) model, it is rather easy to obtain h-step-ahead forecasts of these more complicated models. In the simple GARCH(p, q) case, the optimal h-step-ahead forecast of the conditional variance, i.e. $\hat{\sigma}^2_{t+h|t}$ is given by:

$$\sigma^2_{t+h|t} = \hat{\omega} + \sum_{i=1}^{q} \hat{\alpha}_i \varepsilon^2_{t+h-i|t} + \sum_{j=1}^{p} \hat{\beta}_j \sigma^2_{t+h-j|t}, \qquad (4.21)$$

where $\varepsilon^2_{t+i|t} = \sigma^2_{t+i|t}$ for $i > 0$ while $\varepsilon^2_{t+i|t} = \varepsilon^2_{t+i}$ and $\sigma^2_{t+i|t} = \sigma^2_{t+i}$ for $i \leq 0$. Equation (4.21) is usually computed recursively, even if a closed form solution of $\sigma^2_{t+h|t}$ can be obtained by recursive substitution in Equation (4.21).

Similarly, one can easily obtain the h-step-ahead forecast of the conditional variance of an ARCH, IGARCH and FIGARCH model. By contrast, for thresholds models, the computation of out-of-sample forecasts is more complicated. Indeed, for EGARCH, GJR and APARCH models (as well as for their long-memory counterparts), the assumption made on the innovation process may have an effect on the forecast (especially for $h > 1$).

For instance, for the GJR (p, q) model, we have

$$\hat{\sigma}^2_{t+h|t} = \hat{\omega} + \sum_{i=1}^{q} (\hat{\alpha}_i \varepsilon^2_{t-i+h|t} + \hat{\gamma}_i S^-_{t-i+h|t} \varepsilon^2_{t-i+h|t}) + \sum_{j=1}^{p} \hat{\beta}_j \sigma^2_{t-j+h|t}. \quad (4.22)$$

When $\gamma_i = 0$ for all i, we obtain the forecast of the GARCH model. Otherwise, $S^-_{t-i+h|t}$ has to be computed. Note first that $S^-_{t+i|t} = S^-_{t+i}$ for $i \leq 0$. However, when $i > 0$, $S^-_{t+i|t}$ depends on the choice of the distribution of z_t. When the distribution of z_t is symmetric around 0 (for the Gaussian, Student and GED density), the probability that ε_{t+i} is negative is $S^-_{t+i|t} = 0.5$. If z_t is (standardized) skewed-Student distributed with asymmetry parameter ξ and degree of freedom υ, $S^-_{t+i|t} = \frac{1}{1+\xi^2}$ since ξ^2 is the ratio of probability masses above and below the mode.

For the APARCH (p, q) model,

$$
\begin{aligned}
\hat{\sigma}^{\delta}_{t+h|t} &= E\left(\sigma^{\delta}_{t+h}|\Omega_t\right) \\
&= E\left(\hat{\omega} + \sum_{i=1}^{q} \hat{\alpha}_i \left(|\varepsilon_{t+h-i}| - \hat{\gamma}_i \varepsilon_{t+h-i}\right)^{\hat{\delta}} + \sum_{j=1}^{p} \hat{\beta}_j \sigma^{\hat{\delta}}_{t+h-j} \mid \Omega_t\right) \\
&= \hat{\omega} + \sum_{i=1}^{q} \hat{\alpha}_i E\left[\left(\varepsilon_{t+h-i} - \hat{\gamma}_i \varepsilon_{t+h-i}\right)^{\hat{\delta}}|\Omega_t\right] + \sum_{j=1}^{p} \hat{\beta}_j \sigma^{\hat{\delta}}_{t+h-j|t}, \quad (4.23)
\end{aligned}
$$

where $E\left[\left(\varepsilon_{t+k} - \hat{\gamma}_i \varepsilon_{t+k}\right)^{\hat{\delta}}|\Omega_t\right] = \kappa_i \sigma^{\hat{\delta}}_{t+k|t}$, for $k > 1$ and $\kappa_i = E\left(|z| - \gamma_i z\right)^{\hat{\delta}}$ (see Section 3.6.2).

For the EGARCH (p, q) model,

$$
\begin{aligned}
\log \hat{\sigma}^2_{t+h|t} &= E\left(\log \sigma^2_{t+h}|\Omega_t\right) \\
&= E\left\{\hat{\omega} + \left[1 - \hat{\beta}(L)\right]^{-1} [1 + \hat{\alpha}(L)]\hat{g}(z_{t+h-1}) \mid \Omega_t\right\} \\
&= \left[1 - \hat{\beta}(L)\right]\hat{\omega} + \hat{\beta}(L)\log \hat{\sigma}^2_{t+h|t} + [1 + \hat{\alpha}(L)]\hat{g}(z_{t+h-1|t}) \quad (4.24)
\end{aligned}
$$

where $\hat{g}(z_{t+k|t}) = \hat{g}(z_{t+k})$ for $k \leq 0$ and 0 for $k > 0$.

Finally, the h-step-ahead forecast of the FIAPARCH and FIEGARCH models are obtained in a similar way.

4.9 Constrained Maximum Likelihood and Simulated Annealing

As explained in Section 3.9, it is possible to constrain the parameters to range between a lower and an upper bound by selecting the option MaxBFGS - Bounded Parameters in the Estimate window.

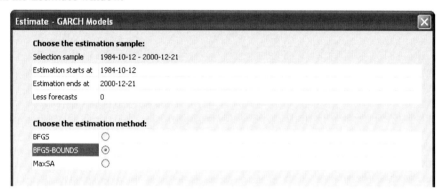

If the user selects the option Select (Individual or Matrix Form) in the Starting Values window, the program automatically opens a new box dialog before launching the estimation. Analogous to the procedure for the starting values, the user can change the bounds manually.

In the following example, an APARCH specification has been used. By default, we propose to impose the constraints $-1 < \gamma_i < 1, \forall i = 1, \ldots, q$ and $0 < \delta < 3$.

Finally, if the option MaxSA - Unbounded Parameters is selected in the Model Settings window, a new box dialog appears before the estimation.[15] In this box dialog, the user may change the default values of the parameters used in the simulated annealing algorithm.

---

[15]This box only appears when the user has selected the option Manually (Individual or Matrix Form) in the Starting Values window.

Simulated annealing is a global optimization method that potentially distinguishes between different local optima. Starting from an initial point, the algorithm takes a step and the function is evaluated. When minimizing a function, any downhill step is accepted and the process repeats from this new point. An uphill step may be accepted. Thus, it can escape from local optima. This uphill decision is made by the Metropolis criteria. As the optimization process proceeds, the length of the steps declines and the algorithm closes in on the global optimum. Since the algorithm makes very few assumptions regarding the function to be optimized, it is quite robust with respect to non-quadratic surfaces. The degree of robustness can be adjusted by the user. In fact, simulated annealing can be used as a local optimizer for difficult functions. This implementation of simulated annealing is used in Goffe, Ferrier, and Rogers (1994). Briefly, it is found to be competitive, if not superior, to multiple restarts of conventional optimization routines for difficult optimization problems. The price to pay is that it is slower than the previous two techniques. A comprehensive help is available on the MaxSA web page:

www.tinbergen.nl/∼cbos/software/maxsa.html.

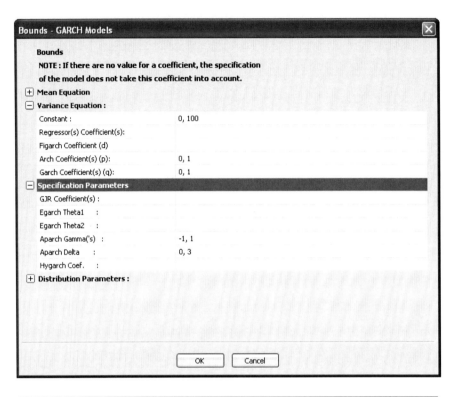

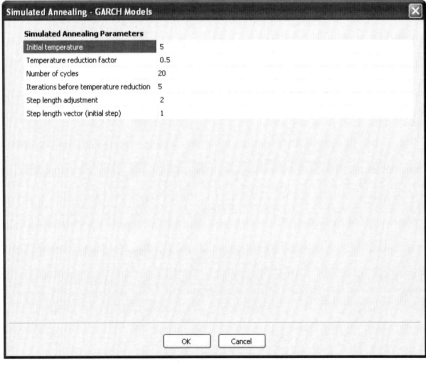

4.10 Accuracy of G@RCH

McCullough and Vinod (1999) and Brooks, Burke, and Persand (2001) use the daily German mark/British pound exchange rate data of Bollerslev and Ghysels (1996) to compare the accuracy of GARCH model estimation among several econometric softwares. They choose the GARCH(1,1) model described in Fiorentini, Calzolari, and Panattoni (1996) (hereafter denoted FCP) as the benchmark. In this section, we use the same methodology with the same dataset to check the accuracy of our procedures. Coefficients and standard errors estimates of G@RCH 4.2 are reported in Table 4.1 together with the results of McCullough and Vinod (1999) (FCP in the table).

	Coefficient		Hessian		Robust Standard Errors	
	G@RCH	FCP	G@RCH	FCP	G@RCH	FCP
μ	-0.006184	-0.006190	0.008462	0.008462	0.009187	0.009189
ω	0.010760	0.010761	0.002851	0.002852	0.006484	0.006493
α_1	0.153407	0.153134	0.026569	0.026523	0.053595	0.053532
β_1	0.805879	0.805974	0.033542	0.033553	0.072386	0.072461

Table 4.1   Accuracy of the GARCH procedure.

G@RCH gives very satisfactory results since the first four digits (at least) are the same as those of the benchmark for all but two estimations.

Moreover, to investigate the accuracy of our forecasting procedures, we have run a 8-step ahead forecasts of the model, similar to Brooks, Burke, and Persand (2001). Table 4 in Brooks, Burke, and Persand (2001) reports the conditional variance forecasts given by six well-known softwares and the correct values. G@RCH hits the benchmarks for all steps to the third decimal.

Finally, Lombardi and Gallo (2001) extends the work of Fiorentini, Calzolari, and Panattoni (1996) to the FIGARCH model of Baillie, Bollerslev, and Mikkelsen (1996) and develops the analytic Hessian matrices of this long memory process. For the same DEM/UKP database as in the previous example, Table 4.2 reports the coefficients estimates and their standard errors for our package (using numerical gradients and the BFGS optimization method) and for Lombardi and Gallo (2001) (using analytical gradients and the Newton-Raphson algorithm).

Results show that G@RCH provides excellent numerical estimates that are quite close to the analytical ones, even for an advanced model such as the FIGARCH.[16]

---

[16]The C code of Lombardi and Gallo (2001) is available at http://www.ds.unifi.it/~mjl/ in the "software" section.

	Coefficient		Hessian	
	G@RCH	LG	G@RCH	LG
μ	0.003606	0.003621	0.009985	0.009985
ω	0.015772	0.015764	0.003578	0.003581
α_1	0.198134	0.198448	0.042508	0.042444
β_1	0.675652	0.675251	0.051800	0.051693
d	0.570702	0.569951	0.075039	0.074762

Table 4.2   Accuracy of the FIGARCH procedure.

4.11 Simulations

G@RCH 6.0 allows the simulation of four models, namely the GARCH, GJR, APARCH and EGARCH models. An ARMA specification is allowed in the conditional mean and four different distributions are available for the error term, i.e. a normal, Student, GED or skewed-student.

Simulation can be done either in ox or through the rolling menus. Simul_Garch.ox is an example of Ox code using the Garch class. Alternatively to simulate a GARCH model using the rolling menus, click on G@RCH in the Modules group in the workspace window on the left-hand side of OxMetrics. Then change the **Category** to Monte Carlo and **Model Class** to Simulation of GARCH Models and click on Formulate.

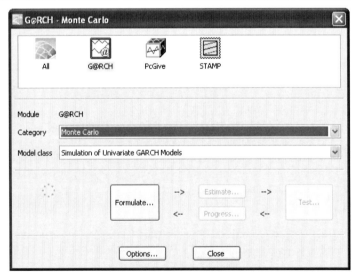

Then, select the model of interest and change the default values of the corresponding parameters (next window). The simulated series can be stored in a separate dataset and are plotted if requested.

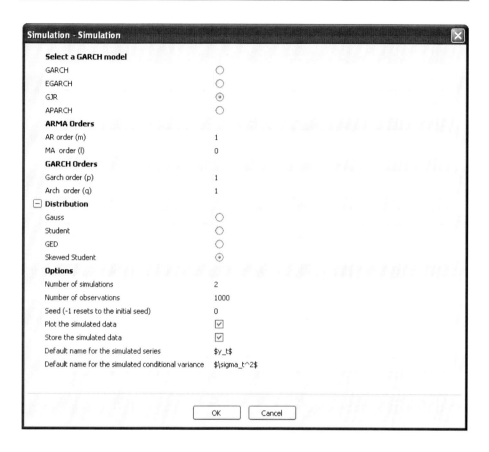

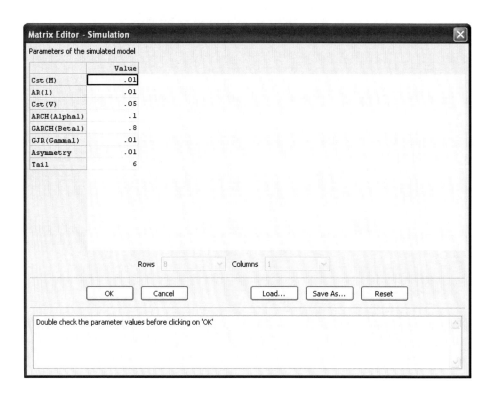

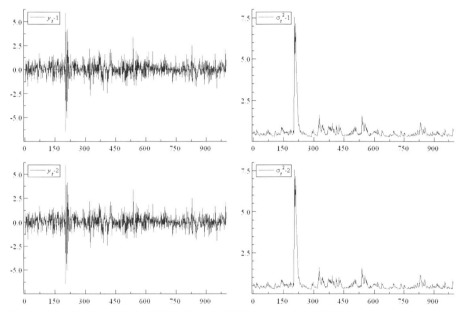

Figure 4.1 DGP: AR(1)-GJR(1,1) with SKST errors. T=1000. The generated series and their conditional variance are plotted on the left and on the right hand side respectively.

Chapter 5

Estimating Univariate Models using the Batch and Ox Versions

G@RCH is primarily a menu-driven module for OxMetrics. However, there are two additional ways of estimating GARCH-type models with G@RCH. The first makes use of the batch facilities of OxMetrics. In the second, an Ox program is written that imports the Garch class code into the program.

This chapter is devoted to the illustration of these two methods. No detailed analysis of the results will be undertaken as we concentrate on the mechanics of the procedures.

5.1 Using the Batch Version

A useful feature in G@RCH 6.0 is the possibility to use the algebra and batch languages in OxMetrics (see the OxMetrics handbook for more details). The batch language gives some control over OxMetrics through a command language. This allows for automating repetitive tasks, or as a quick way to get to a certain point in your analysis. The syntax of these commands is described below.

There are five ways of running Batch commands.

- Batch Editor (Alt+b)
  The Model/Batch... command activates the edit window in which you can edit/load/save a set of batch commands. The file extension used for batch files is .FL.
- Batch from Results windows (Ctrl+b)
  A text selection containing Batch commands can be run directly from that window using the Edit/Run as Batch command (or Ctrl+b as short cut).
- Batch from the File/Open command
  If you use File/Open, and set the file type to Run Batch file (*.fl), then the batch file is run immediately.

- Batch from the Windows Explorer

  You can double click on a .FL file in the Windows Explorer to run the file directly. If OxMetrics is not active yet, it will be started automatically.

- Batch from a Batch file

  A batch file can be called from another batch file using the command `loadbatch("filename");`.

The most intuitive way is probably to estimate a model first and then click on Tools/Batch Editor ... in OxMetrics (or Alt+b). Then, a new box dialog appears with the batch code corresponding to this model. To illustrate, the next picture shows part of the batch code corresponding to a simple (without explanatory variable) ARMA(1,0)-GARCH(1,1) model.

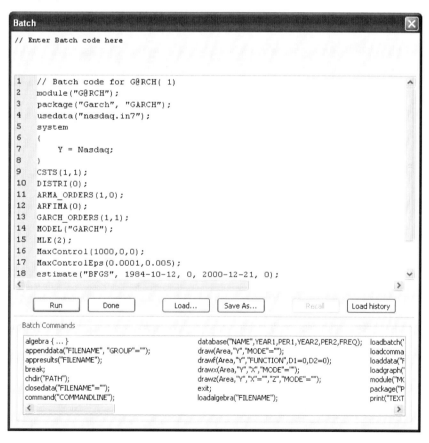

To estimate a slightly different model, one has to change the batch code accordingly. Here is an example batch code used to estimate an ARMA(1,1)-GJR(1,1) model using the same database (note that only the commands `ARMA_ORDERS()` and `MODEL()` have been modified).

```
                                            Batch code for an ARMA(1,1)-GJR(1,1)
// Batch code for G@RCH( 1)
module("G@RCH");
package("Garch", "GARCH");
usedata("nasdaq.xls");
system
{
    Y = Nasdaq;
}
CSTS(1,1);
DISTRI(0);
ARMA_ORDERS(1,0);
ARFIMA(0);
GARCH_ORDERS(0,1);
MODEL("GJR");
MLE(2);
MaxControl(1000,0,1);
MaxControlEps(0.0001,0.005);
estimate("BFGS", 1984-10-12, 0, 2000-12-21, 0);
```

Here is a list of G@RCH specific commands (see Section 10.3 - G@RCH Members Functions for more details on these options).

(1) CSTS: Specifies if constants are wanted respectively in the conditional mean and in the conditional variance equations.

(2) DISTRI: Specifies the desired distribution, i.e. 0 for the Gaussian (Normal) distribution 1, for the Student-t distribution, 2, for the Generalized Error distribution (GED) and 3 for the skewed Student-t.

(3) ARMA_ORDERS: Specifies respectively the AR and MA orders.

(4) ARFIMA: 1 to add a long-memory component in the conditional mean equation, 0 otherwise.

(5) GARCH_ORDERS: Specifies the orders of the GARCH(p, q)-type model.

(6) MODEL: specification choice (string).

- "RISKMETRICS";
- "GARCH";
- "EGARCH";
- "GJR";
- "APARCH";
- "IGARCH";
- "FIGARCH_BBM";
- "FIGARCH_CHUNG";
- "FIEGARCH";
- "FIAPARCH_BBM";

- "FIAPARCH_CHUNG";
- "HYGARCH".

(7) "ARCH_IN_MEAN"; 1 or 2 to add the conditional variance or standard deviation in the conditional mean equation, 0 otherwise.

(8) estimate(method, year1=-1, period1=0, year2=-1, period2=0);
Estimates the model.

The first argument method = "BFGS" for unconstrained ML, "BFGS-BOUNDS" for Constrained ML (lower and upper bounds) and "MaxSA" for Simulated annealing.

year1(period1) – year2(period2) is the estimation sample. Setting year1 to -1 will result in the earliest possible year1(period1), setting year2 to -1 will result in the latest possible year2(period2).

(9) TRUNC, NYBLOM, ITER and Maxsa are used as described in Section 10.3.

(10) KUPIEC_TEST; 1 to apply the KUPIEC test on the in-sample VaR. The VaR levels are specified using option VaR_LEVELS, where the VaR levels are separated by a comma, e.g. VaR_LEVELS(0.95,0.99).

(11) DQT; 1 to apply the Dynamic Quantile test presented in Section 6.2.2. The first argument is one to apply the test and the second is the number of lags of the Hit variable to include in the regression. The VaR levels are also specified using option VaR_LEVELS (see above).

(12) COVAR, BOXPIERCE, ARCHLAGS, RBD, PEARSON, SBT, MLE are also used as described in Section 10.3 except that the lag orders are now separated by a comma, e.g. BOXPIERCE(10,20,30);

(13) Tests(); To launch the miss-specification tests selected above.

(14) FORECAST; The first argument is 1 to run the forecasting procedure, the second argument is the forecasting horizon and the third argument is one to print the forecasts.

(15) Print_VaR_out_of_sample_Forecast; Print the VaR forecasts. The arguments are the VaR levels (see VaR_LEVELS).

(16) For_Graphs. See Chapter 10.

(17) MaxControl and MaxControlEps. See the ox documentation.

Here is another example batch code.

```
                Batch code for an ARMA(1,0)-APARCH(1,1) with various tests
// Batch code for G@RCH( 1)
module("G@RCH");
package("Garch", "GARCH");
usedata("nasdaq.xls");
system
{
    Y = Nasdaq;
}
CSTS(1,1);
DISTRI(0);
ARMA_ORDERS(1,0);
ARFIMA(0);
GARCH_ORDERS(1,1);
MODEL("APARCH");
MLE(2);
MaxControl(1000,0,1);
MaxControlEps(0.0001,0.005);
estimate("BFGS", 1984-10-12, 0, 2000-12-21, 0);
BOXPIERCE(5,10,20,50);
ARCHLAGS(2,5,10);
NYBLOM(1);
SBT(1);
RBD(2,5,10);
PEARSON(40,50,60);
KUPIEC_TEST(1);
DQT(1,5);
VaR_LEVELS(0.95,0.975,0.99,0.995,0.9975);
COVAR(1);
Tests();

TestGraphicAnalysis(1,1,1,1,1,1);
QuantileGraphs(2,0.025,0.975);
FORECAST(1,10, 1);
For_Graphs(0,10,2,2,1);
Print_VaR_out_of_sample_Forecast(0.05,0.95);
```

Feel free to contact us if you need more flexibility for the batch mode.

5.2 Importing the Garch Class in Ox

This section explains how to use the Garch class in Ox. We assume that you have installed Ox (version 5 or later). For more details about Ox, see Jurgen Doornik's web site (http://www.doornik.com).

5.2.1 GarchEstim.ox **example**

G@RCH is build upon the concept of object-oriented programming. For non special-ists, object-oriented programming might sound rather daunting at first. But it is in fact quite easy to get the whole picture.

A major component of object-oriented programming is the "class". Several useful classes are supplied with Ox, such as Database, Modelbase and Simulation classes.

`Garch` is an additional class that helps in the estimation of GARCH-type models. Section 10.1 provides additional details on this concept.

`GarchEstim.ox` is an example of Ox code using the Garch class. As file editor, we strongly recommend to use OxMetrics or OxEdit.[1]

The `GarchEstim.ox` file is displayed in the following Box.

```
                                                                      GarchEstim.ox
#import <packages/Garch6/Garch>

main()
{
    decl garchobj;
    garchobj = new Garch();
//*** DATA ***//
    garchobj.Load("/data/nasdaq.xls");
    garchobj.Info();
    garchobj.Select(Y_VAR, {"Nasdaq",0,0});
    garchobj.SetSelSample(-1, 1, 2000, 1);
//*** SPECIFICATIONS ***//
    garchobj.CSTS(1,1);              // cst in Mean (1 or 0), cst in Variance (1 or 0)
    garchobj.DISTRI(3);             // 0 for Gauss, 1 for Student, 2 for GED, 3 for Skewed-Student
    garchobj.ARMA_ORDERS(0,0);      // AR order (p), MA order (q).
    garchobj.ARFIMA(0);             // 1 if Arfima wanted, 0 otherwise
    garchobj.GARCH_ORDERS(1,1);     // p order, q order
    garchobj.ARCH_in_mean(0);       // ARCH-in-mean: 1 or 2 to add the variance or std. dev.
    garchobj.MODEL("GARCH");        // 0: RISKMETRICS 1:GARCH    2:EGARCH    3:GJR   4:APARCH
                                    // 5:IGARCH 6:FIGARCH-BBM  7:FIGARCH-CHUNG  8:FIEGARCH
                                    // 9:FIAPARCH-BBM 10: FIAPARCH-CHUNG 11: HYGARCH
    garchobj.TRUNC(1000);           // Truncation order (only F.I. models with BBM method)

//*** TESTS & FORECASTS ***//
    garchobj.BOXPIERCE(<10;15;20>); // Lags for the Box-Pierce Q-statistics, <> otherwise
    garchobj.ARCHLAGS(<2;5;10>);    // Lags for Engle's LM ARCH test, <> otherwise
    garchobj.NYBLOM(1);             // 1 to compute the Nyblom stability test, 0 otherwise
    garchobj.SBT(1);                // 1 to compute the Sign Bias test, 0 otherwise
    garchobj.PEARSON(<40;50;60>);   // Cells for the adjusted Pearson Chi-square GoF test,
    garchobj.RBD(<10;15;20>);       // Lags for the Residual-Based Diagnostic test of Tse
    garchobj.FORECAST(0,15,1);      // Arg.1 : 1 to launch the forecasting procedure, 0 otherwize
                                    // Arg.2 : Number of forecasts
                                    // Arg.3 : 1 to Print the forecasts, 0 otherwise
//*** OUTPUT ***//
    garchobj.MLE(2);                // 0 : MLE (Second derivatives), 1 : MLE (OPG Matrix), 2 : QMLE
    garchobj.COVAR(0);              // if 1, prints variance-covariance matrix of the parameters.
    garchobj.ITER(0);               // Interval of iterations between printed intermediary results
    garchobj.TESTS(0,0);            // Arg. 1 : 1 to run tests PRIOR to estimation, 0 otherwise
                                    // Arg. 2 : 1 to run tests AFTER estimation, 0 otherwise
    garchobj.GRAPHS(0,0,"");        // Arg.1 : if 1, displays graphics of the estimations
                                    // Arg.2 : if 1, saves these graphics in a EPS file
                                    // Arg.3 : Name of the saved file.
    garchobj.FOREGRAPHS(1,0,"");    // Same as GRAPHS(p,s,n) but for the graphics of the forecasts.
//*** PARAMETERS ***//
    garchobj.BOUNDS(0);             // 1 if bounded parameters wanted, 0 otherwise
    garchobj.FIXPARAM(0,<0;0;0;0;1;0>);
            // Arg.1 : 1 to fix some parameters to their starting values, 0 otherwize
            // Arg.2 : 1 to fix (see garchobj.DoEstimation(<>)) and 0 to estimate
            //         the corresponding parameter
```

---

[1]OxEdit is a syntax highlighting shareware that allows easy editing of Ox code. See http://www.oxedit.com for details.

```
//*** ESTIMATION ***//
    garchobj.Maxsa(0,5,0.5,20,5,2,1);
            // Arg.1 : 1 to use the MaxSA algorithm of Goffe, Ferrier and Rogers (1994)
            //         and implemented in Ox by Charles Bos
            // Arg.2 : dT=initial temperature
            // Arg.3 : dRt=temperature reduction factor
            // Arg.4 : iNS=number of cycles
            // Arg.5 : iNT=Number of iterations before temperature reduction
            // Arg.6 : vC=step length adjustment
            // Arg.7 : vM=step length vector used in initial step
    garchobj.Initialization(<>);

    garchobj.PrintStartValues(0);      // 1: Prints the S.V. in a table form; 2: Individually;
                                       // 3: in a Ox code to use in StartValues

    garchobj.DoEstimation(<>);
    garchobj.Output();
    garchobj.STORE(0,0,0,1,1,"01",0);  // Arg.1,2,3,4,5 : if 1 -> stored.
                                       // (Res-SqRes-CondV-MeanFor-VarFor)
                                       // Arg.6 : Suffix. The name of the saved series
                                       // will be "Res_ARG6".
                                       // Arg.7 : if 0, saves as an Excel spreadsheet (.xls).
                                       // If 1, saves  as a OxMetrics dataset (.in7)

    delete garchobj;
}
```

Let us study this file more in details. The #import statement indicates that this file is linked to the Garch.oxo and Garch.h files. In the body of the file (after the main() instruction), a new Garch object is first created and a database is loaded. The user has to enter the correct path of the database, but also has to pay attention to the structure of the database to be used. For instance, to use a Microsoft Excel file, the format of the spreadsheet is of crucial importance. The following convention has to be adopted when loading an Excel spreadsheet: variables are in columns, columns with variables are labelled, there is an unlabelled column containing the dates (with the form Year-Period) and the data form a contiguous sample. Here is an example:[2]

	A	**B**	**C**	**D**
1		RET	MON	HOL
2	1990-1	0.0439	1	0
3	1990-2	-0.0302	0	0
4	1990-3	0.0845	0	1

OxMetrics also supports databases having a date variable which provides the dates for daily data (or possibly times for higher frequencies). Then selections are made by date, and the dates shown in the graphics. Dates can be read from and saved to Excel files.

We note then that the dependent variable (Y), the regressor(s) in the mean equation (X) and the regressor(s) in the variance equation (Z) are specified with the Select function. Ox being case-sensitive, the exact name of the variable has to be entered. The second and third arguments denote the starting and ending observations to be consid-

---

[2]See Doornik (2007b) for the supported formats, as well as the Load functions and other related information. Interested reader can also take a look at Chapter 9 of Doornik (2009) and the cac40.xls file included in the package for an example of Excel file ready to be loaded by Ox.

ered. By default, "0" and "0" mean that all the observations are selected. From this selection, a sample can be extracted with the SetSelSample function. The arguments are ordered as (StartYear, StartPeriod, EndYear, EndPeriod2) and the default (-1, 1, -1, 1) means all the selected observations.[3]

The GarchEstim.ox file is made up of six parts:[4]

- the **"Data"** part deals with the database, the sample and the variables selection;
- the **"Specification"** part is related to the choice of the model, the lag orders and the distribution;
- the **"Tests & Forecasts"** part allows computation of different tests and to parameterize the forecasting part. Note that BOXPIERCE, ARCHLAGS, RBD and PEARSON all require a vector of integers corresponding to the lags used in the computation of the statistics;
- the **"Output"** part includes several output options including MLE that refers to the computation method of the standard deviations of the estimated parameters, TESTS that is useful when you want to run some tests on the raw series, prior to any estimation and GRAPHS (resp. FOREGRAPHS) that plots graphs for the estimation (resp. forecasting) process ;
- the **"Parameters"** part consists in two procedures. BOUNDS indicates if constraints are imposed on several parameters (see Section 3.9) while FixParam allows fixing some parameters to their starting values;
- the **"Estimation"** part runs the model. Initialization initializes the model, StartValues is used to modify the starting value of one or more parameter(s), DoEstimation launches the estimation of the model, Output prints results of the estimation, forecasting and tests procedures and, finally, STORE allows storing some series. The argument of DoEstimation is a vector containing starting values of the parameters in a pre-specified order (note that the user has always the possibility to let G@RCH using default values).

5.2.2 Running an Ox Program

If you want to use the "Console Version" of G@RCH 6.0 , all you need is an Ox executable. To illustrate the various ways to run Ox code, we keep our GarchEstim.ox

---

[3]Alternatively, when the database is dated and contains daily observations, the sample can be selected using SetSelDates(const iYear1, const iMonth1, const iDay1, const iYear2, const iMonth2, const iDay2). See example GarchEstim_Dated_Database.ox.

[4]All the functions cited here are described in details in Section 10.3

example.

5.2.2.1 Command Prompt

First, you can type

`oxl GarchEstim`

at the command prompt. This method is mainly for users of Ox Console.

<u>Updating the environment</u>

Skip this section if you managed to run the Ox programs in this booklet. Otherwise, under Windows and Unix you may wish to set the `PATH` environment variable.

The executable (`oxl.exe` etc.) is in the `ox\bin` folder, for example by default it is in:

`C:\Program files\OxMetrics5\Ox\bin`

So, update your `PATH` variable if necessary.[5]

Without these, you can still run `GarchEstim.ox`, but more typing is needed:

`"C:\Program files\OxMetrics5\Ox\bin\oxl"`

`"-iC:\Program files\OxMetrics5\Ox\include"`

`GarchEstim.ox`

The double quotes are required because of the space in the file name.

5.2.2.2 OxEdit

Alternatively, you may use OxEdit.[6] Ox tools should be installed automatically. If not, run `ox\bin\oxedit\oxcons.tool`. To run the program, use the Modules/Ox (for Ox Console) or Modules/OxRun (OxMetrics), as shown below.

---

[5]In Windows XP/NT/2000, you can do it using the Control panel, System: use the environment page in the system properties.

[6]You can download OxEdit at `www.doornik.com/products.html`

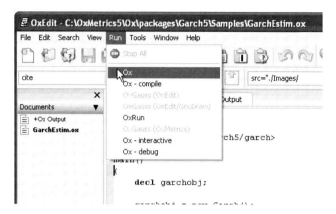

When using OxEdit, OxMetrics is needed to display the graphics but is not manda-tory for running the estimation. Alternatively, graphs can be displayed on the screen using Gnudraw and Gnuplot. Indeed, G@RCH 6.0 can be combined with Gnudraw, an Ox package meant for creating GnuPlot[7] developed by Charles Bos.[8] The interface is completely based on the OxDraw package (even the documentation - `gnudraw.html` - uses the same structure as Jurgen Doornik's `oxdraw.html`).[9] Usage of GnuDraw is intended to be simple as the syntax is similar to the original Ox drawing routines. You just have to add the lines

```
#include <oxstd.h>
#include <packages/gnudraw/gnudraw.h>
```
before
```
#import <packages/Garch6/Garch>.
```
As GnuPlot can be called automatically from within Ox, `ShowDrawWindow` can be used, displaying graphs on screen.

See Cribari-Neto and Zarkos (2003) for a comprehensive overview of the GnuDraw package.

5.2.2.3 OxMetrics

A third possibility is to launch Ox programs directly from OxMetrics, as shown below.[10] There are different ways for running an Ox code under OxMetrics. The first way is to

---

[7]To download Gnuplot, go to http://www.gnuplot.info/

[8]The package can be downloaded at http://www.tinbergen.nl/~cbos/. See the documentation for installation details.

[9]A detailed help file `gnudraw.html` and a few examples are provided with the package, which makes its use very friendly.

[10]Note that we here suppose that Ox and OxMetrics are both correctly installed.

use OxRun.

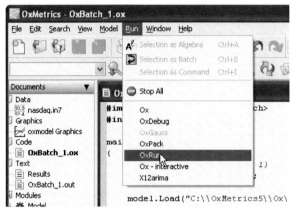

A new feature of G@RCH 6.0 (and OxMetrics 5 in general) is that Ox code can be generated.

The Model/Ox Batch Code command (or Alt+O) activates a new dialog box called 'Generate Ox Code' that allows the user to select an item for which to generate Ox code.

The code is than opened in a new window and provided Ox Professional is available, this code can be run, either from OxMetrics, or from OxEdit or the command line. This option is also available for the 'Descriptive Statistics' and 'Simulation' modules.

OxBatch_1.ox is an example of Ox Batch code generated by G@RCH 6.0 after the estimation of an APARCH model while OxBatch_2.ox and OxBatch_3.ox are two examples of Ox Batch code generated after the use of the 'Descriptive Statistics' and 'Simulation' modules.

```
                                                                              OxBatch_1.ox
#include <oxstd.h>
#import <packages/Garch6/garch>
#include <oxdraw.h>

main()
{
    //--- Ox code for G@RCH( 3)
    decl model = new Garch();

    model.Load("D:\\G@RCH5\\Compilation\\Oxmetrics5\\data\\nasdaq.xls");
    model.Deterministic(-1);

    model.Select(Y_VAR, {"Nasdaq", 0, 0});

    model.CSTS(1,1);
    model.DISTRI(3);
    model.ARMA_ORDERS(2,0);
    model.ARFIMA(0);
    model.GARCH_ORDERS(1,1);
    model.MODEL(APARCH);
    model.MLE(2);
    model.ITER(0);

    model.SetSelSampleByDates(dayofcalendar(1984, 10, 12), dayofcalendar(2000, 12, 21));
    model.Initialization(<>);
    model.DoEstimation(<>);
    model.Output();

    model.INFO_CRITERIA(1);
    model.NORMALITY_TEST(1);
    model.BOXPIERCE(<5;10;20;50>);
    model.ARCHLAGS(<2;5;10>);
    model.NYBLOM(1);
    model.SBT(1);
    model.RBD(<2;5;10>);
    model.PEARSON(<40;50;60>);
    model.KUPIEC_TEST(1);
    model.DQT(1,5);
    model.VaR_LEVELS(<0.95;0.975;0.99;0.995;0.9975>);
    model.COVAR(1);
    model.Tests();

    model.TestGraphicAnalysis(1,1,1,1,1,1,0);
    model.QuantileGraphs(2,<0.025;0.975>,6);
    SetDrawWindow("G@RCH Graphics");
    ShowDrawWindow();

    model.FORECAST(1,10, 1);
    model.Forecasting();
    model.For_Graphs(0,10,2,2,1);
    SetDrawWindow("G@RCH Forecasting");
    ShowDrawWindow();
    model.Print_VaR_out_of_sample_Forecast(<0.05;0.95>);

    model.Append_in(model.m_vE,"Res");
    model.Append_in(model.m_vE.^2,"SqRes");
    model.Append_in(model.m_vStandErrors,"StdRes");
    model.Append_in(model.m_vSigma2,"CondV");
    model.Append_out(model.m_mForc[][0],"ForY");
    model.Append_out(model.m_mForc[][1],"ForVar");
    model.Save("D:\\G@RCH5\\Compilation\\Oxmetrics5\\data\\nasdaq.xls");

    delete model;
}
```

```
                                                                           OxBatch_2.ox
#include <oxstd.h>
#import <packages/Garch6/garch>
#include <oxdraw.h>
#import <lib/testres>
#include <arma.h>
#import <Database>

main()
{
    //--- Ox code for G@RCH( 1)
    decl model = new Garch();

    model.Load("D:\\G@RCH5\\Compilation\\Oxmetrics5\\data\\nasdaq.xls");
    model.Deterministic(-1);

    model.Select(Y_VAR, {"Nasdaq", 0, 0});

    model.SetSelSampleByDates(dayofcalendar(1984, 10, 12), dayofcalendar(2000, 12, 21));
    decl series =   model.GetGroup(Y_VAR),names,y,name;
    model.GetGroupNames(Y_VAR, &names);
    decl m_cT=rows(series);
    decl nbser=columns(series);
    model.Info();
    for (decl i = 0; i < nbser; ++i)
    {
        y=series[][i];
        name=names[i];
        println("Series #", i+1,"/",nbser, ": ", name);
        print("--------");
        model.Normality(y);
        decl m_cLagArch_test=<2;5;10>;
        for (decl l=0; l < sizer(m_cLagArch_test); l++)
            ArchTest(y, 1, m_cLagArch_test'[l],  0, TRUE);
        println("Q-Statistics on Raw data");
        model.BoxPQ(y,<5;10;20;50>, 0);
        println("Q-Statistics on Squared data");
        model.BoxPQ(y.^2,<5;10;20;50>, 0);
        model.ADF(y,name,2,2);
        model.EstimateGSP(y,2046,1);
    }

    delete model;
}
```

```
                                                                           OxBatch_3.ox
#include <oxstd.h>
#import <packages/Garch6/garch>
#include <oxdraw.h>

main()
{
    //--- Ox code for G@RCH( 4)
    decl model = new Garch();

    model.Load("D:\\G@RCH5\\Compilation\\Oxmetrics5\\data\\nasdaq.xls");
    model.Deterministic(-1);

    model.Select(Y_VAR, {"Nasdaq", 0, 0});

    decl z,eps,sigma2,y,y_all=<>,sigma2_all=<>;
    decl new_name_simul_y=new array[3];
    decl new_name_simul_sigma2=new array[3];
    for (decl i=0;i<3;++i)
    {
        z=rann(2000,1);
        model.Simulate_APARCH(0.05,<0.1>,<0.8>,<0.01>,<2>, z, 0, &eps, &sigma2);
        y=eps+0.01;
        y_all~=y;
        sigma2_all~=sigma2;
        new_name_simul_y[i]=sprint("$y_t$","-",i+1);
        new_name_simul_sigma2[i]=sprint("$\sigma_t^2$","-",i+1);
    }
    decl plot=0;
    for (decl i=0;i<3;++i)
    {
        DrawTMatrix(plot++, y_all[][0]', new_name_simul_y[i]);
        DrawTMatrix(plot++, sigma2_all[][0]', new_name_simul_sigma2[i]);
    }
    ShowDrawWindow();
    decl dbase = new Database();
    dbase.Create(1,1,1,rows(y),1);
    dbase.Append(y_all,new_name_simul_y);
    dbase.Append(sigma2_all,new_name_simul_sigma2);
    dbase.Save("simulation.in7");
    delete  dbase;

    delete model;
}
```

5.3 Advanced Ox Usage

5.3.1 Forecast.ox example

To illustrate the potential of writing Ox code based on G@RCH and its Garch class, we also provide Forecast.ox, an example that estimates an ARMA(1,0)-APARCH(1,1) model on the CAC40. In this program, we analyze the French CAC40 stock index for the years 1995-1999 (1249 daily observations). Daily returns in percentage are defined as 100 times the first difference of the log of the closing prices.

After the estimation of the ARMA(1,0)-APARCH(1,1) model with a skewed-student likelihood on the first 800 observations, 448 one-step-ahead forecasts of the conditional mean and conditional variance are computed.

Forecasting Performance

One of the most popular measures to check the forecasting performance of the ARCH-type models is the Mincer-Zarnowitz regression, i.e. ex-post volatility regression:

$$\check{\sigma}_t^2 = a_0 + a_1 \hat{\sigma}_t^2 + u_t, \tag{5.1}$$

where $\check{\sigma}_t^2$ is the ex-post volatility, $\hat{\sigma}_t^2$ is the forecasted volatility and a_0 and a_1 are parameters to be estimated. If the model for the conditional variance is correctly specified (and the parameters are known) and if $E(\check{\sigma}_t^2) = \hat{\sigma}_t^2$, we have $a_0 = 0$ and $a_1 = 1$. The R^2 of this regression is often used as a simple measure of the degree of predictability of the ARCH-type model.

But $\check{\sigma}_t^2$ is never observed. It is thus common to use $\check{\sigma}_t^2 = (y_t - \bar{y})^2$, where $\bar{y}$ is the sample mean of y_t. The R^2 of this regression is often lower than 5% and this could lead to the conclusion that GARCH models produce poor forecasts of the volatility (see, among others, Schwert, 1990, or Jorion, 1996). But, as described in Andersen and Bollerslev (1998a), the reason of these poor results is the choice of what is considered as the "true" volatility. Instead, they propose to compute the daily realized volatility as the sum of squared intraday returns and use it as the "true" volatility. Actually, Andersen and Bollerslev (1998a) show that this measure is a more proper one than squared daily returns. Therefore, using h-minute returns (5-minute for instance), the realized volatility can be expressed as:

$$\sigma_t^2 = \sum_{k=1}^{K} y_{k,t}^2, \tag{5.2}$$

where $y_{k,t}$ is the return of the kth h-minutes interval of the tth day and K is the number of h-minutes intervals per day. See Section 7.3 for more details about realized volatility.

Coming back to our illustration, the CAC40 index is computed by the exchange as a weighted measure of the prices of its components and was originally available in our database on an intraday basis with the price index being computed every 15 minutes. For the time period under review, the opening hours of the French stock market were 10.00 am to 5.00 pm, thus 7 hours of trading per day. This translates into 28 intraday returns used to compute the daily realized volatility.[11] Because the exchange is closed from 5.00 pm to 10.00 am the next day, the first intraday return is the first difference between the log price at 10.15 am and the log price at 5.00 pm the day before. Then, the intraday data are used to compute the daily realized volatility as the sum of the 28 squared intraday returns as shown in Equation (5.2).

Finally, to compare the adequacy of the different distributions in the selected forecasting model, a well-known tool is the density forecasts tests developed in Diebold, Gunther, and Tay (1998). The idea of density forecasts is quite simple.[12] Let $f_i(y_i|\Omega_i)_{i=1}^m$ be a sequence of m one-step-ahead density forecasts produced by a given model, where Ω_i is the conditioning information set, and $p_i(y_i|\Omega_i)_{i=1}^m$ is the sequence of densities defining the Data Generating Process y_i (which is never observed). Testing whether this density is a good approximation of the true density $p(.)$ is equivalent to testing:

$$H_0 : f_i(y_i|\Omega_i)_{i=1}^m = p_i(y_i|\Omega_i)_{i=1}^m. \tag{5.3}$$

Diebold, Gunther, and Tay (1998) use the fact that, under Equation (5.3), the probability integral transform $\hat{\zeta}_i = \int_{-\infty}^{y_i} f_i(t)dt$ is $i.i.d.$ $U(0,1)$, i.e. independent and identically distributed uniform. To check H_0, they propose to use both a goodness-of-fit test and an independence test for $i.i.d.$ $U(0,1)$. The $i.i.d.$-ness property of $\hat{\zeta}_i$ can be evaluated by plotting the correlograms of $\left(\zeta - \overline{\zeta}\right)^j$, for $j = 1,2,3,4,...$, to detect potential dependence in the conditional mean, variance, skewness, kurtosis, etc. Departure from uniformity can also be evaluated by plotting an histogram of $\hat{\zeta}_i$. According to Bauwens, Giot, Grammig, and Veredas (2000), *a humped shape of the $\hat{\zeta}$-histogram would indicate that the issued forecasts are too narrow and that the tails of the true density are not accounted for. On the other hand, a U-shape of the histogram would*

---

[11]Intraday prices are the outcomes of a linear interpolation between the closest recorded prices below and above the time set in the grid. Correspondingly, all returns are computed as the first difference in the regularly time-spaced log prices of the index.

[12]For more details about density forecasts and applications in finance, see the special issue of *Journal of Forecasting* (Timmermann, 2000).

suggest that the model issues forecasts that either under- or overestimate too frequently.
Moreover, Lambert and Laurent (2001) show that an *inverted S* shape of the histogram
would indicate that the errors are skewed, i.e. the true density is probably not symmetric.[13] An illustration is provided in Section 5 with some formal tests and graphical tools.

Results

The Mincer-Zarnowitz regression and some out-of-sample density forecast tests (as
suggested by Diebold, Gunther, and Tay, 1998) are also performed.

The program `Forecast.ox` is printed in the next box. This code has been used
to produce Figure 5.1 and the output labelled "Density Forecast Test on Standardized
Forecast Errors". In the first four panels of Figure 5.1, we show the correlograms of
$\left(\hat{\zeta} - \overline{\hat{\zeta}}\right)^j$, for $j = 1, 2, 3, 4$, where $\hat{\zeta}$ is the probability integral transform for the out-of-
sample period (see the paragraph below Equation (5.3) for more details). This graphical
tool has been proposed by Diebold, Gunther, and Tay (1998) to detect potential remaining dependence in the conditional mean, variance, skewness, kurtosis. In our example,
it seems that the probability integral transform is independently distributed.

```
                                                                    Forecast.ox
#import <packages/Garch6/Garch>

main() {
    decl garchobj;
    garchobj = new Garch();
//*** DATA ***//
    garchobj.Load("/data/CAC40.xls");
    garchobj.Select(Y_VAR, {"CAC40",0,0} );
    garchobj.SetSelSample(-1, 1, 800, 1);
//*** SPECIFICATIONS ***//
    garchobj.DISTRI(3);              // 0 for Gauss, 1 for Student, 2 for GED, 3 for Skewed-Student
    garchobj.ARMA_ORDERS(1,0);      // AR order (p), MA order (q).
    garchobj.GARCH_ORDERS(1,1);     // p order, q order
    garchobj.MODEL(4);              // 0:RISKMETRICS  1:GARCH     2:EGARCH    3:GJR   4:APARCH
                                    // 5:IGARCH 6:FIGARCH-BBM   7:FIGARCH-CHUNG   8:FIEGARCH
                                    // 9:FIAPARCH-BBM  10: FIAPARCH-CHUNG  11: HYGARCH
    garchobj.MLE(1);                // 0 : MLE (Second derivatives), 1 : MLE (OPG Matrix), 2 : QMLE
    garchobj.Initialization(<>) ;
    garchobj.DoEstimation(<>);
    garchobj.Output() ;
//*******************************************************************************
    decl forc=<>,h,yfor=<>,shape=<>;
    decl number_of_forecasts=448; // number of h_step_ahead forecasts
    decl step=1;                  // specify h (h-step-ahead forecasts)
    decl T=garchobj.GetcT();
    println("!!! Please Wait while computing the forecasts !!!");
}
```

---

[13]Confidence intervals for the $\hat{\zeta}$-histogram can be obtained by using the properties of the histogram under the null hypothesis of uniformity.

```
    decl distri=garchobj.GetDistri();
    if (distri==1 || distri==2)
        shape=garchobj.GetValue("m_cV");
    else if (distri==3)
        shape=garchobj.GetValue("m_cA")|garchobj.GetValue("m_cV");
    for (h=0; h<number_of_forecasts; ++h)
    {
        garchobj.FORECAST(1,step,0);
        garchobj.SetSelSample(-1, 1, T+h, 1);
        garchobj.InitData();
        yfor|=garchobj.GetForcData(Y_VAR, step);
        forc|=garchobj.FORECASTING();
    }
    decl Hfor = garchobj.GetVar("REALVOLA")[801:];   // Realized volatility
//  decl Hfor = (yfor - meanc(yfor)).^2;             // Squared returns (in deviation)
    decl cd=garchobj.CD(yfor-forc[][0],forc[][1],garchobj.GetDistri(),shape);
    println("Density Forecast Test on Standardized Forecast Errors");
    garchobj.APGT(cd,20|30,garchobj.GetValue("m_cPar"));
    garchobj.AUTO(cd, number_of_forecasts, -0.1, 0.1, 0);
    garchobj.confidence_limits_uniform(cd,30,0.95,1,4);
    DrawTitle(5, "Conditional variance forecast and realized volatility");
    Draw(5, (Hfor~forc[][1])');
    ShowDrawWindow();
    garchobj.MZ(Hfor, forc[][1], number_of_forecasts);
    garchobj.FEM(forc, yfor~Hfor);
    savemat("MeanFor.xls",forc[][0]);      // Saves the mean forecasts in an Excel file.
    savemat("VarFor.xls",forc[][1]);       // Saves the variance forecasts in an Excel file.
    delete garchobj;
}
```

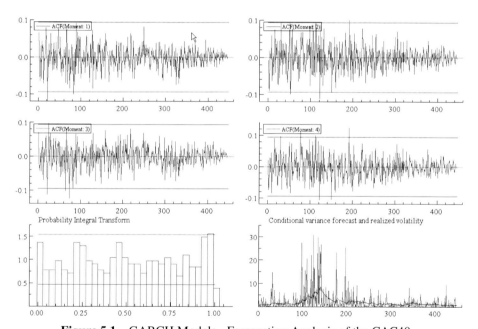

Figure 5.1   GARCH Models - Forecasting Analysis of the CAC40.

Panel 5 of Figure 5.1 also shows the histogram (with 30 cells) of $\hat{\zeta}$ with the 95% confidence bands. From this figure, it is clear that the ARMA(1,0)-APARCH(1,1) model coupled with a skewed-Student distribution for the innovations performs very well with the dataset we have investigated. This conclusion is reinforced by the result reported in the Density Forecast Test on Standardized Forecast Errors box. The adjusted Pearson Chi-square goodness-of-fit test provides a statistical version of the graphical test presented in Figure 5.1. In addition, the program also performs the Mincer-Zarnowitz regression (see Equation (5.1)) that regresses the observed volatility (in our case the realized volatility) on a constant and a vector of 448 one-step-ahead forecasts of the conditional variance (produced by the APARCH model).[14] Theses results suggest that the APARCH model gives good forecasts of the conditional variance. Based on the significance of the β parameter of the regression, one can indeed hardly conclude that the APARCH model provides biased forecasts. Moreover, the R^2 of this regression is about 33%, versus 0.14 when we use the daily squared returns (in deviation) as proxy of the observed volatility.[15]

```
                    Density Forecast Test on Standardized Forecast Errors

Adjusted Pearson Chi-square Goodness-of-fit test

 Cells(g)  Statistic     P-Value(g-1)     P-Value(g-k-1)
    20       21.0179        0.335815          0.020969
    30       26.5089        0.598181          0.149654
Rem.: k = 9 = Number of estimated parameters
---------------
Probability Integral Transform The Lower and Upper bounds are
0.46875 and 1.54018

Mincer-Zarnowitz regression on the forecasted volatility
                    Coefficient  Std.Error  t-value  t-prob
Alpha                 0.027698    0.23253    0.1191   0.9052
Beta                  1.239532    0.16052    7.722    0.0000
R2: 0.329662 Note: S.E. are
Heteroskedastic Consistent (White, 1980)
---------------
```

5.3.2 Imposing Nonlinear Constraints

As mentioned in Section 3.9, the inspected range of the parameter space is $]-\infty; \infty[$ when numerical optimization is used to maximize the log-likelihood function with respect to the vector of parameters Ψ. Sometimes these parameters might have to be constrained in a smaller interval.

We have shown how to impose these lower and upper bounds and how to change these bounds in the OxPack version of G@RCH (see Section 4.9).

The same feature is available for the Console version. Furthermore, the Console version allows the user to impose any nonlinear constraint on the parameters (like the stationarity constraints).

---

[14]The realized volatility and the one-step-ahead forecasts are plotted in the last panel of Figure 5.1.

[15]For a discussion on the improved forecasting performance of GARCH models when using correctly specified proxy of the real volatility, see Andersen and Bollerslev (1998a).

The example `StartValues_Bounds.ox` shows how to print the code needed to change the starting values and the bounds for an ARMA(0,0)-GARCH(1,1) with a Student likelihood.

```
                                              First Step : StartValues_Bounds.ox
#import <packages/Garch6/Garch>

StartValues(const object)
{
    object.GetPara();                         // DO NOT REMOVE THIS LINE
    object.Initialization(object.GetValue("m_vPar"));   // DO NOT REMOVE THIS LINE
}

main()
{
    decl garchobj;
    garchobj = new Garch();
//*** DATA ***//
    garchobj.Load("/data/nasdaq.xls");
    garchobj.Info();
    garchobj.Select(Y_VAR, {"Nasdaq",0,0});
    garchobj.SetSelSample(-1, 1, 2000, 1);
//*** SPECIFICATIONS ***//
    garchobj.CSTS(1,1);                       // cst in Mean (1 or 0), cst in Variance (1 or 0)
    garchobj.DISTRI(1);                       // 0 for Gauss, 1 for Student, 2 for GED, 3 for Skewed-Student
    garchobj.ARMA_ORDERS(0,0);                // AR order (p), MA order (q).
    garchobj.GARCH_ORDERS(1,1);               // p order, q order
    garchobj.MODEL("GARCH");                  // 0:RISKMETRICS 1:GARCH    2:EGARCH    3:GJR   4:APARCH
                                              // 5:IGARCH 6:FIGARCH-BBM   7:FIGARCH-CHUNG   8:FIEGARCH
                                              // 9:FIAPARCH-BBM  10: FIAPARCH-CHUNG  11: HYGARCH
//*** OUTPUT ***//
    garchobj.MLE(2);                          // 0 : MLE (Second derivatives), 1 : MLE (OPG Matrix), 2 : QMLE
//*** PARAMETERS ***//
    garchobj.BOUNDS(1);                       // 1 if bounded parameters wanted, 0 otherwise
//*** ESTIMATION ***//
    garchobj.Initialization(<>);
    StartValues(garchobj);
    garchobj.PrintBounds(2);                  // 1: Prints the bounds in a matrix form,
                                              // 2: to write the Ox code to use in StartValues
    garchobj.PrintStartValues(3);             // 1: Prints the S.V. in a table form;
                                              // 2: Individually;  3: in a Ox code to use in StartValues

    exit(0);
    garchobj.DoEstimation(<>);
    garchobj.Output();
    delete garchobj;
}
```

Let us focus now on the following lines:

```
//*** PARAMETERS ***//
    garchobj.BOUNDS(1);                       // 1 if bounded parameters wanted, 0 otherwise
//*** ESTIMATION ***//
    garchobj.Initialization(<>);
    StartValues(garchobj);
    garchobj.PrintBounds(2);                  // 1: Prints the bounds in a matrix form,
                                              // 2: to write the Ox code to use in StartValues
    garchobj.PrintStartValues(3);             // 1: Prints the S.V. in a table form;
                                              // 2: Individually;  3: in a Ox code to use in StartValues

    exit(0);
```

The function `BOUNDS(1)` selects the constrained optimizer. `PrintBounds(2)` prints the code needed to change the bounds while `PrintStartValues(3)` prints the code needed to change the starting values. The function `exit(0)` stops the program before starting the estimation (since the starting values and the bounds have to be modified).

The output labelled `First Step : Output` indicates that the default starting value of the degree of freedom of the Student density (m_cV) is 6 and that m_calpha0 (i.e. ω, the constant of the GARCH model) is bounded between 0 and 100.

```
                                                              First Step : Output
Bounds
======
object.SetBounds("m_clevel", -100, 100);
object.SetBounds("m_calpha0", 0, 100);
object.SetBounds("m_valphav", 0, 1);
object.SetBounds("m_vbetav", 0, 1);
object.SetBounds("m_cV", 2, 100);
-----------------------------------
Starting Values
===============
object.SetStartValue("m_clevel",0.01);
object.SetStartValue("m_calpha0",0.05);
object.SetStartValue("m_valphav",<0.1>);
object.SetStartValue("m_vbetav",<0.8>);
object.SetStartValue("m_cV",6);
```

To change the starting value of m_cV to say 5 and to fix the bounds of m_calpha0 to [-100;100] (instead of [0;100]), just copy-paste the lines

object.SetBounds("m_calpha0", 0, 100);

object.SetStartValue("m_cV",6);

at the top of the function StartValues(const object) and change the values as shown below:[16]

```
#import <packages/Garch6/Garch>

StartValues(const object)
{
    object.SetBounds("m_calpha0", -100, 100);
    object.SetStartValue("m_cV",5);
    object.GetPara();
    object.Initialization(object.GetValue("m_vPar"));
}
```

Furthermore, nonlinear constraints (like the stationarity constraint of the GARCH $(1,1)$ model, i.e. $\alpha_1 + \beta_1 < 1$) can be imposed during the estimation in the Console version. The example Stat_Constr_GARCH shows how to impose this restriction.

---

[16]Do not forget to remove or comment out exit(0); before launching the program. Notice also that the functions PrintStartValues() and PrintBounds() are not mandatory for the estimation and can be removed.

```
                                                    Stat_Constr_GARCH.ox

#import <packages/Garch6/Garch>

StartValues(const object)
{
    object.GetPara();                        // DO NOT REMOVE THIS LINE
    object.Initialization(object.GetValue("m_vPar")); // DO NOT REMOVE THIS LINE
}

class GARCH_C : Garch                         // CONSTRUCTOR
{                                             // This function defines
    GARCH_C();                                // a new class called GARCH_C
    cfunc_gt0(const avF, const vP);           // and launches the cfunc_gt0 function
};

GARCH_C::GARCH_C()
{
    this.Garch();                             // This function defines GARCH_C
    m_iModelClass = MC_GARCH;                 // as a Garch object that thus inherits
    Init_Globals();                           // all the properties of Garch
}

GARCH_C::cfunc_gt0(const avF, const vP)
{
    SplitPara(vP);  // Do not remove this line
    decl matconstr=new matrix[1][1];
    matconstr[0] = 1.000001 - m_valphav[0] - m_vbetav[0];    // alpha_1 + beta_1 < 1
    avF[0] = matconstr;
    return 1;
}

main()
{
    decl garchobj;
    garchobj = new GARCH_C();
...
    garchobj.GARCH_ORDERS(1,1);    // p order, q order
    garchobj.MODEL(1);             // 0:RISKMETRICS 1:GARCH    2:EGARCH    3:GJR    4:APARCH
                                   // 5:IGARCH 6:FIGARCH(BBM) 7:FIGARCH(Chung) 8:FIEGARCH(BM only)
                                   // 9:FIAPARCH(BBM) 10: FIAPARCH(Chung) 11: HYGARCH(BBM)
//*** OUTPUT ***//
    garchobj.MLE(1);               // 0 : both, 1 : MLE, 2 : QMLE
//*** PARAMETERS ***//
    garchobj.BOUNDS(1);            // 1 if bounded parameters wanted, 0 otherwise
//*** ESTIMATION ***//
    garchobj.Initialization(<>) ;
    garchobj.DoEstimation() ;
    garchobj.Output() ;
    delete garchobj;
}
```

In Stat_Constr_GARCH, a new object GARCH_C is created and inherits all the members and functions of the GARCH class. The option Bounds(1) is selected while the virtual function cfunc_gt0 is replaced by the function that imposes the corresponding restrictions:

```
GARCH_C::cfunc_gt0(const avF, const vP)
{
    SplitPara(vP);  // Do not remove this line
    decl matconstr=new matrix[1][1];
    matconstr[0] = 1.000001 - m_valphav[0] - m_vbetav[0];
                    // alpha_1 + beta_1 < 1
    avF[0] = matconstr;
    return 1;
}
```

In this case the nonlinear constraint $\alpha_1 + \beta_1 < 1$ is evaluated by the cfunc_gt0 function.[17]

Indeed, the cfunc_gt0 argument can be zero, or a function evaluating the nonlinear constraints (which will be constrained to be positive) with the following format:

---

[17]Practically speaking, the constraint is $1.0001 - \alpha_1 - \beta_1 \geq 0$.

```
cfunc_gt0(const avF, const vP);
avF
 in: address
 out: m x 1 matrix with constraints at vP
vP
 in: p x 1 matrix with coefficients
returns
1: successful, 0: constraint evaluation failed
```

In Stat_Constr_FIGARCH.ox, the stationarity constraints of the FIGARCH$(1, d, 0)$ and FIGARCH$(1, d, 1)$ models are imposed during the estimation. Interestingly imposing the constraint was found to speed up the estimation by about 25 % (while the estimates are exactly the same without imposing it).

```
                                                                    Stat_Constr_FIGARCH.ox
...
GARCH_C::cfunc_gt0(const avF, const vP)
{
    SplitPara(vP);  // Do not remove this line
    decl matconstr;
    if ((m_cMod==6)&&(m_cP == 1)&&(m_cQ < 2))            // FIGARCH-BBM
    {
        matconstr=new matrix[3][1];
        decl a,b,c,d;
        // Remark: FIGARCH(1,d,0) --> m_valphav = 0
        a = m_vbetav - m_dD;
        b = ((2-m_dD)/3);
        c = m_dD * (m_valphav - ((1-m_dD)/2));
        d = m_vbetav * (m_valphav - m_vbetav + m_dD);

        matconstr[0][0] =  m_valphav - a + 0.000001;  // beta_1 - d <= phi_1
        matconstr[1][0] =  b - m_valphav + 0.000001;  // phi_1 <= (2-d)/3
        matconstr[2][0] =  d - c + 0.000001;          // d*[phi_1-(1-d)/2] <= beta_1*(phi_1-beta_1+d)
    }
    else if ((m_cMod==7)&&(m_cP == 1)&&(m_cQ < 2))      // FIGARCH-Chung
    {
        // Remark: FIGARCH(1,d,0) --> m_valphav = 0
        if (m_cQ == 0)
        {
            matconstr = new matrix[3][1];
            matconstr[0][0] =  m_vbetav;              // 0 <= beta_1
        }
        else
        {
            matconstr = new matrix[4][1];
            matconstr[0][0] =  m_vbetav - m_valphav;  // phi_1 <= beta_1
            matconstr[3][0] =  m_valphav;             // 0 <= phi_1
        }
        matconstr[1][0] =  m_dD - m_vbetav;           // beta_1 <= d
        matconstr[2][0] =  1 - m_dD;                  // d <= 1
    }
    avF[0] = matconstr;
    return 1;
}
...
```

5.4 G@RCH and OxGauss

OxGauss, is a program available with recent versions of Ox. It provides a way to run Gauss[18] programs in the Ox environment or to call an existing Gauss procedure under Ox.

Depending on the goal of the analysis and the user's experience, both features are noteworthy and useful. From an Ox-G@RCH user point of view, the main objective of OxGauss is to allow existing Gauss programs to be called from Ox with only a minimum number of changes to these programs. This is beneficial to both Ox and Gauss users. It provides more visibility to both and hence increases the potential use of the underlying statistical technique. Furthermore, it can help with the migration from Gauss to Ox.

Running a pure Gauss code with OxGauss is attractive for non-Gauss and potentially even for non-Ox users because it allows the replication of published work using the console version of Ox. This is an interesting feature since the replicability of simulation and empirical results in econometrics is recognized as being an important aspect of research. An increasing number of researchers in econometrics are making their programs and routines freely available to the econometrics community. As such, OxGauss also provides much added value in that it provides the researcher with a free and rather simple solution to run Gauss programs. See Laurent and Urbain (2003) for a review of OxGauss and the M@ximize web site at `http://www.core.ucl.ac.be/~laurent/`.[19]

The main goal of this section is to illustrate the usefulness of OxGauss for G@RCH users.

5.4.1 Calling Gauss Programs from Ox

The first use of OxGauss is to allow Gauss procedures to be called from Ox. This helps in the transition to Ox, and it increases the amount of code available to Ox users.

To illustrate how Gauss programs can be called from Ox, we consider a small project that mixes both Gauss and Ox programs. The first file, `Gaussprocs.src`, consists of a code file that features the procedure `gengarch(omega,alpha,beta,nu,T_0,T,n)`, which simulates a GARCH model. This procedure has been written by Dick van Dijk

---

[18]Gauss is sold by Aptech Systems, 23804 S.E. Kent-Kangley Rd., Maple Valley, WA, 98038, USA; see `http://www.aptech.com/`. Timberlake Consultants is a distributor of Gauss for many countries.

[19]M@ximize is a package for OxGauss, and is designed to bridge the gap between cml, maxlik, optmum and Ox.

(see Franses and van Dijk, 2000) and is downloadable from his web site

http://www.few.eur.nl/few/people/djvandijk/nltsmef/nltsmef.htm.

```
/*
**   gengarch.src (written by dick van dijk)
**   purpose :  generate realizations from garch(p,q) processes
**   format : eps = gengarch(omega,alpha,beta,t_0,t,n);
**
**   input : omega    : scalar, constant in conditional variance equation
**           alpha    : (qx1) vector, parameters of lagged squared residuals
**                      in conditional variance equation
**           beta     : (px1) vector, parameters of lagged conditional variance
**                      in conditional variance equation
**           nu       : scalar, indicating whether disturbances are to be
**                      drawn from standard normal distribution (nu=0), or from
**                      t-distribution with nu degrees of freedom
**           t_0      : scalar, number of initial observations to be discarded
**           t        : scalar, the length of the series to be generated
**           n        : scalar, the number of generated series
**
**   output  : eps   : t x n, the generated series
*/
proc gengarch(omega,alpha,beta,nu,t_0,t,n);
  local p,q,eps_1,h_1,eps,i,z;

p=rows(beta); q=rows(alpha);

if (rows(n) gt 1);
  z=n;
  n=cols(n);
endif;

/* starting values for lagged residuals are set equal to zero, while lagged
   conditional variances are set equal to unconditional variance */
eps_1=zeros(q+1,n);
if (sumc(alpha)+sumc(beta) /= 1);
  h_1=ones(p+1,n)*(omega/(1-sumc(alpha)-sumc(beta)));
else;
  h_1=ones(p+1,n);
endif;
alpha=alpha|0;
beta=beta|0;

eps=zeros(t_0+t,n);
i=0;
do until (i==t_0+t);
  i=i+1;
  h_1=(omega + alpha'(eps_1.*eps_1) + beta'h_1)|trimr(h_1,0,1);

  if (nu==-1);
    eps_1=(sqrt(h_1[1,.]).*z[i,.])|trimr(eps_1,0,1);
  elseif (nu==0);
    eps_1=(sqrt(h_1[1,.]).*rndn(1,n))|trimr(eps_1,0,1);
  else;
    eps_1=(sqrt((nu-2)/nu).*sqrt(h_1[1,.]).*rndn(1,n)./
                 sqrt(sumc(rndn(nu,n).^2)'./nu))|trimr(eps_1,0,1);
  endif;
  eps[i,.]=eps_1[1,.];
endo;

retp(eps[t_0+1:t_0+t,.]);
endp;
```

To call this procedure from Ox codes, one first has to create a header file. This header file allows the declaration of the functions, constants and external variables so that these are known when required. This is also mandatory to avoid compilation errors in Ox, since functions and global variables have to be explicitly declared before their use. The header file corresponding to our example is Gaussprocs.h.

```
                                                        Gaussprocs.h
#include <oxstd.h>
namespace gauss
{
    gengarch(const omega,const alpha,const beta,const nu,const T_0,
            const T, const n);
    // Add new procedures here
}
```

Additional procedures can be added in Gaussprocs.src, but the header file has to be modified accordingly.[20] It is recommended to use the .src extension for the Gauss programs and .h for the header files.

In the example /packages/OxGauss/GarchEstim.ox, we use a Gauss procedure to generate 20,000 observations from a GARCH(1,1) process with Student-t errors. Then, we rely on G@RCH to estimate a GARCH(1,1) model by Gaussian Quasi-Maximum likelihood. To do this, the Gauss code must be imported into the Ox program, along with the G@RCH package. The **#import** command has been extended so that OxGauss imports are defined by prefixing the file name with gauss::.

```
                                                        GarchEstim.ox
#include <oxstd.h>
#import <packages/Garch6/Garch>
#import "gauss::Gaussprocs"                             \\  <---
main()
{
    decl omega=0.2; decl alpha=0.1; decl beta=0.8; decl nu=10;
    decl T_0=1000; decl T=20000; decl n=1;
    decl y=gauss::gengarch(omega,alpha,beta,nu,T_0,T,n);   \\  <---
    decl garchobj;
    garchobj = new Garch();
    garchobj.Create(1, 1, 1, T, 1);
    garchobj.Append(y, "Y");
    garchobj.Select(Y_VAR, {"Y",0,0} );
    garchobj.SetSelSample(-1, 1, -1, 1);
    garchobj.DISTRI(0);             \\ 0 for Normal
    garchobj.GARCH_ORDERS(1,1);     \\ p order, q order
    garchobj.MODEL(1);              \\ 1: GARCH
    garchobj.Initialization(<>);
    garchobj.DoEstimation(<>);
    garchobj.Output();
    delete garchobj;
}
```

Note that when OxGauss functions or variables are accessed, they must also be prefixed with the identifier gauss::.

---

[20] Arguments declared **const** can be referenced, but cannot be changed inside the function.

5.4.2 Understanding OxGauss

When an OxGauss program is run, it automatically includes the ox\include\oxgauss.ox file. This by itself imports the required files:[21]

```
                                                        \include\oxgauss.ox
/*-------------------------------------------------------------------------
 * oxgauss.ox - master file for functions mapped from Gauss to Ox
 *
 *          (C) Jurgen Doornik 2000-2001
 *
 * this file is automatically inserted when OxGauss code is run
 *-----------------------------------------------------------------------*/
#define OX_GAUSS
#import <g2ox>
#import <gauss::oxgauss>
```

These import statements ensure that ox\include\g2ox.h and oxgauss.h are being included. Most of the OxGauss run-time system is in ox\include\g2ox.ox while the keywords are largely in oxgauss.src.

Most of the programs that link Gauss functions to Ox are gathered in the file \include\g2ox.ox. For instance, the output of the Gauss function cumprodc(x) is an $N \times K$ matrix with the cumulative products of the columns of the $N \times K$ matrix x. The Ox code given below (copied from the file g2ox.ox) shows how OxGauss interprets this function.

```
                                                        part of g2ox.ox
cumprodc(const mx)
{
    return ::cumprod(mx);
}
```

As indicated in this example, OxGauss does not translate the Gauss code into Ox. Instead, it makes a link between the Gauss function (here cumprodc) and its Ox counterpart (cumprod). When the corresponding Ox function does not exist, Ox code is written between the brackets which computes what the original Gauss function meant. It is important to note that not all Gauss functions are supported by OxGauss. For instance, there is no equivalent of the Gauss function intgrat2 (for the computation of double integrals) in Ox 5. For this reason, the corresponding procedure in g2ox.ox just reports the error message intgrat2() unsupported (see below). However, if such a function becomes available in a future version of Ox, mapping ingrat2 to the corresponding function in Ox will be very easy.

---

[21] For ease of presentation, the filename is printed in the upper right corner of the window.

5.4.3 Graphics Support in OxGauss

An important aspect of OxGauss is that it supports most of the graphical features of the Gauss library pgraph. As for the standard functions (see Section 5.4.2), the file \oxgauss\src\pgraph.ox now makes the link between pgraph and the Ox graphical package (oxdraw). For instance, the Gauss function xy() is linked to its Ox counterpart DrawXMatrix().

Here is an example of a Gauss program (grGauss.prg) that draws a simple graph.

```
                                                              grGauss.prg
library pgraph;
    x=seqa(1,1,1000);
    y=rndn(1000,1);
    xlabel("X-axis");
    ylabel("Y-axis: Normal(0,1) draws");
    call xy(x, y);
end;
```

However, only Ox Professional for Windows supports on-screen graphics (through Ox-Metrics). By default, non-Windows versions of Ox and Ox Console have no support for graphs. Nevertheless, the user can rely on the Ox package GnuDraw developed by Charles Bos that allows the creation of GnuPlot (see http://www.gnuplot.info) graphics from Ox (see Section 5.2.2.2). Interestingly, GnuDraw allows the use of the console version for a quick check of the graphical output of Gauss code. Therefore, academic institutions do not have to license the full professional version of Ox if Gauss programs only need to be replicated.

Chapter 6

Value-at-Risk (VaR) estimation using G@RCH

In recent years, the tremendous growth of trading activity and the widely publicized trading loss of well-known financial institutions (see Jorion, 2000, for a brief history of these events) has led financial regulators and supervisory authorities to favor quantitative techniques which appraise the possible loss that these institutions can incur. Value-at-Risk has become one of the most sought-after techniques as it provides a simple answer to the following question: with a given probability (say α), what is my predicted financial loss over a given time horizon? The answer is the VaR at level α, which gives an amount in the currency of the traded assets (in dollar terms for example) and is thus easily understandable.

It turns out that the VaR has a simple statistical definition: the VaR at level α for a sample of returns is defined as the corresponding empirical quantile at $\alpha\%$. Because of the definition of the quantile, we have that, with probability $1 - \alpha$, the returns will be larger than the VaR. In other words, with probability $1 - \alpha$, the losses will be smaller than the dollar amount given by the VaR.[1] From an empirical point of view, the computation of the VaR for a collection of returns thus requires the computation of the empirical quantile at level α of the distribution of the returns of the portfolio.

In this section, we show how to use G@RCH to predict the VaR and test the adequacy of the selected model in forecasting the VaR of the investigated series. The material used in the current section is based on Giot and Laurent (2003) and is devoted to show that models that rely on a symmetric density distribution for the error term can underperform with respect to skewed density models when the left and right tails of the distribution of returns must be modelled. Thus, VaR for traders having both long **and** short positions is not adequately modelled using usual normal or Student distributions.

---

[1] Contrary to some wide-spread beliefs, the VaR does not specify the maximum amount that can be lost.

We suggest using an APARCH model based on the skewed-Student distribution to fully take into account the fat left and right tails of the returns distribution. This allows for an adequate modelling of large returns defined on long and short trading positions. The performances of the model is assessed on daily data of the NASDAQ (11/10/1984 - 21/12/2000).

6.1 VaR Models

To characterize the models, we consider a collection of daily returns (in %), $y_t = 100$ $[\log(p_t) - \log(p_{t-1})]$, where $t = 1, \ldots T$, and p_t is the price at time t. Because daily returns are known to exhibit some serial autocorrelation, we fit an $AR(2)$ structure on the y_t series for all specifications. Accordingly, the conditional mean of y_t, i.e. μ_t, is equal to $\mu + \sum_{j=1}^{2} \psi_j(y_{t-j} - \mu)$. We now consider several specifications for the conditional variance of ε_t.

6.1.1 RiskMetrics^{TM}

In its most simple form, it can be shown that the basic RiskMetrics^{TM} model is equivalent to a normal Integrated GARCH (IGARCH) model where the autoregressive parameter is set at a pre-specified value λ and the coefficient of ε_{t-1}^2 is equal to $1 - \lambda$. In the RiskMetrics^{TM} specification for daily data, λ is fixed to 0.94 and we then have:

$$\varepsilon_t = \sigma_t z_t \tag{6.1}$$

where z_t is IID $N(0, 1)$ and σ_t^2 is defined as in Equation (4.14).

The long side of the daily VaR is defined as the VaR level for traders having long positions in the relevant equity index: this is the "usual" VaR where traders incur losses when negative returns are observed. Correspondingly, the short side of the daily VaR is the VaR level for traders having short positions, i.e. traders who incur losses when stock prices increase.[2]

How good a model is at predicting long VaR is thus related to its ability to model large negative returns, while its performance regarding the short side of the VaR is based on its ability to take into account large positive returns.

---

[2] An asset is short-sold by a trader when it is first borrowed and subsequently sold on the market. By doing this, the trader hopes that the price will fall, so that he can then buy the asset at a lower price and give it back to the lender.

For the RiskMetrics^{TM} model, the one-step-ahead VaR computed in $t-1$ for long trading positions is given by $\mu_t + z_\alpha\sigma_t$, for short trading positions it is equal to $\mu_t + z_{1-\alpha}\sigma_t$, with z_α being the left quantile at $\alpha\%$ for the normal distribution and $z_{1-\alpha}$ is the right quantile at $\alpha\%$.[3]

6.1.2 Normal APARCH

The normal APARCH (Ding, Granger, and Engle, 1993) is an extension of the GARCH model of Bollerslev (1986). It is a very flexible ARCH-type model as it nests at least seven GARCH specifications (see Section 4.4). The APARCH$(1,1)$ is:

$$\sigma_t^\delta \;=\; \omega + \alpha_1\left(|\varepsilon_{t-1}| - \gamma_1\varepsilon_{t-1}\right)^\delta + \beta_1\sigma_{t-1}^\delta \tag{6.2}$$

where $\omega, \alpha_1, \gamma_1, \beta_1$ and δ are parameters to be estimated.

For the normal APARCH model, the one-step-ahead VaR is computed as for the RiskMetrics^{TM} model except the computation of the conditional standard deviation σ_t which is now given by Equation (6.2) (evaluated at its MLE).

6.1.3 Student APARCH

Previous empirical studies on VaR have shown that models based on the normal distribution usually cannot fully take into account the 'fat tails' of the distribution of the returns. To alleviate this problem, the Student APARCH (or ST APARCH) is introduced:

$$\varepsilon_t = \sigma_t z_t \tag{6.3}$$

where z_t is IID $t(0,1,\upsilon)$ and σ_t is defined as in Equation (6.2).

For the Student APARCH model, the VaR for long and short positions is given by $\mu_t + st_{\alpha,\upsilon}\sigma_t$ and $\mu_t + st_{1-\alpha,\upsilon}\sigma_t$, with $st_{\alpha,\upsilon}$ being the left quantile at $\alpha\%$ for the (standardized) Student distribution with (estimated) number of degrees of freedom υ and $st_{1-\alpha,\upsilon}$ is the right quantile at $\alpha\%$ for this same distribution. Note that because $z_\alpha = -z_{1-\alpha}$ for the normal distribution and $st_{\alpha,\upsilon} = -st_{1-\alpha,\upsilon}$ for the Student distribution, the forecasted long and short VaR will be equal in both cases.

---

[3]Note that when computing the VaR, μ_t and σ_t are evaluated by replacing the unknown parameters by their maximum likelihood estimates (MLE).

6.1.4 Skewed-Student APARCH

To account for the excess skewness and kurtosis, Fernández and Steel (1998) propose to extend the Student distribution by adding a skewness parameter.[4] Their procedure allows the introduction of skewness in any continuous unimodal and symmetric (about zero) distribution $g(.)$ by changing the scale at each side of the mode. The main drawback of this density is that it is expressed in terms of the mode and the dispersion. In order to keep in the ARCH 'tradition', Lambert and Laurent (2001) re-expressed the skewed-Student density in terms of the mean and the variance, i.e. re-parameterize this density in such a way that the innovation process has zero mean and unit variance. Otherwise, it will be difficult to separate the fluctuations in the mean and variance from the fluctuations in the shape of the conditional density (Hansen, 1994).

The innovation process z is said to be (standardized) skewed-Student distributed if:

$$f(z|\xi, \upsilon) = \begin{cases} \frac{2}{\xi + \frac{1}{\xi}} sg\left[\xi\left(sz + m\right)|\upsilon\right] & \text{if} \quad z < -\frac{m}{s} \\ \frac{2}{\xi + \frac{1}{\xi}} sg\left[\left(sz + m\right)/\xi|\upsilon\right] & \text{if} \quad z \geq -\frac{m}{s} \end{cases} \tag{6.4}$$

where $g(.|\upsilon)$ is the symmetric (unit variance) Student density and ξ is the asymmetry coefficient.[5] m and s^2 are respectively the mean and the variance of the non-standardized skewed-Student and are defined in Section 3.6.2.

Notice also that the density $f(z_t|1/\xi, \upsilon)$ is the "mirror" of $f(z_t|\xi, \upsilon)$ with respect to the (zero) mean, i.e. $f(z_t|1/\xi, \upsilon) = f(-z_t|\xi, \upsilon)$. Therefore, the sign of $\log(\xi)$ indicates the direction of the skewness: the third moment is positive (negative), and the density is skew to the right (left), if $\log(\xi) > 0 \, (< 0)$.

Lambert and Laurent (2000) show that the quantile function $skst^*_{\alpha,\upsilon,\xi}$ of a non standardized skewed-Student density is:

$$skst^*_{\alpha,\upsilon,\xi} = \begin{cases} \frac{1}{\xi} st_{\alpha,\upsilon}\left[\frac{\alpha}{2}(1 + \xi^2)\right] & \text{if} \quad \alpha < \frac{1}{1+\xi^2} \\ -\xi st_{\alpha,\upsilon}\left[\frac{1-\alpha}{2}(1 + \xi^{-2})\right] & \text{if} \quad \alpha \geq \frac{1}{1+\xi^2} \end{cases} \tag{6.5}$$

where $st_{\alpha,\upsilon}$ is the quantile function of the (unit variance) Student-t density. It is straightforward to obtain the quantile function of the standardized skewed-Student: $skst_{\alpha,\upsilon,\xi} = \frac{skst^*_{\alpha,\upsilon,\xi} - m}{s}$.[6]

---

[4] Other (but very similar) asymmetric Student densities have been proposed by Hansen (1994) and Paolella (1997).

[5] The asymmetry coefficient $\xi > 0$ is defined such that the ratio of probability masses above and below the mean is $\frac{\Pr(z \geq 0|\xi)}{\Pr(z < 0|\xi)} = \xi^2$.

[6] In G@RCH, the corresponding function is `INVCDFTA(const p, const logxi, const nu)`, where p = probability (α), logxi = $\log(\xi)$ and nu = degree of freedom (υ).

For the skewed-Student APARCH model, the VaR for long and short positions is given by $\mu_t + skst_{\alpha,v,\xi}\sigma_t$ and $\mu_t + skst_{1-\alpha,v,\xi}\sigma_t$, with $skst_{\alpha,v,\xi}$ being the left quantile at $\alpha\%$ for the skewed-Student distribution with v degrees of freedom and asymmetry coefficient ξ; $skst_{1-\alpha,v,\xi}$ is the corresponding right quantile. If $\log(\xi)$ is smaller than zero (or $\xi < 1$), $|skst_{\alpha,v,\xi}| > |skst_{1-\alpha,v,\xi}|$ and the VaR for long trading positions will be larger (for the same conditional variance) than the VaR for short trading positions. When $\log(\xi)$ is positive, we have the opposite result.

6.2 Application

6.2.1 Model for VaR assessment

The first step of the application consists in estimating the various models. Then, the adequacy in forecasting the in-sample VaR will be tested. The code used to perform this illustration is given in the file `VaR_insample.ox`. The first model to be estimated is an ARMA(2,0)-RiskMetrics^{TM} model (with a normal density). The second, third and fourth are ARMA(2,0)-APARCH(1,1) models with respectively a normal, Student and skewed-Student densities. The results are given in the four boxes below. Several comments are in order:

- the autoregressive effect in the volatility specification is strong as β_1 is around 0.8, suggesting a strong memory effects. Indeed, $\alpha_1 E\left(|z| - \gamma_1 z\right)^\delta + \beta_1$ is around 1 (0.944317 and 0.963684 respectively for the N-APARCH and SKST-APARCH).
- γ_1 is positive and significant, indicating a leverage effect for negative returns in the *conditional* variance specification;
- $\log(\xi)$ (or "Asymmetry" in the output) is negative and significant which implies that the *asymmetry in the Student distribution* is needed to fully model the distribution of returns. Likelihood ratio tests also clearly favor the skewed-Student density compared to the normal and the Student.
- δ is about 1.35, significantly different from 2 but not significantly different from 1. This suggests that, instead of modelling the conditional variance (GARCH), it is more relevant in this case to model the conditional standard deviation. This result is in line with those of Taylor (1986), Schwert (1990) and Ding, Granger, and Engle (1993) who indicate that there is substantially more correlation between absolute returns than squared returns, a stylized fact of high frequency financial returns (often called 'long memory').

- Comparing the likelihoods of the RiskMetrics^{TM} and the N-APARCH models suggests that the additional flexibility of the APARCH specification is empirically relevant (it increases the likelihood of more than 100 points !).

To summarize, these results indicate the need for a model featuring a negative leverage effect (conditional asymmetry) for the conditional variance combined with an asymmetric distribution for the underlying error term (unconditional asymmetry). The skewed-Student APARCH model delivers such specifications.

Does it means that this model improves on symmetric GARCH models when the VaR for long and short returns is needed ?

```
                                                              VaR_insample.ox
#import <packages/Garch5/Garch>

main()
{
    decl garchobj;
    garchobj = new Garch();

//*** DATA ***//
    garchobj.Load("/data/nasdaq.xls"); // -> B4094
    garchobj.Select(Y_VAR, {"Nasdaq",0,0} );
    garchobj.SetSelSample(1, 1, 2000, 1);
    garchobj.Info();

//*** SPECIFICATIONS ***//
    garchobj.CSTS(1,1);             // cst in Mean (1 or 0), cst in Variance (1 or 0)
    garchobj.DISTRI(0);             // 0 for Gauss, 1 for Student, 2 for GED, 3 for Skewed-Student
    garchobj.ARMA_ORDERS(2,0);      // AR order (p), MA order (q).
    garchobj.ARFIMA(0);             // 1 if Arfima wanted, 0 otherwise
    garchobj.GARCH_ORDERS(1,1);     // p order, q order
    garchobj.MODEL(0);              // 0:RISKMETRICS 1:GARCH    2:EGARCH    3:GJR   4:APARCH
                                    // 5:IGARCH 6:FIGARCH(BBM) 7:FIGARCH(Chung) 8:FIEGARCH(BBM only)
                                    // 9:FIAPARCH(BBM) 10: FIAPARCH(Chung) 11: HYGARCH(BBM)

//*** OUTPUT ***//
    garchobj.MLE(0);                // 0 : Second Derivates, 1 : OPG, 2 : QMLE
    garchobj.ITER(0);               // Interval of iterations between printed intermediary
                                    // results (if no intermediary results wanted, enter '0')

//*** PARAMETERS ***//
    garchobj.BOUNDS(0);             // 1 if bounded parameters wanted, 0 otherwise
    garchobj.Initialization(<>);
    garchobj.DoEstimation(<>);
    garchobj.Output();

    decl quan=<0.95,0.975,0.99,0.995,0.9975>; // Quantiles investigated

    decl Y=garchobj.GetGroup(Y_VAR);
    decl T=garchobj.GetcT();
    decl m_cA,m_cV,i,j;
    decl qu_pos,qu_neg,m_vSigma2,dfunc,m_vPar,cond_mean;
    decl m_Dist=garchobj.GetValue("m_cDist");

    println("Infos");
    println("Number of observations: ", T);
    println("Investigated quantiles: ",quan);
    println("In-sample VaR");

    decl emp_quan_in_pos=new matrix[T][columns(quan)];
    decl emp_quan_in_neg=new matrix[T][columns(quan)];
    m_vSigma2=garchobj.GetValue("m_vSigma2");
    cond_mean=Y-garchobj.GetValue("m_vE");
```

```
    if (m_Dist==0)
    {
        qu_pos=quann(quan)';
        qu_neg=quann(1-quan)';
    }
    if (m_Dist==1)
    {
        m_cV=garchobj.GetValue("m_cV");
        qu_pos=sqrt((m_cV-2)/m_cV)*quant(quan,m_cV)';
        qu_neg=sqrt((m_cV-2)/m_cV)*quant(1-quan,m_cV)';
    }
    if (m_Dist==3)
    {
        m_cV=garchobj.GetValue("m_cV");
        m_cA=garchobj.GetValue("m_cA");
        qu_pos=qu_neg=<>;
        for (i = 0; i < columns(quan) ; ++i)
        {
            qu_pos|=garchobj.INVCDFTA(quan[i],m_cA,m_cV);
            qu_neg|=garchobj.INVCDFTA(1-quan[i],m_cA,m_cV);
        }
    }

    emp_quan_in_pos=(cond_mean + sqrt(m_vSigma2).*qu_pos');
    emp_quan_in_neg=(cond_mean + sqrt(m_vSigma2).*qu_neg');

    println("In-sample Value-at-Risk");
    garchobj.VaR_DynQuant(Y, emp_quan_in_pos, emp_quan_in_neg, quan, 5, 0,0);
    garchobj.VaR_Test(Y, emp_quan_in_pos, emp_quan_in_neg, quan);

    delete garchobj;
}
```

```
                                    Output RiskMetrics - VaR_insample.ox
********************
** SPECIFICATIONS **
********************
Dependent variable : Nasdaq
Mean Equation : ARMA (2, 0) model.
No regressor in the mean
Variance Equation : RiskMetrics (lambda=0.94).
 No regressor in the variance
The distribution is a Gauss distribution.

Strong convergence using numerical derivatives
Log-likelihood = -2222.83
Please wait : Computing the Std Errors ...

 Maximum Likelihood Estimation (Std.Errors based on Second derivatives)
                Coefficient  Std.Error  t-value  t-prob
Cst(M)             0.044980   0.020337    2.212  0.0271
AR(1)              0.269636   0.024409    11.05  0.0000
AR(2)             -0.011516   0.024168  -0.4765  0.6338
ARCH(Alpha1)       0.060000
GARCH(Beta1)       0.940000

No. Observations :     2000  No. Parameters  :        5
Mean (Y)         :   0.04326  Variance (Y)    :   0.83876
Skewness (Y)     :  -2.33675  Kurtosis (Y)    :  33.73842
Log Likelihood   : -2222.834

The sample mean of squared residuals was used to start recursion.

Estimated Parameters Vector :
 0.044980; 0.269636;-0.011516; 0.060000; 0.940000

Elapsed Time : 0.21 seconds (or 0.0035 minutes).
```

```
                                    Output N-APARCH(1,1) - VaR_insample.ox
  ********************
  ** SPECIFICATIONS **
  ********************
Dependent variable : Nasdaq
Mean Equation : ARMA (2, 0) model.
No regressor in the mean
Variance Equation : APARCH (1, 1) model.
 No regressor in the variance
The distribution is a Gauss distribution.

Strong convergence using numerical derivatives
Log-likelihood = -2119.06
Please wait : Computing the Std Errors ...

 Maximum Likelihood Estimation (Std.Errors based on Second derivatives)
                Coefficient  Std.Error  t-value  t-prob
Cst(M)             0.047817   0.019917    2.401   0.0165
AR(1)              0.285268   0.025034   11.40    0.0000
AR(2)              0.005233   0.024285    0.2155  0.8294
Cst(V)             0.045054  0.0081194    5.549   0.0000
ARCH(Alpha1)       0.169705   0.018395    9.226   0.0000
GARCH(Beta1)       0.799843   0.024229   33.01    0.0000
APARCH(Gamma1)     0.286858   0.072419    3.961   0.0001
APARCH(Delta)      1.357528    0.24113    5.630   0.0000

No. Observations :     2000  No. Parameters  :        8
Mean (Y)         :   0.04326  Variance (Y)    :   0.83876
Skewness (Y)     :  -2.33675  Kurtosis (Y)    :  33.73842
Log Likelihood   : -2119.063

The sample mean of squared residuals was used to start recursion.
The condition for existence of E(sigma^delta) and E(|e^delta|) is observed.
The constraint equals 0.944317 and should be < 1.

Estimated Parameters Vector :
0.047817; 0.285268; 0.005233; 0.045054; 0.169705; 0.799843; 0.286858; 1.357528

Elapsed Time : 2.654 seconds (or 0.0442333 minutes).
```

```
                                    Output SKST-APARCH(1,1) - VaR_insample.ox
*********************
** SPECIFICATIONS **
*********************
Dependent variable : Nasdaq
Mean Equation : ARMA (2, 0) model.
No regressor in the mean
Variance Equation : APARCH (1, 1) model.
 No regressor in the variance
The distribution is a skewed-Student distribution, with
a tail coefficient of 5.23817 and an asymmetry coefficient of -0.16141.

Strong convergence using numerical derivatives
Log-likelihood = -2001.87
Please wait : Computing the Std Errors ...

Maximum Likelihood Estimation (Std.Errors based on Second derivatives)
                 Coefficient  Std.Error  t-value  t-prob
Cst(M)              0.054586   0.019069    2.863  0.0042
AR(1)               0.268316   0.023425   11.45   0.0000
AR(2)              -0.011101   0.023234   -0.4778 0.6329
Cst(V)              0.037921   0.0098793   3.838  0.0001
ARCH(Alpha1)        0.153786   0.023273    6.608  0.0000
GARCH(Beta1)        0.820957   0.029905   27.45   0.0000
APARCH(Gamma1)      0.219447   0.087570    2.506  0.0123
APARCH(Delta)       1.367004   0.27287     5.010  0.0000
Asymmetry          -0.161410   0.031849   -5.068  0.0000
Tail                5.238169   0.60680     8.632  0.0000

No. Observations :      2000  No. Parameters  :        10
Mean (Y)          :   0.04326  Variance (Y)    :   0.83876
Skewness (Y)      :  -2.33675  Kurtosis (Y)    :  33.73842
Log Likelihood    : -2001.868

The sample mean of squared residuals was used to start recursion.
The condition for existence of E(sigma^delta) and E(|e^delta|) is observed.
The constraint equals 0.963684 and should be < 1.

Estimated Parameters Vector :
0.054586; 0.268316;-0.011101; 0.037921; 0.153786; 0.820957;
0.219447; 1.367004;-0.161410; 5.238169

Elapsed Time : 5.457 seconds (or 0.09095 minutes).
```

Figure 6.1 plots the in-sample VaR for the 5% and 95 % quantiles for the AR(2)-APARCH-SKST model. Using the rolling menus, this graph is easily obtained by using the Test.../Graphic Analysis/In-Sample VaR Forecasts command and choosing option Theoretical Quantiles' with the following quantiles: 0.05; 0.95.

6.2.2 In-sample VaR

All models are tested with a VaR level α which ranges from 5% to 0.25% (quan $= <$ 0.95, 0.975, 0.99, 0.995, 0.9975 $>$) and their performance is then assessed by computing the failure rate for the returns y_t. By definition, the failure rate is the number of times returns exceed (in absolute value) the forecasted VaR. If the VaR model is correctly specified, the failure rate should be equal to the pre-specified VaR level. In our empirical application, we define a failure rate f_l for the long trading positions, which

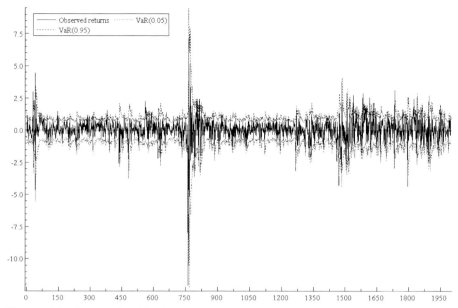

Figure 6.1 In-sample VaR for the NASDAQ given by an AR(2)-APARCH-SKST model.

is equal to the percentage of negative returns smaller than one-step-ahead VaR for long positions. Correspondingly, we define f_s as the failure rate for short trading positions as the percentage of positive returns larger than the one-step-ahead VaR for short positions.

Because the computation of the empirical failure rate defines a sequence of yes/no observations, it is possible to test $H_0 : f = \alpha$ against $H_1 : f \neq \alpha$, where f is the failure rate (estimated by $\widehat{f}$, the empirical failure rate). At the 5% level and if T yes/no observations are available, a confidence interval for $\widehat{f}$ is given by $\left[\widehat{f} - 1.96\sqrt{\widehat{f}(1 - \widehat{f})/T}, \widehat{f} + 1.96\sqrt{\widehat{f}(1 - \widehat{f})/T}\right]$. In the literature on VaR models, this test is also called the Kupiec (1995) LR test when the hypothesis is tested using a likelihood ratio test. The LR statistic is $LR = -2\log\left(\frac{\alpha^N(1-\alpha)^{T-N}}{\widehat{f}^N(1-\widehat{f})^{T-N}}\right)$, where N is the number of VaR violations, T is the total number of observations and α is the theoretical failure rate. Under the null hypothesis that f is the true failure rate, the LR test statistic is asymptotically distributed as a $\chi^2(1)$.

In this application, these tests are successively applied to the failure rate f_l for long trading positions and then to f_s, the failure rate for short trading positions using the procedure VaR_Test.

While an extremely easy-to-understand concept, the Value-at-Risk has however some drawbacks. On of these is that it is not a coherent measure of risk in the sense of Artzner, Delbaen, Eber, and Heath (1999). A somewhat related measure of risk is the so-called expected shortfall (see Scaillet, 2000). Expected shortfall is a coherent measure of risk and it is defined as the expected value of the losses conditional on the loss being larger than the VaR. The average multiple of tail event to risk measure "measures the degree to which events in the tail of the distribution typically exceed the VaR measure by calculating the average multiple of these outcomes to their corresponding VaR measures" (Hendricks, 1996).[7] These measure are reported when calling the procedure VaR_Test and labelled ESF1 and ESF2 respectively.

Complete VaR results for the four models are reported in the following outputs.

		Output RiskMetrics - VaR_insample.ox			
		- Short positions -			
Quantile	Failure rate	Kupiec LRT	P-value	ESF1	ESF2
0.95000	0.96250	7.1752	0.0073918	1.5238	1.3202
0.97500	0.98350	6.7238	0.0095137	1.9570	1.3399
0.99000	0.99000	0.00000	1.0000	2.1653	1.2828
0.99500	0.99300	1.4293	0.23188	2.3557	1.2509
0.99750	0.99450	5.3641	0.020555	2.6115	1.2019
		- Long positions -			
Quantile	Failure rate	Kupiec LRT	P-value	ESF1	ESF2
0.050000	0.056500	1.7103	0.19094	-1.8823	1.6088
0.025000	0.040500	16.648	4.4986e-005	-2.1481	1.5187
0.010000	0.025500	33.969	5.5985e-009	-2.2529	1.4934
0.0050000	0.020000	51.358	7.6961e-013	-2.4338	1.4575
0.0025000	0.015000	57.820	2.8755e-014	-2.8104	1.4673

		Output N-APARCH - VaR_insample.ox			
		- Short positions -			
Quantile	Failure rate	Kupiec LRT	P-value	ESF1	ESF2
0.95000	0.96700	13.757	0.00020807	1.7191	1.2706
0.97500	0.98500	9.5549	0.0019942	1.9285	1.2721
0.99000	0.99250	1.3822	0.23973	2.2827	1.2493
0.99500	0.99550	0.10401	0.74707	2.4319	1.2518
0.99750	0.99700	0.18836	0.66429	2.6958	1.2570
		- Long positions -			
Quantile	Failure rate	Kupiec LRT	P-value	ESF1	ESF2
0.050000	0.053000	0.37198	0.54193	-1.8833	1.5075
0.025000	0.032500	4.2230	0.039879	-2.1592	1.4640
0.010000	0.018000	10.450	0.0012263	-2.7534	1.4800
0.0050000	0.012500	15.928	6.5802e-005	-3.0119	1.5042
0.0025000	0.0095000	22.829	1.7712e-006	-3.2831	1.5016

---

[7] The expected short-fall for the long VaR is computed as the average of the observed returns smaller than the long VaR. The expected short-fall for the short VaR is computed as the average of the observed returns larger than the short VaR. Computations are similar for the average multiple of tail event to risk measure.

```
                            Output ST-APARCH - VaR_insample.ox
                              - Short positions -
     Quantile   Failure rate   Kupiec LRT    P-value        ESF1       ESF2

      0.95000     0.96400        9.1060     0.0025477      1.7063     1.2772
      0.97500     0.98750       15.662    7.5739e-005      2.2696     1.2699
      0.99000     0.99600        9.4119     0.0021558      2.5200     1.2352
      0.99500     0.99900        9.5944     0.0019518      3.7156     1.4563
      0.99750     0.99900        2.3393     0.12614        3.7156     1.2326
                              - Long positions -
     Quantile   Failure rate   Kupiec LRT    P-value        ESF1       ESF2

     0.050000    0.066500       10.434      0.0012371     -1.7154     1.5324
     0.025000    0.034500        6.6333     0.010009      -2.1324     1.4559
     0.010000    0.014000        2.8748     0.089975      -2.9631     1.4620
     0.0050000   0.0080000       3.0582     0.080329      -3.5505     1.4453
     0.0025000   0.0050000       3.8755     0.048996      -4.0783     1.3946
```

```
                            Output SKST-APARCH - VaR_insample.ox
                              - Short positions -
     Quantile   Failure rate   Kupiec LRT    P-value        ESF1       ESF2

      0.95000     0.95050        0.010560    0.91815       1.5490     1.3057
      0.97500     0.98000        2.1997      0.13804       2.0181     1.2966
      0.99000     0.99150        0.47890     0.48892       2.1671     1.2303
      0.99500     0.99700        1.8781      0.17055       2.6958     1.2974
      0.99750     0.99900        2.3393      0.12614       3.7156     1.4868
                              - Long positions -
     Quantile   Failure rate   Kupiec LRT    P-value        ESF1       ESF2

     0.050000    0.051500        0.093853    0.75934      -1.9159     1.5136
     0.025000    0.024500        0.020647    0.88574      -2.4564     1.4604
     0.010000    0.0090000       0.20904     0.64752      -3.3903     1.5069
     0.0050000   0.0060000       0.37773     0.53882      -3.8849     1.4071
     0.0025000   0.0045000       2.5882      0.10766      -4.1698     1.2782
```

These results indicate that:

- VaR models based on the normal distribution (RiskMetrics^{TM} and normal APARCH model) have a difficult job in modelling large positive and negative returns.

- The symmetric Student APARCH model sometimes improves on the performance of normal based models but its performance is still not satisfactory in all cases. Its performance in general is even worse than normal based models. The reason is that the critical values of the Student distribution $t_{\alpha,\upsilon}$ and $t_{1-\alpha,\upsilon}$ are very large in this case, which leads to a high level of long and short VaR: the model is often rejected because it is too conservative.

- the skewed-Student APARCH model improves on all other specifications for both negative and positive returns. The improvement is substantial as the switch to a skewed-Student distribution alleviates almost all problems due to the 'conservativeness' of the symmetric Student distribution. The model performs correctly in 100% of all cases for the negative returns (long VaR) and for the positive returns (short VaR).

Besides the failure rate, a relevant VaR model should feature a sequence of indi-cator functions (VaR violations) that is not serially correlated. With the new variables $Hit_t(\alpha) = I(y_t < VaR_t(\alpha)) - \alpha$ and $Hit_t(1 - \alpha) = I(y_t > VaR_t(1 - \alpha)) - \alpha$, Engle and Manganelli (1999) suggest to test jointly that:

- A1: $E(Hit_t(\alpha)) = 0$ (respectively $E(Hit_t(1 - \alpha)) = 0$) in the case of long trading positions (short trading positions);
- A2: $Hit_t(\alpha)$ (or $Hit_t(1 - \alpha)$) is uncorrelated with the variables included in the information set.

According to Engle and Manganelli (1999), testing A1 and A2 can be done using the artificial regression $Hit_t = X\lambda + \epsilon_t$, where X is a $T \times k$ matrix whose first column is a column of ones, the next p columns are $Hit_{t-1}, \ldots, Hit_{t-p}$ and the $k - p - 1$ remaining columns are additional independent variables (including the VaR itself). Engle and Manganelli (1999) also show that under the null A1 and A2, the Dynamic Quantile test statistic $\frac{\hat{\lambda}' X' X \hat{\lambda}}{\alpha(1-\alpha)} \overset{a}{\sim} \chi^2(k)$, where $\hat{\lambda}$ is the OLS estimate of λ. A small sample version of this test (F-test) is readily obtained but the difference is negligible since the sample size is larger than 1,000 observations. Note that while Engle and Manganelli (1999) only consider long trading positions, we also use this test when computing the VaR of short trading positions.

The G@RCH package also provide a function called VaR_DynQuant implementing this test.

Complete VaR results corresponding to the Dynamic Quantile test are reported in the following outputs.

```
                                          Output RiskMetrics - VaR_insample.ox
           - Short positions -
   Quantile          Stat.       P-value

   0.95000          13.994      0.051297
   0.97500          9.9820       0.18960
   0.99000          4.4913       0.72177
   0.99500          2.4473       0.93101
   0.99750          7.9630       0.33587

           - Long positions -
   Quantile          Stat.       P-value

   0.050000         22.591      0.0020078
   0.025000         44.824    1.4796e-007
   0.010000         95.823       0.00000
   0.0050000        121.21       0.00000
   0.0025000        171.78       0.00000

Remark: In the Dynamic Quantile Regression, p=5.
```

```
                                       Output N-APARCH - VaR_insample.ox
              - Short positions -
       Quantile       Stat.        P-value

       0.95000       15.924        0.025818
       0.97500       10.064        0.18495
       0.99000        6.9102       0.43829
       0.99500        0.31019      0.99989
       0.99750        0.31617      0.99988

              - Long positions -
       Quantile       Stat.        P-value

       0.050000       1.9588       0.96209
       0.025000       5.9063       0.55073
       0.010000      18.798        0.0088448
       0.0050000     32.636        3.0952e-005
       0.0025000     56.664        6.9706e-010

Remark: In the Dynamic Quantile Regression, p=5.
```

```
                                       Output ST-APARCH - VaR_insample.ox
              - Short positions -
       Quantile       Stat.        P-value

       0.95000       13.398        0.062986
       0.97500       15.831        0.026710
       0.99000        7.3396       0.39440
       0.99500        6.4381       0.48962
       0.99750        1.8166       0.96929

              - Long positions -
       Quantile       Stat.        P-value

       0.050000      15.164        0.033953
       0.025000      10.682        0.15308
       0.010000       8.2543       0.31070
       0.0050000     14.335        0.045531
       0.0025000      6.4057       0.49326

Remark: In the Dynamic Quantile Regression, p=5.
```

```
                                       Output SKST-APARCH - VaR_insample.ox
              - Short positions -
       Quantile       Stat.        P-value

       0.95000        3.0185       0.88328
       0.97500       11.787        0.10777
       0.99000        5.2936       0.62418
       0.99500        1.6636       0.97610
       0.99750        1.8136       0.96943

              - Long positions -
       Quantile       Stat.        P-value

       0.050000       1.6258       0.97763
       0.025000       3.0760       0.87789
       0.010000       4.9101       0.67093
       0.0050000      1.6573       0.97636
       0.0025000      4.1900       0.75765

Remark: In the Dynamic Quantile Regression, p=5.
```

The same conclusion holds for the SKST-APARCH model, i.e. it performs very well for the NASDAQ, unlike its symmetric competitors.

6.2.3 Out-of-sample VaR

The testing methodology in the previous subsection is equivalent to back-testing the model on the estimation sample. Therefore it can be argued that this should be favorable to the tested model. In a 'real life situation', VaR models are used to deliver out-of-sample forecasts, where the model is estimated on the known returns (up to time t for example) and the VaR forecast is made for period $[t + 1, t + h]$, where h is the time horizon of the forecasts. In this subsection we implement this testing procedure for the long and short VaR with $h = 1$ day. Note that the code used for this illustration is VaR_outofsample.ox.

We use an iterative procedure where the skewed-Student APARCH model is estimated to predict the one-day-ahead VaR. The first estimation sample is the complete sample for which the data is available less the last five years. The predicted one-day-ahead VaR (both for long and short positions) is then compared with the observed return and both results are recorded for later assessment using the statistical tests. At the *i-th* iteration where i goes from 2 to 5×252 (five years of data), the estimation sample is augmented to include one more day and the VaRs are forecasted and recorded. Whenever i is a multiple of 50, the model is re-estimated to update the skewed-Student APARCH parameters. In other words, we update the model parameters every 50 trading days and we thus assume a 'stability window' of 50 days for our parameters. We iterate the procedure until all days (less the last one) have been included in the estimation sample. Corresponding failure rates are then computed by comparing the long and short forecasted VaR_{t+1} with the observed return y_{t+1} for all days in the five years period. We use the same statistical tests as in the previous subsection.

```
                                                                     VaR_outofsample.ox
#import <packages/Garch5/Garch>

main()
{
    decl garchobj;
    garchobj = new Garch();
//*** DATA ***//
    garchobj.Load("/data/nasdaq.xls"); // -> B4094
    garchobj.Select(Y_VAR, {"Nasdaq",0,0} );
    garchobj.SetSelSample(1, 1, 4093-5*252, 1);
    garchobj.Info();
//*** SPECIFICATIONS ***//
    garchobj.CSTS(1,1);                 // cst in Mean (1 or 0), cst in Variance (1 or 0)
    garchobj.DISTRI(1);                 // 0 for Gauss, 1 for Student, 2 for GED, 3 for Skewed-Student
    garchobj.ARMA_ORDERS(2,0);          // AR order (p), MA order (q).
    garchobj.GARCH_ORDERS(1,1);         // p order, q order
    garchobj.MODEL(4);                  // 0:RISKMETRICS 1:GARCH    2:EGARCH    3:GJR   4:APARCH
                                        // 5:IGARCH 6:FIGARCH(BBM) 7:FIGARCH(Chung) 8:FIEGARCH(BBM only)
                                        // 9:FIAPARCH(BBM) 10: FIAPARCH(Chung) 11: HYGARCH(BBM)
//*** OUTPUT ***//
    garchobj.MLE(0);                    // 0 : Second Derivates, 1 : OPG, 2 : QMLE
    garchobj.ITER(0);
//*** PARAMETERS ***//
    garchobj.Initialization(<>) ;
    garchobj.DoEstimation(<>) ;
    garchobj.Output();

    decl quan=<0.95,0.975,0.99,0.995,0.9975>; // Quantiles investigated
    decl out_of_sample_VaR=1; // 1 to compute the out-of-sample VaR, 0 otherwise
    decl numb_out_of_sample=5*252; // number of observations in the out-of-sample period
    decl reestimate_every=50; // k: to reestimate the model every k observations
    decl Y=garchobj.GetGroup(Y_VAR);
    decl T=garchobj.GetcT();
    decl m_cA,m_cV,i,j;
    decl qu_pos,qu_neg,m_vSigma2,dfunc,m_vPar,cond_mean;
    decl m_Dist=garchobj.GetValue("m_cDist");
    println("Infos");
    println("Number of observations: ", T);
    println("Investigated quantiles: ",quan);
    println("Number of forecasts: ", numb_out_of_sample);
    println("Out-of-sample: re-estimate every ", reestimate_every, " observations");
}
    m_Dist=garchobj.GetValue("m_cDist");
    m_vPar=garchobj.GetValue("m_vPar");
    decl emp_quan_out_pos=new matrix[numb_out_of_sample][columns(quan)];
    decl emp_quan_out_neg=new matrix[numb_out_of_sample][columns(quan)];
    decl k=0;
    for (j = 0; j < numb_out_of_sample ; ++j)
    {
        garchobj.SetSelSample(-1, 1, T+j, 1);
        if (k==reestimate_every-1)
        {
            println("..... Remaining Steps (Out-of-sample): ",numb_out_of_sample-j, " .....");
            garchobj.Initialization(m_vPar) ;
            garchobj.DoEstimation(<>);
            k*=0;
        }
        else
        {
            garchobj.InitData();
            garchobj.FigLL(garchobj.GetFreePar(), &dfunc, 0,0);
            ++k;
        }
        m_vPar=garchobj.GetValue("m_vPar");
        garchobj.SetSelSample(-1, 1, T+j+1, 1);
        garchobj.InitData();
        Y=garchobj.GetGroup(Y_VAR);
        garchobj.Res_Var();
        m_vSigma2=garchobj.GetValue("m_vSigma2")[T+j];
        cond_mean=Y[T+j][]-garchobj.GetValue("m_vE")[T+j][];
        if (m_Dist==0)
        {
            qu_pos=quann(quan)';
            qu_neg=quann(1-quan)';
        }
```

```
                                                          ...VaR_outofsample.ox
    if (m_Dist==1)
    {
        m_cV=garchobj.GetValue("m_cV");
        qu_pos=sqrt((m_cV-2)/m_cV)*quant(quan,m_cV)';
        qu_neg=sqrt((m_cV-2)/m_cV)*quant(1-quan,m_cV)';
    }
    if (m_Dist==3)
    {
        m_cV=garchobj.GetValue("m_cV");
        m_cA=garchobj.GetValue("m_cA");
        qu_pos=qu_neg=<>;
        for (i = 0; i < columns(quan) ; ++i)
        {
            qu_pos|=garchobj.INVCDFTA(quan[i],m_cA,m_cV);
            qu_neg|=garchobj.INVCDFTA(1-quan[i],m_cA,m_cV);
        }
    }
    emp_quan_out_pos[j][]=(cond_mean + sqrt(m_vSigma2).*qu_pos)';
    emp_quan_out_neg[j][]=(cond_mean + sqrt(m_vSigma2).*qu_neg)';
    }
    println("Out-of-sample Value-at-Risk (rolling regression)");
    garchobj.VaR_DynQuant(Y[T:T+numb_out_of_sample-1],emp_quan_out_pos,emp_quan_out_neg,quan,5,0,0);
    garchobj.VaR_Test(Y[T:T+numb_out_of_sample-1],emp_quan_out_pos,emp_quan_out_neg,quan);
    delete garchobj;
}
```

Empirical results for the SKST-APARCH are given below. Broadly speaking, the
results are quite similar (although not as good) to those obtained for the in-sample
testing procedure.

```
                                    Output - VaR_APARCH_SKST_outofsample.ox
              - Short positions -
    Quantile        Stat.       P-value

    0.95000        42.683    3.8399e-007
    0.97500        28.903     0.00015072
    0.99000        6.6717        0.46384
    0.99500       0.32859        0.99986
    0.99750        3.5069        0.83449

              - Long positions -
    Quantile        Stat.       P-value

    0.050000       38.467    2.4696e-006
    0.025000       43.893    2.2419e-007
    0.010000       7.6759        0.36204
    0.0050000      3.5150        0.83363
    0.0025000     0.61369        0.99891

Remark: In the Dynamic Quantile Regression, p=5.

                              - Short positions -
    Quantile   Failure rate   Kupiec LRT    P-value        ESF1       ESF2

    0.95000      0.91667       24.765    6.4776e-007     2.7630     1.3391
    0.97500      0.95635       14.760     0.00012207     3.1518     1.2488
    0.99000      0.98730      0.85382        0.35547     3.7643     1.2290
    0.99500      0.99444     0.075438        0.78358     4.4206     1.1863
    0.99750      0.99683      0.21171        0.64543     2.7719     1.0845
                              - Long positions -
    Quantile   Failure rate   Kupiec LRT    P-value        ESF1       ESF2

    0.050000     0.069048       8.6470      0.0032760    -3.0879     1.4279
    0.025000     0.033333       3.2553      0.071193     -3.5326     1.3442
    0.010000     0.011905      0.43522       0.50944     -4.4876     1.3198
    0.0050000    0.0063492     0.42458       0.51466     -4.5203     1.2693
    0.0025000    0.0031746     0.21171       0.64543     -6.2120     1.2574
```

Chapter 7

Realized Volatility and Intraday Periodicity

(written with the collaboration of Kris Boudt and Jerome Lahaye)

The recent widespread availability of databases providing the intradaily prices of financial assets (stocks, stock indices, bonds, currencies, ...) has led to new developments in applied econometrics and quantitative finance to model daily and intradaily volatility.

The aim of this chapter is to introduce and illustrate several concepts. We first sketch basic notions to understand diffusion models before moving on to an explanation of relevant volatility measures. We introduce the notion of integrated volatility and one popular estimator: realized volatility. We then consider the issues of the presence of jumps in the price process. We then present an important stylized fact of intraday returns, namely intraday periodicity in volatility, and show how to consistently estimate it in the presence and absence of jumps. We also review two estimators of the integrated volatility that are robust in the presence of jumps, i.e. the bi-power variation and the realized outlyingness weighted variation.

We also review two different approaches for jumps detection. The first one tests whether the contribution of jumps to the daily variance is zero. The second one tests at the intraday level whether a given return is affected by price jumps.

While G@RCH 6.0 is primarily a menu-driven module for OxMetrics, it also provides a set of Ox classes that allow the user to write Ox programs that import these classes. G@RCH contains a set of procedures, gathered in the Realized class, devoted to the computation (or estimation) of

- the realized volatility and its univariate and multivariate extensions;
- daily and intradaily jumps;

- intraday or intraweek periodicity in volatility;

and the simulation of continuous-time stochastic volatility processes.

Most concepts are directly implemented in the menu-driven application. As usual, several ox programs are also provided (they are available in
/packages/Realized/samples/).

This chapter has been inspired by several excellent sources of information, namely
Chapter 6 (Continuous-Time Models and Their Applications) of Tsay (2002), the
recent survey of Andersen, Bollerslev, Christoffersen, and Diebold (2006) and more
generally by the seminal papers of Andersen, Bollerslev, Diebold and coauthors,
Barndorff-Nielsen and Shephard, as well as Lee and Mykland (2008). This chapter
is also based on Boudt, Croux, and Laurent (2008a,2008b).

7.1 Introduction to diffusion models

It is useful to think of returns as arising from an underlying continuous-time process.
In particular, suppose that this underlying model involves a continuous sample path
for the (logarithmic) price process. The return process may then, under general
assumptions, be written in standard stochastic differential equation (sde) form as,

$$dp(t) = \mu(t)dt + \sigma(t)dW(t), t \geq 0, \tag{7.1}$$

where $dp(t)$ denotes the logarithmic price increment, $\mu(t)$ the drift, $\sigma(t)$ refers to
the point-in-time or spot volatility, and $W(t)$ is a standard Brownian motion.

7.1.1 Standard Brownian motion / Wiener process

In a discrete-time econometric model, we assume that shocks are driven by a white
noise process, which is not predictable. What is the counterpart of shocks in a
continuous-time model? The answer is *increments* of a Wiener process $W(t)$ (also
known as a standard Brownian motion).

A continuous-time stochastic process $W(t)$ is a Wiener process if it satisfies:

(1) $W(0) = 0$;
(2) $\Delta W(t) \equiv W(t + \Delta) - W(t) = \epsilon\sqrt{\Delta}$, where ϵ is an N(0,1) random variable;
(3) $\Delta W(t)$ is independent of $\Delta W(j), \forall j \leq t$;
(4) $W(t)$ is a continuous process, i.e. there are no jumps in its sample paths,

where Δ is a small increment in time.

To simulate a continuous process, it is of course necessary to discretize time. We simulate the motion at times $0, \Delta, 2\Delta, 3\Delta, ...$ Moreover, the definition of a Brownian motion implies that $\{W(k\Delta) - W((k-1)\Delta) : k \in N\}$ is a collection of *i.i.d.* $N(0,1)$ random variables. So to simulate a trajectory of the Brownian motion up to time $m\Delta$, one needs to generate m independent $N(0,1)$ random variables $\{Z_k : k \in \{1, 2, ..., m\}\}$.

Since $W_0 \equiv 0$, and $W(k\Delta) \equiv W([k-1]\Delta) + \Delta^{1/2}Z_k, k \in \{1, 2, ..., m\}$, we simulate:

$$W_0 \equiv 0, W_{k\Delta} \equiv W_{(k-1)\Delta} + (\Delta)^{1/2}Z_k, k \in \{1, 2, ..., m\}.$$

This is called the Euler method to simulate a Brownian motion.

The example file `Simul_wiener.ox` uses the procedure `Simul_Wiener_process(const m, const deltat)` to simulate four Wiener processes consisting of 5 days with 10,000 observations per day ($m = 5 \times 10,000 = 50,000$ and $\Delta = 1/10,000$). This procedure is available in `/packages/Realized/samples/procs_simul.ox`.

Figure 7.1 represents the four simulated Wiener processes starting with $W(0) = 0$.

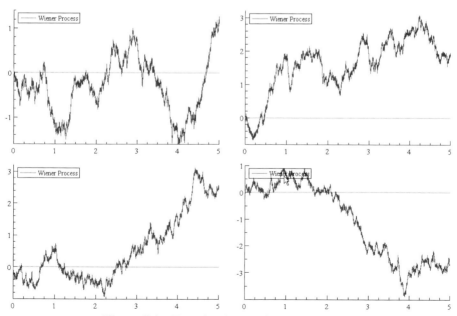

Figure 7.1   Four simulated Wiener processes.

The Wiener process is a special stochastic process with zero drift and variance proportional to the length of time interval. This means that the rate of change in expectation is 0 and the rate of change in variance is 1. Even though this process is of crucial importance in finance, it is desirable to generalize it and allow the mean and the variance to evolve over time in a more realistic manner.

7.1.2 Generalized Wiener Process

Let us now consider the generalized Wiener process $p^*(t)$: its expectation has a drift rate μ while the rate of variance change is σ^2.

The generalized Wiener process can be written as follows:

$$dp^*(t) = \mu dt + \sigma dW(t), t \geq 0, \tag{7.2}$$

where $W(t)$ is a Wiener process, and $p^*(t)$ is the price (and not its log). Then, $E[p^*(t) - p^*(0)] = \mu t$ and $\text{Var}[p^*(t) - p^*(0)] = \sigma^2 t$. μ and σ^2 are often referred to as the drift and volatility parameters of the generalized Wiener process $p^*(t)$.

The main limitation of the generalized Wiener process is that both the drift and volatility parameters (μ and σ^2) are constant over time while it is well known that daily returns for instance (i.e. $t = 1$) are heteroscedastic.

The Ito process overcomes this drawback, allowing both the drift and volatility parameters to be time-varying. It is usually written as follows:

$$dp^*(t) = \mu(p^*(t), t)dt + \sigma(p^*(t), t)dW(t), t \geq 0, \tag{7.3}$$

where $W(t)$ is a Wiener process. This process can be rewritten $p^*(t) = p^*(0) + \int_0^t \mu(p^*(s), s)ds + \int_0^t \sigma(p^*(s), s)dW(s)$.

A particular version of this process is commonly used in the literature to describe the behavior of prices and is known as geometric Brownian motion:

$$dp^*(t) = p^*(t)\mu dt + p^*(t)\sigma dW(t), t \geq 0. \tag{7.4}$$

In other words, a geometric Brownian motion is a continuous-time stochastic process in which the logarithm of the randomly varying quantity follows a Brownian motion. It is easy to show that the random variable $\log(p^*(t)/p^*(0))$ is normally distributed with mean $(\mu - \sigma^2/2)t$ and variance $\sigma^2 t$, which reflects the fact that increments of a geometric Brownian motion are normal relative to the current price, reason for which it is called geometric Setting $t = 1$, e.g. daily data, we have that the one-period-ahead returns are normally distributed, with mean $(\mu - \sigma^2/2)$ and variance σ^2. See Chapter 6 of Tsay (2002) for more details.

7.2 Integrated Volatility

A drawback of the geometric Brownian motion is that it is not able to generate the well know ARCH effects (volatility clustering). It is thus desirable to make both μ and σ^2 time varying.

7.2.1 Theoretical background

Let us now consider the following diffusion process for the logarithmic price $p(t) = log(p^*(t))$:

$$dp(t) = \mu(t)dt + \sigma(t)dW(t), t \geq 0, \tag{7.5}$$

where $\mu(t)$ denotes the drift, $\sigma(t)$ refers to the point-in-time or spot volatility, and $W(t)$ denotes a standard Brownian motion. Intuitively, over (infinitesimal) small time intervals,

$$r(t, \Delta) \equiv p(t) - p(t - \Delta) \approx \mu(t - \Delta)\Delta + \sigma(t - \Delta)\Delta W(t), \tag{7.6}$$

where $\Delta W(t) = W(t) - W(t - \Delta) \sim N(0, \Delta)$.

For the one-period daily return,

$$r_t \equiv p(t) - p(t - 1) = \int_{t-1}^{t} \mu(s)ds + \int_{t-1}^{t} \sigma(s)dW(s). \tag{7.7}$$

From Equation (7.7), it is clear that the volatility for the continuous-time process over $[t - 1, t]$ is linked to the evolution of the spot volatility $\sigma(t)$. Furthermore, conditional on the sample path of the drift and the spot volatility processes,

$$r_t \sim N\left(\int_{t-1}^{t} \mu(s)ds, IV_t\right), \tag{7.8}$$

where IV_t denotes the so-called integrated variance (volatility), and is defined as follows:

$$IV_t \equiv \int_{t-1}^{t} \sigma^2(s)ds.$$

7.2.2 Illustration of the concept of integrated volatility

To visualize the difference between the spot volatility, the integrated volatility, the conditional volatility of a GARCH(1,1) model and daily squared returns, let us consider the following simulation study.

The simulated model is designed to induce temporal dependencies consistent with the GARCH(1,1) model. The simulated continuous-time GARCH diffusion is formally defined by

$$dp(t) \quad = \quad \sigma(t)dW_p(t) \tag{7.9}$$

$$d\sigma^2(t) \quad = \quad \theta[\omega - \sigma^2(t)]dt + (2\lambda\theta)^{1/2}\sigma^2(t)dW_d(t), \tag{7.10}$$

where $W_p(t)$ and $W_d(t)$ denote two independent Brownian motions.[1]

The Realized class contains a function `Simul_Continuous_GARCH` devoted to the simulation of the above continuous-time GARCH diffusion process. This procedure uses a standard Euler discretization scheme to generate the continuous-time GARCH diffusion process, i.e. $p(t + \Delta) = p(t) + \sigma(t)\sqrt{\Delta}Z_p(t)$ and $\sigma^2(t + \Delta) = \theta\omega\Delta + \sigma^2(t)\left[1 - \theta\Delta + \sqrt{2\lambda\theta\Delta}Z_d(t)\right]$, where $Z_p(t)$ and $Z_d(t)$ denote two independent standard normal variables.

In the example file `Simul_Continuous_GARCH.ox`, a continuous-time GARCH diffusion process is generated for which the constants are set to $\theta = 0.035$, $\omega = 0.636$ and $\lambda = 0.296$. The same model has previously been analyzed in Andersen and Bollerslev (1998a). To simulate exchange rates, we choose $\Delta = 1/2880$, corresponding to 10 observations per 5-minute interval. The number of simulated days $= 510$ but the first ten days have been discarded, giving a total of 500 simulated days. Furthermore, we use the following initial values for the log-price and spot volatility: $p(0) = 1$ and $\sigma^2(0) = 0.1$.

Figure 7.2 graphs the simulated instantaneous log-prices, 5-min prices and daily prices.

Figure 7.3 plots the corresponding returns, i.e. instantaneous returns, 5-min returns and daily returns.

Finally, Figure 7.4 plots five volatility measures:

(1) The top left panel of Figure 7.4 displays the simulated spot volatility $\sigma^2(s)$. The spot variance is $\sigma^2(t+\Delta) = \theta\omega\Delta + \sigma^2(t)\left[1 - \theta\Delta + \sqrt{2\lambda\theta\Delta}Zd(t)\right]$. We thus have 2880 values per day.

(2) The top right panel displays the corresponding daily integrated volatility, i.e. IV_t. Given the fact that $IV_t \equiv \int_{t-1}^{t} \sigma^2(s)ds$, the 'daily' IV_t is computed as $\sum_{i=1}^{1/\Delta} \sigma^2(t - j/\Delta)\Delta$, where $1/\Delta = 2880$.

---

[1]See Andersen and Bollerslev (1998a) for more details.

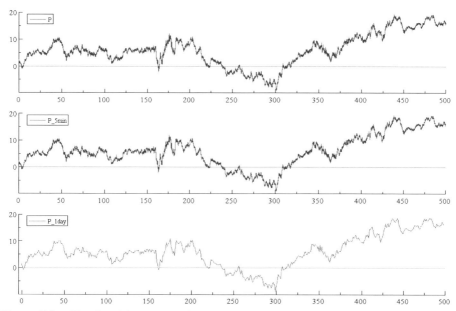

Figure 7.2 Simulated log-prices of a continuous-time GARCH diffusion model. The figure plots respectively the instantaneous log-prices, 5-min prices and daily prices.

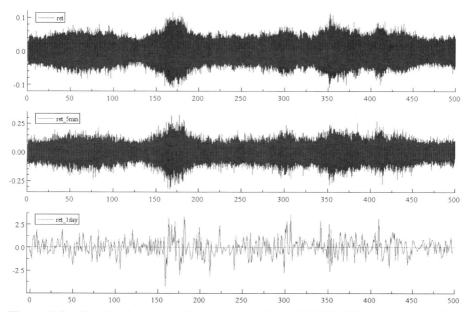

Figure 7.3 Simulated returns of a continuous-time GARCH diffusion model. The figure plots respectively the instantaneous returns, 5-min returns and daily returns.

(3) The bottom left panel displays the conditional variance obtained by estimating a GARCH(1,1) model on the daily returns.

(4) Finally, the bottom right panel plots the squared daily returns.

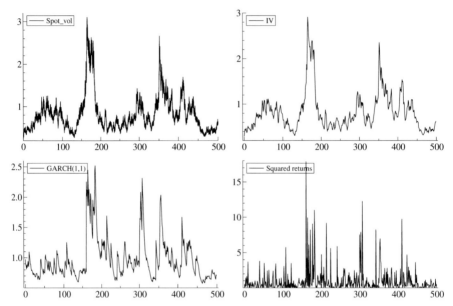

Figure 7.4 Four volatility measures: Spot volatility, Integrated Volatility, GARCH(1,1) on daily returns and daily squared returns.

Two comments are in order.

- Even though the daily squared return are known to be an unbiased measure of the volatility, it is extremely noisy.
- Unlike daily squared returns, the conditional variance of the GARCH(1,1) is much less noisy. Indeed, it generally tracks the level of the spot volatility very well.

We have seen in Section 5.3.1 that one of the most popular measures to check the forecasting performance of the ARCH-type models is the Mincer-Zarnowitz regression, i.e. ex-post volatility regression:

$$\check{\sigma}_t^2 = a_0 + a_1 \hat{\sigma}_t^2 + u_t, \tag{7.11}$$

where $\check{\sigma}_t^2$ is the ex-post volatility, $\hat{\sigma}_t^2$ is the forecasted volatility and a_0 and a_1 are parameters to be estimated. Recall that if the model for the conditional variance is correctly specified (and the parameters are known) and if $E(\breve{\sigma}_t^2) = \hat{\sigma}_t^2$, we have $a_0 = 0$ and $a_1 = 1$. Furthermore, the R^2 of this regression is often used as a simple measure of the degree of predictability of the ARCH-type model.

To judge the quality of the GARCH forecasts it is common to use $\breve{\sigma}_t^2 = (r_t - \bar{r})^2$, where $\bar{r}$ is the sample mean of r_t (daily return at time t). The R^2 of this regression is often lower than 5% and this could lead to the conclusion that GARCH models produce poor forecasts of the volatility (see, among others, Schwert, 1990, or Jorion, 1996). In their seminal paper, Andersen and Bollerslev (1998a) have shown that if r_t follows a GARCH(1,1), the R^2 of this regression is nothing but $\frac{\text{Var}(\breve{\sigma}_t^2)}{\text{Var}(r_t^2)} = \frac{\alpha_1^2}{(1-\beta_1^2-2\alpha_1\beta_1)}$. If κ is the kurtosis of z_t, we have that $\kappa\alpha_1^2 + \beta_1^2 + 2\alpha_1\beta_1 < 1$ to ensure the existence of the unconditional kurtosis of r_t. It follows then that $\kappa\alpha_1^2 < 1 - \beta_1^2 - 2\alpha_1\beta_1$ and,

$$R^2 \equiv \frac{\alpha_1^2}{(1 - \beta_1^2 - 2\alpha_1\beta_1)} < \frac{1}{\kappa}.$$

If the innovations (z_t) are $i.i.d$ $N(0,1)$, the R^2 is thus necessarily lower than $\frac{1}{3}$.

In example file `Simul_Continuous_GARCH_R2.ox`, we simulate the same diffusion process as before and run the above regression to illustrate the findings of Andersen and Bollerslev (1998a). When using the daily squared returns to measure the observed daily volatility, the R^2 of the regression is found to be extremely low, i.e. 0.0374596 even though a_0 and a_1 are not significantly different from 0 and 1 respectively. However, if we consider the integrated volatility instead of the squared daily returns as an ex-post volatility measure, the R^2 now equals 0.421871 suggesting that the GARCH model explains more than 40% of the variability of the true volatility.

7.3 Realized Volatility

It is clear from Section 7.2 that the integrated volatility is an ideal ex-post measure of volatility and thus useful for assessing the quality of conditional volatility forecasts. In other words, it is the ideal measure for assessing the quality of conditional volatility forecasts, like GARCH models. However, the integrated volatility is never observed in practice.

Inspired by the recent widespread availability of intraday prices of various financial assets, Andersen and Bollerslev (1998a) have proposed to proxy the integrated volatility by the so-called realized volatility.

The most fundamental feature of realized volatility is that it provides a *consistent non parametric* estimate of the price variability that has transpired over a given discrete interval.

The intuition behind the use of realized volatility is most readily conveyed within the popular continuous-time diffusion presented in Equation (7.5) for which the key quantity of daily volatility is the integral of the squared spot variance. This integral is called the integrated variance.

We assume we dispose of T days of $M \equiv \lfloor 1/\Delta \rfloor$ equally-spaced intraday returns. Now denote the i-th return of day t by $r_{t,i} \equiv p(t + i\Delta) - p(t + (i - 1)\Delta)$, where $i = 1, \ldots, M$. The daily Realized Variance (RVar) of day t, denoted $RV_t(\Delta)$, is then defined as:

$$RV_t(\Delta) \equiv \sum_{i=1}^{M} r_{t,i}^2. \tag{7.12}$$

By the theory of quadratic variation, when $\Delta \to 0$ and when the true diffusion process belongs to the family of processes presented in Equation (7.5) (i.e. absence of jumps):

$$RV_t(\Delta) \to \int_{t-1}^{t} \sigma^2(s)ds. \tag{7.13}$$

In other words, under suitable conditions (like the absence of serial correlation in the intraday returns)[2], the realized volatility is consistent for the integrated volatility in the sense that when $\Delta \to 0$, $RV_t(\Delta)$ measures the latent integrated volatility IV_t perfectly.

G@RCH contains a set of procedures devoted to the computation of the realized volatility (and other related concepts that we will review in the next sections) gathered in the Realized class. For instance, the example file `Simul_Continuous_GARCH_RV.ox` simulates the previous GARCH-diffusion process and uses the procedure `Compute_RV` to compute the realized volatility from the simulated 5-minute returns, i.e. 288 returns per day.

Figure 7.5 plots four volatility measures obtained when running `Simul_Continuous_GARCH_RV.ox`.

---

[2]However, in practice, at very high frequencies, returns are polluted by microstructure noise (bid-ask bounce, unevenly spaced observations, discreteness,...). This "errors-in-variables" problem causes the high-frequency returns to be autocorrelated. Recall that bid-ask bounce occurs in all high-frequency transaction data as successive quotes tend to bounce between buys and sells, and sampling these as proxies for the mid-price gives an impression that markets are moving more than they actually are, adding an upward bias to the measured volatility.

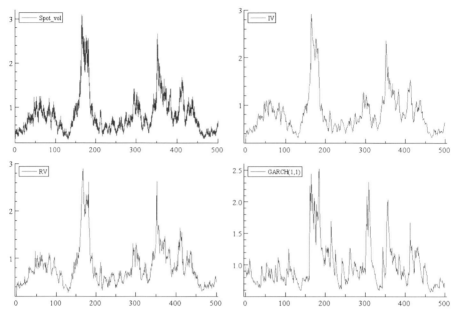

Figure 7.5 Four volatility measures: Spot volatility, Integrated Volatility, realized volatility based on 5-min returns and GARCH(1,1) on daily returns.

(1) The top left panel displays the simulated spot volatility $\sigma^2(t)$.

(2) The top right panel displays the corresponding daily integrated volatility.

(3) The bottom left panel plots the daily realized volatility.

(4) And finally, the bottom right panel displays GARCH(1,1) conditional variance.

The quality of the approximation of IV_t by $RV_t(\Delta)$ is evident from this graph.

Note that the example file `Simul_Continuous_GARCH_R2.ox` also reported the R^2 of the Mincer-Zarnowitz regression using the realized volatility as endogenous variable. Not surprisingly, the R^2 is very close to the previous value obtained for the IV_t, i.e. 0.4219 vs. 0.4121.

7.4 Jumps

Empirical studies have shown that a continuous diffusion model as in Equation (7.5) fails to explain some characteristics of asset returns. Furthermore, standard GARCH models are not able to fully explain the excess kurtosis found in most financial time series. In a continuous time framework, the inadequacy of the standard stochastic diffusion model has led to developments of alternative models. Jump diffusion and stochastic volatility models have been proposed in the literature to overcome this inadequacy.

As common in the literature on non parametric estimation of the continuous and jump components in the quadratic variation (QVar), we suppose that the log-price process belongs either to the Brownian SemiMartingale (BSM) or the BSM with Jumps (BSMJ) families of models. Under the BSMJ model, the diffusion component captures the smooth variation of the price process, while the jump component accounts for the rare, large discontinuities in the observed prices. Andersen, Bollerslev, and Dobrev (2007) cite the work of several authors who found that this is a realistic model for the price series of many financial assets.

A BSMJ log-price diffusion admits the representation

$$dp(t) = \mu(t)dt + \sigma(t)dW(t) + \kappa(t)dq(t), 0 \leq t \leq T, \tag{7.14}$$

where $\mu(t)$ is a continuous locally bounded variation process, $\sigma(t)$ is a strictly positive and càdlàg (right-continuous with left limits) stochastic volatility process, $W(t)$ is a standard Brownian motion, $dq(t)$ is a counting process with $dq(t) = 1$ corresponding to a jump at time t and $dq(t) = 0$ otherwise. The (possibly time-varying) jump intensity is $l(t)$ and $\kappa(t)$ is the size of the corresponding jump.

Jumps in stock prices are often assumed to follow a probability law. For instance, the jumps may follow a Poisson process, which is a continuous-time discrete process. For a given time t, let X_t be the number of times a special event occurs during the time period $[0, t]$. Then X_t is a Poisson process if:

$$\Pr(X_t = m) = \frac{l^m t^m}{m!} exp(-lt), l > 0.$$

The l parameter governs the occurrence of the special event and is referred to as the *rate* or *intensity* of the process. Recall also that $E(X_t) = l$.

G@RCH also provides a procedure `Simul_Continuous_GARCH_JUMPS` to simulate a continuous-time GARCH diffusion process with jumps, formally defined by

$$dp(t) = \sigma(t)dW_p(t) + \kappa(t)dq(t), \tag{7.15}$$

$$d\sigma^2(t) = \theta[\omega - \sigma^2(t)]dt + (2\lambda\theta)^{1/2}\sigma^2(t)dW_d(t), \tag{7.16}$$

$$\kappa(t) \sim \sigma(t)\sqrt{m}([-2, -1] \cup [1, 2]) \tag{7.17}$$

$$dq(t) \sim Poisson(l). \tag{7.18}$$

The jump size $\kappa(t)$ is modeled as the product between $\sigma(t)$ and a uniformly distributed random variable on $\sqrt{m}([-2,-1]\cup[1,2])$. The parameter m determines the magnitude of the jumps.

Figure 7.6 plots IV_t and RV_t for 500 days of simulated intraday returns. The DGP is given by Equations (7.15)-(7.18) with the same GARCH parameters as before, but m is set to 0.5 and l is chosen such that there is on average one jump every 5 days. The ox code used to get this figure is `Simul_Continuous_GARCH_JUMPS_IV_RV.ox`.

Importantly, it is clearly visible that the realized volatility does not match the spot and integrated volatility.

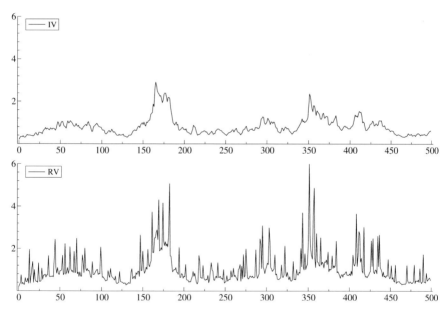

Figure 7.6 Integrated Volatility based and Realized Volatility for a continuous-time GARCH model with jumps.

This result is not surprising since we know by the theory of quadratic variation that for $\Delta \to 0$, we have the following convergence in probability:

$$RV_t(\Delta) \to \int_{t-1}^{t} \sigma^2(s)ds + \sum_{t-1<s\leq t} \kappa^2(s). \qquad (7.19)$$

In other words, in the absence of jumps, the realized volatility is a consistent estimator of the integrated volatility. But not in the presence of jumps. Alternatives to the realized volatility that are robust to jumps are discussed in Section 7.6.

7.5 Intraday Periodicity

Temporal dependence in volatility is one of the most striking features of financial series recorded at various frequencies. Interestingly, new phenomena become visible as one proceeds from daily returns to intraday returns.

The aim of this section is to show how G@RCH can be used to estimate the intraday (or intraweek) periodicity in volatility.

The codes used to prepare this section are also available in the folder /packages/Realized/samples/.

Note that the dataset has been simulated in such a way that the outputs and graphs obtained when running this example should be very similar to the ones reported in this section.

7.5.1 Data

Like Andersen and Bollerslev (1997), Andersen and Bollerslev (1998a), Martens, Chang, and Taylor (2002) and Taylor and Xu (1997), we study the periodicity in intraday volatility of 5-minute EUR/USD returns.[3]

Our data set ranges from January 2000 to October 2004 and time is expressed in Easter Time (EST, EST = GMT - 5), taking into account the daylight saving time shifts in Europe and the USA. All the returns from Friday 16.05 EST through Sunday 16.00 EST are excluded. We also exclude from the sample some regular (Christmas, New Year...) and irregular (Easter...) holidays. We finally delete days where the data quality is dubious. We are left with $T = 1175$ days of $M = 288$ equally-spaced and continuously compounded 5-minute return observations $r_{t,i}$, as currencies are traded around the clock. The data consists of the last mid point of the interval (last average of log(bid) and log(ask)). The first interval of day t is 16.05 EST, the last is 16.00 EST.

7.5.2 Evidence of intraday periodicity

Figure 7.7 (obtained by running example file Periodicity.ox plots the lag 1 through 1440 (i.e. $288 \times 5 = 5$ days) sample autocorrelations for the five-minute absolute returns $|r_{t,i}|$.

---

[3]Unfortunately due to the fact that the intraday data are copyrighted, we are not allowed to provide this dataset. However, all the results reported here have been obtained by running the examples files on the simulated dataset 5-min-ret.in7. The simulated data is such that its intraday volatility closely matches the pattern of the EUR/USD.

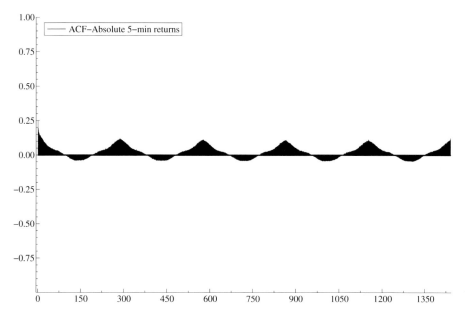

Figure 7.7   ACF of 5-minute absolute returns of the EUR-USD from January 2000, through October 2004.

This graph displays a distinct U-shaped pattern in the ACF of absolute returns. Standard ARCH models imply a geometric decay in the absolute return autocorrelation structure and simply cannot accommodate strong regular cyclical patterns of the sort displayed in Figure 7.7.

The volatility dynamics of intraday financial time series are complex. There are intraday volatility patterns, reflecting the daily activity cycle of the regional centers as well as weekend, the macroeconomic announcement effects (immediately following the release) and standard volatility clustering at the daily level.

The behaviour of a time series is called periodic if it shows a periodic structure in addition to less regular movements. The foreign exchange (FX) market shows strong periodic effects caused by the presence of the traders in the three major markets according to the hour of the day, the day of the week and the Daylight Saving Times. The global FX market consists of three major markets, i.e., Asia, Europe and North America, and the major movements of intradaily return volatility can be attributed to the passage of market activity around the globe.

Figure 7.8 depicts the average absolute returns over the (288) five-minute intervals. This intraday pattern is quite similar across all days of the week with discrete

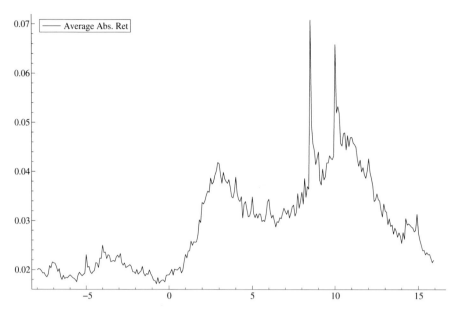

Figure 7.8   Intraday average absolute returns for the EUR-USD.

changes in quoting activity marking the opening and closing of business hours in the three major regional centres, all of which have their own activity pattern.

The following hours can be used as indicative: the Far East is open from 16:00 EST (21:00 GMT) to 1:00 EST (6:00 GMT), Europe trades between 2:00 EST (7:00 GMT) and 11:00 EST (16:00 GMT) and trading in North America occurs from 7:00 EST (12:00 GMT) to 16:00 EST (21:00 GMT). Using the discussion of market opening and closures presented above, we explain the intraday periodic volatility as follows. At 19:00 EST, the Far Eastern market has already been trading for around three hours and market activity is high. From 19:00 EST until about 22:00 EST, activity levels and volatility remain high. The lunchtime in Tokyo (22:00 EST- 23:45 EST) is the point of the day corresponding to the most prominent feature of the series. Volatility drops sharply and regains its former value at about 0:00 EST. Generally, Europe begins to contribute to activity at around 2:00 EST as the Far Eastern market begins to wane: there is a small peak in volatility. During European lunch hours (starting around 6:30 EST), both activity and volatility show a slight lull. The most active period of the day is clearly when both the European and North American markets are open (between 7:00 EST and 11:00 EST). Volatility starts to decline as first the European and then US markets wind down. At around 16:00

EST, the pacific market begins to trade again and the daily cycle is repeated after midnight. This intraday pattern is consistent with previous evidence reported in the literature, see Andersen and Bollerslev (1998b) among others.

Failure to take account of this intra-daily periodicity is likely to result in misleading statistical analyses as shown by Andersen and Bollerslev (1997) (in the sense that intraday returns do not conform at all to the theoretical aggregation results for the GARCH models).

The periodic phenomena in the volatility of FX markets can be modelled in a variety of ways. GARCH specification with dummy variables can be used for modelling the conditional volatility. For our dataset, this would require estimating 288 time-of-day parameters, if one dummy variable were created for each five-minute interval. The number of variables required is very large and it is unlikely to be effective in capturing the complexity of the periodic patterns.

7.5.3 Classical and robust estimation of intraday periodicity

Recall that we dispose of T days of M equally-spaced and continuously compounded intraday returns and that $r_{t,i}$ is the i-th return of day t. We assume the log-price follows a Brownian SemiMartingale with Finite Activity Jumps (BSMFAJ) diffusion.

We assume also that, for small values of Δ, the returns $r_{t,i}$ in an interval without jumps in the underlying price diffusion, are conditionally normally distributed with mean zero and variance $\sigma_{t,i}^2 = \int_{t+(i-1)\Delta}^{t+i\Delta} \sigma^2(s)ds$.

Due to the weekly cycle of opening, lunch and closing times of the financial centers around the world, the high-frequency return variance $\sigma_{t,i}^2$ has a periodic component $f_{t,i}^2$.

Depending on the nature of the analysis, there exists a natural window length for which almost all variation in $\sigma_{t,i}^2$ during the window can be attributed to $f_{t,i}^2$ such that $s_{t,i}^2 \equiv \sigma_{t,i}^2/f_{t,i}^2$ is approximately constant over the local window. Henceforth G@RCH follow the suggestion Andersen and Bollerslev (1997, 1998b), Andersen, Bollerslev, and Dobrev (2007) and Lee and Mykland (2008) to use local windows of one day.[4]

---

[4]There is a tradeoff in choosing the window size, say K, over which the stochastic part of the continuous volatility is assumed to be constant. While larger values impose a greater computational burden, K must be large enough to retain the advantage of bipower variation as a robust-to-jump estimator. A range of values satisfy the condition for K ($K = O_p(\Delta^\alpha)$, with $-1 < \alpha < -0.5$). Lee and Mykland (2008) recommend the smallest possible window size within the range given by α, as their simulations show that greater windows only increase the computational burden. So K is chosen as $\Delta^{-0.5}$. For example, suppose $\Delta = \frac{1}{252 \times nobs}$, $nobs$

Andersen and Bollerslev (1997, 1998b) suggest to estimate $s_{t,i}$ by $\hat{s}_t = \sqrt{\frac{1}{M} h_t}$ $\forall i = 1, \ldots, M$, where h_t is the conditional variance of day t obtained by estimating a GARCH model on daily returns. Under the BSM model, a more efficient estimator for $s_{t,i}$ is $\hat{s}_t = \sqrt{\frac{1}{M} RV_t}$.

As we will see in Section 7.6.1, under the BSMJAJ model, $s_{t,i}$ is better approximated using a normalized version of Barndorff-Nielsen and Shephard (2004b)'s realized bi-power variation, i.e. $\hat{s}_{t,i} = \sqrt{\frac{1}{M-1} BV_t}$ where BV_t is the bi-power variation computed on all the intraday returns of day t (see Equation (7.38)).

To ensure identifiability of the periodicity factor $f_{t,i}$ with respect to the average variance of day t, we impose that the squared periodicity factor has mean one over the local window.

Under this model we have that when $\Delta \to 0$ and if $r_{t,i}$ is not affected by jumps, the standardized high-frequency return $\bar{r}_{t,i} = r_{t,i}/\hat{s}_{t,i}$ is conditionally normally distributed with mean zero and variance equal to the squared periodicity factor. This result suggests to estimate the periodicity factor using either a non parametric or parametric estimator of the scale of the standardized returns. The estimator has to be robust to price jumps.

7.5.3.1 Non parametric estimation of periodicity

The non parametric periodicity estimator is based on a scale estimate of the standardized returns $\bar{r}_{t,i} = r_{t,i}/\hat{s}_{t,i}$ that share the same periodicity factor.

Let $\bar{r}_{1;t,i}, \ldots, \bar{r}_{n_{t,i};t,i}$ be the set of $n_{t,i}$ returns having the same periodicity factor as $r_{t,i}$. If we condition the estimation of the periodicity factor only on the calendar effects, $\bar{r}_{1;t,i}, \ldots, \bar{r}_{n_{t,i};t,i}$ are the returns observed on the same time of the day and day of the week as $r_{t,i}$.

The classical periodicity estimator is based on the standard deviation

$$\hat{f}_{t,i}^{\text{SD}} = \frac{\text{SD}_{t,i}}{\sqrt{\frac{1}{M} \sum_{j=1}^{M} \text{SD}_{t,j}^2}}, \tag{7.20}$$

where $\text{SD}_{t,i} = \sqrt{\frac{1}{n_{t,i}} \sum_{j=1}^{n_{t,i}} \bar{r}_{j;t,i}^2}$. This estimator is similar to Taylor and Xu (1997)'s periodicity estimate based on averages of squared returns.

---

being the number of observations per day, then the integers between 15.87 and 252 are within the required range. More specifically, they recommend the following window sizes for sampling at frequencies of one week, one day, one hour, 30 minutes, 15 minutes and 5 minutes: 7, 16, 78, 110, 156, and 270, respectively. In G@RCH, K is set to the M, i.e. the number of intraday observations per day.

In absence of jumps, the standard deviation is efficient if the standardized returns are normally distributed. In the presence of jumps, this estimator is useless, since it suffices that one observation in the sample is affected by a jump to make the periodicity estimate arbitrarily large.

Because of the non-robustness of the previous estimator in the presence of jumps, Boudt, Croux, and Laurent (2008b) propose to replace the standard deviation in (7.20) by a robust non parametric estimator.

A first candidate is the so-called median absolute deviation (MAD). The MAD of a sequence of observations $y_1, \ldots, y_n$ is defined as

$$1.486 \cdot \text{median}_i |y_i - \text{median}_j y_j|, \tag{7.21}$$

where 1.486 is a correction factor to guarantee that the MAD is a consistent scale estimator at the normal distribution. The MAD estimator for the periodicity factor of $r_{t,i}$ equals

$$\hat{f}_{t,i}^{\text{MAD}} = \frac{\text{MAD}_{t,i}}{\sqrt{\frac{1}{M} \sum_{j=1}^{M} \text{MAD}_{t,j}^2}}. \tag{7.22}$$

Amongst the large number of robust scale estimators available in the literature (see Maronna, Martin, and Yohai 2006, for an overview), Boudt, Croux, and Laurent (2008b) also recommend the use of the Shortest Half scale estimator proposed by Rousseeuw and Leroy (1988), because it remains consistent in the presence of infinitesimal contaminations by jumps in the data. Importantly, it has the property of being, among a wide class of scale estimators, the estimator for which jumps can cause the smallest maximum bias possible. Under normality, it has the same efficiency as the MAD and the interquartile range. A final advantage is that it is computationally convenient and does not need any location estimation. For the definition of the Shortest Half scale estimator, we need the corresponding order statistics $\bar{r}_{(1);t,i}, \ldots, \bar{r}_{(n_{t,i});t,i}$ such that $\bar{r}_{(1);t,i} \leq \bar{r}_{(2);t,i} \leq \ldots \leq \bar{r}_{(n_{t,i});t,i}$. The shortest half scale is the smallest length of all "halves" consisting of $h_{t,i} = \lfloor n_{t,i}/2 \rfloor + 1$ contiguous order observations. These halves equal $\{\bar{r}_{(1);t,i}, \ldots, \bar{r}_{(h_{t,i});t,i}\}$, $\ldots$, $\{\bar{r}_{(n_{t,i}-h_{t,i}+1);t,i}, \ldots, \bar{r}_{(n_{t,i});t,i}\}$, and their length is $\bar{r}_{(h_{t,i});t,i} - \bar{r}_{(1);t,i}$, $\ldots$, $\bar{r}_{(n_{t,i});t,i} - \bar{r}_{(h_{t,i});t,i}$, respectively. The corresponding scale estimator (corrected for consistency under normality) equals the minimum of these lengths:

$$\text{ShortH}_{t,i} = 0.741 \cdot \min\{\bar{r}_{(h_{t,i});t,i} - \bar{r}_{(1);t,i}, \ldots, \bar{r}_{(n_{t,i});t,i} - \bar{r}_{(n_{t,i}-h_{t,i}+1);t,i}\}. \tag{7.23}$$

The Shortest Half estimator for the periodicity factor of $r_{t,i}$ equals

$$\hat{f}_{t,i}^{\text{ShortH}} = \frac{\text{ShortH}_{t,i}}{\sqrt{\frac{1}{M} \sum_{j=1}^{M} \text{ShortH}_{t,j}^2}}. \tag{7.24}$$

The shortest half dispersion is highly robust to jumps, but it has only a 37% efficiency under normality of the $\bar{r}_{t,i}$'s. Boudt, Croux, and Laurent (2008b) show that a better trade-off between the efficiency of the standard deviation under normality and the high robustness to jumps of the shortest half dispersion is offered by the standard deviation applied to the returns weighted in function of their outlyingness under the ShortH estimate, i.e.

$$\hat{f}_{t,i}^{\text{WSD}} = \frac{\text{WSD}_{t,i}}{\sqrt{\frac{1}{M} \sum_{j=1}^{M} \text{WSD}_{t,j}^2}}, \tag{7.25}$$

where

$$\text{WSD}_{t,j} = \sqrt{1.081 \cdot \frac{\sum_{l=1}^{n_{t,j}} w[(\bar{r}_{l;t,j}/\hat{f}_{t,j}^{\text{ShortH}})^2] \bar{r}_{l;t,j}^2}{\sum_{l=1}^{n_{t,j}} w[(\bar{r}_{l;t,j}/\hat{f}_{t,j}^{\text{ShortH}})^2]}}.$$

Because the weighting is applied to the squared standardized returns which are extremely large in the presence of jumps, Boudt, Croux, and Laurent (2008b) recommend the use of the hard rejection with threshold equal to the 99% quantile of the χ^2 distribution with one degree of freedom, i.e.

$$w(z) = \begin{cases} 1 & \text{if } z \leq 6.635 \\ 0 & \text{else.} \end{cases} \tag{7.26}$$

The factor 1.081 is needed to ensure consistency of the estimator under normality. The Weighted Standard Deviation (WSD) in (7.25) has a 69% efficiency under normality of the $\bar{r}_{t,i}$'s.

Note that when the dataset is 'dated', the length of the periodicity filter equals 5 days, otherwise it is equal to one day.

7.5.3.2 Parametric estimation of periodicity

The non parametric estimators for the periodic component of intraday volatility use only the subset of the data for which the returns have the same periodicity factor. Andersen and Bollerslev (1997) show that more efficient estimates can be obtained if the whole time series dimension of the data is used for the estimation of the periodicity process. Andersen and Bollerslev (1997) use the result that under the assumption that returns are not affected by jumps (i.e. BSM model): $r_{t,i} \approx f_{t,i} s_{t,i} u_{t,i}$, where $u_{t,i} \sim N(0,1)$ and so $\log(\frac{|r_{t,i}|}{s_{t,i}}) \approx \log f_{t,i} + \log |u_{t,i}|$, which allows to isolate $f_{t,i}$ as follows,

$$\log(|r_{t,i}/s_{t,i}|) - c = \log f_{t,i} + \varepsilon_{t,i}, \tag{7.27}$$

where the error term $\varepsilon_{t,i}$ is i.i.d. distributed with mean zero and has the density function of the centered absolute value of the log of a standard normal random variable, i.e.

$$g(z) = \sqrt{2/\pi} \exp[z + c - 0.5 \exp(2(z+c))]. \tag{7.28}$$

The parameter $c = -0.63518$ equals the mean of the log of the absolute value of a standard normal random variable. Andersen and Bollerslev (1997) then propose to model $\log f_{t,i}$ as a function h of a vector of variables x (such as sinusoid and polynomial transformations of the time of the day) that is linear in the parameter vector θ

$$\log f_{t,i} = h(x_{t,i}; \theta) = x'_{t,i} \theta. \tag{7.29}$$

Combining (7.27) with (7.29), we obtain the following regression equation

$$\log(|\bar{r}_{t,i}|) - c = x'_{t,i} \theta + \varepsilon_{t,i}. \tag{7.30}$$

It is common to estimate the parameter θ in (7.30) by the OLS estimator. This approach is neither efficient nor robust, since the error terms are not normally distributed. Denote the loss functions of the OLS and Maximum Likelihood (ML) estimators by $\rho^{\text{OLS}}(z) = z^2$ and by

$$\rho^{\text{ML}}(z) = -0.5 \log(2/\pi) - z - c + 0.5 \exp(2(z+c)),$$

respectively. The OLS and ML estimates equal

$$\hat{\theta}^{\text{OLS}} = \operatorname{argmin} \frac{1}{MT} \sum_{t=1}^{T} \sum_{i=1}^{M} \rho^{\text{OLS}}(\varepsilon_{t,i}) \text{ and } \hat{\theta}^{\text{ML}} = \operatorname{argmin} \frac{1}{MT} \sum_{t=1}^{T} \sum_{i=1}^{M} \rho^{\text{ML}}(\varepsilon_{t,i}),$$
$$\tag{7.31}$$

where $\varepsilon_{t,i}$ is a function of θ (see Equation (7.30)).

Boudt, Croux, and Laurent (2008b) find that the ML estimator has a large bias in the presence of jumps. The non-robustness of the OLS and ML estimators to jumps is due to the unbounded effect an observation can have on their loss function. These loss functions are plotted in Figure 7.9. As mentioned by Martens, Chang,

Figure 7.9 Loss functions associated to the OLS and ML estimators. The vertical lines denotes the likelihood threshold and the upper and lower truncation levels based on the 99.5% quantile, used by the truncated ML estimator.

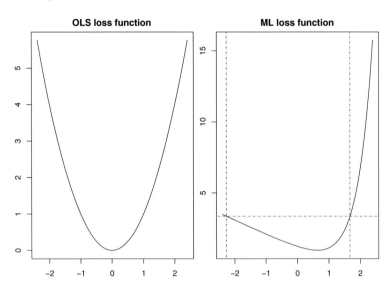

and Taylor (2002), the effect of jumps on the OLS and ML estimators is attenuated because the regression is based on the log of the standardized returns.

As an alternative to the OLS and ML estimators, Boudt, Croux, and Laurent (2008b) propose to use the *Truncated Maximum Likelihood* (TML) estimator introduced by Marazzi and Yohai (2004). This estimator gives a zero weight to observations that are outliers according to the value of the ML loss function evaluated at the corresponding residual computed under the robust non parametric estimator $\hat{f}^{\text{WSD}}$ in (7.25). Let

$$e_{t,i}^{\text{WSD}} = \log \bar{r}_{t,i} - c - \log \hat{f}_{t,i}^{\text{WSD}}. \tag{7.32}$$

Observations for which $\rho^{\text{ML}}(e_{t,i}^{\text{WSD}})$ is large, have a low likelihood and are therefore likely to be outliers (Marazzi and Yohai, 2004). Denote q an extreme upper quantile of the distribution of $\varepsilon_{t,i}$. The TML estimator is defined as

$$\hat{\theta}^{\text{TML}} = \frac{1}{\sum_{t=1}^{T} \sum_{i=1}^{M} w_{t,i}} \sum_{t=1}^{T} \sum_{i=1}^{M} w_{t,i} \rho(\varepsilon_{t,i}), \tag{7.33}$$

with

$$w_{t,i} = \begin{cases} 1 & \text{if } \rho^{\text{ML}}(e_{t,i}^{\text{WSD}}) \le \rho^{\text{ML}}(q) \\ 0 & \text{else.} \end{cases}$$

The truncation on the basis of the value of the ML-function is illustrated in Figure 7.9 for the 99.5% quantile. All observations with $\rho^{\text{ML}}(e_i^{\text{WSD}}) > 3.36$ receive a zero weight in the objective function of the TML estimator.

Like for the non parametric periodicity estimators, we impose that the squared periodicity factor has mean one in the local window. The parametric estimate for the periodicity factor thus equals

$$\hat{f}_{t,i}^{\text{TML}} = \frac{\exp x_{t,i}' \hat{\theta}^{\text{TML}}}{\sqrt{\frac{1}{M} \sum_{j=1}^{M} (\exp x_{t,j}' \hat{\theta}^{\text{TML}})^2}}, \qquad (7.34)$$

and similarly for $\hat{f}_{t,i}^{\text{OLS}}$ and $\hat{f}_{t,i}^{\text{ML}}$.

7.5.4 First illustration on simulated data

In this section we show how to use G@RCH 6.0 to estimate the periodicity filters presented above on simulated data.

The non parametric periodicity filters presented in Section 7.5.3.1 are implemented in the functions `TaylorXu(...)` and `Robust_periodicity(...)`. Their use is illustrated in example file `NP_periodicity_filters.ox`. This example uses the simulated data obtained by running the files `Store_Cont_GARCH_...ox` available in the directory `/packages/Realized/samples/`. There are four different files simulating 5-min (FX) returns from a continuous-time GARCH(1,1) diffusion with or without intraday periodicity in volatility and with or without jumps. The simulated data are then stored in the directory `/packages/Realized/samples/data/`.

Let us concentrate first on `Store_Cont_GARCH_FFF.ox`. The aim of this program is to generate 5-minute returns following a continuous-time stochastic volatility model without drift and spot volatility $\sigma(s)$ specified as a multiplicative process of the periodicity function f, which depends only on the time of the day $s - \lfloor s \rfloor$ and a GARCH diffusion process (see Equation 7.9), i.e.

$$\sigma(s) = f(s - \lfloor s \rfloor) \sigma_{\text{garch}}(s), \qquad (7.35)$$

where $log(s - \lfloor s \rfloor) = \theta x(s - \lfloor s \rfloor)s - \lfloor s \rfloor$ is intraday time.

$\sigma_{\text{garch}}(s)$ is generated using the values $\theta = 0.035$, $\omega = 0.636$ and $\lambda = 0.296$. The function $f(s - \lfloor s \rfloor)$ used in the simulation is based on $\log f(s - \lfloor s \rfloor) = \theta' x(s)$ with $x(s)$ a vector holding sinusoid transformations of s, i.e.

$$\log f_{t,i} = \sum_{j=1}^{P} \left(\gamma_j \cos \frac{2ij\pi}{M} + \delta_j \sin \frac{2ij\pi}{M} \right), \qquad (7.36)$$

where $M = 1/\Delta$, P is set to 4 and $\theta = (\gamma_1, \delta_1, \ldots, \gamma_4, \delta_4) = (-0.24422; -0.49756; -0.054171; 0.073907; -0.26098; 0.32408; -0.11591; -0.21442)$. In this case, the length of the periodicity cycle is one day and the periodicity is thus the same for all the days of the week. To simulate exchange rates, we choose $\Delta = 1/2880$, corresponding to 10 observations per 5-minute interval. The number of simulated days $= 3010$ but the first ten days have been discarded, which leads actually to a total of 3000 simulated days.

After running this file, the simulated data are automatically saved to ./data/Simulated_cont_GARCH_no_jumps_FFF.in7.

Figure 7.10 plots the true periodicity (dotted line) and the estimated periodicity (solid line) obtained by applying the four non parametric filters on 3000 days of 5-min simulated returns (288 returns per day). This model being compatible with the BSM model, the four methods should provide good estimates of the periodicity. As expected, we see that the four methods provide excellent estimates of the periodicity. In a more comprehensive Monte Carlo study, Boudt, Croux, and Laurent (2008b) have shown that in the class of non parametric estimators, the SD is the most efficient estimator.

Figure 7.11 plots the true periodicity (dotted line) and the estimated periodicity (solid line) obtained by applying the three parametric filters on the same data (using the file P_periodicity_filters.ox). Table 7.1 reports the estimated values for the three methods.

As expected, we see that the three methods provide excellent estimates of the periodicity.

Table 7.1   Estimation results for the periodicity filter. DGP is a GARCH(1,1) with periodicity.

	TRUE	OLS	ML	TML
cos(2PI1i/M)	-0.24422	-0.24059	-0.23810	-0.23804
sin(2PI1i/M)	-0.49756	-0.49946	-0.49561	-0.49699
cos(2PI2i/M)	-0.054171	-0.055155	-0.055193	-0.054463
sin(2PI2i/M)	0.073907	0.073229	0.072583	0.073019
cos(2PI3i/M)	-0.26098	-0.27287	-0.27080	-0.27080
sin(2PI3i/M)	0.32408	0.31672	0.31546	0.31562
cos(2PI4i/M)	-0.11591	-0.10828	-0.10778	-0.10728
sin(2PI4i/M)	-0.21442	-0.21937	-0.21617	-0.21666

Boudt, Croux, and Laurent (2008b) also show that all parametric estimators are more precise that the non parametric estimators. For the parametric estimators, they find that the ML estimator is efficient. The TML estimator is found to be only slightly less efficient than the ML estimator and, as expected, the OLS estimator (Gaussian QML) is the least precise of all parametric estimators.

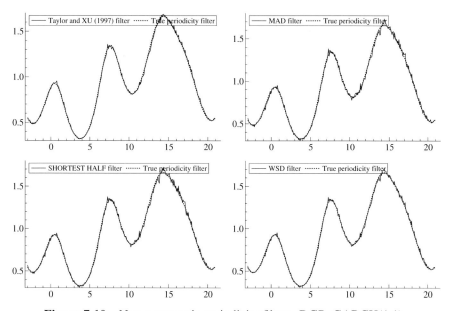

Figure 7.10 Non parametric periodicity filters. DGP=GARCH(1,1).

Let us now consider the case of a BSMJ model (see Equations (7.15)-(7.18)) with the same GARCH parameters as before) with $\mu(s) = 0$ and $\sigma(s)$ specified as the same multiplicative process as in (7.35) (with the same parameter values as in the previous simulation).

The jump size $\kappa(s)$ is modeled as the product between $\sigma(s)$ and a uniformly distributed random variable on $\sqrt{m}([-2, -1] \cup [1, 2])$. The parameter m determines the magnitude of the jumps. We set m equal to 0.3 (rather small jumps). Finally, the jump occurrences $q(s)$ are specified as a Poisson process with on average $K = 2$ jumps per day. Importantly, occurrences of jumps are concentrated on the parts of the day when volatility is periodically very low ($f < 0.45$). Figure 7.12 plots the number of simulated jumps per intraday period of time. The simulated data, i.e. `Simulated_cont_GARCH_jumps_FFF_K_2_M_0.3.in7` are obtained by running `Store_Cont_GARCH_Jumps_FFF.ox` with the options $K = 2$, $M = 0.3$ and $threshold = 0.45$.[5]

---

[5]To generate uniformly distributed jumps (across the day), set $threshold$ to a value greater

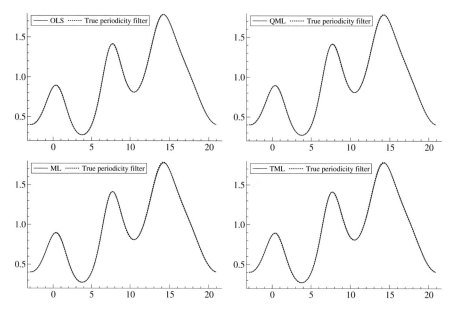

Figure 7.11   Parametric periodicity filters. DGP=GARCH(1,1).

Figure 7.13 plots the estimated periodicity obtained by applying the four non parametric filters on the simulated 5-min returns (using NP_periodicity_filters.ox).

In this case the SD is expected to be inappropriate because of its non robustness to jumps. This is illustrated in Figure 7.13, where we see that Taylor and Xu (1997)'s periodicity filter (i.e. based on the SD) is very inaccurate while the three robust alternatives are as good as in the previous case of no jump. Again, in a more comprehensive Monte Carlo study, Boudt, Croux, and Laurent (2008b) show that the robust non parametric estimators are little affected by the inclusion of jumps in the price process.

Figure 7.14 plots the true periodicity (dotted line) and the estimated periodicity (solid line) obtained by applying the three parametric filters on the same data (using the file P_periodicity_filters.ox). Table 7.2 reports the estimated values for the three methods. The ML estimator is found to be extremely sensitive to jumps. The optimality of the ML estimator is thus restricted to the model without jumps. Since jumps do occur in practice, we do not recommend its use in practice.

The robustness of the OLS estimator is surprising at first sight, but it corroborates

---

than $max(f_{t,i})$, e.g. $threshold = 100$.

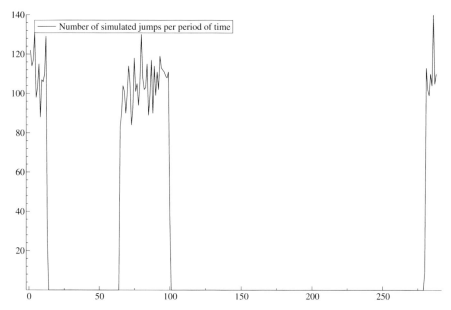

Figure 7.12 Number of simulated jumps per intraday period of time. Jumps only occur when $f < 0.45$.

Martens, Chang, and Taylor (2002)'s intuition that the log-transformation shrinks the outliers and makes the estimators based on a regression of the log absolute returns more robust to jumps. However, while being much better than the ML estimator, the OLS (or Gaussian QML) estimator is quite affected by jumps, which is apparently not the case for the TML estimator (for which the fit is again almost perfect).

The main message of this simulation study is that the non parametric WSD and parametric TML estimators have a relatively high efficiency in the absence of jumps. If jumps are present in the process, they are the most accurate of all non parametric and parametric estimators considered, respectively. In all cases considered here, the TML estimator based on the correctly specified periodicity function is more efficient than the WSD estimator. While the advantage of the TML over the WSD is clear when the functional form of the periodicity is known, its major drawbacks are that this functional form is not known a priori in practical applications and its estimation is much more time consuming.

Table 7.2   Estimation results for the periodicity filter. DGP is a GARCH(1,1) with periodicity and jumps.

	TRUE	OLS	ML	TML
cos(2PI1i/M)	-0.24422	-0.24059	-0.23810	-0.23804
sin(2PI1i/M)	-0.49756	-0.49946	-0.49561	-0.49699
cos(2PI2i/M)	-0.054171	-0.055155	-0.055193	-0.054463
sin(2PI2i/M)	0.073907	0.073229	0.072583	0.073019
cos(2PI3i/M)	-0.26098	-0.27287	-0.27080	-0.27080
sin(2PI3i/M)	0.32408	0.31672	0.31546	0.31562
cos(2PI4i/M)	-0.11591	-0.10828	-0.10778	-0.10728
sin(2PI4i/M)	-0.21442	-0.21937	-0.21617	-0.21666

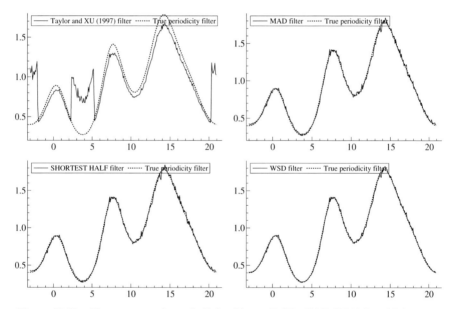

Figure 7.13   Non parametric periodicity filters. DGP=GARCH(1,1) with jumps.

7.5.5 Second illustration on EUR/USD data

In this section, we use the dataset described in Section 7.5.1, i.e. 5-min returns of the Euro - US dollar (EUR-USD) exchange rate from January 2000 to October, 2004.

To model the periodic component, we use a slightly more general specification

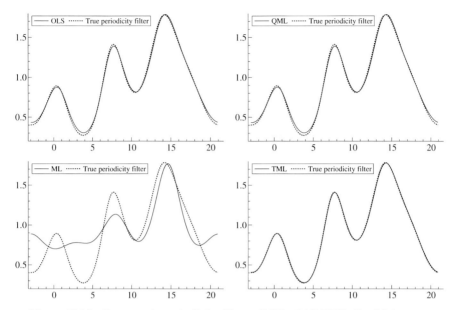

Figure 7.14   Parametric periodicity filters. DGP=GARCH(1,1) with jumps.

than the one used in the previous simulation studies, i.e.

$$\log f_{t,i} = \mu_{1,j}\frac{i}{N_1} + \mu_{2,j}\frac{i^2}{N_2} + \sum_{j=1}^{P}\left(\gamma_j\cos\frac{2ij\pi}{M} + \delta_j\sin\frac{2ij\pi}{M}\right) + \sum_{k=1}^{D}\lambda_k I(k)_{t,i},$$
(7.37)

where $M = 1/\Delta$, P is set to 4, $N_1 = (M+1)/2$ and $N_2 = (2M^2 + 3M + 1)/6$ are normalizing constants. Note that Andersen and Bollerslev (1997) originally used the normalizing constant $N_2 = (M+1)(M+2)/6$. However, the analytic solution for a sum of squares of integers $\sum_{k=1}^{M}k^2 = (2M^3 + 3M^2 + M)/6$ which leads to the value reported above when computing the mean instead of the sum.

The smooth periodicity generated from the Fourier terms is unlikely to cope well with the sharp drop in volatility, for instance, around lunch in the Far East and the day of the week dependencies. To fill this gap, the term $\sum_{k=1}^{D}\lambda_k I(k)_{t,i}$ is included, where $I(k)_{t,i}$ is an indicator variable for event k during interval i of day t. The events may be calendar (day of the week dummies, etc.) as well as announcement effects. For instance to account for the announcement effects we have included two dummies that equal one on Friday 8:35 and 8:40 EST.[6]

---

[6]A better choice would certainly be to use the International Money Market Service data

Figure 7.15 plots $\hat{f}_{t,i}^{\text{SD}}$, $\hat{f}_{t,i}^{\text{ShortH}}$ and $\hat{f}_{t,i}^{\text{WSD}}$ from Monday to Friday (i.e. 288×5 values) while Figure 7.16 plots $\hat{f}_{t,i}^{\text{OLS}}$, $\hat{f}_{t,i}^{\text{ML}}$ and $\hat{f}_{t,i}^{\text{TML}}$. These graphs have been obtained by running example file Periodicity.ox. Note that for ease of comparison between non parametric and parametric methods, Figure 7.16 also plots $\hat{f}_{t,i}^{\text{WSD}}$ on each graph.

We see that while not being radically different, the three non parametric estimates are not equivalent. For instance, the periodicity factor is found to be much higher on Friday at 8h35 (peak around observation 1350) for the non-robust $\hat{f}_{t,i}^{\text{SD}}$ estimator than for the robust ones.

The same comment applies for the parametric estimates. $\hat{f}_{t,i}^{\text{TML}}$ and $\hat{f}_{t,i}^{\text{OLS}}$ seem to overestimate the periodicity on that particular interval. Looking at Table 7.3 we see that the estimated coefficient for the 'Friday 8:35' dummy is about $1, 1.3$, and 0.55 for the OLS, ML and TML methods respectively.

Note also that it seems that while the parametric and non parametric estimates are very close to each other it is clear that the specification chosen for the parametric methods does not fully capture the intraday periodicity and needs more refinement.

7.6 Robust to jumps volatility measures

We have seen in Section 7.4 that in absence of jumps, realized volatility is a consistent estimator of integrated volatility. However, in presence of jumps it is no longer consistent. Furthermore, it has been shown in the literature (see Andersen, Bollerslev, and Diebold, 2007) that jumps are much less persistent (and predictable) than the continuous sample path, or integrated volatility, component of the quadratic variation process. It is thus useful to separate the two components of the quadratic variation process. This was first done by Barndorff-Nielsen and Shephard (2004b) through the use of the so-called Bi-Power Variation (BPVar). In this section we also review an alternative to the BPVar, namely Realized Outlyingness Weighted Variation (ROWVar), recently proposed by Boudt, Croux, and Laurent (2008a).

---

on surveyed and realized macroeconomic fundamentals to compute standardized surprises. The standardized surprise for announcement h, at time i of day t, is defined by $N(h)_{t,i} = \frac{R(h)_{t,i} - E(h)_{t,i}}{\hat{\sigma}(h)}$, where $R(h)_{t,i}$ is the realization of announcement h, $E(h)_{t,i}$ is its survey expectation and $\hat{\sigma}(h)$ is the standard deviation of that difference. It has been shown in the literature that the expected value of macro news predicts the announcement in an approximately unbiased manner.

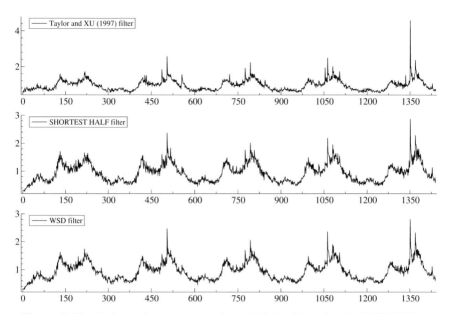

Figure 7.15   Estimated non parametric periodicity filters for the EUR-USD.

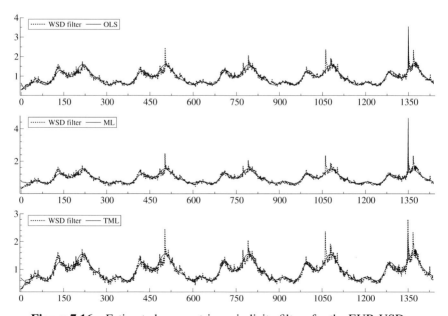

Figure 7.16   Estimated parametric periodicity filters for the EUR-USD.

7.6.1 Bi-Power Variation

Barndorff-Nielsen and Shephard (2004b) show that, for a subclass of BSMJ price diffusions (i.e. BSM with Finite Activity Jumps), the normalized sum of products

Table 7.3 Estimation results for the parametric periodicity filters .

	OLS	ML	TML
Monday Morning	-0.033321	0.0025972	-0.0050530
Tuesday	0.0066779	-0.019706	-0.015382
Wednesday	0.026778	-0.020484	-0.0056105
Thursday	0.014360	-0.028472	-0.022191
Friday	-0.036773	-0.058797	-0.047153
Friday 8:35	1.0090	1.3076	0.55753
Friday 8:40	0.44006	0.42802	0.33174
i/N1	-0.99591	-0.072911	-0.45299
i^2/N2	0.69094	0.055195	0.33335
cos(2PI1i/M)	-0.37557	-0.13875	-0.24023
sin(2PI1i/M)	-0.36311	-0.31468	-0.30830
cos(2PI2i/M)	-0.088932	-0.040887	-0.061628
sin(2PI2i/M)	-0.052102	-0.036089	-0.037174
cos(2PI3i/M)	-0.17503	-0.11762	-0.13831
sin(2PI3i/M)	0.083212	0.071998	0.084067
cos(2PI4i/M)	0.061097	0.069227	0.066619
sin(2PI4i/M)	-0.080584	-0.067013	-0.070710

of the absolute value of contiguous returns (i.e. bi-power variation) is a consistent estimator for the IVar.

The BPVar (implemented in the procedure Compute_BV()) is defined as:

$$BV_t(\Delta) \equiv \mu_1^{-2} \sum_{i=2}^{M} |r_{t,i}||r_{t,i-1}|,$$ (7.38)

where $\mu_1 \equiv \sqrt{2/\pi} \simeq 0.79788$ and $M = 1/\Delta$.

Unlike the RVar, the BPVar is designed to be robust to jumps because its building block is the product between two consecutive returns instead of the squared return. If one of the returns corresponds to a jump and the next one follows the BSM diffusion process, then the product has a small impact on the BPVar, being the sum of many of these building blocks. If the jump process has finite activity[7] then a.s. jumps cannot affect two contiguous returns for $\Delta \to 0$ (or equivalently $M \to \infty$) and the jump process has a negligible impact on the probability limit of the BPVar, which coincides with the IVar. Under the BSM with Finite Activity Jumps (BSMFAJ) one has

$$\operatorname*{plim}_{\Delta \to 0} BV_t(\Delta) = \int_{t-1}^{t} \sigma^2(s)ds.$$ (7.39)

---

[7]A jump process is defined to be of finite activity if the number of jumps in *any* interval of time is finite.

To illustrate the applicability of the above results, let us consider the following picture, obtained by running the example file `Simul_Continuous_GARCH_Jumps_1.ox`. Note that the DGP is a continuous-time GARCH(1,1) with on average one jump every 5 days (with $m = 0.5$).

Looking at Figure 7.17, we see that that unlike $RV_t(\Delta)$ (see Figure 7.6), $BV_t(\Delta)$ is a much better estimate of the integrated volatility (IV_t) in presence of jumps.

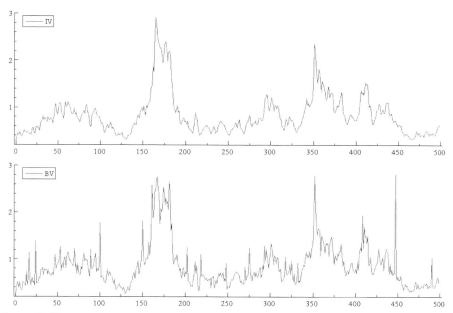

Figure 7.17   Integrated Volatility and Bi-Power Variation for a continuous-GARCH jump process.

7.6.2 Realized Outlyingness Weighted Variance

For the impact of jumps on the BPVar to be negligible, the high-frequency returns need to be observed over extremely short time intervals ($\Delta \to 0$) in order to avoid that jumps affect two contiguous returns and the effect of jumps on the price process may not be smeared out over these short intervals. When returns are computed over longer time intervals such as 5 or 15 minutes, these conditions may be violated. Furthermore, the BPVar is sensitive to the occurrence of "zero" returns in the sample.[8] The multivariate extension of the BPVar has the additional disadvantage

---

[8]In applications the prevalence of zero returns is often substantial due to the rounding of prices to a discrete price grid.

that it is not affine equivariant and it is not necessarily positive semidefinite, which are undesirable properties for covolatility estimators. For theses reasons, Boudt, Croux, and Laurent (2008a) have proposed an alternative to the BPVar that is robust to jumps affecting two or more contiguous returns. This estimator, called Realized Outlyingness Weighted Variance (ROWVar) is also more efficient than the BPVar under the BSM model and its multivariate extension has some nice properties.

The computation of the ROWVar proceeds as follows.

Step 1: Estimation of local outlyingness

Boudt, Croux, and Laurent (2008a) measure the outlyingness $d_{t,i}$ of return $r_{t,i}$ as the square of the robustly studentized return:[9]

$$d_{t,i} = \left(\frac{r_{t,i}}{\hat{\sigma}_{t,i}} \right)^2, \tag{7.40}$$

where $\hat{\sigma}_{t,i}$ is a robust estimate of the instantaneous volatility computed from all the returns belonging to the same local window as $r_{t,i}$. In Boudt, Croux, and Laurent (2008a), $\hat{\sigma}_{t,i}$ is the Median Absolute Deviation about the median (MAD)[10] of all the returns belonging to the same local window, which is here equal to one day.[11]

Because of the presence of a strong intraday periodicity in volatility (see Section 7.5.3), this assumption does not hold when the length of that window is greater than a few minutes. Recall that following Andersen and Bollerslev (1997, 1998b), Andersen, Bollerslev, and Dobrev (2007) and Lee and Mykland (2008) G@RCH uses local windows of length M, i.e. one day.

For this reason, in their empirical application, Boudt, Croux, and Laurent (2008b) propose to compute $d_{t,i}$ on filtered returns $\tilde{r}_{t,i} = \frac{r_{t,i}}{\hat{f}_{t,i}}$ instead of the raw returns $r_{t,i}$, where $\hat{f}_{t,i}$ is any of the robust periodicity filters presented in Section 7.5.3.

For practical reasons, G@RCH only considers non parametric estimates for $\hat{f}_{t,i}$, i.e. $\hat{f}_{t,i}^{MAD}$, $\hat{f}_{t,i}^{ShortH}$ and $\hat{f}_{t,i}^{WSD}$. Note that when the dataset is 'dated', the length of the periodicity filter is set to 5 days, otherwise it is equal to one day.

---

[9]As usual in this literature, the drift is assumed to be negligible and thus set to 0.

[10]Recall that the MAD of a sequence of observations $y_1, \ldots, y_n$ is defined as $1.486 \cdot \text{median}_i |y_i - \text{median}_j y_j|$, where 1.486 is a correction factor to guarantee that the MAD is a consistent scale estimator at the normal distribution.

[11]Note that other choices than the MAD like the normalized realized bi-power variation presented in Section 7.5.3 are possible, i.e. $\sqrt{\frac{1}{M-1} BV_t}$ where BV_t is the bi-power variation computed on all the intraday returns of day t.

Step 2: Computation of ROWVar

Once one has such an outlyingness measure $d_{t,i}$ for all the high-frequency returns in the interval $[t-1, t]$, a weight function has to be chosen. This weight function equals one for returns for which the outlyingness $d_{t,i}$ does not raise any suspicion that the corresponding return $r_{t,i}$ might be affected by jumps and goes to 0 the more extreme $d_{t,i}$ is. Popular weight functions are the hard Rejection weight function

$$w_{\mathrm{HR}}(z) = \begin{cases} 1 & \text{if } z \le k \\ 0 & \text{otherwise,} \end{cases} \tag{7.41}$$

and the Soft Rejection Huber weight function

$$w_{\mathrm{SR}}(z) = \min\{1, k/z\}, \tag{7.42}$$

with k a tuning parameter to be selected. Under the BSM model and some weak assumptions stated in Boudt, Croux, and Laurent (2008a), the outlyingness measure is asymptotically chi-squared distributed with 1 degree of freedom (χ_1^2). The outlyingness of a return affected by a jump will then be in the extreme tails of the χ_1^2 distribution. Consequently, for the ROWVar the rejection threshold k can be set to $\chi_1^2(\beta)$, the β quantile of the χ_1^2 distribution function. Boudt, Croux, and Laurent (2008a) strongly recommend to use the SR weight function with $\beta = 95\%$ as a good compromise between robustness and efficiency.

Given a series of high-frequency returns, their estimated outlyingness and a weight function, one can then compute the ROWVar as follows:

$$\mathrm{ROWVar}_t(\Delta) = c_w \frac{\sum_{i=1}^{M} w(d_{t,i}) r_{t,i}^2}{\frac{1}{M} \sum_{i=1}^{M} w(d_{t,i})}. \tag{7.43}$$

The correction factor c_w in (7.43) ensures that the ROWVar is consistent for the IVar under the BSM model. Table 7.4 (see below) reports the correction factors for the hard and soft rejection weight functions for several values of the critical level β.

Let us now compute ROWVar on the same simulated data than in the previous section. Figure 7.18, obtained by running the example file `Simul_Continuous_GARCH_Jumps_2.ox`, suggests that $ROWVar_t(\Delta)$ also does a good job in estimating the integrated volatility (IV_t) in presence of jumps.

A more formal comparison between bi-power variation and ROWVar will be presented in Section 7.7.

β	1	0.99	0.975	0.95	0.925	0.90	0.85	0.80
c_w HR	1	1.081	1.175	1.318	1.459	1.605	1.921	2.285
c_w SR	1	1.017	1.041	1.081	1.122	1.165	1.257	1.358
θ HR	2	2.897	3.707	4.674	5.406	5.998	6.917	7.592
θ SR	2	2.072	2.184	2.367	2.539	2.699	2.989	3.245
d_w HR	0.333	0.440	0.554	0.741	0.945	1.177	1.760	2.566

Table 7.4 c_w, θ and d_w for different critical levels β (such that the threshold $k = \chi_1^2(\beta)$, with $\chi_1^2(\beta)$ the β quantile of the χ_1^2).

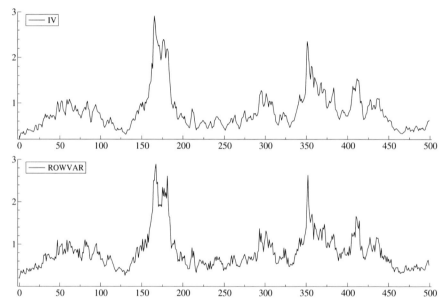

Figure 7.18   Integrated Volatility and ROWVar for a continuous-GARCH jump process.

7.7 Daily jump tests

Evidently, the difference between RV_t and any robust to jumps estimator of IV_t, denoted $\hat{IV}_t(\Delta)$, is an estimate of the jump contribution or realized jumps.

More formally,

$$RJ_t(\Delta) \equiv RV_t(\Delta) - \hat{IV}_t(\Delta) \rightarrow \sum_{t-1 < s \le t} \kappa^2(s), \qquad (7.44)$$

where $\hat{IV}_t(\Delta)$ is for instance $BV_t(\Delta)$ or $ROWVar_t(\Delta)$.

Based on the theoretical results of Barndorff-Nielsen and Shephard (2006) that

$$\sqrt{\Delta} \left(\begin{array}{c} RV_t(\Delta) - IV_t \\ \hat{IV}_t(\Delta) - IV_t \end{array} \right) \xrightarrow{d} MN \left(0, \left(\begin{array}{cc} 2 & 2 \\ 2 & \theta \end{array} \right) IQ_t \right) \text{ if } \Delta \to 0,$$

Andersen, Bollerslev, and Diebold (2007) have developed a formal test for (daily) jumps, i.e.

$$Z_t \equiv \frac{RV_t(\Delta) - \hat{IV}_t(\Delta)}{\sqrt{(\theta - 2) \frac{1}{M} \hat{IQ}_t}}, \tag{7.45}$$

where $\hat{IQ}_t$ is a robust to jumps estimate of the integrated quarticity $IQ_t \equiv \int_{t-1}^{t} \sigma^4(s) ds$.

Andersen, Bollerslev, and Diebold (2007) consider the case $\hat{IV}_t(\Delta) = BV_t(\Delta)$ and use the so-called Tri-power quarticity $TQ_t(\Delta)$ to estimate IQ_t, where

$$TQ_t(\Delta) \equiv M \mu_{4/3}^{-3} \sum_{i=3}^{M} |r_{t,i}|^{4/3} |r_{t,i-1}|^{4/3} |r_{t,i-2}|^{4/3}, \tag{7.46}$$

with $\mu_{4/3} \equiv 2^{2/3} \Gamma(7/6) \Gamma(1/2)^{-1}$.

Another popular estimator for IQ_t, in the spirit of the bi-power (or multi-power) variation, is the Quad-power quarticity $QQ_t(\Delta)$, i.e.

$$QQ_t(\Delta) \equiv M \mu_1^{-4} \sum_{i=4}^{M} |r_{t,i}| |r_{t,i-1}| |r_{t,i-2}| |r_{t,i-3}|. \tag{7.47}$$

When $\hat{IV}_t(\Delta) = BV_t(\Delta)$, $\theta = \mu_1^{-4} + 2\mu_1^{-2} - 3 \approx 2.609$. Note that $TQ_t(\Delta)$ and $QQ_t(\Delta)$ are implemented in the procedures Compute_TQ() and Compute_QQ(), respectively.

The main drawback of $TQ_t(\Delta)$ and $QQ_t(\Delta)$ is that like $BV_t(\Delta)$ they are downward biased in the presence of zero returns. Furthermore, the bias is expected to be even larger in finite sample than for $BV_t(\Delta)$ because they are made up of products of respectively three and four consecutive absolute returns.

To overcome this problem, Boudt, Croux, and Laurent (2008a) have proposed to replace $\hat{IV}_t(\Delta)$ in Equation (7.45) by $ROWVar_t(\Delta)$ and $\hat{IQ}_t(\Delta)$ by the Realized Outlyigness Weighted Quarticity

$$\text{ROWQuarticity}_t(\Delta) = d_w \frac{\sum_{i=1}^{M} w(d_{t,i}) r_{t,i}^4}{\sum_{i=1}^{M} w(d_{t,i})}, \tag{7.48}$$

where $w(.)$ is the hard rejection weight function. The correction factor d_w and the asymptotic variance of the ROWVar θ are reported in Table 7.4 for several choices of the critical level β (used to get the outlyingness threshold k).

Barndorff-Nielsen and Shephard (2006) advocated the use of a log version of the Z_t statistics. According to them, the following statistic

$$log Z_t \equiv \frac{\log(RV_t(\Delta)) - \log(\hat{IV}_t(\Delta))}{\sqrt{(\theta - 2)\frac{1}{M}\hat{IQ}_t(\Delta)\hat{IV}_t(\Delta)^{-2}}}, \tag{7.49}$$

has better finite sample properties.

They also proposed a max version of $log Z_t$, denoted $maxlog Z_t$, where

$$maxlog Z_t \equiv \frac{\log(RV_t(\Delta)) - \log(\hat{IV}_t(\Delta))}{\sqrt{(\theta - 2)\frac{1}{M}max\{1, \hat{IQ}_t(\Delta)\hat{IV}_t(\Delta)^{-2}\}}}. \tag{7.50}$$

Under the null of no jump on day t, Z_t, $log Z_t$ and $maxlog Z_t$ are asymptotically (as $\Delta \to 0$) standard normal. The sequences $\{Z_t(\Delta)\}_{t=1}^{T}$, $\{log Z_t\}_{t=1}^{T}$ and $\{maxlog Z_t\}_{t=1}^{T}$ provide evidence on the daily occurrence of jumps in the price process.

The outlyingness measure $d_{t,i}$ can also be used to build a statistic for daily jump detection. Indeed, under the null of no jump during day t, $d_{t,i} \sim \chi^2(1)$, $\forall i = 1, \dots, M$ (see Equation 7.40). In the spirit of the test proposed by Lee and Mykland (2008) (see next section), we can show that $\max_{i=1,\dots,M} \sqrt{d_{t,i}}$ follows a Gumbel distribution under the null. More specifically, we reject the null of no jump during day t at the $\alpha\%$ critical level if

$$\max_{i=1,\dots,M} \sqrt{d_{t,i}} > G^{-1}(1 - \alpha)S_n + C_n,$$

where $G^{-1}(1-\alpha)$ is the $1-\alpha$ quantile function of the standard Gumbel distribution, $C_n = (2 \log n)^{0.5} - \frac{\log(\pi)+\log(\log n)}{2(2 \log n)^{0.5}}$ and $S_n = \frac{1}{(2 \log n)^{0.5}}$. When $n = M$ or $n = MT$, the expected number of spurious (daily) detected jumps respectively equals αT and α.

If $I_{t,\alpha}(\Delta)$ is a dummy variable that equals 1 if a jump has been detected on day t at the α (e.g. 0.999) significance level (using any of the tests presented above) and 0 otherwise, a better estimate of the realized jumps is given by:

$$J_{t,\alpha}(\Delta) = I_{t,\alpha}(\Delta) \cdot [RV_t(\Delta) - \hat{IV}_t(\Delta)]. \tag{7.51}$$

To make sure that the jump component added to the continuous one equals the realized volatility, we define as an estimator of the integrated variance

$$C_{t,\alpha}(\Delta) = [1 - I_{t,\alpha}(\Delta)] \cdot RV_t(\Delta) + I_{t,\alpha}(\Delta) \cdot I\hat{V}_t(\Delta). \qquad (7.52)$$

Note that when $\alpha = 0, C_{t,\alpha}(\Delta) = I\hat{V}_t(\Delta), \forall t$.

7.8 Intraday jump tests

So far, we have considered the estimation of functions of jumps over given time intervals. The approach taken in this section is different. We explain how we can test whether any given intra-day return $r_{t,i}$ is from a purely continuous diffusion or is rather due to a jump in the price process. What follows is mainly based on the work of Lee and Mykland (2008) and Boudt, Croux, and Laurent (2008b).

The idea of Lee and Mykland (2008) for jump estimation is intuitive. If a return contains a jump component, it should be abnormally big. However, what constitutes an abnormally big return depends on the volatility condition prevailing at the time of the tested return. Indeed, in times of high volatility, an abnormal return is bigger than an abnormal return in times of low volatility. Hence, Lee and Mykland (2008) study the properties of the ratio of the tested return over a measure of local volatility. They derive asymptotic theory for the statistic and a rejection region under the null of no jump at tested time. In short, they propose a powerful, parsimonious methodology that allows to test whether any return contains a jump component, to know the sign of the jumps and its exact timing.

The statistic $J_{t,i}$ tests whether a jump occurred between intradaily time periods $i - 1$ and i of day t. It is defined as the absolute return divided by an estimate of the local standard deviation $\hat{\sigma}_{t,i}$, i.e.

$$J_{t,i} = \frac{|r_{t,i}|}{\hat{\sigma}_{t,i}}. \qquad (7.53)$$

Under the null of no jump at the testing time, that the process belongs to the family of BSMJ models described in Equation (7.14), and a suitable choice of the window size for local volatility, $\frac{r_{t,i}}{\hat{\sigma}_{t,i}}$ asymptotically follows a standard normal distribution.

Note that Lee and Mykland (2008) recommend replacing $\hat{\sigma}_{t,i}$ by $\hat{s}_{t,i} = \sqrt{\frac{1}{M-1}BV_t}$ where BV_t is the bi-power variation computed on all the intraday returns of day t. Boudt, Croux, and Laurent (2008b) propose to account for the strong periodicity in volatility and show that replacing $\hat{\sigma}_{t,i}$ by $\hat{f}_{t,i}\hat{s}_{t,i}$ is more appropriate. They show that ignoring periodic volatility patterns leads to spurious jump identification. Indeed, the original Lee/Mykland statistic (that neglects the periodicity) tends to overdetect (underdetect) jumps in periods of high (low) intraday periodic volatility. G@RCH 6.0 gives the choice between the three robust non parametric estimation methods described in Section 7.5.3.1 to estimate $\hat{f}_{t,i}$, i.e. $\hat{f}_{t,i}^{\text{MAD}}$, $\hat{f}_{t,i}^{\text{ShortH}}$ and $\hat{f}_{t,i}^{\text{WSD}}$. Recall that when the dataset is 'dated', the length of the periodicity filter is set to 5 days, otherwise it is equal to one day.

Under the null of no jump and a consistent estimate $\hat{\sigma}_{t,i}$, $J_{t,j}$ follows the same distribution as the absolute value of a standard normal variable. Brownlees and Gallo (2006) propose comparing $J_{t,i}$ with the $1 - \alpha/2$ quantile of the standard normal distribution. This rule might spuriously detect many jumps, however. Andersen, Bollerslev, and Dobrev (2007) use a Bonferroni correction to minimize spurious jump detection. To minimize the risk of falsely finding jumps, Lee and Mykland (2008) propose inferring jumps from a conservative critical value, which they obtain from the distribution of the statistic's maximum over the sample size. If the statistic exceeds a plausible maximum, one rejects the null of no jump. Under the stated assumptions and no jump in the interval $i - 1, i$ of day t, then when $\Delta \to 0$, the sample maximum of the absolute value of a standard normal variable (i.e. the jump statistic $J_{t,i}$) follows a Gumbel distribution. We reject the null of no jump if

$$J_{t,i} > G^{-1}(1 - \alpha)S_n + C_n, \tag{7.54}$$

where $G^{-1}(1-\alpha)$ is the $1-\alpha$ quantile function of the standard Gumbel distribution, $C_n = (2\log n)^{0.5} - \frac{\log(\pi) + \log(\log n)}{2(2\log n)^{0.5}}$ and $S_n = \frac{1}{(2\log n)^{0.5}}$. When $n = 1$, the test is similar to the one of Brownlees and Gallo (2006) in the sense that the expected number of spurious detected jumps (under the null) can be extremely large, i.e. αMT. When $n = M$ (i.e. number of observations per day) and $n = MT$ (i.e. total number of observations), this number equals respectively αT and α (i.e. ≈ 0). So if we choose a significance level of $\alpha = 0.0001$, then we reject the null of no jump at testing time if $J_{t,i} > S_n\beta^* + C_n$ with β^* such that $P(\psi \le \beta^*) = exp(-e^{-\beta^*}) = 0.9999$, i.e. $\beta^* = -log(-log(0.9999)) = 9.21$.

The L&M test is implemented in the function `Compute_LeeMykJump` of the Realized class. An example is provided in the file `Jumps_JumpDetection_LeeMykland.ox`. In this example, we simulate a GARCH diffusion with jumps and intraday periodicity (see Section 7.4) and apply the L&M

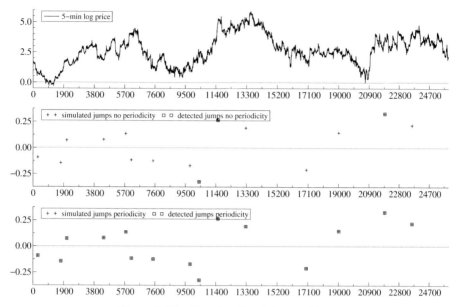

Figure 7.19 Simulated and detected jumps.

test.

The first graph on Figure 7.19 shows the simulated 5-min log-prices. The other graphs plot the simulated (plus) and detected (squares) jumps using the L&M test. Note that the presence of intraday periodicity is ignored in the second graph. The third graph corresponds to the filtered L&M test that implements the correction proposed by Boudt, Croux, and Laurent (2008b), i.e. $\hat{\sigma}_{t,i}$ by $\hat{f}_{t,i}\hat{s}_{t,i}$ where in this example we chose the WSD periodicity filter $\hat{f}_{t,i}^{\mathrm{WSD}}$.

We see that neglecting the presence of intraday periodicity has a strong impact on the power of the test. Indeed, while all the simulated jumps are correctly detected for the filtered L&M test, most jumps (i.e. small ones) are not detected when ignoring the intraday periodicity. See Boudt, Croux, and Laurent (2008b) for a more comprehensive simulation study.

7.9 Multivariate case

In the case where $r_{t,i}$ is an N-dimensional return vector generated by the multivariate counterpart of the BSMJ price diffusion model in (7.14), the processes $p(s)$, $\mu(s)$ and $q(s)$ are all N-dimensional vector processes and $w(s)$ is a vector of N independent

Brownian motions. Denote by $\Omega(s)$ the $N \times N$ càdlàg process such that $\Sigma(s) = \Omega(s)\Omega'(s)$ is the spot covariance matrix process of the continuous component of the price diffusion. Let K be the $N \times N$ process controlling the magnitude and transmission of jumps such that $K(s)dq(s)$ is the contribution of the jump process to the price diffusion. We then have that a N-dimensional log-price diffusion can be decomposed as follows:

$$\text{BSMJ:} \quad dp(s) \quad = \quad \mu(s)ds + \Omega(s)dw(s) + K(s)dq(s). \tag{7.55}$$

The integrated covariance matrix (ICov) over $[t-1, t]$ is the matrix

$$\text{ICov}_t = \int_{t-1}^{t} \Sigma(s)ds. \tag{7.56}$$

Denote by κ_j the contribution of the j-th jump in $[t-1, t]$ to the price diffusion.

7.9.1 Realized Quadratic Covariation

Andersen, Bollerslev, Diebold, and Labys (2003) have shown that the Realized quadratic covariation (RCov)

$$\text{RCov}_t(\Delta) \equiv \sum_{i=1}^{M} r_{t,i}r'_{t,i} \tag{7.57}$$

is a consistent estimator for the sum of the ICov and the realized jump variability

$$\underset{\Delta \to 0}{\text{plim}} \, \text{RCov}_t(\Delta) = \text{ICov}_t + \sum_{j=1}^{j_t} \kappa_j \kappa'_j, \tag{7.58}$$

where $j_t = \int_{t-1}^{t} dq^*(s)$, with $q^*(s)$ the univariate counting process derived from $q(s)$ such that $q^*(s)$ increases by 1 whenever $q(s)$ changes.

7.9.2 Realized BiPower Covariation

For disentangling the continuous and jump components in the RCov, we need an additional estimator for the ICov that is robust to jumps. To this purpose, Barndorff-Nielsen and Shephard (2004a) introduce the Realized BiPower Covariation process (RBPCov) as the process whose value at time t is the N-dimensional square matrix with k, l-th element equal to

$$\frac{\pi}{8} \left(\sum_{i=2}^{M} \left| r_{(k)t,i} + r_{(l)t,i} \right| \left| r_{(k)t,i-1} + r_{(l)t,i-1} \right| \right.$$

$$\left. - \left| r_{(k)t,i} - r_{(l)t,i} \right| \left| r_{(k)t,i-1} - r_{(l)t,i-1} \right| \right), \tag{7.59}$$

where $r_{(k)t,i}$ is the k-th component of the return vector $r_{t,i}$. The factor $\pi/8$ ensures that the RBPCov converges to the ICov under the BSMFAJ model:

$$\operatorname*{plim}_{\Delta \to 0} \mathrm{RBPCov}_t(\Delta) = \int_{t-1}^{t} \Sigma(s)ds. \tag{7.60}$$

Like the BPVar, the RBPCov is highly affected by jumps when these jumps affect two contiguous returns. The RBPCov, being a multivariate scale estimator, has the additional disadvantage that it is not affine equivariant and it is not necessarily positive semidefinite, which are undesirable properties for covolatility estimators.

In the next subsection, we show that the inclusion of an appropriate weight function in the RCov, that downweights extreme returns, leads to an estimator that has the following properties:

1. it is affine equivariant and yields positive semidefinite matrices;
2. at the BSM model it is consistent for the ICov and has a high efficiency;
3. at the BSMFAJ model it is consistent for the ICov.

7.9.3 ROWQCov

The computation of the ROWQCov is analogous to the computation of the ROW-Var, but here $r_{t,i}$ is a return vector of dimension N.

Step 1: estimation of local multivariate outlyingness

We estimate the multivariate outlyingness of the return vector $r_{t,i}$ by the Mahalanobis distance between $r_{t,i}$ and 0 using a highly robust estimator of the multivariate scale $S(r_{t,i})$ of the returns belonging to the same local window as $r_{t,i}$.[12] Formally, the outlyingness of $r_{t,i}$ equals

$$d_{t,i} = r'_{t,i}S^{-1}(r_{t,i})r_{t,i}. \tag{7.61}$$

Under the BSM model and some weak assumptions stated in Boudt, Croux, and Laurent (2008a), the Mahalanobis outlyingness measure is asymptotically chi squared distributed with N degrees of freedom (χ_N^2) provided that the spot covariance matrix is constant over the local window.

For the same reasons as the ones evoked in Sections 7.6.2 and 7.8, the assumption of constancy of the covariance is not realistic for local windows of length one day.

---

[12] Like for the ROWVar, G@RCH considers local windows of length one day.

For that reason, the choice is given to the user to computed $d_{t,i}$ on raw returns (i.e. Equation (7.61)) but also on filtered returns. The three non parametric techniques discussed in Section 7.5.3 are offered, i.e. $\hat{f}_{t,i}^{MAD}$, $\hat{f}_{t,i}^{ShortH}$ or $\hat{f}_{t,i}^{WSD}$. Note that the N periodicity filters are estimated separately.

A common choice for a highly robust multivariate scale estimator is the Minimum Covariance Determinant (MCD) covariance estimate proposed by Rousseeuw and Driessen (1999). It is defined as follows. We call a halfsample of a local window a subsample of $h = \lfloor 0.5(M + N + 1) \rfloor$ returns belonging to that local window. Denote now S the covariance matrix computed from the halfsample having the smallest value of the determinant of the covariance matrix computed from it.[13] Compute then for the i-th return belonging to the same local window as $r_{t,i}$ the weight $w_i = w_{HR}[r'_{t,i}(c_{0.5}S)^{-1}r_{t,i}]$. The MCD multivariate scale estimator is then given by the weighted covariance matrix of all returns belonging to the local window

$$S^{MCD}(r_{t,i}) = \frac{c_{0.95}}{\sum_{i=1}^{M} w_i} \sum_{i=1}^{M} w_i r_{t,i} r'_{t,i}.$$

The scalars $c_{0.5}$ and $c_{0.95}$ are the correction factors needed for consistency at the multivariate normal distribution. One has that $c_\beta = \beta / F_{\chi^2_{N+2}}(\chi^2_N(\beta))$, where $F_{\chi^2_{N+2}}(\cdot)$ is the χ^2_{N+2} distribution function (Croux and Haesbroeck, 1999).

The MCD covariance estimator is our preferred choice to construct the outlyingness. However, one can also use other robust multivariate scale estimators, such as the average RBPCov (see above). Note the positive semidefiniteness of ROWQCov is preserved when $d_{t,i}$ is build upon the RBPCov.

Step 2: computation of ROWQCov

Because the Mahalanobis outlyingness are scalar-valued and asymptotically χ^2_N distributed, one can use the hard and soft rejection weight functions in (7.41)-(7.42) with threshold equal to an extreme quantile of the χ^2_N distribution, to downweight

---

[13] We find this subset using the fast MCD algorithm of Rousseeuw and Driessen (1999) which takes many initial choices of halfsamples. For each initial choice, the covariance of the subsample is computed and then used to calculate the outlyingness of all observations. Next the observations in the halfsample with highest outlyingness are replaced by those with lowest outlyingness. This is called a "C-step", where C stands for concentration. This step is repeated, but with the outlyingness computed using the covariance matrix of the new subset. For each initial halfsample, this procedure is repeated until convergence. The MCD estimate is then the one with lowest determinant over all considered halfsamples.

Table 7.5 Correction factors c_w when the dimension of the series is N and for the hard and soft rejection weight functions with threshold k.

N	$k = \chi_N^2(0.95)$				$k = \chi_N^2(0.99)$			
	1	2	5	10	1	2	5	10
HR	1.318	1.187	1.099	1.063	1.081	1.049	1.026	1.016
SR	1.081	1.041	1.017	1.009	1.017	1.009	1.004	1.002

the high-frequency returns that are outlying with respect to the majority of the returns in their local window. The ROWQCov is then defined as follows.

Definition 2 *Let $r_{t,i}$, for $i = 1, \ldots, M$, be a sample of M high-frequency returns and $d_{t,i}$ their outlyingness value based on local windows of length one day. For a given weight function $w(\cdot)$, the Realized Outlyingness Weighted Quadratic Covariation is defined as*

$$\text{ROWQCov}_t(\Delta) = c_w \frac{\sum_{i=1}^{M} w(d_{t,i}) r_{t,i} r_{t,i}'}{\frac{1}{M} \sum_{i=1}^{M} w(d_{t,i})}. \tag{7.62}$$

7.9.4 Correction factor for ROWVar and ROWQCov

The correction factor c_w in (7.62) ensures that the ROWQCov is consistent for the ICov at the BSM and BSMFAJ models. It depends on the dimension N of the process and on the weight function used. Denote $E[g(u)]$ the expectation of $g(u)$ where u is standard normal distributed. The correction factor c_w is then given by

$$c_w = N \frac{E\left[w(u'u)\right]}{E\left[w(u'u)u'u\right]}. \tag{7.63}$$

For the HR weight function defined in (7.41) with threshold $k = \chi_N^2(1 - \alpha)$, $c_w = (1-\alpha)/F_{\chi_{N+2}^2}(\chi_N^2(1-\alpha))$, where $F_{\chi_{N+2}^2}(\cdot)$ is the χ_{N+2}^2 distribution function. Table 7.5 reports the correction factors for the hard and soft rejection weight functions. For $N = 1$, the correction factor c_w is identical to the one used in (7.43).

Chapter 8

Getting started with RE@LIZED

The aim of this section is to explain how to apply most concepts reviewed in this chapter using the rolling-menu facilities of G@RCH 6.0.

G@RCH cannot operate without data. Once OxMetrics is activated, the very first step is to load data. To be used with the RE@LIZED package, the database has to be formatted has follows:

- It must contain equally spaced intraday returns (e.g. 1-, 5- 15-min returns) without missing values.
- Each row must correspond to a trading period (e.g. one day) over which the realized moments are going to be computed.
- Each column must contain all the intraday returns of that trading period, e.g. 288 columns for 5-min FX data.
- The database must be dated. The simplest way to make a 'dated' database is to add a variable labelled "Date" containing the date in ISO format of yyyy-mm-dd. The year is always four digits, the month one or two digits (1=January) and the date also one or two digits. For example: 1965-1-31 to 1985-9-5. If the date is not recognised, this can be done (provided the format is correct) by double clicking on the name of the date variable in the database. This produces the dialog for editing the description of that variable. The variable can be renamed in this field. The type of the variable can be modified. Choose type Date for a variable that contains dates and/or times.

8.1 Univariate non parametric volatility

Let us illustrate how to compute RVar, BV and ROWVar using G@RCH through a concrete example. The dataset used in this section is
`Simulated_cont_GARCH_jumps_FFF_K_0.2_M_0.3.in7`. This dataset is obtained

by running the program `Store_Cont_GARCH_Jumps_FFF.ox` with the options $K = 0.2$, $M = 0.3$ and $threshold = 100$. These data correspond to simulated 5-min returns following a GARCH(1,1) diffusion with jumps and intraday periodicity. There are 288 observations per day. The number of simulated jumps is 640 and the number of days with at least one significant jump is 571 which corresponds indeed to about one jump per week.

The first column is the (hypothetical) date, the next 288 ones, `Ret_1,....,Ret_288`, are the 5-min returns and the last columns are the daily Returns (`DRet`), Integrated Variance (`IV`) and Integrated Quarticity (`IQ`).

	Date	Ret_1	Ret_2	Ret_3	Ret_4	Ret_5
1987-01-05	1987-01-05	0	.0184402	.0193936	.0104924	.0198455
1987-01-06	1987-01-06	-.00186872	.00925856	.0119589	-.015263	.0261916
1987-01-07	1987-01-07	-.0141159	.00302196	.000730676	.0129537	.0284517
1987-01-08	1987-01-08	-.0160593	.00318442	.0283071	.0030291	-.00455868
1987-01-09	1987-01-09	-.00849092	.00817128	-.0149588	-.0137111	.000493532
1987-01-12	1987-01-12	.00792566	.0595319	-.0330976	.00389996	-.0181739
1987-01-13	1987-01-13	-.00398106	-.00953188	.0159848	-.0253668	-.0104024
1987-01-14	1987-01-14	-.0103388	.0185602	-.00660191	.0213089	.0342919
1987-01-15	1987-01-15	-.00741353	-.00827331	-.0311291	.0200857	.0286914
1987-01-16	1987-01-16	.00457011	.00858188	-.0178295	-.00565585	.0384398
1987-01-19	1987-01-19	-.00906838	-.0300256	.01035	.00752573	.015055
1987-01-20	1987-01-20	.00273451	-.014531	.00822023	-.0216218	.00504507
1987-01-21	1987-01-21	.0165497	-.00886311	.00686709	.0282351	-.000693958
1987-01-22	1987-01-22	.0285036	.00242323	-.00389603	.000672253	.0367912
1987-01-23	1987-01-23	-.0328161	-.0121218	-.0128129	.0107459	-.00100829
1987-01-26	1987-01-26	.0216111	-.0196284	.00609833	.0207729	.0225407
1987-01-27	1987-01-27	-.00696781	.0160026	-.0156777	-.0407403	-.0295558
1987-01-28	1987-01-28	.00314417	.0415355	.00126986	-.00860144	.017322

To start RE@LIZED, click on G@RCH in the Modules group in the workspace window on the left-hand side of OxMetrics. Next change the **Category** to Other models and the **Model class** to Realized Volatility using G@RCH, then click on Formulate.

A list with all the variables of the database appears in the Database frame. Select all the intraday return series, i.e. Ret_1,....,Ret_288, by clicking on the variable names and then click on the $<<$ button.

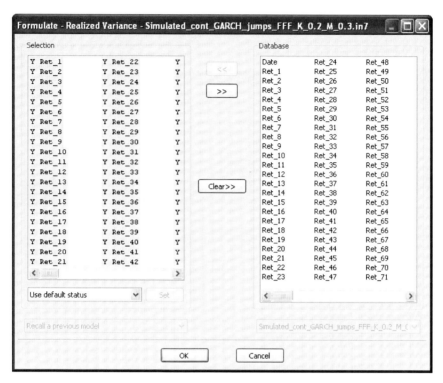

Once the OK button is pressed, the Settings box automatically appears.

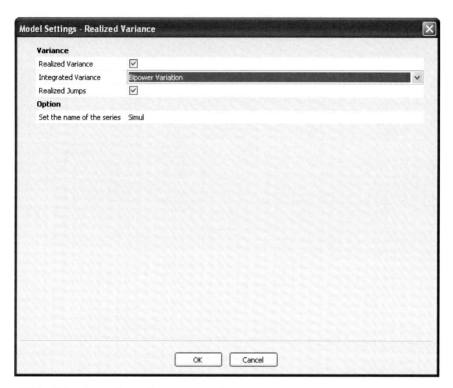

This dialog box allows the user to select the non parametric volatility measures to compute. 'Realized Variance' refers to RVar, 'Integrated Variance' to IVar and 'Realized Jumps' to RJ.

When the option 'Integrated Variance' is set to 'No' the IVar is not computed. When it is set to 'Bipower Variation' or 'ROWVar', IVar is computed using Equation (7.38) or (7.43) respectively.

The last option allows to change the label of the series. By default it is the name of the dataset (without the extension).

The subsequent window displays options related to the sample period.

Case 'Bipower Variation'

When 'Realized Variance' and 'Realized Jumps' are enabled and 'Integrated Variance' equals 'Bipower Variation', and once the OK button is pressed, a new dialog box pops up with some options about the test for jumps.

The option 'Integrated Quarticity' corresponds to $IQ_t = \int_{t-1}^{t} \sigma^4(s)ds$. When this option is set to 'Tripower Quarticity', IQ_t is computed using Equation (7.46) while when it is set to 'Quadpower Quarticity' it is computed using Equation (7.47).

The option 'Test Statistics' proposes three different Z statistics for jumps:

(1) 'Z on RV' corresponds to Equation (7.45);

(2) 'Z on log(RV)' corresponds to Equation (7.49);

(3) 'Z on log(RV) with max adjustment' corresponds to Equation (7.50).

Finally, the critical level α of the test has to be chosen.

Let us consider the options 'Tripower Variation', 'Z on log(RV) with max adjustment' and $\alpha = 0.999$.

Once the OK button is pressed, a new dialog appears and proposes to select the estimation sample. When the variable corresponding to the date is correctly formatted, the sample can conveniently be fixed based on starting and ending date (see Chapter 9 of Doornik, (2009), for details).

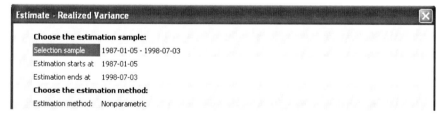

Here is the output generated by G@RCH:

```
Z Jump Statistic on log(RV) with max adjustment using Tripower Quarticity
Expected number of spurious detected jumps (under H0=no jump): 3
Number of detected jumps: 405
Proportion of detected jumps: 0.135
Critical level: 0.001
Critical value: 3.09023
```

While 571 days contain at least one jump, the test detects only 405 jumps, i.e. 13.5% of jumps at the 1% critical level.

Case 'ROWVAR'

Let us now consider the case where option 'Integrated Variance' is set to 'ROWVar' in the Model Settings box. Once the OK button is pressed, a new dialog box pops up with some options about ROWVar.

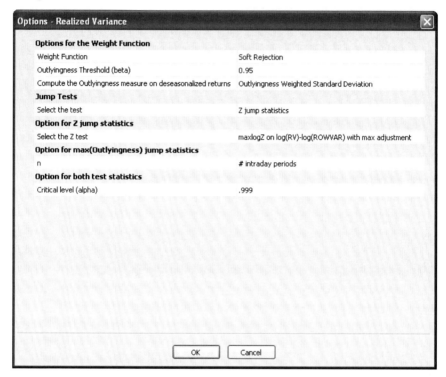

This dialog box is divided into 5 parts.

(1) Options for the weight function $w(.)$ in Equation (7.43).

- The first option gives the choice between the hard and soft rejection functions given in Equations (7.41) and (7.42) respectively.
- The second option concerns the critical level β used to compute the outlyingness threshold k. Recall that both rejection functions contain a tuning parameter k equal to the $\beta = 1 - \alpha$ quantile of the χ_1^2 distribution function. Usually, β is set to 0.95 which corresponds to the 95% quantile of the χ_1^2 distribution function.
- When the third option is set to 'NO', the outlyingness measure $d_{t,i}$ is computed on $r_{t,i}$. When it is set to 'MAD', 'ShortH' or 'WSD', $d_{t,i}$ is computed on filtered returns $\tilde{r}_{t,i} = \frac{r_{t,i}}{\hat{f}_{t,i}}$, where $\hat{f}_{t,i}$ is $\hat{f}_{t,i}^{MAD}$, $\hat{f}_{t,i}^{ShortH}$ or $\hat{f}_{t,i}^{WSD}$ respectively. See Section 7.5.3 for more details about robust non parametric

estimates of the periodicity in volatility. Note that the estimated periodicity factor $\hat{f}_{t,i}$ used in the filtering of the data can be plotted and stored (see menus Tests/Graphical Analysis and Tests/Store).

(2) Choice between Z-statistics or test based on $\max_{i=1,\ldots,M} \sqrt{d_{t,i}}$ (see Section 7.7 for more details).

(3) Choice between three Z-statistics:

- 'Z on RV' corresponds to Equation (7.45);
- 'Z on log(RV)' corresponds to Equation (7.49);
- 'Z on log(RV) with max adjustment' Equation (7.50).

(4) The next option is n. This parameter is needed in the test based on $\max_{i=1,\ldots,M} \sqrt{d_{t,i}}$. The choice is given between two values. '# intraday periods' corresponds to $n = M$ while '# intraday observations' corresponds to $n = MT$. Recall that when $n = M$ or $n = MT$, the expected number of spurious (daily) detected jumps respectively equals αT and α (i.e. ≈ 0).

(5) The critical level of the test.

The three outputs below correspond respectively to 'Z on log(RV) with max adjustment' and the max outlyingness statistics $\max_{i=1,\ldots,M} \sqrt{d_{t,i}}$ with $n = M$ and $n = MT$ respectively.

```
maxlogZ Jump Statistic on log(RV)-log(ROWVAR) with max adjustment
Expected number of spurious detected jumps (under H0=no jump): 3
Number of detected jumps: 479
Proportion of detected jumps: 0.159667
Critical level: 0.001
Critical value: 3.09023
```

```
Jump Statistic of Boudt, Croux and Laurent (2008) based on max(Outlyingness)
with n = 288
Robust non-parametric periodicity filter: WSD
Expected number of spurious detected jumps (under H0=no jump): 3
Number of detected jumps: 574
Proportion of detected jumps: 0.191333
Critical level: 0.001
Critical value: 4.99015
```

```
Jump Statistic of Boudt, Croux and Laurent (2008) based on max(Outlyingness)
with n = 864000
Robust non-parametric periodicity filter: WSD
Expected number of spurious detected jumps (under H0=no jump): 0.001
Number of detected jumps: 571
Proportion of detected jumps: 0.190333
Critical level: 0.001
Critical value: 6.19013
```

These results clearly suggest that the test based on $\max_{i=1,\ldots,M} \sqrt{d_{t,i}}$ better performs than the ones based on the Z statistics.

<u>Menu Tests...</u>

Three additional options are also available in the Tests... menu.

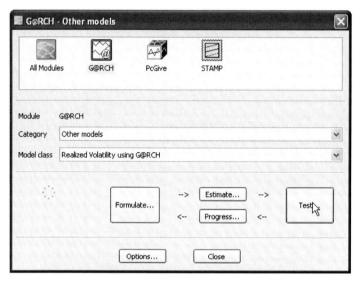

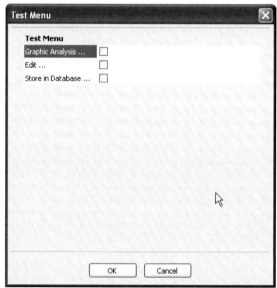

The first one, Tests/Graphic Analysis... allows to plot several graphs concerning the following series (provided these quantities have been calculated):

Realized Moments

(1) Realized Returns $RR_t = \sum_{i=1}^{M} r_{t,i}$;

(2) Realized Variance, see Equation (7.12);

(3) $C_{t,\alpha}(\Delta)$ with $\hat{IV}_t(\Delta) = BV_t(\Delta)$, i.e. Bipower Variation. See Equations (7.38) and (7.52);

(4) $C_{t,\alpha}(\Delta) =$ with $\hat{IV}_t(\Delta) = ROWVar_t(\Delta)$. See Equations (7.43) and (7.52);

(5) Realized Jumps $J_{t,\alpha}(\Delta) = I_{t,\alpha}(\Delta) \cdot [RV_t(\Delta) - \hat{IV}_t(\Delta)]$. See Equation (7.51);

Standardized Realized Returns

(1) Using Realized Variance $= RR_t/\sqrt{RV_t}$;

(2) Using Bipower Variation or ROWVar $= RR_t/\sqrt{C_{t,\alpha}(\Delta)}$.

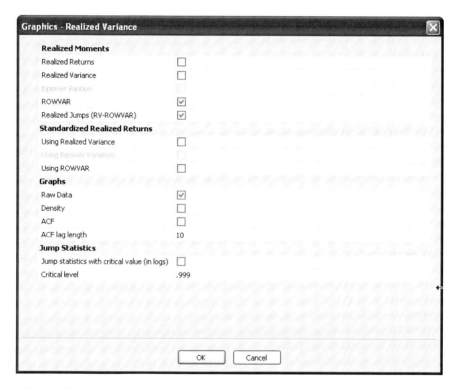

The available graphs of the above series are a time series plot of the raw series, density (unconditional distribution) and ACF (with a specified lag length).

Figure 8.1 plots the estimated bi-power variation $C_{t,\alpha}(\Delta)$ with $\hat{IV}_t(\Delta) = BV_t(\Delta)$ and $\alpha = 0.999$.

The second option, Tests/Edit... allows to edit RV_t, BV_t, $ROWVar_t$ and RJ_t in a basic matrix editor. It also enables you to save the contents of the editor in an matrix file, so that it can be used again.

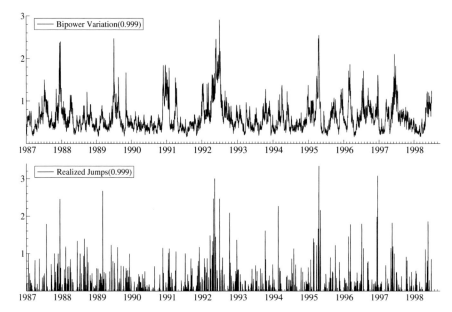

Figure 8.1 BV_t and significant jumps with $\alpha = 0.999$.

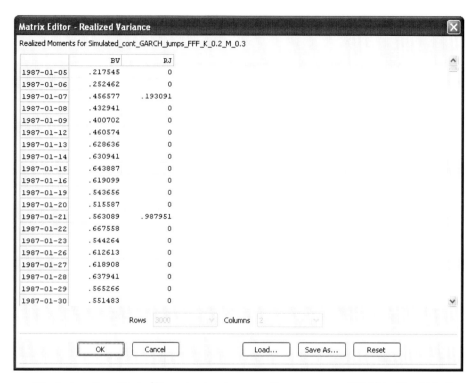

The last option, Tests/Store in database... allows to store $RV_t(\Delta)$, $C_{t,\alpha}(\Delta)$ (for $I\hat{V}_t(\Delta) = BV_t(\Delta)$ or $ROWVar_t(\Delta)$ and $J_{t,\alpha}(\Delta)$ (among others) in the database as new variables. When selecting this option, a first window appears and the user selects the series to be stored.

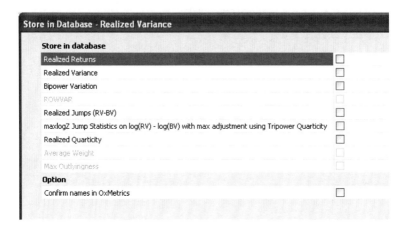

8.2 Intraday tests for jumps

To apply the intraday tests for jumps reviewed in Section 7.8, click on G@RCH in the Modules group in the workspace window on the left-hand side of OxMetrics. Next change the **Category** to Other models and the **Model class** to Lee and Mykland tests for jumps using G@RCH, then click on Formulate.

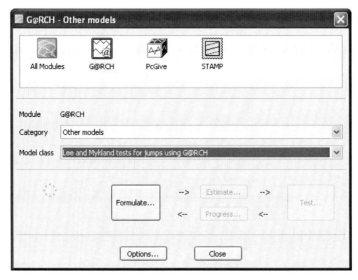

A list with all the variables of the database appears in the Database frame. Select all the intraday return series, i.e. Ret_1,....,Ret_288, by clicking on the variable names and then click on the $<<$ button.

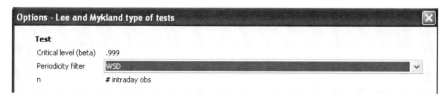

Once the OK button is pressed, the Options box automatically appears.
There are three options.

(1) The critical level of the test, e.g. $\beta = 0.999$.

(2) The second option concerns the choice of the periodicity filter. 'NO' means that
the local variance $\hat{\sigma}_{t,i} = \hat{s}_{t,i} \equiv \sqrt{\frac{1}{M-1}BV_t}$. When choosing 'MAD', 'ShortH'
or 'WSD', $\hat{\sigma}_{t,i} = \hat{f}_{t,i}\hat{s}_{t,i}$ where $\hat{f}_{t,i} = \hat{f}_{t,i}^{MAD}$, $\hat{f}_{t,i}^{ShortH}$ or $\hat{f}_{t,i}^{WSD}$ respectively.
See Section 7.5.3 for more details about robust non parametric estimates of the
periodicity in volatility.

(3) The third option is n. Three values are possible: 1, '# intraday periods', i.e.
$n = M$ and '# intraday observations' i.e. $n = MT$. Recall that when $n = 1$,
$n = M$ or $n = MT$, the expected number of spurious (daily) detected jumps
respectively equals αMT, αT and α (i.e. ≈ 0).

Once the OK button is pressed, a new dialog appears and proposes to select the
estimation sample.

The output printed here below corresponds to the L&M test with $\beta = 0.999$,
$\hat{\sigma}_{t,i} = \hat{f}_{t,i}^{ShortH}\hat{s}_{t,i}$ and $n = MT$. 639 intraday jumps have been detected (out of 640
simulated jumps) and 571 days contain at least one jump (which is the exact number of
days with jumps).

```
Lee and Mykland type of test for jump arrival times.
Local robust variance = Average Bipower variation
Robust non-parametric periodicity filter: WSD
Critical level of the test: 0.999
n: 864000

Number of detected jumps: 639
Proportion of detected jumps: 0.000739583
Number of periods (typically days) with at least one significant jump: 571
Proportion of periods with at least one significant jump: 0.190333
Critical value, i.e. G(Beta)*Sn+Cn: 6.19013
Expected number of spurious detected jumps (under H0=no jumps): 0.001
```

<u>Menu Tests...</u>

Three additional options are also available in the Tests... menu.

The menu, Tests/Graphic Analysis... allows to plot first the number of detected
jumps per period of time and the estimated periodicity factor $\hat{f}_{t,i}$.

Figures 8.2 and 8.3 have been obtained after applying respectively the L&M test
without and with the (WSD) periodicity filter option on the same data as before.

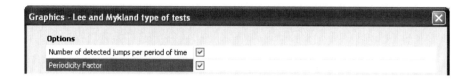

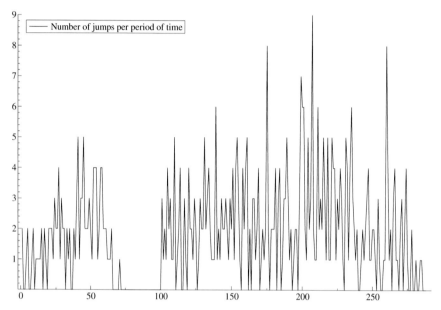

Figure 8.2   L&M test without periodicity filter.

Recall first that the jumps have been generated independently from $f_{t,i}$ and thus the number of detected jumps per period of time is expected to be independent from the intraday time interval. This is however not the case for the version of the test that does not account for intraday periodicity because it never detects jumps when periodicity is low (intervals 70 to 100 corresponding to the lunch of Tokyo). This is essentially due to the fact that when periodicity is low, this version of the test overestimates the spot volatility which leads to a size distortion and a loss of power.

The second option, Tests/Edit... allows to edit

(1) intraday returns $r_{t,i}$;

(2) the L&M statistic $J_{t,i}$;

(3) a binary variable that equals 1 for significant jumps, 0 otherwise, i.e. $(J_{t,i} > G^{-1}(1 - \alpha)S_n + C_n)$;

(4) and the estimated periodicity filter $\hat{f}_{t,i}$.

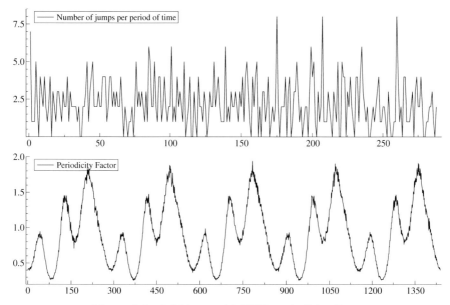

Figure 8.3 L&M test with WSD periodicity filter.

in a basic matrix editor (each variable is edited in a $TM \times 1$ vector). It also enables you to save the contents of the editor in an matrix file, so that it can be used again.

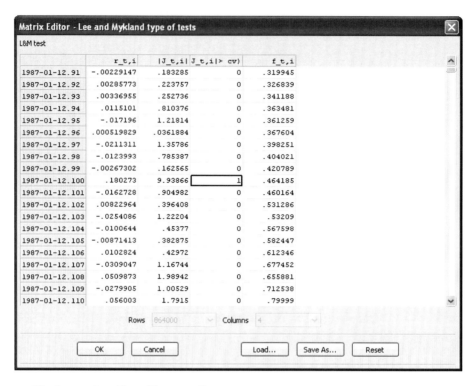

The last option, Tests/Store... allows to store

(1) daily aggregated jumps, i.e. $\sum_{i=1}^{M} r_{t,i}^2 I(J_{t,i} > G^{-1}(1 - \alpha)S_n + C_n)$;

(2) the L&M statistic $J_{t,i}$;

(3) and significant intraday returns, i.e. $r_{t,i}I(J_{t,i} > G^{-1}(1 - \alpha)S_n + C_n)$;

in the database as new variables. When selecting this option, a first window appears and the user selects the series to be stored. Daily aggregated jumps are stored in the same datafile than the one containing the intraday returns while the others are stored in separate datafiles.

8.3 Multivariate non parametric volatility

Let us illustrate how to compute RCov, RBPCov and ROWQCov using G@RCH through a concrete example. Once again, G@RCH cannot operate without data. The very first step is to load data. The datasets used in this section are `ret1.in7` and `ret2.in7`. These data correspond 3000 days of simulated 5-min returns (288 observations per day) following a bivariate CCC-GARCH(1,1) diffusion with jumps. The true correlation between the two series is 0.8 while the number of simulated jumps is 150 (i.e. 5%).

The first column of each file is the (hypothetical) date, the next 288 ones, `ret1`,....,`ret288`, are the 5-min returns. Importantly, the two datasets are dated in such a way that the two separated files can be matched when computing the covariance estimates.

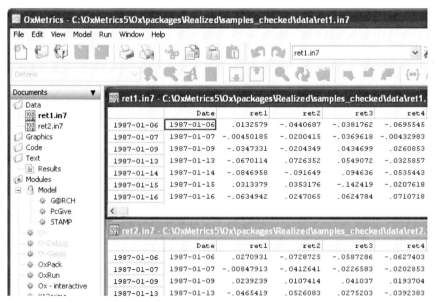

To start RE@LIZED, click on G@RCH in the Modules group in the workspace window on the left-hand side of OxMetrics. Next change the **Category** to Other models and the **Model class** to Realized Covariance using G@RCH, then click on Formulate.

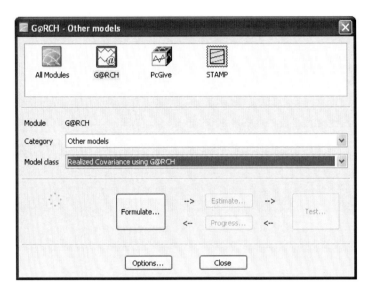

A list with the name of all the loaded databases appears in the Select the datafiles - Realized Covariance frame. Select the files containing the intraday returns (at least two) and then click on the OK button.

A list with all the variables of the currently selected database appears in the Database frame. Select all the intraday return series, i.e. ret1,....,ret288, by clicking on the variable names and then click on the << button. If the datafiles are not dated, select a variable corresponding to the Date and change its status to Date (D).[1]

Once the OK button is pressed, the Settings box automatically appears.

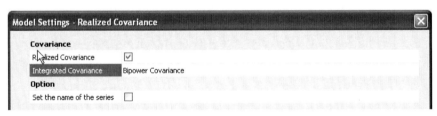

This dialog box allows the user to select the non parametric Covariance measures to compute. 'Realized Covariance' refers to RCov and 'Integrated Covariance' to ICov.

When the option 'Integrated Covariance' is set to 'No' the ICov is not estimated.

---

[1]All the files are expected to contain this variable.

When it is set to 'Bipower Covariance' or 'ROWQCov', IVar is computed using Equation (7.59) or (7.62) respectively.

The last option allows to change the label of the series. By default it is the name of the dataset (without the extension).

The subsequent window displays options related to the sample period.

Let us now consider the case when option 'Integrated Variance' is set to 'ROWQCov' in the Model Settings box. Once the OK button is pressed, a new dialog box pops up with some options about ROWQCov.

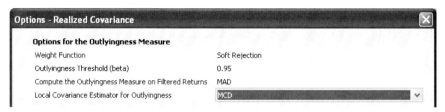

(1) The first option concerns the choice of the weight function $w(.)$ in Equation (7.43), i.e. hard or soft rejection functions (see Equations (7.41) and (7.42) respectively).

(2) The second option concerns the outlyingness threshold k. Recall that both rejection functions contain a tuning parameter k equal to the $\beta = 1 - \alpha$ quantile of the χ^2_N distribution function. This option allows the chose β. Usually, β is set to 0.95 which corresponds to the 95% quantile of the χ^2_N distribution function.

(3) When the third option is set to 'NO', the outlyingness measure $d_{t,i}$ is computed on $r_{t,i}$. When it is set to 'MAD', 'ShortH' or 'WSD', $d_{t,i}$ is computed on filtered returns $\tilde{r}_{t,i} = \frac{r_{t,i}}{\hat{f}_{t,i}}$, where $\hat{f}_{t,i}$ is $\hat{f}^{MAD}_{t,i}$, $\hat{f}^{ShortH}_{t,i}$ or $\hat{f}^{WSD}_{t,i}$ respectively. Note that since $r_{t,i}$ is now an $N \times 1$ vector, $\hat{f}_{t,i}$ is also an $N \times 1$, where the different periodicity filters are estimated separately. See Section 7.5.3 for more details about robust non parametric estimates of the periodicity in volatility.

(4) The fourth option concerns the choice of the local covariance estimator for outlyingness. The first option is the empirical variance, the second is the MCD and the third one is Pairwise covariance.

Menu Tests...

Three additional options are also available in the Tests... menu.

The menu, Tests/Graphic Analysis... allows to plot the following series (provided these quantities have been calculated):

(1) RVar: Realized variances, i.e. diagonal elements of $RCov_t$;

(2) RCov: Realized covariance(s), i.e. upper diagonal elements (excluding the diagonal) of $RCov_t$;

(3) RCorr: Realized correlation(s), i.e. upper diagonal elements (excluding the diagonal) of $diag(\sqrt{RVar_t})^{-1}RCov_t diag(\sqrt{RVar_t})^{-1}$;

(4) BPVar: bi-power variations, i.e. diagonal elements of $RBPCov_t$;

(5) RBPCov: Realized bi-power covariation(s), i.e. upper diagonal elements (excluding the diagonal) of $RBPCov_t$;

(6) RBPCorr: Realized bi-power correlation(s), i.e. upper diagonal elements (excluding the diagonal) of $diag(\sqrt{BPVar_t})^{-1}RBPCov_t diag(\sqrt{BPVar_t})^{-1}$;

(7) ROWVar: Realized outlyingness weighted variations, i.e. diagonal elements of $ROWQCov_t$;

(8) ROWCov: Realized outlyingness weighted covariation(s), i.e. upper diagonal elements (excluding the diagonal) of $ROWQCov_t$;

(9) ROWCorr: Realized outlyingness weighted correlation(s), i.e. upper diagonal elements (excluding the diagonal) of
$diag(\sqrt{ROWVar_t})^{-1}ROWQCov_t diag(\sqrt{ROWVar_t})^{-1}$.

Figures 8.4, 8.5 and 8.6 plot the estimated correlation extracted from the Realized Correlation, RBPCov and ROWQCov respectively.

It is clear from Figure 8.4 that RCorr is affected by the presence of jumps.

8.4 The Realized class

In the previous section we have seen how to use the rolling-menu facilities of G@RCH to compute different measures and test statistics related to the concept of realized volatility. The aim of this section is now to show how to do the same things in Ox.

A nice feature of G@RCH 6.0 is that Ox code can be generated.

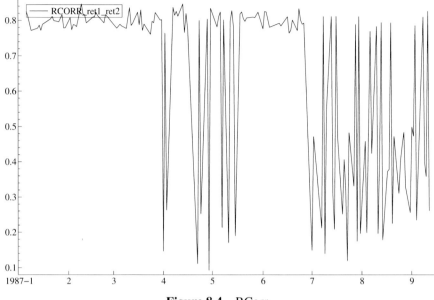

Figure 8.4 RCorr.

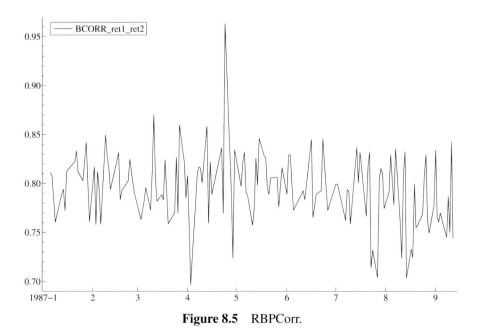

Figure 8.5 RBPCorr.

The Model/Ox Batch Code command (or Alt+O) activates a new dialog box called 'Generate Ox Code' that allows the user to select an item for which to generate Ox

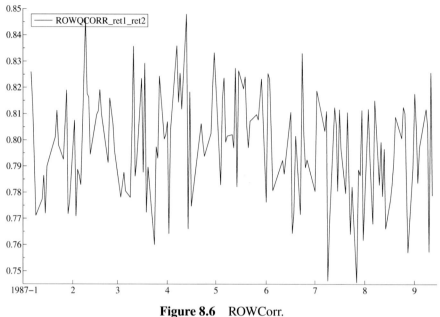

Figure 8.6   ROWCorr.

code.

The code is then opened in a new window and provided Ox Professional is available, this code can be run, either from OxMetrics, or from OxEdit or the command line. This option is also available for the 'Realized Volatility using G@RCH', 'Lee and Mykland tests for jumps using G@RCH' and 'Realized Covariance using G@RCH' modules.

OxBatch_1.ox is an example of Ox Batch code generated by G@RCH 6.0 after the replication of the first example of Section 8.1.

```
                                                                    OxBatch_1.ox
main()
{
//--- Ox code for REALIZED
decl model = new Realized();

model.Load("C:\\Data\\Simulated_cont_GARCH_jumps_FFF_K_0.2_M_0.3.in7");
model.Deterministic(-1);

model.Select(Y_VAR, {"Ret_1", 0, 0});
...
model.Select(Y_VAR, {"Ret_288", 0, 0});

model.SetModelClass(MC_RV);
model.RV(1);
model.IV(1);
model.OPTIONS_JUMPS_TEST_BV(1,0,2,0.999);

model.SetSelSampleByDates(dayofcalendar(1987, 1, 5), dayofcalendar(1998, 7, 3));
model.Estimate();
model.Graphs_RV(0,0,1,0,0,0,0,1,1,0,0,10,0,0.999);
model.Append_in(model.m_vIV,"BV");
model.Append_in(model.m_vRJ,"RJ_BV");
model.Save("C:\\Data\\Simulated_cont_GARCH_jumps_FFF_K_0.2_M_0.3.in7");

delete model;
}
```

The output obtained after running `OxBatch_1.ox` is reported here below.

```
maxlogZ Jump Statistic on log(RV)-log(BV) with max adjustment using Tripower Quarticity
Expected number of spurious detected jumps (under H0=no jumps): 3
Number of detected jumps: 405
Proportion of detected jumps: 0.135
Critical level: 0.001
Critical value: 3.09023
```

`OxBatch_2.ox` and `OxBatch_3.ox` are two examples of Ox Batch codes generated by G@RCH 6.0 after the computation of the L&M statistic and ROWQCov.

```
                                                                    OxBatch_2.ox
main()
{
//--- Ox code for REALIZED
decl model = new Realized();

model.Load("C:\\temp\\Simulated_cont_GARCH_jumps_FFF_K_0.2_M_0.3.in7");
model.Deterministic(-1);

model.Select(Y_VAR, {"Ret_1", 0, 0});
...
model.Select(Y_VAR, {"Ret_288", 0, 0});

model.SetModelClass(MC_LM);
model.OPTIONS_LM_TEST(0.999,864000,3);
model.SetSelSampleByDates(dayofcalendar(1987, 1, 5), dayofcalendar(1998, 7, 3));
model.Estimate();
model.Graphs_LM(1,1);
model.Append_in(sumr(model.m_mLMsigJumps.*(model.m_mY.^2)),"LM_RJ");
model.Save("C:\\temp\\Simulated_cont_GARCH_jumps_FFF_K_0.2_M_0.3.in7");
model.Store_LM(model.m_mLMstat,"|J_ti|",,"C:\\temp\\abs_Jti.in7");
model.Store_LM(model.m_mLMsigJumps.*model.m_mY,"LM_sign_ret","C:\\temp\\LM_sign_ret.in7");

delete model;
}
```

```
                                                                           OxBatch_3.ox
main()
{
//--- Ox code for RE@LIZED
decl model = new Realized();

decl path_datafiles=new array[2];
path_datafiles[0]="C:\\OxMetrics6\\Ox\\packages\\Realized\\samples\\data\\ret1.in7";
path_datafiles[1]="C:\\OxMetrics6\\Ox\\packages\\Realized\\samples\\data\\ret2.in7";
model.Set_path_datafiles(path_datafiles);

model.SetModelClass(MC_RCOV);
model.Select(Y_VAR, {"ret1", 0, 0});
...
model.Select(Y_VAR, {"ret288", 0, 0});

model.RCOV(1);
model.ICOV(2,1,1);
model.SetSelSampleByDates(dayofcalendar(1987, 1, 6), dayofcalendar(1987, 9, 14));
model.Estimate();
model.Graphs_RCOV(-1,0,0,1,0,0,1);

delete model;
}
```

Chapter 9

Multivariate GARCH Models

(written with the collaboration of Francesco Violante)

9.1 Introduction

It is now widely accepted that financial volatilities move together over time across assets and markets.

To illustrate, Figure 9.1 plots the daily returns (in %) of two major US indices, namely the Dow Jones and Nasdaq (from 1989-09-28 to 2004-09-27). The unconditional correlation between the two series is about 70%.

Recognizing this feature through a multivariate modeling framework leads to more relevant empirical models than working with separate univariate models. From a financial point of view, it opens the door to better decision tools in various areas, such as asset pricing, portfolio selection, option pricing, hedging, and risk management. Indeed, unlike at the beginning of the 1990s, several institutions have now developed the necessary skills to use the econometric theory in a financial perspective.

The most obvious application of MGARCH (multivariate GARCH) models is the study of the relations between the volatilities and co-volatilities of several markets.[1] Is the volatility of a market leading the volatility of other markets? Is the volatility of an asset transmitted to another asset directly (through its conditional variance) or indirectly (through its conditional covariances)? Does a shock on a market increase the volatility on another market, and by how much? Is the impact the same for negative and positive shocks of the same amplitude? A related issue is whether the correlations between asset returns change over time.[2] Are they higher during periods of higher

---

[1] Kearney and Patton (2000) and Karolyi (1995) exemplify such studies.
[2] See Bollerslev (1990) and Longin and Solnik (1995).

219

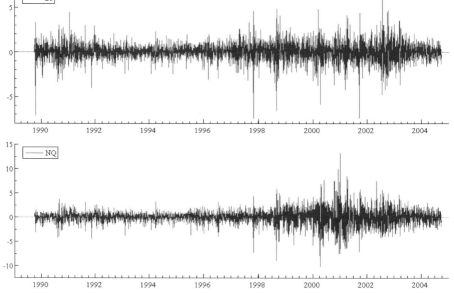

Figure 9.1   Dow Jones and Nasdaq indices. Daily returns in % from 1989-09-28 to 2004-09-27.

volatility (sometimes associated with financial crises)? Are they increasing in the long run, perhaps because of the globalization of financial markets? Such issues can be directly studied by using a multivariate model, and raise the question of the specification of the dynamics of covariances or correlations.

Another application of MGARCH models is the computation of time-varying hedge ratios. Traditionally, constant hedge ratios are estimated by OLS as the slope of a regression of the spot return on the futures return, because this is equivalent to estimating the ratio of the covariance between spot and futures over the variance of the futures. Since a bivariate MGARCH model for the spot and futures returns directly specifies their conditional variance-covariance matrix, the hedge ratio can be computed as a by-product of estimation and updated by using new observations as they become available. See Lien and Tse (2002) for a survey on hedging and additional references.

Given an estimated univariate GARCH model on a return series, we have seen in Chapter 6 that one can forecast the value-at-risk (VaR) of a long or short position. When considering a portfolio of assets, the portfolio return can be directly computed from the asset shares and returns. A GARCH model can be fitted to the portfolio returns for given weights. If the weight vector changes, the model has to be estimated again. On the contrary, if a multivariate GARCH model is fitted, the multivariate distribution of the returns can be directly used to compute the implied distribution of any portfolio. There is no need to re-estimate the model for different weight vectors. The multivariate approach is illustrated by Giot and Laurent (2003) using a trivariate example with a time-varying correlation model.

9.2 Estimating MGARCH Models with G@RCH

Estimating MGARCH models with G@RCH 6.0 is intended to be very simple. First click on G@RCH in the Modules group in the workspace window on the left-hand side of OxMetrics. Next change the **Category** to Models for financial data and the **Model class** to Multivariate GARCH models using G@RCH, then click on Formulate.

A list with all the variables of the database appears in the Database frame. To select variables that will enter your model, click on the variable name and then click on the << button. There are three possible statuses for each variable (see the list of statuses under the Selection frame): dependent variable (Y variable), regressor in the conditional mean (Mean), or regressor in the conditional variance (Variance). Several variables can be included in the conditional mean and the conditional variance equations and the same variable can be a regressor in both equations. Once the OK button is pressed, the Settings box automatically appears.

G@RCH 6.0 proposes seven different MGARCH models, namely the scalar BEKK, diagonal BEKK, RiskMetrics, CCC, DCC, OGARCH and GOGARCH models. These models are described in the next section.

Let us choose a scalar BEKK model on the two series presented in Section 9.1.

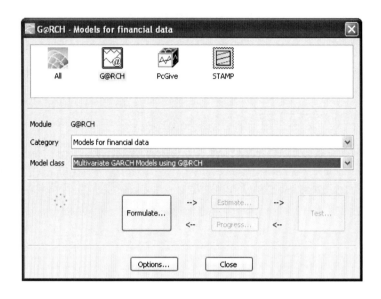

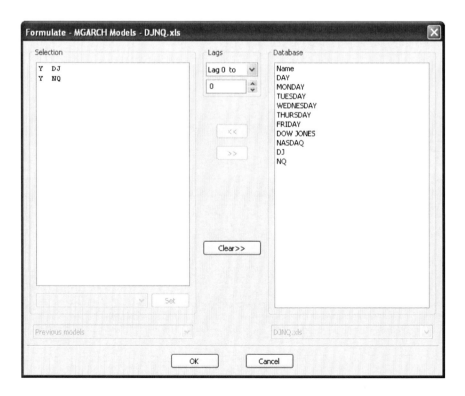

The program automatically opens a new dialog box Additional Settings before launching the estimation.

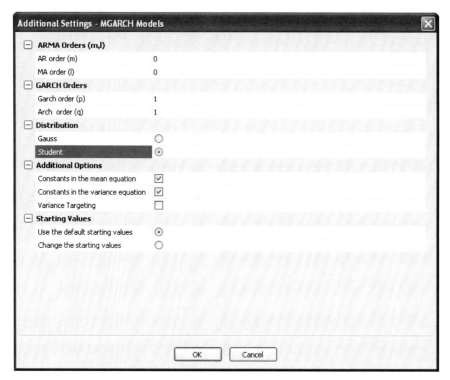

For the Scalar-BEKK model, the user is asked to chose the ARMA and GARCH orders, as well as the distribution for the error term (Normal or Student). There are also two options to control for the inclusion of a constant in the conditional mean and/or conditional variance-covariance equations. Analogous to the univariate package, the user can chose to apply variance targeting and change the starting values.

Finally, if default starting values are chosen, the program automatically opens the Estimate window and proposes options about the sample size.

When the variable corresponding to the date is correctly formatted, the sample can conveniently be fixed based on starting and ending date (see Chapter 9 of Doornik, 2007, for details). The number of forecasts can be also subtracted when out-of-sample forecasting is to be performed.

The models are estimated using a constrained maximum likelihood (ML) approach. The output "Box 1" corresponds to the one obtained after the estimation of a Scalar-BEKK(1,1) with a Student distribution.

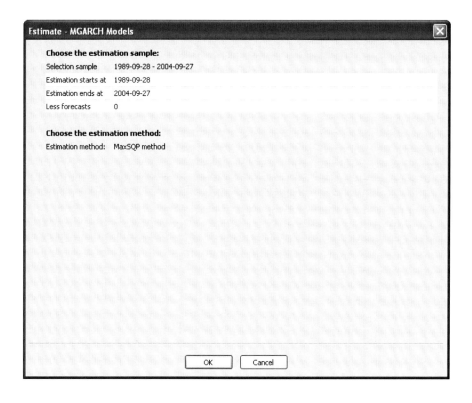

```
               Box 1 - Output of a Scalar-BEKK(1,1) with a Student distribution
    ********************************
    ** MG@RCH( 1) SPECIFICATIONS **
    ********************************
    Conditional Mean : ARMA (0, 0) model.
    No regressor in the conditional mean.
    Conditional Variance : Scalar BEKK (1, 1).
    No regressor in the conditional variance
    Multivariate Student distribution, with 8.04272 degrees of freedom.

    Strong convergence using numerical derivatives
    Log-likelihood = -9700.53
    Please wait : Computing the Std Errors ...

     Robust Standard Errors (Sandwich formula)
                    Coefficient  Std.Error  t-value  t-prob
    Cst1               0.064727   0.011457    5.649   0.0000
    Cst2               0.095830   0.014274    6.714   0.0000
    C_11               0.070598   0.0098203   7.189   0.0000
    C_12               0.053370   0.010987    4.858   0.0000
    C_22               0.061664   0.0077886   7.917   0.0000
    b_1                0.972292   0.0030826   315.4   0.0000
    a_1                0.226364   0.012753    17.75   0.0000
    df                 8.042718   0.75720     10.62   0.0000
    No. Observations :    3913   No. Parameters  :         8
    No. Series       :       2   Log Likelihood  : -9700.529
```

Ex-post, it is desirable to test the adequacy of the MGARCH model. New options are thus available after the estimation of the model when clicking on the Test... button of the main G@RCH box: Tests, Graphic Analysis, Forecasts, Exclusion Restrictions, Linear Restrictions and Store.

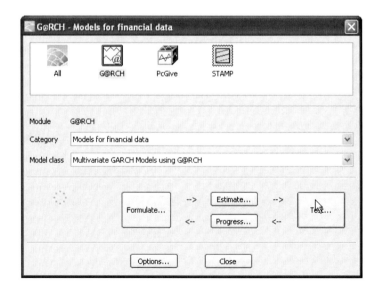

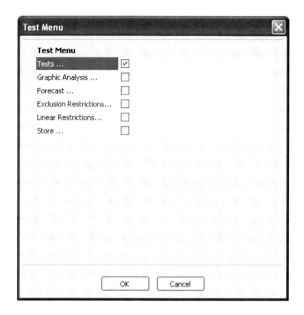

9.2.1 Misspecification Tests

The Tests... option allows to print some information criteria and to run different several misspecification tests. A distinction is made between univariate tests applied sequentially on the standardized residuals and multivariate tests. The following tests are available in G@RCH 6.0.

Univariate Tests

- Normality tests.
- Box/Pierce tests on standardized residuals.
- Box/Pierce tests on squared standardized residuals.

For more details about these tests, see Section 3.8.

Multivariate Tests

- A multivariate normality test.
- Hosking's Portmanteau test on standardized residuals.
- Hosking's Portmanteau test on squared standardized residuals.
- Li and McLeod test on standardized residuals.
- Li and McLeod test on squared standardized residuals.
- And two constant correlation tests (only after the estimation of a CCC model).

The multivariate tests are described in Section 9.7.

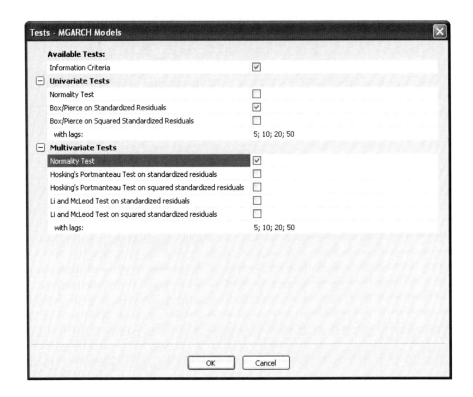

9.3 Graphics

The Graphic Analysis... option allows to plot different graphics, i.e. raw series, standardized residuals, conditional variances, conditional covariances and conditional correlation (for all or a subset of series).

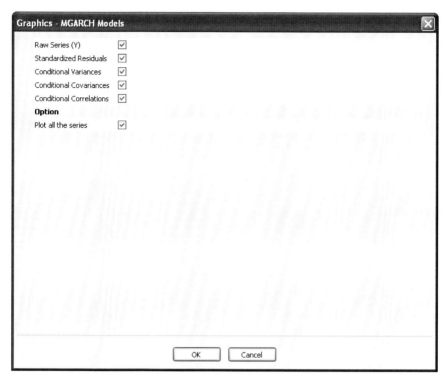

Figure 9.2 plots the conditional variances of the Dow Jones and NASDAQ given by the estimated Scalar-BEKK(1,1). Figures 9.3 and 9.4 plot respectively the conditional covariance and correlation between these two series.

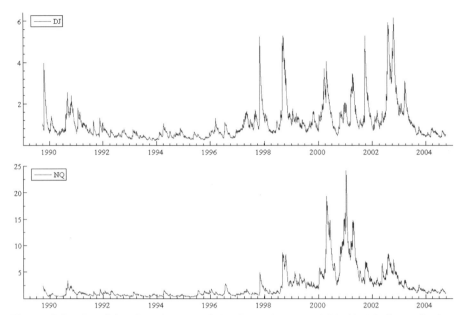

Figure 9.2   Conditional variances of the Dow Jones and NASDAQ for a Scalar-BEKK(1,1).

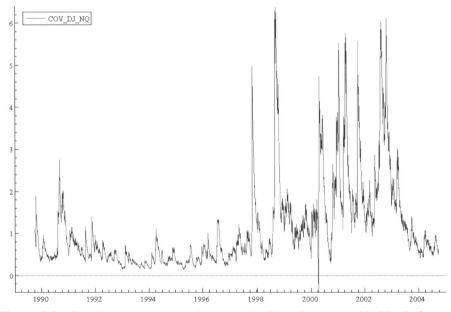

Figure 9.3   Conditional covariance between the Dow Jones and NASDAQ for a Scalar-BEKK(1,1).

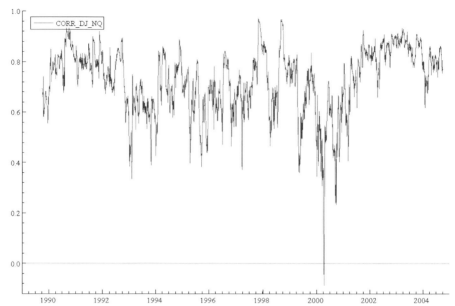

Figure 9.4 Conditional correlation between the Dow Jones and NASDAQ for a Scalar-BEKK(1,1).

Just as any other graphs in the OxMetrics environment, all graphs plotted from G@RCH can be easily edited (color, size,...) and exported in many formats (.eps, .ps, .wmf, .emf and .gwg).

9.4 Forecasts

With the Forecast... option, G@RCH 6.0 also provides forecasting tools: forecasts of both the conditional mean and the conditional variance-covariance matrix are available.

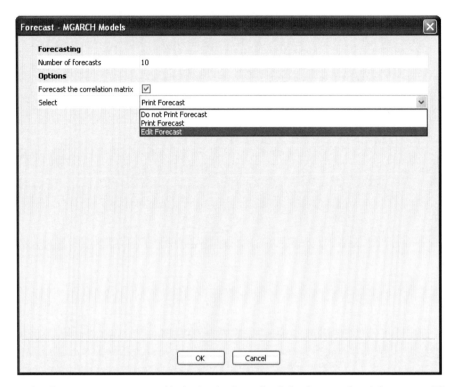

The first parameter to specify is the horizon h of the h-step-ahead forecasts. The default value is 10. Three options are available:

(1) Do not Print Forecast: to run the forecasting procedure without printing the fore-casts (useful if the user just want to store the forecasts);

(2) Print Forecasts: to print the forecasts in the output file;

(3) or Edit Forecasts: to edit the conditional mean forecasts in a MATRIX editor and the conditional variance-covariance forecasts in an ARRAY editor.

The next captures show 10 out-of-sample forecasts of the conditional mean and correlation (of an AR(1)-Scalar-BEKK(1,1) estimated on the Dow Jones-Nasdaq series) obtained via the option 'Edit Forecasts'.

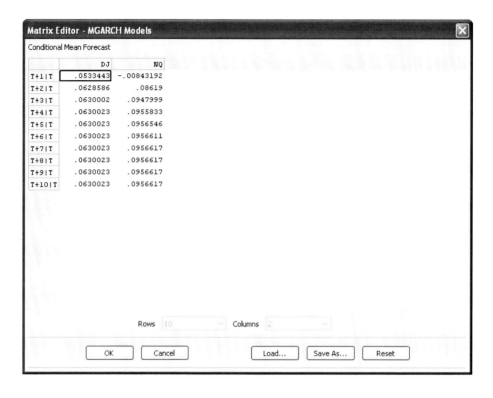

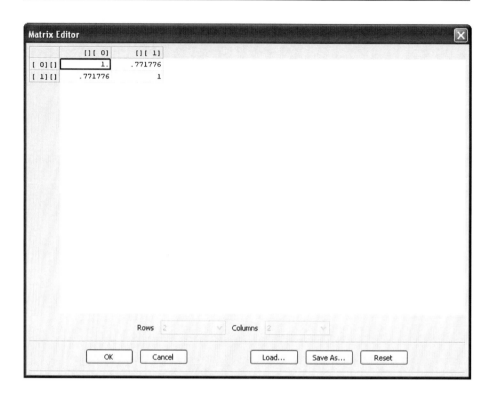

9.4.1 Exclusion Restrictions Dialog Box

The Exclusion Restrictions dialog box option allows you to select explanatory variables and test whether they are jointly significant. A more general form is the test for linear restrictions.

Mark all the variables you wish to include in the test in this Multiple-Selection List box. G@RCH tests whether the selected variables can be deleted from the model.

Note that this option is not vailable for some models (like the OGARCH).

9.4.2 Linear Restrictions Dialog Box

Tests for linear restrictions are specified in the form of a matrix R, and a vector r. These are entered as one matrix $[R : r]$ in the dialog. (This is more general than testing for exclusion restrictions).

The first four columns are the columns of R, specifying two restrictions. The last column is r, which specifies what the restrictions should add up to.

The dimensions of the matrix must be specified in the rows and columns fields. It is your responsibility to specify the right values, G@RCH will not try to work it out (because elements of a row may be spread over several lines).

Note that this option is not vailable for some models (like the OGARCH).

- **Rows** : The number of rows in the matrix.
- **Columns** : The number of columns in the matrix.
- **Matrix** : This window is a basic text editor in which you can edit a matrix file. Here you can enter the R:r matrix as in the above example.
- **Set to zero** : This could be useful to create an initial matrix. Select variables in the model box (this is a this multiple-selection list box) and press this button to specify the $R : r$ matrix which corresponds to the restriction that each selected variable has coefficient zero (so one row for each selected variable).
- **Load** : Enables you to load an existing matrix file into the editor. Any existing matrix in the editor will be lost.
- **Save** : Enables you to save the contents of the editor in an matrix file, so that it can be used again.

9.4.3 Store in Database Dialog

Finally, the residuals, standardized residuals, conditional means, conditional variances, conditional covariances, conditional correlations, and the h-step-ahead forecasts (of the conditional mean, variances, covariances and correlations) can be stored in the database as new variables. When selecting this option, a first window appears and the user selects the series to be stored. A default name is then proposed for this series but this name can be changed by selecting option 'Confirm names in OxMetrics'.

9.5 Overview of models

MGARCH models were initially developed in the late eighties and the first half of the nineties, and after a period of tranquility in the second half of the nineties, this area seems to be experimenting again a quick expansion phase. See Bauwens, Laurent, and Rombouts (2006) for a recent survey on MGARCH models.

Consider a vector stochastic process $\{y_t\}$ of dimension $N \times 1$. As usual, we condition on the sigma field, denoted by Ω_{t-1}, generated by the past information (here the y_t's) until time $t - 1$. We denote by θ a finite vector of parameters and we write:

$$y_t = \mu_t(\theta) + \epsilon_t, \tag{9.1}$$

where $\mu_t(\theta)$ is the conditional mean vector and,

$$\epsilon_t = H_t^{1/2}(\theta)z_t, \tag{9.2}$$

where $H_t^{1/2}(\theta)$ is a $N \times N$ positive definite matrix. Furthermore, we assume the $N \times 1$

random vector z_t to have the following first two moments:

$$E(z_t) = 0$$
$$Var(z_t) = I_N, \tag{9.3}$$

where I_N is the identity matrix of order N. We still have to explain what $H_t^{1/2}$ is (for convenience we leave out θ in the notation). To make this clear we calculate the conditional variance matrix of y_t:

$$
\begin{aligned}
Var(y_t|\Omega_{t-1}) = Var_{t-1}(y_t) &= Var_{t-1}(\epsilon_t) \\
&= H_t^{1/2} Var_{t-1}(z_t)(H_t^{1/2})' \\
&= H_t. \tag{9.4}
\end{aligned}
$$

Hence $H_t^{1/2}$ is any $N \times N$ positive definite matrix such that H_t is the conditional variance matrix of y_t, e.g. $H_t^{1/2}$ may be obtained by the Cholesky factorization of H_t. Both H_t and μ_t depend on the unknown parameter vector θ, which can in most cases be split into two disjoint parts, one for μ_t and one for H_t. A case where this is not true is that of GARCH-in-mean models, where μ_t is functionally dependent on H_t.

In the next subsections we review different specifications of H_t implemented in G@RCH 6.0. They differ in various aspects. We distinguish three non mutually exclusive approaches for constructing multivariate GARCH models: (i) direct generalizations of the univariate GARCH model of Bollerslev (1986), (ii) linear combinations of univariate GARCH models, (iii) conditional correlation models. In the first category we have BEKK and RiskMetrics models.In the second category we have (generalized) orthogonal models. The last category contains constant and dynamic conditional correlation models.

9.5.1 Conditional mean specification

Recall that the conditional mean equation is specified as follows:

$$y_t = \mu_t(\theta) + \epsilon_t, \tag{9.5}$$

where $\mu_t(\theta) = \{\mu_{1t}, \ldots, \mu_{Nt}\}$ is the conditional mean vector of y_t.

ARMAX specifications are available for all the MGARCH models described in the next sections. G@RCH 6.0 provides diagonal ARMAX models in the sense that an ARMAX specification is fitted on each univariate series, i.e.

$$\Psi_i\left(L\right)\left(y_{it} - \mu_{it}\right) = \Theta_i\left(L\right)\epsilon_{it}$$
$$\mu_{it} = \mu_i + \sum_{j=1}^{n_1} \delta_{ji} x_{j,t}, \tag{9.6}$$

where L is the lag operator[3], $\Psi_i\left(L\right) = 1 - \sum_{j=1}^{n} \psi_{ij} L^j$ and $\Theta_i\left(L\right) = 1 + \sum_{j=1}^{s} \theta_{ij} L^j$.

Note that an ARFIMA specification (see equation (3.8) in Chapter 3) is also available for CCC, DCC, OGARCH and GOGARCH models.

9.5.2 Generalizations of the univariate standard GARCH model

The models in this category are multivariate extensions of the univariate GARCH model. When we consider VARMA models for the conditional mean of several time series the number of parameters increases rapidly. The same happens for multivariate GARCH models as straightforward extensions of the univariate GARCH model. Furthermore, since H_t is a variance matrix, positive definiteness has to be ensured. To make the model tractable for applied purposes, additional structure may be imposed, for example in the form of factors or diagonal parameter matrices. This class of models lends itself to relatively easy theoretical derivations of stationarity and ergodicity conditions, and unconditional moments (see *e.g.* He and Teräsvirta, 2002a).

9.5.2.1 RiskMetrics and BEKK models

J.P.Morgan (1996) uses the exponentially weighted moving average model (EWMA) to forecast variance and covariances. Practitioners who study volatility processes often observe that their model is very close to the unit root case. To take this into account, Riskmetrics defines the variances and covariances as IGARCH type models (Engle and Bollerslev, 1986):

Definition 1. *The RiskMetrics model is defined as:*

$$H_t = (1 - \lambda)\epsilon_{t-1}\epsilon'_{t-1} + \lambda H_{t-1}, \tag{9.7}$$

or alternatively

$$H_t = \frac{(1 - \lambda)}{(1 - \lambda)^{t-1}} \sum_{i=1}^{t-1} \lambda^{i-1} \epsilon_{t-1}\epsilon'_{t-1}. \tag{9.8}$$

---

[3]Recall that $L^k y_t = y_{t-k}$.

The decay factor λ $(0 < \lambda < 1)$ proposed by Riskmetrics is equal to 0.94 for daily data and 0.97 for monthly data. The decay factor is not estimated but suggested by Riskmetrics. In this respect, this model is easy to work with in practice. However, imposing the same dynamics on every component in a multivariate GARCH model, no matter which data are used, is difficult to justify.

Engle and Kroner (1995) propose a parametrization for H_t that easily imposes its positivity, i.e. the BEKK model (the acronym comes from synthesized work on multivariate models by Baba, Engle, Kraft and Kroner).

Definition 2. *The BEKK(p,q) model is defined as:*

$$H_t = C'C + \sum_{i=1}^{q} A'_i \epsilon_{t-i} \epsilon'_{t-i} A_i + \sum_{j=1}^{p} G'_i H_{t-j} G_j, \tag{9.9}$$

where C, the A's and the G's matrices are of dimension $N \times N$ but C is upper triangular.

The original BEKK model is a bit more general since it involves a summation over K terms. We restrict K to be equal to 1. The BEKK model is actually a special case of the VEC model of Bollerslev, Engle, and Wooldridge (1988).

The number of ARCH and GARCH parameters in the BEKK(1,1) model is $N(5N+1)/2$. To reduce this number, and consequently to reduce the generality, one can impose a diagonal BEKK model, *i.e.* A_i and G_j in (9.9) are diagonal matrices.

Another way to reduce the number of parameters is to use a scalar BEKK model, *i.e.* A_i and G_j are equal to a scalar times a matrix of ones.

G@RCH 6.0 provides two of these models, i.e. the Diag-BEKK and Scalar-BEKK model. The Full-BEKK model will be available in the next release of G@RCH.

The Diag-BEKK and Scalar-BEKK (without explanatory variables) are covariance-stationary if $\sum_{i=1}^{q} a_{nn,i}^2 + \sum_{j=1}^{p} g_{nn,j}^2 < 1, \forall n = 1, \ldots, N, \sum_{i=1}^{q} a_i^2 + \sum_{j=1}^{p} g_j^2 < 1$, respectively. These conditions are imposed during the estimation.

When it exists, the unconditional variance matrix $\Sigma \equiv E(H_t)$ of the BEKK model (again without explanatory variables), is given by

$$vec(\Sigma) = \left[I_{N^2} - \sum_{i=1}^{q}(A_i \otimes A_i)' - \sum_{j=1}^{p}(G_j \otimes G_j)' \right]^{-1} vec(C'C), \tag{9.10}$$

where vec denotes the operator that stacks the columns of a matrix as a vector.

Similar expressions can be obtained for the Diag-BEKK and Scalar-BELL models.

Explanatory Variables in RiskMetrics and BEKK Models

As for univariate models, explanatory variables can be included in the volatlity equation. For RiskMetrics and BEKK models, we extend equations (9.7) and (9.9) by adding the folling term:

$$+F \cdot diag(|Z_t|) \cdot F', \tag{9.11}$$

where F is a $N \times n_2$ matrix and $diag(|Z_t|)$ is a $n_2 \times n_2$ diagonal matrix with $|Z_t|$ on the diagonal. The positivity of $|Z_t|$ and the quadratic form ensures the positive definiteness of the conditional variance-covariance.

Variance Targeting

What renders most MGARCH models difficult for estimation is their high number of parameters. A simple trick to ensure a reasonable value of the model-implied unconditional covariance matrix, which also helps to reduce the number of parameters in the maximization of the likelihood function, is referred to as variance targeting by Engle and Mezrich (1996). The conditional variance matrix of the BEKK model (and all its particular cases), may be expressed in terms of the unconditional variance matrix and other parameters. Doing so one can reparametrize the model using the unconditional variance matrix and replace it by a consistent estimator (before maximizing the likelihood).

Applying variance targeting to the BEKK models implies replacing CC' by unvec $\left[I_{N^2} - \sum_{i=1}^{q} (A_i \otimes A_i)' - \sum_{j=1}^{p} (G_j \otimes G_j)' \right] \bar{\Sigma}$, where $\bar{\Sigma}$ is the unconditional variance-covariance matrix of ϵ and unvec is the reverse of the vec operator.[4]

The difficulty when estimating a BEKK model is the high number of unknown parameters, even after imposing several restrictions. It is thus not surprising that these models are rarely used when the number of series is larger than 3 or 4.

To illustrate, we consider daily returns of three major exchange rates (available in /data/TXCH.xls), namely the EUR/USD, YEN/USD and GBP/USD from 1989 to 2001(3065 observations). We estimate three models by Gaussian-QMLE: RiskMetrics (with $\lambda = 0.94$), a Scalar-BEKK(1,1) and a Diag-BEKK(1,1).

The outputs are printed in the following box, respectively models MG@RCH(1), MG@RCH(2) and MG@RCH(3).

---

[4]When explanatory variables appear in the BEKK equaton and the variance targeting option is selected, these variables are simply centered as explained in Section 3.5.3.

```
                                                                 Box 2 - RiskMetrics
********************************
** MG@RCH( 1) SPECIFICATIONS **
********************************
Conditional Mean : ARMA (0, 0) model.
No regressor in the conditional mean.
Conditional Variance : RiskMetrics with lambda = 0.94.
No regressor in the conditional variance
Multivariate Normal distribution.

Strong convergence using numerical derivatives
Log-likelihood = -7316.96
Please wait : Computing the Std Errors ...

 Robust Standard Errors (Sandwich formula)
              Coefficient  Std.Error  t-value  t-prob
Cst1           -0.000114   0.016922 -0.006710  0.9946
Cst2            0.004883   0.017731   0.2754   0.7830
Cst3            0.008012   0.014596   0.5489   0.5831
No. Observations :    3065 No. Parameters  :       3
No. Series       :       3 Log Likelihood  : -7316.959
```

```
                                                                 Box 3 - Scalar-BEKK
********************************
** MG@RCH( 2) SPECIFICATIONS **
********************************
Conditional Mean : ARMA (0, 0) model.
No regressor in the conditional mean.
Conditional Variance : Scalar BEKK (1, 1).
No regressor in the conditional variance
Multivariate Normal distribution.

Strong convergence using numerical derivatives
Log-likelihood = -7107.94
Please wait : Computing the Std Errors ...

 Robust Standard Errors (Sandwich formula)
              Coefficient  Std.Error  t-value  t-prob
Cst1           -0.001123   0.010507  -0.1069   0.9149
Cst2           -0.005100   0.010189  -0.5005   0.6167
Cst3            0.003196   0.0092426  0.3458   0.7295
C_11            0.083025   0.013269   6.257    0.0000
C_12           -0.043454   0.0086911 -5.000    0.0000
C_13           -0.051536   0.0084118 -6.127    0.0000
C_22            0.069801   0.011343   6.153    0.0000
C_23            0.004576   0.0048022  0.9529   0.3407
C_33            0.046755   0.0098481  4.748    0.0000
b_1             0.962326   0.0074751  128.7    0.0000
a_1             0.255909   0.025445   10.06    0.0000
No. Observations :    3065 No. Parameters  :      11
No. Series       :       3 Log Likelihood  : -7107.941
```

```
                                                                 Box 3 - Diag-BEKK
********************************
** MG@RCH( 3) SPECIFICATIONS **
********************************
Conditional Mean : ARMA (0, 0) model.
No regressor in the conditional mean.
Conditional Variance : Diagonal BEKK (1, 1).
No regressor in the conditional variance
Multivariate Normal distribution.

Strong convergence using numerical derivatives
Log-likelihood = -7101.29
Please wait : Computing the Std Errors ...

 Robust Standard Errors (Sandwich formula)
              Coefficient  Std.Error  t-value  t-prob
Cst1           -0.001710   0.010564  -0.1619   0.8714
Cst2           -0.005196   0.010402  -0.4995   0.6174
Cst3            0.003640   0.0097962  0.3716   0.7102
C_11            0.080764   0.013027   6.200    0.0000
C_12           -0.047269   0.0093742 -5.042    0.0000
C_13           -0.054690   0.016212  -3.374    0.0008
C_22            0.072533   0.011347   6.392    0.0000
C_23            0.002792   0.0040173  0.6949   0.4872
C_33            0.047637   0.011798   4.038    0.0001
b_1.11          0.966493   0.0055223  175.0    0.0000
b_1.22          0.958830   0.0064010  149.8    0.0000
b_1.33          0.959691   0.015326   62.62    0.0000
a_1.11          0.236666   0.018056   13.11    0.0000
a_1.22          0.268682   0.021555   12.46    0.0000
a_1.33          0.263990   0.050038   5.276    0.0000
No. Observations :    3065 No. Parameters  :      15
No. Series       :       3 Log Likelihood  : -7101.289
```

The three models are nested and thus LRT tests or information criteria can be used to select the most appropriate one.

A useful tool is available in G@RCH to compare nested models. Clicking on the Progress... button in the main G@RCH box launches a new dialog box with some information about the previously estimated models, i.e. MG@RCH(1) for RiskMetrics, MG@RCH(2) for Scalar-BEKK and MG@RCH(3) for Diag-BEKK. This box allows to select the models to be compared in terms of information criteria.

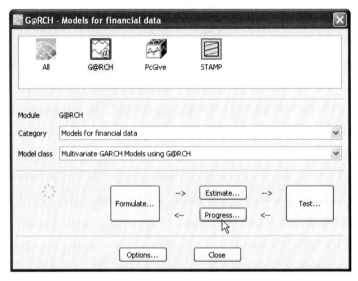

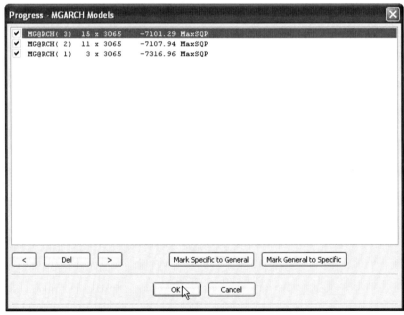

The output given in the next box suggest that the second model (Scalar-BEKK) is preferred by the Schwarz and Hannan-Quinn criteria while the Diag-BEKK is chosen by the Akaike criterion (know to favour the less parsimonious specification).

```
                                                                    Box 4 - Progress
Progress to date
Model        T     p      log-likelihood        SC         HQ        AIC
MGØRCH( 1)  3065   3  MaxSQP    -7316.9591     4.7824     4.7786     4.7765
MGØRCH( 2)  3065  11  MaxSQP    -7107.9414     4.6669<    4.6531<    4.6453
MGØRCH( 3)  3065  15  MaxSQP    -7101.2893     4.6731     4.6542     4.6436<
```

9.5.3 Linear combinations of univariate GARCH models

In this category, we consider models that are linear combinations of several univariate models, each of which is not necessarily a standard GARCH (*e.g.* the EGARCH model of Nelson, 1991, the APARCH model of Ding, Granger, and Engle, 1993, the fractionally integrated GARCH of Baillie, Bollerslev, and Mikkelsen, 1996).

In the orthogonal GARCH model, the observed data are assumed to be generated by an orthogonal transformation of N (or a smaller number of) univariate GARCH processes. The matrix of the linear transformation is the orthogonal matrix (or a selection) of eigenvectors of the population unconditional covariance matrix of the standardized returns. In the generalized version, this matrix must only be invertible. The orthogonal models can also be considered as factor models, where the factors are univariate GARCH-type processes.

In the orthogonal GARCH model of Kariya (1988) and Alexander and Chibumba (1997), the $N \times N$ time-varying variance matrix H_t is generated by $m \leq N$ univariate GARCH models.

Definition 3. *The O-GARCH$(1, 1, m)$ model is defined as:*

$$y_t = \mu_t + \epsilon_t \tag{9.12}$$

$$\epsilon_t = V^{1/2} u_t \tag{9.13}$$

$$u_t = Z_m f_t, \tag{9.14}$$

where $V = \text{diag}\,(v_1, v_2, \ldots, v_N)$, with v_i the population variance of ϵ_{it}, and Z_m is a matrix of dimension $N \times m$ given by:

$$Z_m = P_m L_m^{1/2} = P_m \text{diag}\,(l_1^{1/2} \ldots l_m^{1/2}), \tag{9.15}$$

$l_1 \geq \ldots \geq l_m > 0$ being the m largest eigenvalues of the population correlation matrix of ϵ_t (or of the covariance matrix of u_t), and P_m the $N \times m$ matrix of associated *(mutually orthogonal) eigenvectors. The vector $f_t = (f_{1t} \ldots f_{mt})'$ is a random process such that:*

$$\mathrm{E}_{t-1}(f_t) = 0 \quad and \quad \mathrm{Var}_{t-1}(f_t) = \Sigma_t = diag\left(\sigma^2_{f_{1t}}, \ldots, \sigma^2_{f_{mt}}\right), \qquad (9.16)$$

$$\sigma^2_{f_{it}} = (1 - \alpha_i - \beta_i) + \alpha_i f^2_{i,t-1} + \beta_i \sigma^2_{f_{i,t-1}} \qquad i = 1, \ldots, m. \qquad (9.17)$$

Consequently,

$$H_t = \mathrm{Var}_{t-1}(\epsilon_t) = V^{1/2} V_t V'^{1/2} \quad where \quad V_t = \mathrm{Var}_{t-1}(u_t) = Z_m \Sigma_t Z'_m. \quad (9.18)$$

The parameters of the model are V, L_m, and the parameters of the GARCH factors (α_i's and β_i's). The number of parameters is N(N+5)/2 (if $m = N$). In practice, V and L_m are replaced by their sample counterparts, and m is chosen by principal component analysis applied to the standardized residuals $\hat{u}_t$. Alexander (2001a, section 7.4.3) illustrates the use of the O-GARCH model. She emphasizes that using a small number of principal components compared to the number of assets is the strength of the approach (in one example, she fixes m at 2 for 12 assets). However, when $m < N$, the conditional variance matrix has reduced rank and is very likely to be singular (not invertible). In this case, diagnostic tests based on standardized residuals (which depend on the inverse of H_t) are not reported. Provided that H_t is invertible, standardized residuals are computed as follows $\epsilon_t = H_t^{-1/2}(y_t - \mu_t)$.

Note also that equation (9.17) is a GARCH(1,1) model with unit unconditional variance. Interestingly, G@RCH 6.0 permits the choice of all the specifications presented in Chapter 4 rather than just restricting to the standard GARCH model. Furthermore, explanatory variable can be included in the conditional variance of the m factors. For instance, for a GARCH(1,1) with an explanatory variable x_t, equation (9.17) becomes

$$\sigma^2_{f_{it}} = \sigma^*_i + \gamma x_t + \alpha_i f^2_{i,t-1} + \beta_i \sigma^2_{f_{i,t-1}}, \qquad (9.19)$$

where $\sigma^*_i = (1 - \alpha_i - \beta_i) - \gamma \bar{x}_i$ and $\bar{x}_i$ is the sample average of x_t (recalling that by construction the unconditional variance of $f_{it} = 1$).[5]

Estimation of the OGARCH model is done in three steps.

(1) The conditional mean equation (μ_t) is obtained by estimating N models by QMLE with normal errors. If $\mu_t = \mu$ the sample average of y_t is used instead.

---

[5]Alternatively, the GARCH(1,1) can be rewritten $\sigma^2_{f_{it}} = (1 - \alpha_i - \beta_i) + \gamma(x_t - \bar{x}) + \alpha_i f^2_{i,t-1} + \beta_i \sigma^2_{f_{i,t-1}}$.

Note that explanatory variables can be included in the μ_t as well as an AR(FI)MA specification.[6]

(2) P_m and L_m are computed by means of a principal component analysis (a scree plot is provided to help the user to chose m if the relevant option is selected).

(3) Finally, m GARCH-type models are estimated on $f_{it}, i = 1, \ldots, M$ by QMLE (note that standard errors are not corrected for the uncertainty of the first two steps).

To illustrate the OGARCH model, let us consider the daily return series of the Dow Jones and Nadaq series (`/data/DJNQ.xls`).

First, the variables are selected. A dummy variable FRIDAY is considered for the conditional variance of the m factors.

Then the OGARCH model is selected.

We chose an AR(1) term for the conditional mean and instead of the GARCH (1,1) of equation (9.19), we select a GJR(1,1) for the variance of the factors. In the Option 'Principal Components Options', We set the number of principal component (or factors) to $m = 0$ and enable option 'Scree Plot' to plot the scree plot before choising m. The scree plot is given below. We chose $m = N = 2$.

The conditional variance, covariance and correlation produced by the fitted model are plotted respectively in Figures 9.5,9.6,9.7.

---

[6]OGARCH models do not allow for ARCH-in-Mean effects.

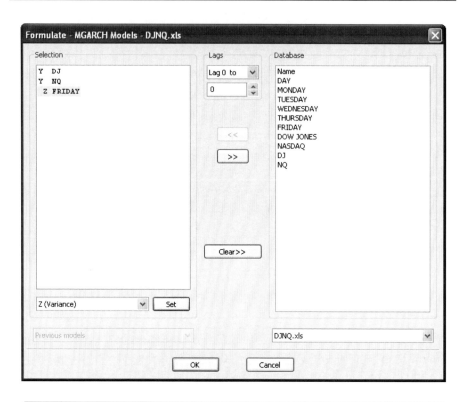

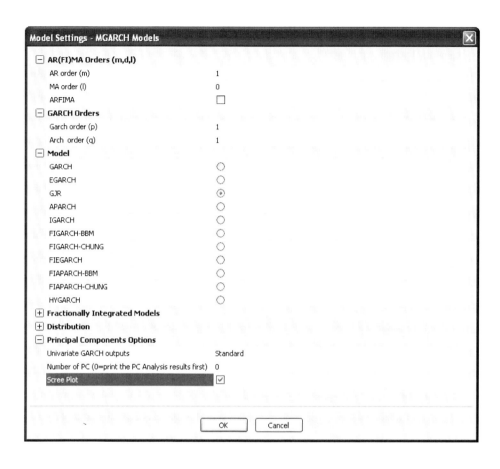

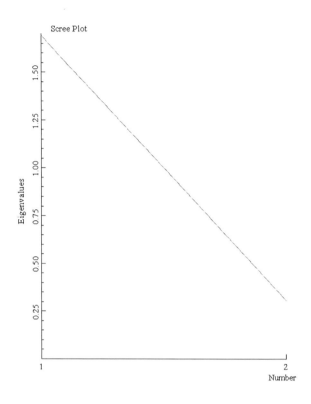

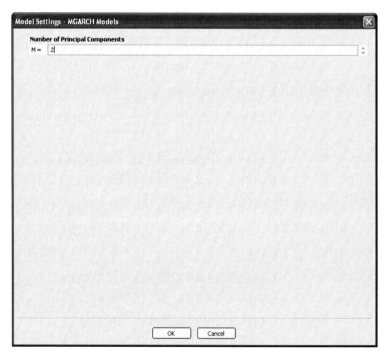

```
                           Box 5 - OGARCH STEP 1: AR(1)
-------------------------Estimating the univariate GARCH model for DJ-------------------------


  ********************
  ** SPECIFICATIONS **
  ********************
Dependent variable : DJ
Mean Equation : ARMA (1, 0) model.
No regressor in the conditional mean
Variance Equation : GARCH (0, 0) model.
No regressor in the conditional variance
Normal distribution.


Strong convergence using numerical derivatives
Log-likelihood = -5596.64
Please wait : Computing the Std Errors ...

  Robust Standard Errors (Sandwich formula)
                  Coefficient  Std.Error  t-value  t-prob
Cst(M)              0.033489    0.016156    2.073   0.0383
AR(1)              -0.001076    0.023241  -0.04630  0.9631
Cst(V)              1.022913    0.043648   23.44    0.0000

No. Observations :     3913  No. Parameters  :       3
Mean (Y)         :   0.03369  Variance (Y)    :   1.02307
Skewness (Y)     :  -0.30325  Kurtosis (Y)    :   8.12068
Log Likelihood   : -5596.639

Estimated Parameters Vector :
 0.033489;-0.001076; 1.022913

-------------------------Estimating the univariate GARCH model for NQ-------------------------


  ********************
  ** SPECIFICATIONS **
  ********************
Dependent variable : NQ
Mean Equation : ARMA (1, 0) model.
No regressor in the conditional mean
Variance Equation : GARCH (0, 0) model.
No regressor in the conditional variance
Normal distribution.


Strong convergence using numerical derivatives
Log-likelihood = -7248.07
Please wait : Computing the Std Errors ...

  Robust Standard Errors (Sandwich formula)
                  Coefficient  Std.Error  t-value  t-prob
Cst(M)              0.035089    0.025376    1.383   0.1668
AR(1)               0.027975    0.026912    1.040   0.2986
Cst(V)              2.379124    0.10661    22.32    0.0000

No. Observations :     3913  No. Parameters  :       3
Mean (Y)         :   0.03527  Variance (Y)    :   2.38111
Skewness (Y)     :  -0.01238  Kurtosis (Y)    :   8.76442
Log Likelihood   : -7248.073

Estimated Parameters Vector :
 0.035089; 0.027975; 2.379124
```

```
                         Box 6 - OGARCH STEP 2: PC
PC Analysis
-----------------


Principal Components Analysis on the Correlation matrix


    Component    Eigenvalue   Proportion   Cumulative
       1.0000       1.6929      0.84647      0.84647
       2.0000       0.30706     0.15353      1.0000

Eigenvectors


              PC_1         PC_2
DJ         -0.70711      0.70711
NQ         -0.70711     -0.70711

Correlation between the PC and the variables

              PC_1         PC_2
DJ         -0.92004      0.39183
NQ         -0.92004     -0.39183

O-GARCH rotation matrix
-----------------------
Rotation matrix (Z_m = P_m L_m^1/2 with m=2)
     -0.92004      0.39183
     -0.92004     -0.39183
```

```
                         Box 7 - OGARCH STEP 3: GARCH on PC
ML Estimation of the GARCH-type models on the unobserved factors
--------------------------------------------------------------------------------------------

--------------------------Estimating the univariate GARCH model for PC(1)--------------------------


********************
** SPECIFICATIONS **
********************
Dependent variable : PC(1)
Mean Equation : ARMA (0, 0) model.
No regressor in the conditional mean
Variance Equation : GJR (1, 1) model.
          Variance Targeting
1 regressor(s) in the conditional variance.
Normal distribution.

Strong convergence using numerical derivatives
Log-likelihood = -4916.33
Please wait : Computing the Std Errors ...

  Robust Standard Errors (Sandwich formula)
                Coefficient  Std.Error  t-value  t-prob
FRIDAY (V)         0.155899   0.064006    2.436   0.0149
ARCH(Alpha1)       0.112544   0.026261    4.286   0.0000
GARCH(Beta1)       0.923963   0.017442   52.97    0.0000
GJR(Gamma1)       -0.093986   0.026911   -3.492   0.0005
sigma^2           -0.020710

No. Observations :     3913  No. Parameters  :        4
Mean (Y)         :  0.00000  Variance (Y)    :  1.00000
Skewness (Y)     :  0.15700  Kurtosis (Y)    :  7.66192
Log Likelihood   : -4916.333

The sample mean of squared residuals was used to start recursion.
Positivity & stationarity constraints are not computed because there are
explanatory variables in the conditional variance equation.

Estimated Parameters Vector :
 0.155899; 0.112544; 0.923963;-0.093986
```

```
--------------------------Estimating the univariate GARCH model for PC(2)--------------------------


*********************
** SPECIFICATIONS **
*********************
Dependent variable : PC(2)
Mean Equation : ARMA (0, 0) model.
No regressor in the conditional mean
Variance Equation : GJR (1, 1) model.
          Variance Targeting
1 regressor(s) in the conditional variance.
Normal distribution.

Strong convergence using numerical derivatives
Log-likelihood = -4804.16
Please wait : Computing the Std Errors ...

 Robust Standard Errors (Sandwich formula)
               Coefficient  Std.Error  t-value  t-prob
FRIDAY (V)        0.061350   0.053089    1.156  0.2479
ARCH(Alpha1)      0.037768   0.010111    3.735  0.0002
GARCH(Beta1)      0.952159  0.0098491   96.67   0.0000
GJR(Gamma1)       0.013421   0.010270    1.307  0.1914
sigma^2          -0.008914

No. Observations :      3913  No. Parameters  :        4
Mean (Y)         : -0.00000  Variance (Y)    :  1.00000
Skewness (Y)     :  0.36774  Kurtosis (Y)    : 10.02964
Log Likelihood   : -4804.160

The sample mean of squared residuals was used to start recursion.
Positivity & stationarity constraints are not computed because there are
explanatory variables in the conditional variance equation.

Estimated Parameters Vector :
 0.061350; 0.037768; 0.952159; 0.013421

Summary Statistics
--------------------
No. Observations :      3913  No. Parameters  :       12
No. Series       :         2  Log Likelihood  :-10180.531
```

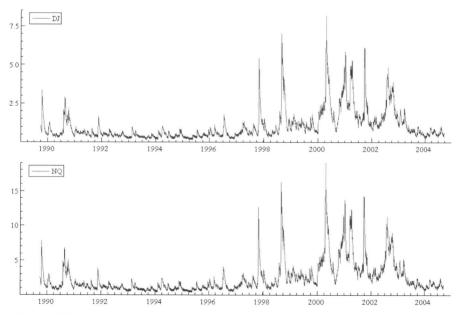

Figure 9.5   Conditional variances of the AR(1)-GJR(1,1)-OGARCH(2) model.

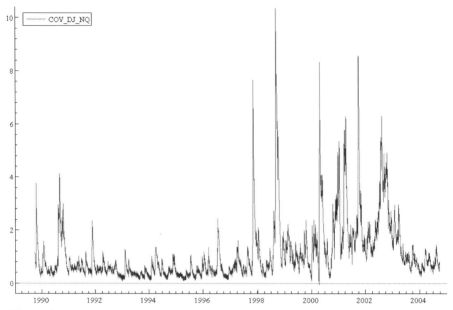

Figure 9.6   Conditional covariance of the AR(1)-GJR(1,1)-OGARCH(2) model.

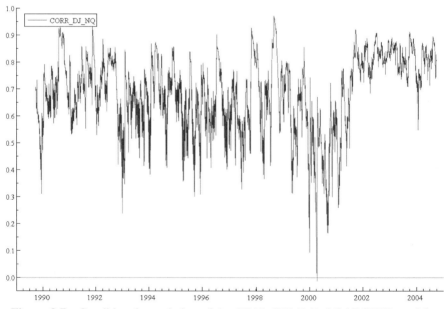

Figure 9.7   Conditional correlation of the AR(1)-GJR(1,1)-OGARCH(2) model.

van der Weide (2002) proposes a generalization of the OGARCH model. In the
G(eneralized)O-GARCH, the orthogonality condition assumed in the O-GARCH model

is relaxed by assuming that the matrix Z in the relation $u_t = Zf_t$ is square and invertible, rather than orthogonal. The matrix Z has N^2 parameters and is not restricted to be triangular.

Definition 4. *The GO-GARCH(1, 1) model is defined as in Definition 3, where $m = N$ and $Z_m = Z = PL^{1/2}U$ is a non-singular matrix of parameters and U is orthogonal. The implied conditional correlation matrix of ϵ_t can be expressed as:*

$$R_t = J_t^{-1}V_tJ_t^{-1}, \quad \text{where } J_t = (V_t \odot I_m)^{1/2} \text{ and } V_t = Z\Sigma_tZ'. \tag{9.20}$$

P and L are defined as above (from the eigenvectors and eigenvalues). The O-GARCH model (when $m = N$) corresponds to the particular choice $U = I_N$. More generally, van der Weide (2002) expresses U as the product of $N(N - 1)/2$ rotation matrices:

$$U = \prod_{i<j} G_{ij}(\delta_{ij}), \quad -\pi \le \delta_{ij} \le \pi, \quad i, j = 1, 2, \dots n, \tag{9.21}$$

where $G_{ij}(\delta_{ij})$ performs a rotation in the plane spanned by the i-th and the j-th vectors of the canonical basis of $\mathbb{R}^N$ over an angle δ_{ij}. For example, in the trivariate case,

$$G_{12} = \begin{pmatrix} \cos\delta_{12} & \sin\delta_{12} & 0 \\ -\sin\delta_{12} & \cos\delta_{12} & 0 \\ 0 & 0 & 1 \end{pmatrix}, \quad G_{13} = \begin{pmatrix} \cos\delta_{13} & 0 & -\sin\delta_{13} \\ 0 & 1 & 0 \\ -\sin\delta_{13} & 0 & \cos\delta_{13} \end{pmatrix},$$
$$\tag{9.22}$$

and G_{23} has the block with $\cos\delta_{23}$ and $\sin\delta_{23}$ functions in the right low corner. The $N(N - 1)/2$ rotation angles are parameters to be estimated.

For estimation, van der Weide (2002) replaces in a first step P and L by their sample counterparts and the remaining parameters (those of U) are estimated together with the parameters of the GARCH factors in a second step.

The orthogonal models are particular F-GARCH models and thus are nested in the BEKK model. As a consequence, their properties follow from those of the BEKK model. In particular, it is obvious that the (G)O-GARCH model is covariance-stationary if the m univariate GARCH processes are themselves stationary.

Estimation of the GO-GARCH model is done in three steps.

(1) The conditional mean equation (μ_t) is obtained by estimating N models by QMLE with normal errors. If $\mu_t = \mu$ the sample average of y_t is used instead. Note that explanatory variables can be included in the μ_t as well as an AR(FI)MA specification.

(2) P_m and L_m are computed by means of a principal component analysis. Note that the GO-GARCH imposes $m = N$.

(3) Finally, U' and the GARCH parameters are estimated by QMLE. Note also that $f_t = U'L^{-1/2}P'u_t$, where u_t and f_t are $m \times 1$ vectors and U is a function of δ.

To illustrate this model, we extend the previous model by considering the GO-GARCH instead of the OGARCH. Since we already chose $m = N = 2$ for the OGARCH model, the first two steps are identical and thus we only report the results of the last step.

```
                              Box 8 - GO-GARCH STEP 3
GO-GARCH of Van der Weide (JAE, 2002)

*****************************************
Warning: Maximization of the full model
*****************************************

Estimated U matrix
        0.77391        -0.63329
        0.63329         0.77391

Non-singular matrix (Z = P L^1/2 U)
       -0.96017        -0.27941
       -0.46389        -0.88589

Strong convergence using numerical derivatives
Log-likelihood = -9430.15
Please wait : Computing the Std Errors ...

  Robust Standard Errors (Sandwich formula)
                  Coefficient  Std.Error  t-value  t-prob
Part: U Matrix
delta_1             0.685800    0.036040    19.03   0.0000
Part: PC_1
FRIDAY (V)          0.218058    0.090096     2.420  0.0156
ARCH(Alpha1)        0.092194    0.018685     4.934  0.0000
GARCH(Beta1)        0.932575    0.013351    69.85   0.0000
GJR(Gamma1)        -0.075669    0.019852    -3.812  0.0001
Part: PC_2
FRIDAY (V)         -0.033401    0.026854    -1.244  0.2136
ARCH(Alpha1)        0.084264    0.016095     5.236  0.0000
GARCH(Beta1)        0.928573    0.011515    80.64   0.0000
GJR(Gamma1)        -0.031396    0.013741    -2.285  0.0224

No. Observations :    3913  No. Parameters   :         9
No. Series       :       2  Log Likelihood   : -9430.152

Summary Statistics
---------------------
No. Observations :    3913  No. Parameters   :        13
No. Series       :       2  Log Likelihood   : -9890.189
```

Comparing the summary statistics of the OGARCH and GO-GARCH models, we conclude that the later model clearly outperforms the former in terms of log-likelihood (-9890.189 vs. -10180.53 for one more parameter). Interestingly, since the OGARCH model corresponds to the particular choice $U = I_N$, we can easily test the null hypothesis of an orthogonal linkage by testing $H_0 : \delta_1 = 0$. The p-value of the corresponding t-test reported in the above output is 0.0000. This is another indication of the primacy of the GO-GARCH model.

As pointed out recently by Boswijk and van der Weide (2006), the practical power of the O-GARCH has been lost in the GO-GARCH of van der Weide (2002), i.e. the fact that all GARCH parameters can be conveniently estimated by appealing to univariate

GARCH model for the the principal components of the original series.

Boswijk and van der Weide (2006) have proposed an alternative method for estimating the GO-GARCH model that makes it more attractive from a purely practical point of view. The price to pay is a loss of efficiency.

Let us recall from Definition 3 that $u_t = Z f_t$ (when $m = N$) and from the GO-GARCH model that $Z = PL^{1/2}U$. Thus, $u_t = PL^{1/2}U f_t = PL^{1/2}s_t$, where $s_t = U f_t$ is the standardized and orthogonalized version of u_t. It is straightforward to show that $s_t = L^{-1/2}P'u_t$.

The idea of Boswijk and van der Weide (2006) is to identify U from the (cross-) autocorrelation structure of $s_t s_t'$.

Consider the linear projection of $f_t f_t'$ on $f_{t-1}f_{t-1}'$

$$
\begin{bmatrix}
f_{1t}^2 & \cdots & f_{1t}f_{mt} \\
\vdots & \ddots & \vdots \\
f_{mt}f_{1t} & \cdots & f_{mt}^2
\end{bmatrix}
=
\begin{bmatrix}
a_1 & \cdots & 0 \\
\vdots & \ddots & \vdots \\
0 & \cdots & a_m
\end{bmatrix}
+
\begin{bmatrix}
b_1^2 f_{1,t-1}^2 & \cdots & 0 \\
\vdots & \ddots & \vdots \\
0 & \cdots & b_m^2 f_{m,t-1}^2
\end{bmatrix}
+ e_t,
$$

or in matrix form,

$$
f_t f_t' = D_a + D_b \odot f_{t-1}f_{t-1}' \odot D_b + e_t, \tag{9.23}
$$

where $\odot$ denotes the Hadamar product, D_a and D_b are diagonal, and e_t is uncorrelated to $f_{t-1}f_{t-1}'$.

Now suppose that we estimate the following model:

$$
f_t f_t' = A + B f_{t-1}f_{t-1}' B + v_t, \tag{9.24}
$$

by means of NLS, i.e. by minimizing $\sum_{t=1}^{T} tr(v_t^2)$ over symmetric matrices A and B. Then the pseudo-true values of A and B will be diagonal (under some conditions on fourth-order moments; see Boswijk and van der Weide, 2006), although not equal to D_a and D_b.

Therefore, using $s_t = U f_t$, if we estimate:

$$
s_t s_t' = C + Q s_{t-1}s_{t-1}' Q + w_t, \tag{9.25}
$$

over symmetric matrices C and Q, then the pseudo-true values will satisfy $C = U A U'$ and $Q = U B U'$ for diagonal matrices A and B. This implies that we may estimate U as eigenvectors from $\hat{Q}$ (or $\hat{C}$).

The resulting estimator $\hat{U}$ may be used to construct $\hat{Z} = \hat{P}\hat{L}^{1/2}\hat{U}$, and hence $\hat{f}_t = \hat{Z}^{-1}u_t$.

The diagonal variance matrix V_t may be estimated from $\hat{f}_t$ using univariate GARCH models. In principle different models for the different components are possible. Some empirical applications and simulations suggest that the new procedure is worth considering. A formal (asymptotic) theory of inference is not yet available.

To illustrate this model, we estimate again the same model on the Dow Jones and Nasdaq series with the NLS estimation procedure for the GO-GARCH model.

The first step (conditional mean) is the same than for the OGARCH and GO-GARCH-ML models and thus not reported.

Let us now concentrate on the next two steps. The output reported in Box 9 corresponds to the NLS part. This output contains the estimated Q matrix of equation (9.25), the estimated U matrix (eigenvectors of $\hat{Q}$) and the rotation matrix $\hat{Z} = \hat{P}\hat{L}^{1/2}\hat{U}$.

```
                          Box 9 - GO-GARCH STEP 2 : NLS
NLS Estimation of the rotation matrix
----------------------------------------------

NLS function value: -21.9209
Estimated Q matrix (symmetric)
    -0.39786      -0.053886
    -0.053886     -0.44841
Estimated U matrix
     0.84398      -0.53637
    -0.53637      -0.84398
Non-singular matrix (Z = P L^1/2 U)
    -0.98666       0.16279
    -0.56633       0.82418
```

The last part of the output concern the estimation of the $m = N$ univariate GJR models estimatd on $\hat{f}_t = \hat{Z}^{-1}u_t$.

```
                          Box 10 - GO-GARCH STEP 3
ML Estimation of the GARCH-type models on the unobserved factors
--------------------------------------------------------------------

---------------------------Estimating the univariate GARCH model for PC(1)---------------------------


*********************
** SPECIFICATIONS **
*********************
Dependent variable : PC(1)
Mean Equation : ARMA (0, 0) model.
No regressor in the conditional mean
Variance Equation : GJR (1, 1) model.
             Variance Targeting
1 regressor(s) in the conditional variance.
Normal distribution.

Strong convergence using numerical derivatives
Log-likelihood = -5128.23
Please wait : Computing the Std Errors ...

  Robust Standard Errors (Sandwich formula)
                  Coefficient  Std.Error  t-value  t-prob
FRIDAY (V)          0.223481    0.087390    2.557   0.0106
ARCH(Alpha1)        0.095263    0.018765    5.077   0.0000
GARCH(Beta1)        0.932051    0.013465   69.22    0.0000
GJR(Gamma1)        -0.081431    0.019808   -4.111   0.0000
sigma^2            -0.031317

No. Observations :      3913  No. Parameters  :        4
Mean (Y)          :  -0.00000  Variance (Y)    :  1.00001
Skewness (Y)      :   0.28444  Kurtosis (Y)    :  8.23344
Log Likelihood    : -5128.230

The sample mean of squared residuals was used to start recursion.
Positivity & stationarity constraints are not computed because there are
explanatory variables in the conditional variance equation.

Estimated Parameters Vector :
  0.223481; 0.095263; 0.932051;-0.081431
```

```
-------------------------Estimating the univariate GARCH model for PC(2)-------------------------

*********************
** SPECIFICATIONS **
*********************
Dependent variable : PC(2)
Mean Equation : ARMA (0, 0) model.
No regressor in the conditional mean
Variance Equation : GJR (1, 1) model.
               Variance Targeting
1 regressor(s) in the conditional variance.
Normal distribution.

Weak convergence (no improvement in line search) using numerical derivatives
Log-likelihood = -4321.13
Please wait : Computing the Std Errors ...

 Robust Standard Errors (Sandwich formula)
                Coefficient  Std.Error  t-value  t-prob
FRIDAY (V)        -0.025539   0.027898  -0.9154  0.3600
ARCH(Alpha1)       0.052197  0.0084970    6.143  0.0000
GARCH(Beta1)       0.932751   0.010955    85.14  0.0000
GJR(Gamma1)        0.024557   0.012732    1.929  0.0538
sigma^2            0.007884

No. Observations :      3913  No. Parameters  :        4
Mean (Y)         :  -0.00000  Variance (Y)    :  1.00000
Skewness (Y)     :  -0.17151  Kurtosis (Y)    : 12.14008
Log Likelihood   : -4321.129

The sample mean of squared residuals was used to start recursion.
Positivity & stationarity constraints are not computed because there are
explanatory variables in the conditional variance equation.

Estimated Parameters Vector :
-0.025539; 0.052197; 0.932751; 0.024557

Summary Statistics
--------------------
No. Observations :      3913  No. Parameters  :       13
No. Series       :         2  Log Likelihood  : -9909.396
```

The log-likelihood value of this model (-9909.396, see Summary Statistics) is is lower than the one of the ML-GOGARCH of van der Weide (2002) but is much bigger than the OGARCH model.

9.5.4 Conditional correlation models

This section collects models that may be viewed as nonlinear combinations of univariate GARCH models. This allows for models where one can specify separately, on the one hand, the individual conditional variances, and on the other hand, the conditional correlation matrix. For models of this category, theoretical results on stationarity, ergodicity and moments may not be so straightforward to obtain as for models presented in the preceding sections. Nevertheless, they are less greedy in parameters than the models of the first category, and therefore they are more easily estimable.

The conditional variance matrix for this class of models is specified in a hierarchical way. First, one chooses a GARCH-type model for each conditional variance. Second, based on the conditional variances one models the conditional correlation matrix (imposing its positive definiteness $\forall t$).

Bollerslev (1990) proposes a class of MGARCH models in which the conditional correlations are constant and thus the conditional covariances are proportional to the product of the corresponding conditional standard deviations. This restriction highly reduces the number of unknown parameters and thus simplifies estimation.

Definition 5. *The CCC model is defined as:*

$$H_t = D_t R D_t = \left(\rho_{ij} \sqrt{h_{iit} h_{jjt}} \right), \tag{9.26}$$

where

$$D_t = \text{diag} \left(h_{11t}^{1/2} \ldots h_{NNt}^{1/2} \right), \tag{9.27}$$

h_{iit} *can be defined as any univariate GARCH model, and*

$$R = (\rho_{ij}) \tag{9.28}$$

is a symmetric positive definite matrix with $\rho_{ii} = 1, \forall\, i.$

R is the matrix containing the constant conditional correlations ρ_{ij}. The original CCC model has a GARCH(1,1) specification for each conditional variance in D_t:

$$h_{iit} = \omega_i + \alpha_i \epsilon_{i,t-1}^2 + \beta_i h_{ii,t-1} \quad i = 1, \ldots, N. \tag{9.29}$$

This CCC model contains $N(N+5)/2$ parameters. H_t is positive definite if and only if all the N conditional variances are positive and R is positive definite. The unconditional variances are easily obtained, as in the univariate case, but the unconditional covariances are difficult to calculate because of the nonlinearity in (9.26).

The assumption that the conditional correlations are constant may seem unrealistic in many empirical applications.[7] Engle (2002) and Tse and Tsui (2002) propose a generalization of the CCC model by making the conditional correlation matrix time dependent. The model is then called a dynamic conditional correlation (DCC) model. An additional difficulty is that the time dependent conditional correlation matrix has to be positive definite $\forall t$. The DCC models guarantee this under simple conditions on the parameters.

Definition 6. *The DCC model of Tse and Tsui (2002) is defined as:*

$$H_t = D_t R_t D_t, \tag{9.30}$$

---

[7]Several tests have been proposed in the literature to check this assumption. Two of theses tests, i.e. the tests of Tse (2000) and Engle and Sheppard (2001), are available in G@RCH. See Section 9.7.2 for more details about these tests.

where D_t is defined in (9.27), h_{iit} can be defined as any univariate GARCH model, and

$$R_t = (1 - \theta_1 - \theta_2)R + \theta_1\Psi_{t-1} + \theta_2 R_{t-1}. \tag{9.31}$$

In (9.31), θ_1 and θ_2 are non-negative parameters satisfying $\theta_1 + \theta_2 < 1$, R is a symmetric $N \times N$ positive definite parameter matrix with $\rho_{ii} = 1$, and Ψ_{t-1} is the $N \times N$ correlation matrix of ϵ_τ for $\tau = t - M, t - M + 1, \ldots, t - 1$. Its i, j-th element is given by:

$$\psi_{ij,t-1} = \frac{\sum_{m=1}^{M} u_{i,t-m} u_{j,t-m}}{\sqrt{(\sum_{m=1}^{M} u_{i,t-m}^2)(\sum_{h=1}^{M} u_{j,t-m}^2)}}, \tag{9.32}$$

where $u_{it} = \epsilon_{it}/\sqrt{h_{iit}}$. The matrix Ψ_{t-1} can be expressed as:

$$\Psi_{t-1} = B_{t-1}^{-1} L_{t-1} L'_{t-1} B_{t-1}^{-1}, \tag{9.33}$$

where B_{t-1} is a $N \times N$ diagonal matrix with i-th diagonal element given by $(\sum_{h=1}^{M} u_{i,t-h}^2)^{1/2}$ and $L_{t-1} = (u_{t-1}, \ldots, u_{t-M})$ is a $N \times M$ matrix, with $u_t = (u_{1t}\ u_{2t}\ \ldots u_{Nt})'$.

A necessary condition to ensure the positivity of Ψ_{t-1}, and therefore also of R_t, is that $M \geq N$.[8] Then R_t is itself a correlation matrix if R_{t-1} is also a correlation matrix (notice that $\rho_{iit} = 1\ \forall i$).

Alternatively, Engle (2002) proposes a different DCC model (see also Engle and Sheppard, 2001).

Definition 7. *The DCC model of Engle (2002) is defined as in (9.30) with*

$$R_t = \text{diag}\,(q_{11,t}^{-1/2} \ldots q_{NN,t}^{-1/2})\, Q_t\, \text{diag}\,(q_{11,t}^{-1/2} \ldots q_{NN,t}^{-1/2}), \tag{9.34}$$

where the $N \times N$ symmetric positive definite matrix $Q_t = (q_{ij,t})$ is given by:

$$Q_t = (1 - \alpha - \beta)\overline{Q} + \alpha u_{t-1} u'_{t-1} + \beta Q_{t-1}, \tag{9.35}$$

with u_t as in Definition 6. $\overline{Q}$ is the $N \times N$ unconditional variance matrix of u_t, and α and β are nonnegative scalar parameters satisfying $\alpha + \beta < 1$.

The elements of $\overline{Q}$ can be estimated or alternatively set to their empirical counterpart to render the estimation even simpler (see Section ??).

---

[8]Note that when $M = 1$, Ψ_{t-1} is equal to a matrix of ones.

To show more explicitly the difference between the two DCC models, we write the expression of the correlation coefficient in the bivariate case: for the DCC of Tse and Tsui (2002),

$$\rho_{12t} = (1 - \theta_1 - \theta_2)\, \rho_{12} + \theta_2\, \rho_{12,t-1} + \theta_1\, \frac{\sum_{m=1}^{M} u_{1,t-m} u_{2,t-m}}{\sqrt{(\sum_{m=1}^{M} u_{1,t-m}^2)(\sum_{h=1}^{M} u_{2,t-m}^2)}}, \tag{9.36}$$

and for the DCC of Engle (2002),

$$\rho_{12t} = \frac{(1 - \alpha - \beta)\, \bar{q}_{12} + \alpha\, u_{1,t-1} u_{2,t-1} + \beta\, q_{12,t-1}}{\sqrt{\left((1 - \alpha - \beta)\, \bar{q}_{11} + \alpha\, u_{1,t-1}^2 + \beta\, q_{11,t-1}\right)\left((1 - \alpha - \beta)\, \bar{q}_{22} + \alpha\, u_{2,t-1}^2 + \beta\, q_{22,t-1}\right)}}. \tag{9.37}$$

Unlike Tse and Tsui (2002), Engle (2002) formulates the conditional correlation as a weighted sum of past correlations. Indeed, the matrix Q_t is written like a GARCH equation, and then transformed to a correlation matrix. However, for both DCC models, one can test $\theta_1 = \theta_2 = 0$ or $\alpha = \beta = 0$ respectively to check whether imposing constant conditional correlations is empirically relevant.

A drawback of the DCC models is that θ_1, θ_2 and α, β are scalars, so that all the conditional correlations obey the same dynamics. This is necessary to ensure that R_t is positive definite $\forall t$ through sufficient conditions on the parameters. If the conditional variances are specified as GARCH(1,1) models then the DCC models contain $(N + 1)(N + 4)/2$ parameters.

Interestingly, CCC and DCC models can be estimated consistently in two steps (see Section 9.6.2) which makes this approach feasible when N is high. Of course, when N is large, the restriction of common dynamics gets tighter, but for large N the problem of maintaining tractability also gets harder.

To conclude, DCC models open the door to using flexible GARCH specifications in the variance part. Indeed, as the conditional variances (together with the conditional means) can be estimated using N univariate models, one can easily extend the DCC-GARCH models to more complex GARCH-type structures (as mentioned in the beginning of Section 9.5.3). One can also extend the bivariate CCC FIGARCH model of Brunetti and Gilbert (2000) to a model of the DCC family.

Definition 8. *The DECO model of Engle and Kelly (2008) is defined as in (9.30) with*

$$R_t = (1 - \rho_t)I_N + \rho_t J_{N \times N}, \tag{9.38}$$

$$\rho_t = \frac{1}{N(N-1)} \sum_{i \neq j} \frac{q_{ij,t}}{\sqrt{q_{ii,t} q_{jj,t}}} \tag{9.39}$$

where ρ_t is the equicorrelation, $q_{ij,t}$ is the i,jth element of Q_t in Equation (9.35), I_N denotes the N-dimensional identity matrix and $J_{N \times N}$ is an $N \times N$ matrix of ones.

According Engle and Kelly (2008) (see Lemma 2.1), R_t^{-1} exists if and only if $\rho_t \neq 1$ and $\rho_t \neq -1/(N-1)$ and R_t is positive definite if and only if $-1/(N-1) < \rho_t < 1$.

The estimation of a CCC, DCC and DECO models is extremely simple. Select 'CCC', 'DCC (Engle)', 'DCC (TSE and TSUI)' or 'DCC-DECO' in the Settings dialog box. A new dialog box Model Settings is launched and the user is asked to chose the specification of the model. We select an AR(1)-GJR(1,1)-CCC with a normal distribution for the error term.

Other options

Variance Targeting is accessible through the menu 'Additional options/Variance Targeting' of the the Settings dialog box. If this option is enabled, the unconditional correlation matrix of u_t is used in place of R or $\bar{Q}$.

The next three options are self explanatory. Finally the last option concerns the estimation method. 2-step corresponds to the 2-step ML estimation method presented in Section 9.6.2 and 1-step to the traditional one-step maximum likelihood procedure (presented in Section 9.6.1). Note that when option '1-step' is selected, the model is first estimated via the two-step procedure to get accurate starting value for the estimation of the full model.

The output of the two univariate AR(1)-GJR(1,1) models is reported in Box 11 and the CCC part in Box 12.

```
                              Box 11 - CCC STEP 1
  *********************
  **   FIRST STEP   **
  *********************

  --------------------------Estimating the univariate GARCH model for DJ--------------------------


  *********************
  ** SPECIFICATIONS **
  *********************
  Dependent variable : DJ
  Mean Equation : ARMA (1, 0) model.
  No regressor in the conditional mean
  Variance Equation : GJR (1, 1) model.
  No regressor in the conditional variance
  Normal distribution.

  Weak convergence (no improvement in line search) using numerical derivatives
  Log-likelihood = -5150.9
  Please wait : Computing the Std Errors ...

  Robust Standard Errors (Sandwich formula)
                  Coefficient  Std.Error  t-value  t-prob
  Cst(M)            0.029764   0.013591    2.190   0.0286
  AR(1)             0.021967   0.017049    1.288   0.1977
  Cst(V)            0.011930   0.0047754   2.498   0.0125
  ARCH(Alpha1)      0.008823   0.0068322   1.291   0.1966
  GARCH(Beta1)      0.936954   0.016569   56.55    0.0000
  GJR(Gamma1)       0.081739   0.024269    3.368   0.0008


  No. Observations :      3913  No. Parameters  :        6
  Mean (Y)         :   0.03369  Variance (Y)    :  1.02307
  Skewness (Y)     :  -0.30325  Kurtosis (Y)    :  8.12068
  Log Likelihood   : -5150.903

  The sample mean of squared residuals was used to start recursion.
  The condition for existence of the second moment of the GJR is observed.
  This condition is alpha(1) + beta(1) + k gamma(1) < 1 (with k = 0.5 with this distribution.)
  In this estimation, this sum equals 0.986647.
  The condition for existence of the fourth moment of the GJR is observed.
  The constraint equals 0.983421 (should be < 1).  => See Ling & McAleer (2001) for details.

  Estimated Parameters Vector :
   0.029764; 0.021967; 0.011930; 0.008823; 0.936954; 0.081739
```

```
--------------------------Estimating the univariate GARCH model for NQ--------------------------


********************
** SPECIFICATIONS **
********************
Dependent variable : NQ
Mean Equation : ARMA (1, 0) model.
No regressor in the conditional mean
Variance Equation : GJR (1, 1) model.
No regressor in the conditional variance
Normal distribution.

Strong convergence using numerical derivatives
Log-likelihood = -6245.8
Please wait : Computing the Std Errors ...

  Robust Standard Errors (Sandwich formula)
                Coefficient  Std.Error  t-value  t-prob
Cst(M)            0.044543   0.017815    2.500   0.0125
AR(1)             0.110349   0.017202    6.415   0.0000
Cst(V)            0.015383   0.0059041   2.605   0.0092
ARCH(Alpha1)      0.039653   0.010897    3.639   0.0003
GARCH(Beta1)      0.912374   0.018410   49.56    0.0000
GJR(Gamma1)       0.079668   0.024063    3.311   0.0009

No. Observations :     3913  No. Parameters  :         6
Mean (Y)         :   0.03527 Variance (Y)    :   2.38111
Skewness (Y)     :  -0.01238 Kurtosis (Y)    :   8.76442
Log Likelihood   : -6245.795

The sample mean of squared residuals was used to start recursion.
The condition for existence of the second moment of the GJR is observed.
This condition is alpha(1) + beta(1) + k gamma(1) < 1 (with k = 0.5 with this distribution.)
In this estimation, this sum equals 0.99186.
The condition for existence of the fourth moment of the GJR is not observed.
The constraint equals 1.00118 (should be < 1).  => See Ling & McAleer (2001) for details.

Estimated Parameters Vector :
  0.044543; 0.110349; 0.015383; 0.039653; 0.912374; 0.079668
```

```
                             Box 12 - CCC STEP 2
        ********************
     **   SECOND STEP   **
        ********************


        *************
     ** SERIES **
        *************


             #
DJ      1
NQ      2

        *********************************
     ** MGØRCH( 1) SPECIFICATIONS **
        *********************************
Conditional Variance : Constant Correlation Model
Multivariate Normal distribution.

Strong convergence using numerical derivatives
Log-likelihood = -9990.85
Please wait : Computing the Std Errors ...

  Robust Standard Errors (Sandwich formula)
                Coefficient  Std.Error  t-value  t-prob
rho_21            0.714655   0.0088963   80.33   0.0000
No. Observations :     3913  No. Parameters  :         1
No. Series       :        2  Log Likelihood  : -9990.846
```

The next box corresponds to the output of the second step of the CCC model with
the variance targeting option. We see that the unconditional correlation of the Dow
Jones and the Nasdaq is about 70 % and very closed the the estimated value reported in
the previous box.

```
                                Box 13 - CCC STEP 2 (Variance Targeting)
**********************
**   SECOND STEP    **
**********************

**********************
** SPECIFICATION  **
**********************
Constant Correlation Model

Unconditional Correlation (CCC)
rho_21              0.692362
No. Observations :      3913   No. Parameters  :         0
No. Series       :         2   Log Likelihood  : -9996.411
```

The next box reports the output of an AR(1)-GJR(1,1)-DCC using the
DCC specification of Tse and Tsui (2002) with $M = 2$. A quick look
at the significance of the conditional correlation coefficients (α and β) and
at the log-likelihood indicates that the DCC model dominates the CCC.

```
                           Box 14 -DCC of TSE and TSUI
Strong convergence using numerical derivatives
Log-likelihood = -9867.88
Please wait : Computing the Std Errors ...

 Robust Standard Errors (Sandwich formula)
                  Coefficient  Std.Error  t-value  t-prob
Part: DJ
Cst(M)             0.032070   0.00017264   185.8   0.0000
AR(1)              0.030809   0.00020060   153.6   0.0000
Cst(V)             0.009702   0.0028714    3.379   0.0007
ARCH(Alpha1)       0.016149   0.0073525    2.196   0.0281
GARCH(Beta1)       0.945016   0.011370     83.12   0.0000
GJR(Gamma1)        0.054073   0.013762     3.929   0.0001
Part: NQ
Cst(M)             0.046630   0.0089878    5.188   0.0000
AR(1)              0.104576   0.0095936    10.90   0.0000
Cst(V)             0.011978   0.0039631    3.022   0.0025
ARCH(Alpha1)       0.047534   0.0097686    4.866   0.0000
GARCH(Beta1)       0.922509   0.014204     64.95   0.0000
GJR(Gamma1)        0.043626   0.013933     3.131   0.0018
Part: Correlation
rho_21             0.853228   0.037576     22.71   0.0000
alpha              0.025793   0.0047618    5.417   0.0000
beta               0.951086   0.010230     92.97   0.0000

No. Observations :      3913   No. Parameters  :        15
No. Series       :         2   Log Likelihood  : -9867.885
```

To conclude with this family of MGARCH models, the conditional correlation estimated by the CCC, DCC of Tse and Tsui (2002) and DCC of Engle (2002) are plotted
in Figures 9.8, 9.9 and 9.10 respectively.

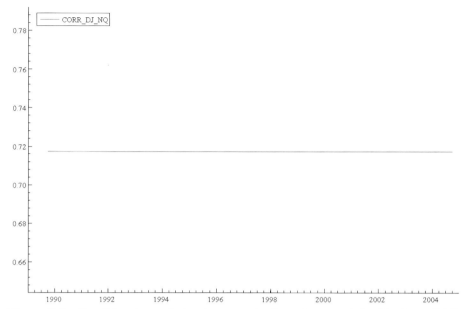

Figure 9.8 Conditional correlation between the Dow Jones and the Nasdaq - CCC model.

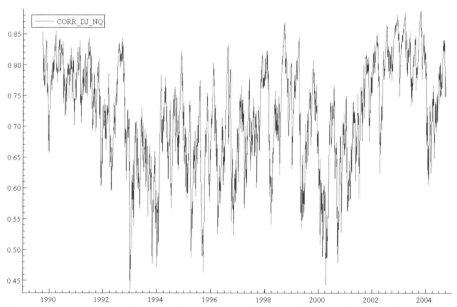

Figure 9.9 Conditional correlation between the Dow Jones and the Nasdaq - CCC model.

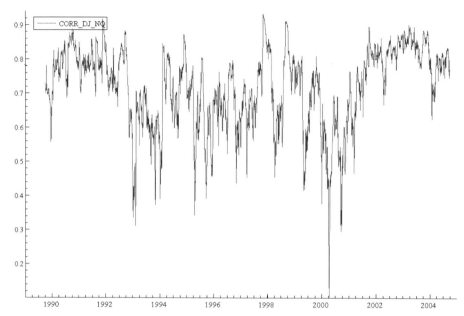

Figure 9.10   Conditional correlation between the Dow Jones and the Nasdaq - CCC model.

9.6 Estimation

In the previous section we have defined existing specifications of conditional variance matrices that enter the definition either of a data generating process (DGP) or of a model to be estimated. In Section 9.6.1 we discuss maximum likelihood (ML) estimation of these models, and in Section 9.6.2 we explain a two-step approach for estimating conditional correlation models. Finally, we review briefly the variance targeting issue in Section 9.6.3.

9.6.1 Maximum Likelihood

Suppose the vector stochastic process $\{y_t\}$ (for $t = 1, \ldots, T$) is a realization of a DGP whose conditional mean, conditional variance matrix and conditional distribution are respectively $\mu_t(\theta_0)$, $H_t(\theta_0)$ and $p(y_t|\zeta_0, \Omega_{t-1})$, where $\zeta_0 = (\theta_0 \ \eta_0)$ is a r-dimensional parameter vector and η_0 is the vector that contains the parameters of the distribution of the innovations z_t (there may be no such parameter). Importantly, to justify the choice of the estimation procedure, we assume that the model to be estimated encompasses the true formulations of $\mu_t(\theta_0)$ and $H_t(\theta_0)$.

   The procedure most often used in estimating θ_0 involves the maximization of a likelihood function constructed under the auxiliary assumption of an $i.i.d.$ distribution for the standardized innovations z_t. The $i.i.d.$ assumption may be replaced by the weaker assumption that z_t is a martingale difference sequence with respect to Ω_{t-1}, but this type of assumption does not translate into the likelihood function. The likelihood function for the $i.i.d.$ case can then be viewed as a quasi-likelihood function.

Consequently, one has to make an additional assumption on the innovation process by choosing a density function, denoted $g(z_t(\theta)|\eta)$ where η is a vector of nuisance parameters. The problem to solve is thus to maximize the sample log-likelihood function $L_T(\theta, \eta)$ for the T observations (conditional on some starting values for μ_0 and H_0), with respect to the vector of parameters $\zeta = (\theta, \eta)$, where

$$L_T(\zeta) = \sum_{t=1}^{T} \log f(y_t|\zeta, \Omega_{t-1}), \tag{9.40}$$

with

$$f(y_t|\zeta, \Omega_{t-1}) = |H_t|^{-1/2} g\left(H_t^{-1/2}(y_t - \mu_t)|\eta\right), \tag{9.41}$$

and the dependence with respect to θ occurs through μ_t and H_t. The term $|H_t|^{-1/2}$ is the Jacobian that arises in the transformation from the innovations to the observables.

The most commonly employed distribution in the literature is the multivariate normal, uniquely determined by its first two moments (so that $\zeta = \theta$ since η is empty). In this case, the sample log-likelihood is:

$$L_T(\theta) = -\frac{1}{2}\sum_{t=1}^{T}\left[N \log(2\pi) + \log | H_t | +(y_t - \mu_t)' H_t^{-1}(y_t - \mu_t)\right]. \tag{9.42}$$

It is well-known that the normality of the innovations is rejected in most applications dealing with daily or weekly data. In particular, the kurtosis of most financial asset returns is larger than three, which means that they have too many extreme values to be normally distributed. Moreover, their unconditional distribution has often fatter tails than what is implied by a conditional normal distribution: the increase of the kurtosis coefficient brought by the dynamics of the conditional variance is not usually sufficient to match adequately the unconditional kurtosis of the data.

However, as shown by Bollerslev and Wooldridge (1992), a consistent estimator of θ_0 may be obtained by maximizing (9.42) with respect to θ *even* if the DGP is not conditionally Gaussian. This estimator, called (Gaussian) quasi-maximum likelihood (QML) or pseudo-maximum likelihood (PML) estimator, is consistent provided the conditional mean and the conditional variance are specified correctly. Jeantheau (1998) proves the strong consistency of the Gaussian QML estimator of multivariate GARCH models. He also provides sufficient identification conditions for the CCC model. See Gourieroux (1997) for a detailed description of the QML method in a MGARCH context and its asymptotic properties. For these reasons and as far as the purpose of the analysis is to estimate consistently the first two conditional moments, estimating MGARCH models by QML is justified.

Nevertheless, in certain situations it is desirable to search for a better distribution for the innovation process. For instance, when one is interested in obtaining density forecasts, (see Diebold, Gunther, and Tay, 1998, in the univariate case and Diebold, Hahn, and Tay, 1999, in the multivariate case) it is natural to relax the normality assumption, keeping in mind the risk of inconsistency of the estimator (see Newey and Steigerwald, 1997).

A natural alternative to the multivariate Gaussian density is the Student density, see Harvey, Ruiz, and Shephard (1992) and Fiorentini, Sentana, and Calzolari (2003). The latter has an extra scalar parameter, the degrees of freedom parameter, denoted ν hereafter. When this parameter tends to infinity, the Student density tends to the normal density. When it tends to zero, the tails of the density become thicker and thicker. The parameter value indicates the order of existence of the moments, *e.g.* if $\nu = 2$, the second order moments do not exist, but the first order moments exist. For this reason, it is convenient (although not necessary) to assume that $\nu > 2$, so that H_t is always interpretable as a conditional covariance matrix. Under this assumption, the Student density can be defined as:

$$g(z_t|\theta, \nu) = \frac{\Gamma\left(\frac{\nu+N}{2}\right)}{\Gamma\left(\frac{\nu}{2}\right)[\pi(\nu - 2)]^{\frac{N}{2}}} \left[1 + \frac{z_t'z_t}{\nu - 2}\right]^{-\frac{N+\nu}{2}}, \tag{9.43}$$

where $\Gamma(.)$ is the Gamma function. Note that in this case $\eta = \nu$. The density function of y_t is easily obtained by applying (9.41).

The asymptotic properties of ML and QML estimators in multivariate GARCH models are not yet firmly established, and are difficult to derive from low level assumptions. As mentioned previously, consistency has been shown by Jeantheau (1998). Asymptotic normality of the QMLE is not established generally. Gourieroux (1997, Section 6.3) proves it for a general formulation using high level assumptions. Comte and Lieberman (2003) prove it for the BEKK formulation. Since (G)O-GARCH models are special cases of the BEKK model, this result holds also for these models (see van der Weide, 2002). Researchers who use MGARCH models have generally proceeded as if asymptotic normality holds in all cases. Asymptotic normality of the MLE and QMLE has been proved in the univariate case under low level assumptions, one of which being the existence of moments of order four or higher of the innovations (see Lee and Hansen, 1994, Lumsdaine, 1996, and Ling and McAleer, 2003).

Finally, it is worth mentioning that the conditional mean parameters may be consistently estimated in a first stage, prior to the estimation of the conditional variance parameters, for example for a VARMA model, but not for a GARCH-in-mean model. Estimating the parameters simultaneously with the conditional variance parameters would increase the efficiency at least in large samples (unless the asymptotic covariance matrix is block diagonal between the mean and variance parameters), but this is computationally more difficult. For this reason, one usually takes either a very simple model for the conditional mean or one considers $y_t - \hat{\mu}_t$ as the data for fitting the MGARCH model.[9]

A detailed investigation of the consequences of such a two step procedure on properties of estimators has still to be conducted.

9.6.2 Two-step estimation

A useful feature of the CCC and DCC models presented in Section 9.5.4 is that they can be estimated consistently using a two-step approach. Engle and Sheppard (2001) show that in the case of a DCC model, the log-likelihood can be written as the sum of a mean and volatility part (depending on a set of unknown parameters θ_1^*) and a correlation part (depending on θ_2^*).

Indeed, recalling that the conditional variance matrix of a DCC model can be expressed as $H_t = D_t R_t D_t$, an inefficient but consistent estimator of the parameter θ_1^* can be found by replacing R_t by the identity matrix in (9.42). In this case the quasi-loglikelihood function corresponds to the sum of loglikelihood functions of N univariate models:

$$QL1_T(\theta_1^*) = -\frac{1}{2} \sum_{t=1}^{T} \sum_{i=1}^{N} \left[\log(2\pi) + \log(h_{iit}) + \frac{(y_{it} - \mu_{it})^2}{h_{iit}} \right]. \qquad (9.44)$$

Given θ_1^* and under appropriate regularity conditions, a consistent, but inefficient, estimator of θ_2^* can be obtained by maximizing:

$$QL2_T(\theta_2^* | \theta_1^*) = -\frac{1}{2} \sum_{t=1}^{T} \left(\log |R_t| + u_t' R_t^{-1} u_t \right), \qquad (9.45)$$

---

[9]Note that VARMA models are available in PcGive.

where $u_t = D_t^{-1}(y_t - \mu_t)$. Note that for the DECO model of Engle and Kelly (2008) (see Definition 8), Equation (9.45) can be simplified as follows:

$$
\begin{aligned}
QL2_T(\theta_2^*|\theta_1^*) &= -\frac{1}{2}\sum_{t=1}^{T}\{\log[(1-\rho_t)^{N-1}(1+(N-1)\rho_t)] \\
&+ \frac{1}{1-\rho_t}[\sum_i u_{it}^2 - \frac{\rho_t}{1+(N-1)\rho_t}(\sum_i u_{it})^2]\}.
\end{aligned}
\tag{9.46}
$$

Engle and Kelly (2008) mention that "*The payoff from making the equicorrelation assumption can now be appreciated. In DCC, the conditional correlation matrices must be recorded and inverted for all t and their determinants calculated; further, these T inversions and determinant calculations are repeated for each of the many iterations required in a numeric optimization program. This is costly for small cross sections and potentially infeasible for very large ones. With DECO, only the scalar equicorrelation parameter for each t is recorded, and the compact analytical forms for the determinant and inverse of a covariance matrix under the assumption of equicorrelation, as presented in Lemma 2.1, make the computational demands for solving the likelihood optimization problem manageable for large cross sections.*"

The sum of the likelihood functions in (9.44) and (9.45) or (9.46), plus half of the total sum of squared standardized residuals ($\sum_t u_t' u_t/2$, which is almost equal to $NT/2$), is equal to the log-likelihood in (9.42). It is thus possible to compare the log-likelihood of the two-step approach with that of the one-step approach and of other models.

Engle and Sheppard (2001) explain that the estimators $\hat{\theta}_1^*$ and $\hat{\theta}_2^*$, obtained by maximizing (9.44) and (9.45) separately, are not fully efficient (even if z_t is normally distributed) since they are limited information estimators.

G@RCH 6.0 implements the two-step approach described above (for the CCC and DCC models) but also allows the estimation of these model in one-step. Note that when choosing the one-step approach, the model is first estimated with the two-step approach to get accurate starting values.

Importantly, G@RCH 6.0 allows the selection of non-standard ARCH models for the conditional variances (like APARCH, GJR, etc., including covariates) and an AR(FI)MAX specification for the conditional mean.

Note that in the rolling menu version the same specification is chosen for the conditional mean and conditional variance of all the series (e.g. an AR(2)-GJR(1,1) for the N series). This restriction is relaxed in the MGarch class where for instance and ARMA(1,0)-GARCH(1,1) can be selected for the first series and an ARMA(0,0)-FIGARCH(0,d,1) can be selected for the others.

9.6.3 Variance Targeting

We have seen that what renders most MGARCH models difficult for estimation is their high number of parameters. A simple trick to ensure a reasonable value of the model-implied unconditional covariance matrix, which also helps to reduce the number of parameters in the maximization of the likelihood function, is referred to as variance targeting by Engle and Mezrich (1996). For example, in the VEC model (and all its particular cases), the conditional variance matrix may be expressed in terms of the unconditional variance matrix (see Section 9.5.2.1) and other parameters. Doing so one can reparametrize the model using the unconditional variance matrix and replace it by a consistent estimator (before maximizing the likelihood). When doing this, one should correct the covariance matrix of the estimator of the other parameters for the uncertainty in the preliminary estimator. In DCC models, this can also be done with the constant matrix of the correlation part, *e.g.* $\overline{Q}$ in (9.35). In this case, the two-step estimation procedure explained in Section 9.6.2 becomes a three-step procedure.

9.7 Diagnostic Checking

Since estimating MGARCH models is time consuming, both in terms of computations and their programming (if needed), it is desirable to check *ex ante* whether the data present evidence of multivariate ARCH effects. *Ex post*, it is also of crucial importance to check the adequacy of the MGARCH specification. However, compared to the huge body of diagnostic tests devoted to univariate models, only few tests are specific to multivariate models.

In the current literature on MGARCH models, one can distinguish two kinds of specification tests, namely univariate tests applied independently to each series and multivariate tests applied to the vector series as a whole. We deliberately leave out the first kind of tests and refer interested readers to Chapter 3 for univariate tests. As emphasized by Kroner and Ng (1998), the existing literature on multivariate diagnostics is sparse compared to the univariate case. However, although univariate tests can provide some guidance, contemporaneous correlation of disturbances entails that statistics from individual equations are not independent. As a result, combining test decisions over all equations raises size control problems, so the need for joint testing naturally arises

(Dufour, Khalaf, and Beaulieu, 2003).

9.7.1 Portmanteau Statistics

The most widely used diagnostics to detect ARCH effects are probably the Box-Pierce/Ljung-Box portmanteau tests. Following Hosking (1980), a multivariate version of the Ljung-Box test statistic is given by:

$$HM(m) = T^2 \sum_{j=1}^{m} (T-j)^{-1} tr\{C_{y_t}^{-1}(0)C_{y_t}(j)C_{y_t}^{-1}(0)C'_{y_t}(j)\}, \qquad (9.47)$$

where y_t is the vector of observed returns and $C_{y_t}(j)$ is the sample autocovariance matrix of order j. Under the null hypothesis of no serial correlation in y_t, $HM(m)$ is distributed asymptotically as a $\chi^2(N^2 m)$.

In G@RCH 6.0, this test is used to detect misspecification in the conditional mean or the variance matrix H_t. To detect misspecification in the conditional mean, y_t is replaced by $\hat{z}_t = \hat{H}_t^{-1/2}\hat{\epsilon}_t$ and to detect misspecification in the conditional variance, y_t is replaced by $\hat{z}_t^2$. The asymptotic distribution of the portmanteau statistics is, however, unknown in this case since $\hat{z}_t$ has been estimated. We apply an ad hoc adjustments of degrees of freedom for the ARMA and GARCH orders. In such a case, portmanteau tests should be interpreted with care even if simulation results reported by Tse and Tsui (1999) suggest that they provide a useful diagnostic in many situations.

Li and McLeod (1981) propose an alternative portmanteau statistic to detect misspecification in the conditional mean of an ARMA model (i.e. it is applied on $\hat{z}_t$). Following their notation, the modified version of their statistic $Q_m^* = Q_m + \frac{k^2 m(m+1)}{2n}$ is asymptotically χ^2 distributed with $k^2(m-s)$ degrees of freedom, where m is the lag order, $k = N$ and s is the ARMA order (AR+MA orders). Similar to Hosking's statistic, G@RCH 6.0 proposes to apply the test on $\hat{z}_t^2$ to detect misspecification in the conditional variance (in this case $s = p + q$).

9.7.2 CCC Tests

To reduce the number of parameters in the estimation of MGARCH models, it is usual to introduce restrictions. For instance, the CCC model of Bollerslev (1990) assumes that the conditional correlation matrix is constant over time. It is then desirable to test this assumption afterwards. Tse (2000) proposes a test for constant correlations. The null is $h_{ijt} = \rho_{ij}\sqrt{h_{iit}h_{jjt}}$ where the conditional variances are GARCH-type models, the alternative is $h_{ijt} = \rho_{ijt}\sqrt{h_{iit}h_{jjt}}$. The test statistic is a LM statistic which under the null is asymptotically $\chi^2(N(N-1)/2)$.

Engle and Sheppard (2001) propose another test of the constant correlation hypothesis, in the spirit of the DCC models presented in Section 9.5.4. The null $H_0 : R_t = \overline{R}$ $\forall t$ is tested against the alternative $H_1 : \text{vech}(R_t) = \text{vech}(\overline{R}) + \beta_1^* \text{vech}(R_{t-1}) + \ldots + \beta_p^* \text{vech}(R_{t-p})$. The test is easy to implement since H_0 implies that coefficients in the regression $X_t = \beta_0^* + \beta_1^* X_{t-1} + \ldots + \beta_p^* X_{t-p} + u_t^*$ are equal to zero, where $X_t = \text{vech}^u(\hat{z}_t \hat{z}_t' - I_N)$, vech^u is like the vech operator but it only selects the elements under the main diagonal, $\hat{z}_t = \hat{\overline{R}}^{-1/2} \hat{D}_t^{-1} \hat{\epsilon}_t$ is the $N \times 1$ vector of standardized residuals (under the null), and $D_t = \text{diag}(h_{11t}^{1/2} \ldots h_{NNt}^{1/2})$.

9.8 Batch code

Up to now, we have seen that MGARCH models can be estimated via the rolling menus. However, like for univariate models, there are two additional ways of estimating MGARCH models with G@RCH. The first makes use of the batch facilities of OxMetrics. In the second, an Ox program is written that imports the MGarch class code into the program.

This section is devoted to the illustration of the first method.

A useful feature in G@RCH is the possibility to use the algebra and batch languages in OxMetrics (see the OxMetrics handbook for more details). The batch language gives some control over OxMetrics through a command language. This allows for automating repetitive tasks, or as a quick way to get to a certain point in your analysis. The syntax of these commands is described below.

There are five ways of running Batch commands.

- Batch Editor (Alt+b)

  The Model/Batch... command activates the edit window in which you can edit/load/save a set of batch commands. The file extension used for batch files is .FL.

- Batch from Results windows (Ctrl+b)

  A text selection containing Batch commands can be run directly from that window using the Edit/Run as Batch command (or Ctrl+b as short cut).

- Batch from the File/Open command

  If you use File/Open, and set the file type to Run Batch file (*.fl), then the batch file is run immediately.

- Batch from the Windows Explorer

  You can double click on a .FL file in the Windows Explorer to run the file directly. If OxMetrics is not active yet, it will be started automatically.

- Batch from a Batch file

  A batch file can be called from another batch file using the command

  ```
  loadbatch("filename");.
  ```

The most intuitive way is probably to estimate a model first and then click on Tools/Batch Editor ... in OxMetrics (or Alt+b). Then, a new box dialog appears with the batch code corresponding to this model. To illustrate, the next picture shows part of the batch code corresponding to a simple (without explanatory variable) ARMA(1,0)-GJR(1,1)-CCC model.

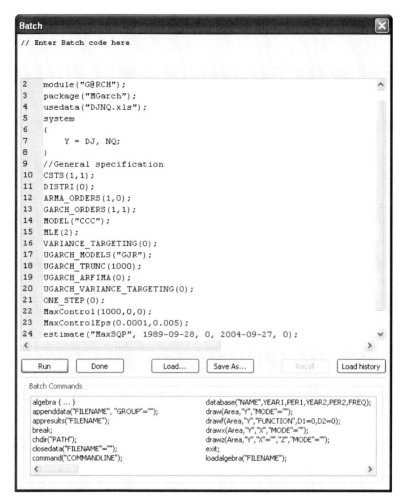

To estimate a slightly different model, one has to change the batch code accordingly. Here is a list of MG@RCH specific batch commands.

(1) CSTS: Specifies if constants are wanted respectively in the conditional mean and in the conditional variance equations.

(2) DISTRI: Specifies the desired distribution, i.e. 0 for the Gaussian (Normal) distribution, 1 for the Student-t distribution.

(3) ARMA_ORDERS: Specifies respectively the AR and MA orders.

(4) GARCH_ORDERS: Specifies the orders of the MGARCH(p, q)-type model.

(5) MODEL: specification choice (string).

- "SCALAR_BEKK";
- "DIAG_BEKK";
- "RiskMetrics";

- "CCC";
- "DCC";
- "DCC_TSE";
- "OGARCH";
- "GOGARCH_ML";
- "GOGARCH_NLS".

(6) estimate(method, year1=-1, period1=0, year2=-1, period2=0);
Estimates the model.

The first argument method = "MaxSQP" . year1(period1) – year2(period2) is the estimation sample. Setting year1 to -1 will result in the earliest possible year1(period1), setting year2 to -1 will result in the latest possible year2(period2).

(7) MLE: 0, standard errors based on second derivatives. 1 standard errors based on numerical OPG matrix. 2, robust standard errors (QMLE) are computed (irrespectively of the density choice).

(8) VARIANCE_TARGETING: 1 to apply variance targeting.

(9) OGARCH_M: number of factors (M) for the OGARCH model.

(10) UGARCH_MODELS: specification choice (string) of the univariate GARCH models (for CCC, DCC, OGARCH and GOGARCH models)

- "GARCH";
- "EGARCH";
- "GJR";
- "APARCH";
- "IGARCH";
- "FIGARCH_BBM";
- "FIGARCH_CHUNG";
- "FIEGARCH";
- "FIAPARCH_BBM";
- "FIAPARCH_CHUNG";
- "HYGARCH".

(11) UGARCH_ARFIMA: 1 to add a long-memory component in the conditional mean equation, 0 otherwise (for CCC, DCC, OGARCH and GOGARCH models).

(12) UGARCH_TRUNC: truncation order of FIGARCH-type models (for CCC, DCC, OGARCH and GOGARCH models).

(13) UGARCH_VARIANCE_TARGETING: 1 to apply variance targeting on the univariate GARCH-type models (for CCC, DCC, OGARCH and GOGARCH models).

(14) ONE_STEP: 1 for 1-step MLE estimation, 0 for 2-step (for CCC and DCC models).

(15) INFO_CRITERIA: 1 to print the information criteria, 0 otherwise.

(16) NORMALITY_TEST: 1 to print the univariate normality tests, 0 otherwise.

(17) Q_TEST: lag orders of the univariate Box-Pierce tests on $\hat{z}_t$, e.g. verb"Q_TEST(5,10);" to run the test with 5 and 10 lags.

(18) M_NORMALITY_TEST: 1 to print the multivariate normality test, 0 otherwise.

(19) HOSKING_TEST: lag orders of Hosking's tests of misspecification of the conditional mean and conditional variance-covariance.

(20) LI_MCLEOD_TEST: lag orders of Li and McLeod tests of misspecification of the conditional mean and conditional variance-covariance.

(21) LMC_TEST: 1 to run the LM test of CCC of TSE (2000) (for CCC models only).

(22) ENGLE_SHEPPARD_TEST: the first argument is 1 to run the test of CCC of Engle and Sheppard (2001). The second argument is the number of lags (for CCC models only).

(23) Tests(): To launch the missspecification tests selected above.

(24) FORECAST: The first argument is 1 to run the forecasting procedure, the second argument is the forecasting horizon h.

(25) PLOT_RAW, PLOT_STAND_RES, PLOT_VAR, PLOT_COV, PLOT_CORR: 1 to plot the raw data, standardised residuals, conditional variances, conditional covariances and conditional correlations respectively, 0 otherwise.

(26) PLOT_IN_SAMPLE: 1 to plot the selected graphs.

The next box contains the batch code of an AR(1)-GJR(1,1)-CCC model with various tests and graphs

```
                   Batch code for an AR(1)-GJR(1,1)-CCC with various tests and graphs
// Batch code for MG@RCH( 1)
module("G@RCH");
package("MGarch");
usedata("DJNQ.xls");
system
{
    Y = DJ, NQ;
}
//General specification
CSTS(1,1);
DISTRI(0);
ARMA_ORDERS(1,0);
GARCH_ORDERS(1,1);
MODEL("CCC");
MLE(2);
VARIANCE_TARGETING(1);
UGARCH_MODELS("GJR");
UGARCH_TRUNC(1000);
UGARCH_ARFIMA(0);
UGARCH_VARIANCE_TARGETING(0);
ONE_STEP(0);
MaxControl(1000,0,0);
MaxControlEps(0.0001,0.005);
estimate("MaxSQP", 1989-09-28, 0, 2004-09-27, 0);
INFO_CRITERIA(1);
NORMALITY_TEST(1);
Q_TEST(5,10,20,50);
M_NORMALITY_TEST(1);
HOSKING_TEST(5,10,20,50);
LI_MCLEOD_TEST(5,10,20,50);
LMC_TEST(1);
ENGLE_SHEPPARD_TEST(1,5,10);
Tests();
PLOT_RAW(1);
PLOT_STAND_RES(1);
PLOT_VAR(1);
PLOT_COV(1);
PLOT_CORR(1);
PLOT_IN_SAMPLE(1);
FORECAST(1,10);
```

9.9 Importing the MGarch Class in Ox

This section explains how to use the MGarch class in Ox. We assume that you have installed Ox (version 5 or later). For more details about Ox, see Jurgen Doornik's web site (http://www.doornik.com).

9.9.1 MGarchEstim.ox **example**

MG@RCH is build upon the concept of object-oriented programming.

A major component of object-oriented programming is the "class". Several useful classes are supplied with Ox. Garch is an additional class that come along with G@RCH 6.0. This class, described in Section 9.9 is useful for the estimation of univariate GARCH-type models.

MGarch is another class devoted to MGARCH models.

`MGarchEstim.ox` is an example of Ox code using the MGarch class. As file editor, we strongly recommend to use OxMetrics or OxEdit.

The `/OxMetrics5/Ox/packages/MGarch1/Samples/MGarchEstim.ox` file is displayed in the following box.

```
                                                              MGarchEstim.ox
#include <oxstd.h>
#include <oxdraw.h>
#import <packages/MGarch1/mgarch>

main()
{
//*** CREATE OBJECT ***//
decl mgarchobj = new MGarch();

//*** DATA ***//
decl data="/data/DJNQ.xls";
mgarchobj.Load(sprint(data));
mgarchobj.Info();
mgarchobj.Select(Y_VAR, {"DJ",0,0} );    // Endogenous variables
mgarchobj.Select(Y_VAR, {"NQ",0,0} );
// mgarchobj.Select(X_VAR, {"MONDAY",1,1} );  // Explanatory variables in the conditional mean
// mgarchobj.Select(Z_VAR, {"MONDAY",1,2} );  // Explanatory variables in the conditional variance (...
// mgarchobj.SetSelSample(-1, 1, 2000, 1);    // Selects a sample for the variables previously selected
   mgarchobj.SetSelDates(1989, 9, 28, 1995, 12, 29); // Selects a sample for the variables previously ...

//*** SPECIFICATIONS ***//
mgarchobj.CSTS(1,1);  // 1 to add a Cst in the conditional mean and in ...
mgarchobj.DISTRI(0);  // 0 for Gauss, 1 for Student
mgarchobj.ARMA_ORDERS(1,0);  // AR order(s) and MA order (q). ...
mgarchobj.GARCH_ORDERS(1,1);  // p order(s) and q order(s). ...
mgarchobj.VARIANCE_TARGETING(0);   // 1 for Variance Targeting, 0 otherwise
mgarchobj.MODEL(CCC); // Model: SCALAR_BEKK, DIAG_BEKK, RiskMetrics, CCC, DCC, DCC_TSE, ...
// FOR CCC, DCC and (G)OGARCH models only
//mgarchobj.UGARCH_MODELS(EGARCH); // Univariate Models: GARCH, EGARCH, GJR, APARCH, IGARCH, FIGARCH_BBM, ...
mgarchobj.UGARCH_TRUNC(1000); // Truncation order of FIGARCH-type models
mgarchobj.UGARCH_PrintOutput(1); // 1 to print the output of the univariate GARCH models in ...
mgarchobj.UGARCH_ARFIMA(0);    // 1 to add an ARFIMA component in the univariate GARCH models

// FOR CCC, DCC  models only
mgarchobj.ONE_STEP(0);       // 1 to estimate the model in one step ...
mgarchobj.TSE_LAGS(4);    // Number of lags to compute Psi_t-1 in the DCC of TSE and TSUI (2002)

// For the OGARCH model
mgarchobj.OGARCH_M(2);    // Number of factors

//*** V-C MATRIX OF ESTIMATES ***//
mgarchobj.MLE(QMLE);    // Variance-Covariance matrix of estimates: HESS, CROSSPRODUCT or QMLE

//*** FORCASTING ***//
mgarchobj.FORECAST(1,5);

//*** MISSPECIFICATION TESTS ***//
// Univariate tests
mgarchobj.INFO_CRITERIA(1);
mgarchobj.NORMALITY_TEST(1);
mgarchobj.Q_TEST(1,<1;3;10>);  // 1 to apply the Box-Pierce test of serial correlation on the standardized ...
mgarchobj.Q2_TEST(1);  // 1 to apply the Box-Pierce test of serial correlation on the squared ...
// Multivariate tests
mgarchobj.M_NORMALITY_TEST(1);
mgarchobj.HOSKING_TEST(1);  // 1 to apply the Hosking test of serial correlation on the ...
mgarchobj.HOSKING2_TEST(1,<1;10>);  // 1 to apply the Hosking test of serial correlation on the squared...
mgarchobj.LI_MCLEOD_TEST(1);  // 1 to apply the Li and McLeod test of serial correlation on the ...
mgarchobj.LI_MCLEOD2_TEST(1);  // 1 to apply the Li and McLeod test of serial correlation on the...
mgarchobj.LMC_TEST(1);  // LM test for constant correlation of TSE (for CCC models only)
mgarchobj.ENGLE_SHEPPARD_TEST(1,<2;5>);  // Test for constant correlation of ENGLE and SHEPPARD ...
mgarchobj.RUNTESTS(1);     // 1 to run the selected misspecification tests

mgarchobj.Initialization(<>);  // Do not remove this line. Initialization.
mgarchobj.PrintStartValues(3);    // 1 to print the starting values in a table form, 2 for variable by...
mgarchobj.PrintOutput(1);  // 1 to print the output after the estimation. 0 otherwize

mgarchobj.DoEstimation();  // To launch the estimation
delete mgarchobj;
}
```

A new feature of G@RCH 6.0 (an of other OxMetrics 5 modules) is that Ox code can be generated. The Model/Ox Batch Code command (or Alt+O) activates a new dialog box called 'Generate Ox Code' that allows the user to select an item for which to generate Ox code.

The code is than opened in a new window and, provided Ox Professional is available, this code can be run, either from OxMetrics, or from OxEdit or the command line.

OxBatch_4.ox is an example of Ox Batch code generated by G@RCH 6.0 after the estimation of an AR(1)-GJR(1,1)-CCC model. In the example we perform all kinds of tests, graphs and forecasts and we store the conditional means, variances and covariances.

```
                                                                OxBatch_4.ox
#include <oxstd.h>
#include <oxdraw.h>
#import <packages/MGarch1/mgarch>

main()
{

//--- Ox code for MG@RCH( 1)
decl model = new MGarch();

model.Load("C:\\OxMetrics5\\CASS\\Data\\DJNQ.xls");
model.Deterministic(-1);

model.Select(Y_VAR, {"DJ", 0, 0});
model.Select(Y_VAR, {"NQ", 0, 0});

model.CSTS(1,1);
model.DISTRI(NORMAL);
model.ARMA_ORDERS(1,0);
model.GARCH_ORDERS(1,1);
model.MODEL(CCC);
model.MLE(QMLE);
model.UGARCH_MODELS(GJR);
model.UGARCH_TRUNC(1000);
model.UGARCH_PrintOutput(1);
model.UGARCH_ARFIMA(0);
model.ONE_STEP(0);
model.TSE_LAGS(0);
model.SetSelSampleByDates(dayofcalendar(1989, 9, 28), dayofcalendar(2004, 9, 27));
model.Initialization(<>);
model.PrintOutput(1);
model.DoEstimation();

decl cov_vec,cor_vec,Varf,covf_vec,corf_vec;
model.INFO_CRITERIA(1);
model.NORMALITY_TEST(1);
model.Q_TEST(1,<5;10;20;50>);
model.Q2_TEST(1,<5;10;20;50>);
model.M_NORMALITY_TEST(1);
model.HOSKING_TEST(1,<5;10;20;50>);
model.HOSKING2_TEST(1,<5;10;20;50>);
model.LI_MCLEOD_TEST(1,<5;10;20;50>);
model.LI_MCLEOD2_TEST(1,<5;10;20;50>);
model.LMC_TEST(1);
model.ENGLE_SHEPPARD_TEST(1,<5;10>);
model.Tests();
model.PLOT_RAW(1);
model.PLOT_STAND_RES(1);
model.PLOT_VAR(1);
model.PLOT_COV(1);
model.PLOT_CORR(1);
model.Graphs_in_sample(-1);
model.FORECAST(1,10);
model.FORECASTING();

cov_vec=model.GetCov_vec();
for (decl i=0;i<columns(cov_vec);++i)
model.Append_in(cov_vec[][i],model.GetCovNames()[i]);
covf_vec=model.GetCovf_vec();
for (decl i=0;i<columns(covf_vec);++i)
model.Append_out(covf_vec[][i],model.GetCovfNames()[i]);
model.Save("C:\\OxMetrics5\\CASS\\Data\\DJNQ.xls");

delete model;
}
```

The MGarch class offers more flexibility than the rolling menus. When using the rolling menus, the same ARMA order is applied on each series. The previous code can be modified to allow different ARMA orders. Similarly, different GARCH orders and different GARCH-type models can be chosen for CCC, DCC, OGARCH and GOGA-RCH models.

For instance, to select an AR(1)-GJR(1,1) for the Dow Jones and an MA(1)-GARCH(1,2) for the Nasdaq, the previous code has simply to be modified as follows:

```
model.ARMA_ORDERS(<1;0>,<0;1>);
model.GARCH_ORDERS(<1;1>,<1;2>);
...
model.UGARCH_MODELS(<GJR;GARCH>);
```

Here is a list of MG@RCH specific Ox commands.

(1) CSTS: Specifies if constants are wanted respectively in the conditional mean and in the conditional variance equations.

(2) DISTRI: Specifies the desired distribution, i.e. 0 for the Gaussian (Normal) distribution, 1 for the Student-t distribution.

(3) ARMA_ORDERS: Specifies respectively the AR and MA orders.

(4) GARCH_ORDERS: Specifies the orders of the MGARCH(p, q)-type model.

(5) MODEL: specification choice (string).

- SCALAR_BEKK;
- DIAG_BEKK;
- RiskMetrics;
- CCC;
- DCC;
- DCC_TSE;
- OGARCH;
- GOGARCH_ML;
- GOGARCH_NLS.

(6) MLE: 0, standard errors based on second derivatives. 1 standard errors based on numerical OPG matrix. 2, robust standard errors (QMLE) are computed (irrespectively of the density choice).

(7) VARIANCE_TARGETING: 1 to apply variance targeting.

(8) OGARCH_M: number of factors (M) for the OGARCH model.

(9) UGARCH_MODELS: specification choice (string) of the univariate GARCH models (for CCC, DCC, OGARCH and GOGARCH models)

- GARCH;
- EGARCH;
- GJR;
- APARCH;
- IGARCH;
- FIGARCH_BBM;
- FIGARCH_CHUNG;
- FIEGARCH;

- FIAPARCH_BBM;
- FIAPARCH_CHUNG;
- HYGARCH.

(10) UGARCH_ARFIMA: 1 to add a long-memory component in the conditional mean equation, 0 otherwise (for CCC, DCC, OGARCH and GOGARCH models).

(11) UGARCH_TRUNC: truncation order of FIGARCH-type models (for CCC, DCC, OGARCH and GOGARCH models).

(12) UGARCH_VARIANCE_TARGETING: 1 to apply variance targeting on the univariate GARCH-type models (for CCC, DCC, OGARCH and GOGARCH models).

(13) ONE_STEP: 1 for 1-step MLE estimation, 0 for 2-step (for CCC and DCC models).

(14) INFO_CRITERIA: 1 to print the information criteria, 0 otherwise.

(15) NORMALITY_TEST: 1 to print the univariate normality tests, 0 otherwise.

(16) Q_TEST: lag orders of the univariate Box-Pierce tests on $\hat{z}_t$, e.g. verb"Q_TEST(¡5;10¿);" to run the test with 5 and 10 lags.

(17) Q2_TEST: lag orders of the univariate Box-Pierce tests on $\hat{z}_t^2$

(18) M_NORMALITY_TEST: 1 to print the multivariate normality test, 0 otherwise.

(19) HOSKING_TEST: lag orders of Hosking's tests of misspecification of the conditional mean.

(20) HOSKING2_TEST: lag orders of Hosking's tests of misspecification of the conditional variance-covariance.

(21) LI_MCLEOD_TEST: lag orders of Li and McLeod tests of misspecification of the conditional mean.

(22) LI_MCLEOD2_TEST: lag orders of Li and McLeod tests of misspecification of the conditional variance-covariance.

(23) LMC_TEST: 1 to run the LM test of CCC of TSE (2000) (for CCC models only).

(24) ENGLE_SHEPPARD_TEST: the first argument is 1 to run the test of CCC of Engle and Sheppard (2001). The second argument is the number of lags (for CCC models only).

(25) Tests(): To launch the missspecification tests selected above.

(26) FORECAST: The first argument is 1 to run the forecasting procedure, the second argument is the forecasting horizon h.

(27) FORECASTING(): To launch the forecasting procedure.

(28) PLOT_RAW, PLOT_STAND_RES, PLOT_VAR, PLOT_COV, PLOT_CORR: 1 to plot the raw data, standardised residuals, conditional variances, conditional covariances and conditional correlations respectively, 0 otherwise.

(29) PLOT_IN_SAMPLE: 1 to plot the selected graphs.

9.10 Simulations

G@RCH 6.0 allows the simulation of several MGARCH models, namely BEKK, CCC and DCC models.

Unlike for univariate GARCH models, simulation of these models is only available by calling the MGarch class within an Ox code.

The relevant functions for the simulation of MGARCH models are: Simul_BEKK, Simul_CCC, Simul_DCCE and Simul_DCCTSE. These functions are described in Chapter 10.

Simul_CCC_DCC.ox is an example of Ox code using the MGarch class that simulates the DCC-GARCH(1,1) of Tse and Tsui (2002) and estimate the same model on the simulated data.

The most relevant lines of code are reported below.

```
                                                          Simul_CCC_DCC.ox
#include <oxstd.h>
#import <packages/MGarch1/mgarch>

main()
{
//*** CREATE OBJECT ***//
decl T=2500;
decl T0=500;
decl N=2;

decl Model={GARCH,GARCH};
decl omega=<0.010312;0.013054>;
decl beta={<0.940037>,<0.925923>};
decl alpha={<0.048645>,<0.066936>};
decl rho=<1,0.606273;0.606273,1>;
decl vtheta_q=0.015423;
decl vtheta_p=0.980941;
decl lags_TSE=N;

decl mgarchobj = new MGarch();
decl mv=rann(T+T0,N);
decl my,Ht;

// mgarchobj.Simul_CCC(Model, omega, alpha, beta, rho, 0, 0, 0, mv, T0, &my, &Ht);
// mgarchobj.Simul_DCCE(Model, omega, alpha, beta, rho, vtheta_q, vtheta_p, 0, 0, 0, mv, T0, &my, &Ht);
mgarchobj.Simul_DCCTSE(Model, omega, alpha, beta, rho, vtheta_q, vtheta_p, lags_TSE, 0, 0, 0, mv, T0, &my, &Ht);
...
}
```

Simul_BEKK.ox is another example of Ox code that simulates (and estimates) a Diagonal BEKK(1,1) with normal errors.

```
                                                          Simul_BEKK.ox
#include <oxstd.h>
#import <packages/MGarch1/mgarch>

main()
{
decl T=2500;
decl T0=500;
decl N=2;

decl C=<0.051162,0.034084;0,0.115097>;
decl beta={<0.981700,0;0,0.938498>};
decl alpha={<0.129161,0;0,0.302027>};

decl mgarchobj = new MGarch();
decl mv=rann(T+T0,N);
decl my,Ht;

mgarchobj.Simul_BEKK(C, beta, alpha, mv, T0, &my, &Ht);
...
}
```

Finally, examples Simul_OGARCH.ox and Simul_GOGARCH.ox illustrate how to simulate OGARCH and GOGARCH models respectively. Note that the only difference between the two programs is the matrix Z. For the OGARCH model, Z is restricted to be orthogonal while for the OGARCH it is only assumed to be square and invertible.

Part of the code is given below.

```
                                                          Simul_GOGARCH.ox
#include <oxstd.h>
#include <oxdraw.h>
#import <packages/Garch5/garch>
#import <packages/MGarch1/mgarch>

main()
{
decl T=2500;
decl T0=500;
decl N=2;

decl Model={<GARCH>,<GARCH>};
decl beta=<0.820603;0.799506>;
decl alpha=<0.085153;0.084490>;
decl omega=ones(N,1)-alpha-beta;
decl Z=<-0.99653,-0.083293;-0.66127,-0.75014>;
// --> U=<0.89345,-0.44917;0.44917,0.89345>;
// --> abs(delta)=0.465835;
decl V=<0.58514,0;0,0.69618>;

decl mgarchobj = new MGarch();
decl garchobj = new Garch();
decl mv=rann(T+T0,N);
decl my=zeros(T,N),fct=<>,f_tmp,sigma2;

for(decl j=0; j<N; ++j)
{
garchobj.Simulate_GARCH(omega[j], alpha[j], beta[j], mv[][j], T0, &f_tmp, &sigma2);
fct~=f_tmp;
}
for(decl j=0; j<T; ++j)
my[j][]=(sqrt(V)*Z*fct[j][]' )';
...
}
```

Chapter 10

Structure of the Program

10.1 Classes and Functions

Ox provides support for object-oriented programming. An interesting concept is therefore the "Classes". Indeed, one can create new classes based on other existing parent-classes and use the functions of these parents, therefore avoiding to rewrite these procedures for derived classes. In our case, the Garch, MGarch and Realized classes are defined as Modelbase type of classes. This Modelbase class derives itself from the Database class.

The Database class is dedicated to the handling of the database, the sample, the names of the variables, the selection of the variables... The Modelbase class implements model estimation features. It is not intended to be used directly but as a base for a more specialized class, such as the Garch, MGarch and Realized classes or already available classes such as ARFIMA, DPD (Panel Data estimation), SVPack (Stochastic Volatility models) or SsfPack (State space forms).

See Doornik (2007b) for more details about the notion of "Classes".

10.2 Garch **Member Functions List**

Here is the list of the Garch member functions and a brief description for each of them.

Constructor and Destructor

Garch	Constructor
~Garch	Destructor

Model Formulation (used in the "Console Version")

ARCH_IN_MEAN	Allows to introduce the ARCH effect in the mean equation
ARCHLAGS	Specifies the desired lags for the Engle's LM test for ARCH

ARFIMA	Specifies if ARFIMA is wanted in the mean
ARMA_ORDERS	Specifies the AR and MA orders in the mean
BOUNDS	Specifies if estimated parameters are bounded with the lower and upper bounds entered in `startingvalues.txt`
BOXPIERCE	Specifies the desired lags for the Box-Pierce test
COVAR	Specifies if the Variance-Covariance matrix of the estimated parameters is printed in the output
CSTS	Specifies if constants are wanted in the mean and in the variance
DISTRI	Specifies the desired distribution
DQT	Specifies if the Dynamic Quantile Test is wanted and the number of lags of the Hit variable
FIXPARAM	Allows to fix some parameters to their starting values
FORECAST	Specifies if forecasts are wanted and the number of forecasts
FOREGRAPHS	Plots and saves various forecast-related graphs in OxMetrics Desktop
GARCH_ORDERS	Specifies the p and q orders of the GARCH(p, q)
GRAPHS	Plots and saves various estimation related graphs in OxMetrics Desktop
INFO_CRITERIA	1 to print the information criteria
ITER	Specifies the number of iterations between prints of intermediary results
KUPIEC_TEST	1 to apply the KUPIEC Test
MLE	Specifies the estimation method of the standard errors
MODEL	Specifies the GARCH-type of models in the conditional variance.
NORMALITY_TEST	1 to apply the normality tests
NYBLOM	Specifies if the Nyblom stability test is wanted
PEARSON	Specifies the desired lags for the adjusted Pearson goodness-of-fit test
RISKMETRICS	Specifies the value of $lambda$ for the RiskMetrics model
RBD	Specifies if the Residual-Based Diagnostic test is wanted
SAVEPAR	Saves the parameters estimates, their standard errors and their t-statistics in an Excel spreadsheet
SBT	Specifies if the Sign Bias Test is wanted
STORE	Allows storing estimated ε_t, ε_t^2 and σ_t^2 series
TESTS	Allows to run tests either on raw data (prior to estimation) or after the estimation
TRUNC	Truncation order for the F.I. models using the method of Baillie, Bollerslev, and Mikkelsen (1996)

VaR_LEVELS	Specifies the VaR levels of the Kupiec and DQT tests
VARIANCE_TARGETING	1 to apply variance targeting (not possible with all models)

Model Information

Get_T1	Returns the value of m_iT1est (modelbase global variable)
Get_T2	Returns the value of m_iT2est (modelbase global variable)
GetcT	Gets the number of observations
GetDistri	Gets the index of the selected distribution
	(0: Normal, 1: Student, 2: GED, 3: skewed-Student)
GetModelName	Returns the index (or string version) of the ARCH model used
GetNbPar	Gets the number of parameters
GetParNames	Gets the names of the parameters
GetSeries	Returns a matrix with the Y series, the mean residuals
	and the conditional variance
GetValue	Returns the value of a variable
GetXNames	Gets the names of the regressors in the mean equation
GetYNames	Gets the name of the dependent variable
GetZNames	Gets the names of the regressors in the variance equation

Parameters management

GetPara	Constructs the parameters vector
	errors and their t-statistics
SplitPara	Allocates the value of each element of the parameters vector to
	the correct variable

Initialization

CheckPara	Checks initial values
CheckValue	Checks the format and size of the concerned parameter
FixBounds	Fixes the values of the lower and upper bounds of the estimated
	parameters
InitGlobals	Initializes the class member variables
InitData	Initializes the characteristics of the model (sample, regressors...
InitStartValues	Initializes the starting values of the parameters to estimate
Initialization	Initializes the model and the associated parameters
MatrixToString	Transforms a matrix into its string counterpart

ReleaseBounds	Sets the bounds to $< -\infty; \infty >$ for all parameters
SetBounds	Allows to change default bounds of a parameter
SetStartValue	Allows to change the default starting value of a parameter

Estimation Process

cfunc_gt0	Function evaluating a set of nonlinear constraints or 0 if not
Covar	Computes and stores the variance-covariance matrix of the estimated parameters
DoEstimation	Estimates the model ("Light version")
Estimate	Estimates the model ("Full version")
FigLL	Defines the function to be optimized
FigLL2	Launches the FigLL function. Used in the Covar function as as first argument of NumJacobianEx
GetRes	Get $y_t - \mu_t$, see Equation (9.6)
GetXB	Get $\mu_t = \mu + \sum_{i=1}^{n_1} \delta_i x_{i,t}$, see Equation (9.6)
GetZB	Get $\omega_t = \omega + \sum_{i=1}^{n_2} \omega_i x_{i,t}$, see Equation (3.14)
Maxsa	Function specifying that the model is estimated using the MaxSA algorithm
MLEMeth	Prints the estimated parameters
Positivity	Checks the positivity constraints with the estimated parameters
Stationarity	Checks the stationarity constraints of the conditional variance

Filters

Aparch	APARCH filter
Aparch_in_mean	APARCH-in-mean filter
Egarch	EGARCH filter
Egarch_in_mean	EGARCH-in-mean filter
Fiaparch_BBM_in_mean	FIAPARCH-in-mean filter with the method of Baillie *et al.*(1996)
Fiaparch_Chung_in_mean	FIAPARCH-in-mean filter with the method of Chung(1999)
Fiegarch	FIEGARCH filter
Fiegarch_in_mean	FIEGARCH-in-mean filter
Figarch_BBM	FIGARCH filter with the method of Baillie *et al.*(1996)
Figarch_BBM_in_mean	FIGARCH-in-mean filter with the method of Baillie *et al.*(1996)
Figarch_Chung	FIGARCH filter with the method of Chung(1999)

Figarch_Chung_in_mean	FIGARCH-in-mean filter with the method of Chung(1999)
Garch_Filter	GARCH filter
Garch_in_mean	GARCH-in-mean filter
GJR_Filter	GJR filter
GJR_in_mean	GJR-in-mean filter
KiAparch	Computes κ_i in the APARCH model. See Section 4.4.

Distributions

CD	Computes the Cumulative Distribution Function of the standardized residuals
CDFGED	Computes the CDF of the GED
CDFTA	Computes the CDF of the (skewed) Student distribution
E_abseps	Computes $E(|z_t|)$ for the corresponding distribution
GaussLik	Computes the log-likelihood for the Gaussian distribution
GEDLik	Computes the log-likelihood for the GED
INVCDFGED	Computes the Inverse CDF of the GED
INVCDFTA	Computes the Inverse CDF of the (skewed) Student-t distribution
mom_trst	Computes the non-centered first moment of the standardized Student-t distribution
SkStudentLik	Computes the log-likelihood for the skewed-Student-t distribution
StudentLik	Computes the log-likelihood for the Student-t distribution

Forecasting

Forecasting	Launches the forecasting procedure
For_Aparch	Forecasts filter of the APARCH process
For_Arma	Forecasts filter of the ARMA process
For_Arfima	Forecasts filter of the ARFIMA process
For_Egarch	Forecasts filter of the EGARCH process
For_Fiaparch_BBM	Forecasts filter of the FIAPARCH process (BBM method)
For_Fiaparch_Chung	Forecasts filter of the FIAPARCH process (Chung method)
For_Fiegarch	Forecasts filter of the FIEGARCH process.
For_Figarch_BBM	Forecasts filter of the FIGARCH process (BBM method)
For_Figarch_Chung	Forecasts filter of the FIGARCH process (Chung method)
For_Garch	Forecasts filter of the GARCH process
For_GJR	Forecasts filter of the GJR process

`For_Graphs`	Draws the forecasts graphics
`GetForcData`	Gets all the post-estimation data (if any)
`GetXBetaForc`	Gets the post-estimation values of the regressor(s) in the mean
`GetZBetaForc`	Gets the post-estimation values of the regressor(s) in the variance

Tests

`absha`	Computes frequencies in an interval defined by upper and lower bounds
`ADF`	Computes the ADF unit root test
`auto`	Plots the correlograms of $\left(\zeta - \overline{\zeta}\right)^j$, for $j = 1, 2, 3, 4$, where ζ is the probability integral transform
`BoxPQ`	Computes and prints the modified Box-Pierce Q-statistics and the associated p-values
`CL_uniform`	Computes the confidence bounds of a confidence interval from the vector of assumed uniform 0-1 "z series"
`EstimateGPH`	Estimate d (long-memory parameter) using the log-periodogram method
`EstimateGSP`	Estimate d (long-memory parameter) using the Gaussian semi-parametric method
`FEM`	Computes and prints 10 forecasts errors measures
`FigLL3`	Launches the FigLL function. Used in the RBD_test function as as first argument of NumJacobianEx
`ICriterion`	Computes four Information Criteria (Akaike, Hannan-Quinn, Schwarz and Shibata)
`KPSS`	Computes the KPSS unit root test
`MZ`	Computes and prints the Mincer and Zarnowitz (1969) regression for the conditional variance
`Normality`	Computes the skewness, kurtosis and Jarque and Bera (1987) test, with associated t-test and p-values
`Nyblom`	Computes and prints the Nyblom (1989) stability test
`PearsonTest`	Computes adjusted Pearson Chi-square Goodness-of-fit test (see Vlaar and Palm, 1993)
`R_test`	Computes the Rescaled Range tests of Mandelbrot (1972) and Lo (1991)
`runs_test`	Computes the Runs (or Wald-Wolfowitz) test on a three-valued data sequence
`RBD_test`	Computes the Residual-Based Diagnostic for Conditional

	Heteroskedasticity of Tse (2002)
SCHMIDT_PHILLIPS	Computes the SCHMIDT-PHILLIPS unit root test
SignBiasTest	Computes the sign bias test, the negative size bias test, the positive size bias test and a joint test of the three
Tests	Launches the selected tests and prints their results
VaR_DynQuant	Computes the Dynamic Quantile Test of Engle and Manganelli (1999
VaR_Test	Computes the Kupiec LR test and the expected shortfall
VR_test	Computes the Variance-ratio test of Lo and MacKinlay (1988)

Output

Append_in	Appends new variables to the database (starting at obs m_iT1est)
Append_out	Appends new variables to the database (starting at obs m_iT2est +1)
Output	Prints the model specification and launches other post-estimation procedures
PrintBounds	Prints the bounds of the parameters to be optimized
PrintStartValues	Prints the starting values of the parameters to be optimized
TestGraphicAnalysis	Draws the graphics of the estimation

High Frequency

Compute_Returns	Computes intra-daily returns
Compute_RV	Computes realized volatility
Compute_BV	Computes bi-power variation
Compute_BVStag	Computes bi-power variation, staggered version (skip-one)
Compute_LeeMykJump	Computes Lee-Mykland statistics for jump detection
Compute_TQ	Computes tri-power quarticity
Compute_TQStag	Computes tri-power quarticity, staggered version (skip-one)
FFF_filter	Flexible fourier form filter
HourNames	Give names that correspond to intra-day hour, returns an array of string containing the hour names
InterpolateMissingValues	
	Replaces missing points with a linear interpolation of the closest available points
SigJumpZTestStat	Compute Z-statistic (log version) for statistical significance of jumps
SigJumpZTestStat2	Compute Z-statistic (relative difference version)

	for statistical significance of jumps
`Simul_Wiener_process`	Simulation of a Wiener process
`Simul_Continuous_GARCH`	Simulation of a continuous-time GARCH diffusion process
`Simul_Continuous_GARCH_JUMPS`	
	Simulation of a continuous-time GARCH diffusion process with jumps
`SplitDate`	Splits dates with format yyyymmdd, returns yyyy, mm, and dd in three variables

10.3 Garch Members Functions

Garch::ADF

```
ADF(const series, const names, const lags, const option);
```

`series`	in: m_cT x k matrix, series to be tested
`names`	in: array of dimension k with the name of the series to be tested
`lags`	in: integer, number of lags in the ADF test
`option`	in: integer, 1 for No intercept and no time trend,
	2 for Intercept and no time trend and 3 for Intercept and time trend.

Return value

Description

Computes the ADF unit root test. See Section 9.3 for more details about this test.

Garch::Aparch, Garch::Egarch, Garch::Figarch_BBM, Garch::Figarch_Chung, Garch::Fiegarch, Garch::Garch_Filter, Garch::GJR_Filter

```
Aparch (const e, const level, const p, const q, const par);
Egarch (const e, const level, const p, const q, const par, const dist);
Garch_Filter (const e, const level, const p, const q, const par);
GJR_Filter (const e, const level, const p, const q, const par);
Figarch_BBM (const e, const level, const p, const q, const laglamb, const par);
Figarch_Chung (const e, const level, const p, const q, const par);
Fiegarch (const e, const level, const p, const q, const laglamb, const par);
```

`e`	in: m_cT x 1 matrix, residuals series (from the mean)

level	in: m_cT x 1 matrix, level term of the conditional variance
p	in: integer, GARCH order
q	in: integer, ARCH order
laglamb	in: integer, truncation order (BBM method)
par	in: m_cPar x 1 matrix, parameters values.

Return value

Returns a m_cT x 1 matrix with the estimated conditional variance (i.e. σ_t^2).

Description

These are the filters of the different models. If there are explanatory variables (or regressors) in the conditional variance equation, level is similar to ω_t in Equation (3.14). If there is no regressor, level is a vector of constant term (ω).

Recall that two methods are available for the FIGARCH models: the Baillie, Bollerslev, and Mikkelsen (1996) method (BBM) that includes a truncation order and the Chung (1999) method that does not. The FIEGARCH process uses BBM's method.

In Figarch_BBM, if the last element of par is 0, we have the regular FIGARCH. Otherwise, we have the HYGARCH model of Davidson (2001) and the last element of par is $\log(\alpha)$.

Finally, the FIAPARCH model is estimated through the FIGARCH procedure. For instance, for a FIAPARCH(1,d,1) with the method of BBM, we have:

Figarch_BBM(sqrt(G),level,p,q,laglamb,alpha|beta|d|hy).^(2/delta)

with $G = (|\varepsilon_t| - \gamma\varepsilon_t)^\delta$.

The elements of the par argument have to be entered in a specific order. Here is the order :

Garch_Filter	$\Rightarrow$ par = <m_valphav | m_vbetav>
Figarch_BBM	$\Rightarrow$ par = <m_valphav|m_vbetav|m_dD|m_vHY>
Figarch_Chung	$\Rightarrow$ par = <m_valphav|m_vbetav|m_dD>
Egarch	$\Rightarrow$ par = <m_valphav|m_vbetav|m_vtheta1|m_vtheta2>
Fiegarch	$\Rightarrow$ par = <m_valphav|m_vbetav|m_vtheta1|m_vtheta2|m_dD>
GJR_Filter	$\Rightarrow$ par = <m_valphav|m_vbetav|m_vleverage>
Aparch	$\Rightarrow$ par = <m_valphav|m_vbetav|m_vgamma|m_ddelta>

Garch::Aparch_in_mean, Garch::Egarch_in_mean,
Garch::Fiaparch_BBM_in_mean, Garch::Fiaparch_Chung_in_mean,
Garch::Fiegarch_in_mean, Garch::Figarch_BBM_in_mean,
Garch::Figarch_Chung_in_mean, Garch::Garch_in_mean,

Garch::GJR_in_mean

Aparch_in_mean (const y, const Xb_mean, const ARMA_orders, const ARMA_coef, const ARFIMA, const d_arfima, const Xb_var, const p, const q, const par_APARCH, const in_mean_type, const in_mean);

Egarch_in_mean (const y, const Xb_mean, const ARMA_orders, const ARMA_coef, const ARFIMA, const d_arfima, const Xb_var, const p, const q, const par_EGARCH, const Cst, const in_mean_type, const in_mean);

Fiaparch_BBM_in_mean (const y, const Xb_mean, const ARMA_orders, const ARMA_coef, const ARFIMA, const d_arfima, const Xb_var, const p, const q, const par_fiaparch, const laglamb, const in_mean_type, const in_mean);

Fiaparch_Chung_in_mean (const y, const Xb_mean, const ARMA_orders, const ARMA_coef, const ARFIMA, const d_arfima, const Xb_var, const p, const q, const par_fiaparch, const in_mean_type, const in_mean);

Fiegarch_in_mean (const y, const Xb_mean, const ARMA_orders, const ARMA_coef, const ARFIMA, const d_arfima, const Xb_var, const p, const q, const par_FIEGARCH, const laglamb, const Cst, const in_mean_type, const in_mean);

Figarch_BBM_in_mean (const y, const Xb_mean, const ARMA_orders, const ARMA_coef, const ARFIMA, const d_arfima, const Xb_var, const p, const q, const par_figarch, const laglamb, const in_mean_type, const in_mean);

Figarch_Chung_in_mean (const y, const Xb_mean, const ARMA_orders, const ARMA_coef, const ARFIMA, const d_arfima, const Xb_var, const p, const q, const par_figarch, const in_mean_type, const in_mean);

Garch_in_mean (const y, const Xb_mean, const ARMA_orders, const ARMA_coef, const ARFIMA, const d_arfima, const Xb_var, const p, const q, const par_garch, const in_mean_type, const in_mean);

GJR_in_mean (const y, const Xb_mean, const ARMA_orders, const ARMA_coef, const ARFIMA, const d_arfima, const Xb_var, const p, const q, const par_gjr, const in_mean_type, const in_mean);

y	in: m_cT x 1 matrix, the dependent variable (i.e. y_t)
Xb_mean	in: m_cT x 1 matrix, the level term of the mean equation

ARMA_orders	in: (2 x 1) vector, the ARMA orders: <m_cAR;m_cMA>
ARMA_coef	in: (m_cAR + m_cMA) x 1 vector, the ARMA coefficients
ARFIMA	in: integer, 1 if ARFIMA process wanted in the mean, 0 otherwise
d_arfima	in: double, fractional coefficient (d) of the ARFIMA(p, d, q) process
Xb_var	in: m_cT x 1 matrix, the level term of the variance equation
p	in: integer, GARCH order
q	in: integer, ARCH order
par_MODEL	in: m_cPar x 1 matrix, parameters values
laglamb	in: integer, truncation order (BBM method)
Cst	in: m_cT x 1 matrix, expected value of the standardized residuals (i.e. $E\|z_t\|$)
in_mean_type	in: integer, "in-mean" option (1: add the conditional variance in the mean equation, 2 : add the conditional standard errors)
in_mean	in: double, ARCH-in-mean parameter, ϑ in Equation (3.10)

Return value

Returns a m_cT x 2 matrix with the residuals and the estimated conditional variance, (i.e. $\epsilon_t \sim \sigma_t^2$).

Description

These are the "in-mean" filters of the different models. Just as with the variance equation, the HYGARCH model is launched with the FIGARCH function: the last element of par is $\log(\alpha)$ (to use the original FIGARCH model, just fix it to 0).

Moreover Xb_mean is equivalent to $\mu_t = \mu + \sum_{i=1}^{n_1} \delta_i x_{i,t}$ in Equation (9.6), while Xb_var is $\omega_t = \omega + \sum_{i=1}^{n_2} w_i x_{i,t}$, for $t = 1, \ldots, m_{cT}$ in Equation (3.14). If there is no independent variables, Xb_mean and Xb_var are m_cT x 1 vectors composed of the same value for each observations (i.e. μ and ω).

Garch::ARCH_IN_MEAN

ARCH_IN_MEAN(const type);

| type | in: integer, 1 to add the conditional variance in the conditional mean equation, 2 to add the conditional standard deviation, and 0 otherwise |

No return value

Description

Allows to include σ_t or σ_t^2 in the conditional mean (as an additional regressor) by allocating the value of `type` to the class member variable `m_c_in_mean` (which is used in the various "in-mean" filters).

Garch::ARCHLAGS

```
ARCHLAGS(const lags);
```

       `lags`   in: l x 1 matrix, vector containing the l desired lags for the test

No return value

Description

    Fix the lags for Engle's LM test for ARCH processes. The required format of `lags` is $< lag_1; lag_2; ...; lag_l >$ and its default value is $< 2; 5; 10 >$. This means that three Engle's LM tests for ARCH are computed, at lags 2, 5 and 10, respectively. If `lags` is $<>$, the test will not be reported (this code line can also be removed as it is optional).

Garch::ARFIMA

```
ARFIMA(const type);
```

       `type`   in: integer, 1 to add a fractionally integrated coefficient in the
                           conditional mean equation, 0 otherwise

No return value

Description

    Allows to include a fractionally integrated element in the mean equation, as illustrated in Equation (3.8).

Garch::ARMA_ORDERS, Garch::GARCH_ORDERS

```
ARMA_ORDERS(const cAR, const cMA);
GARCH_ORDERS(const cP, const cQ);
```

       `cAR`   in: integer, AR order, p

       `cMA`   in: integer, MA order, q

       `cP`   in: integer, GARCH order, p

       `cQ`   in: integer, ARCH order, q

No return value

Description

    Fixes the ARMA and GARCH orders.

Garch::Append_in

```
Append_in(const variable, const name);
```

```
variable      in: T × k matrix with the new variables
name          in: array with k variable names of the new variables
```
No return value

Description

Appends new variables to the database (starting at obs m_iT1est)

Garch::Append_out

```
Append_in(const variable, const name);
```
```
variable      in: T × k matrix with the new variables
name          in: array with k variable names of the new variables
```
No return value

Description

Appends new variables to the database (starting at obs m_iT2est + 1)

Garch::Auto

```
Auto(const z, const ncor, const min, const max, const plot);
```
```
z             in: N x 1 matrix, probability integral transform
ncor          in: integer, number of lags
min, max      in: integer, coordinates of the Y-axis (for the 4 graphs)
plot          in: integer, area wherein the first graph is plotted
```
No return value

Description

Plots the correlograms of $\left(\zeta - \overline{\zeta}\right)^{j}$, for $j = 1, 2, 3, 4$, where ζ is the probability integral transform.

Garch::BOUNDS

```
BOUNDS(const method);
```
```
method        in: integer, 1 to bound parameters, 0 otherwise
```
No return value

Description

If method is 1, the estimated parameters are bounded between lower and upper values (these bounds can be edited, see Section 3.9). If it is equal to 0, the parameters are not bounded (i.e. they are said to be "free").

Garch::BOXPIERCE

```
BOXPIERCE(const lags);
```

lags   in: l x 1 matrix, vector containing the l desired lags for the test.

No return value

Description

 Fixes the desired lags when computing Box-Pierce statistics. The required format of lags is $< lag_1; lag_2; ...; lag_l >$ and its default value is is $< 5; 10; 20 >$. This means that BP(5), BP(10) and BP(20) are computed for the standardized residuals and squared standardized residuals. If lags is $<>$, the test will not be reported (this code line can also be removed as it is optional).

Garch::BoxPQ

```
BoxPQ(const eh, const ncor, const adj);
```
   eh   in: m_cT x 1 matrix, series to be tested
   ncor   in: k x 1 matrix, vector of lags
   adj   in: integer, number of degrees of freedom lost (to compute the
           p-values)

Return value

 Returns 1 if the test is successfully run.

Description

 Computes and prints Box-Pierce Q-statistics on the series eh. See Section 9.3 for more details about this test.

Garch::CD

```
CD (const e, const var, const dist, const par);
```
   e   in: m_cT x 1 matrix, the residuals series
   var   in: m_cT x 1 matrix, the variance series
   dist   in: integer, the distribution (0:normal, 1:Student-t, 2:GED or
           3:skewed-Student-t)
   par   in: 2 x 1 matrix, $\log(\xi); \upsilon >$, i.e. the asymmetry coefficient
           and the degree of freedom.

Return value

 A m_cT x 1 vector with the CD.

Description

 Computes $F(z_t)$, where $F(.)$ is the CDF of the selected distribution. Note that par is $<>$ if dist $= 0$ and par is $< 0; \upsilon >$ if dist $= 1$ or 2.

Garch::CDFGED, Garch::CDFTA

```
CDFGED (const ee, const nu);
```

```
CDFTA (const ee, const logxi, const nu);
```
       `ee`   in: m_cT x 1 matrix, the series

       `logxi`   in: double, logarithm of the skewness parameter

       `nu`   in: double, degree of freedom

Return value

A m_cT x 1 matrix with the CDF of the selected distribution.

Description

Computes the CDF of the GED (CDFGED) and the skewed-Student (CDFTA).

Garch::cfunc_gt0

```
virtual cfunc_gt0(const avF, const vP);
```
      `avF`   in: address

                     out: m x 1 matrix with the constraints at vP

      `vP`   in: p x 1 matrix with the coefficients

Return value

Returns 1 if successfully run.

Description

The `cfunc_gt0` argument can be zero, or a function evaluating the nonlinear constraints (which will be constrained to be positive). By default this function does nothing. It is a virtual function and has to be replaced by the user to impose the corresponding constrains. See Section 5.3.2.

Garch::CheckPara

```
CheckPara();
```
No return value

Description

Checks the validity of some basic constraints in the model specification.

Garch::CheckValue

```
CheckValue(const name, const stval, const type);
```
      `name`   in: string, name (cfr. `garch.h`) of the variable to be checked

      `stval`   in: value to be checked (can be of different types: constant, vector, matrix,...)

      `type`   in: integer, 1: starting values, 2: bounds

Return value

Returns 1 if value has the correct format corresponding to name.

Description

Checks if value corresponds to the correct format of the variable name (size, type,...). If type = 1, the format of name itself if checked. If type = 2, the format of the bounds imposed on name are checked.

Garch::Compute_Returns

Compute_Returns(const mPriceData, const ONRet);

>mPriceData   in: $T \times 2$ matrix with the date and intraday prices.

>ONRet   in: integer, 1 if you want to set all overnight returns to zero,
>   0 otherwise.

Return value

Returns a matrix of intradaily returns, i.e. $100[log(s(t)) - log(s(t - \Delta))] \equiv 100[p(t) - p(t - \Delta)]$ with same format as the original price matrix.

Description

The first column of the returned matrix is the date vector (yyyymmdd format). The first return reported by the function is set to zero. If day $t - 1$ is missing (i.e. non-consecutive days), the first intra-day return of day t is set to zero. The input ONRet allows to set all overnight returns (first intradaily return of the day) to 0.

Garch::Compute_RV

Compute_RV(const mRet_table);

>mRet_table   in: $T \times k$ matrix with intraday returns

Return value

Returns a $T \times 1$ vector with realized volatility.

Description

Computes realized volatility as defined in Equation (7.12). Note that each row of mRet_table corresponds to one day. The first column corresponds to the first return of the day. There are $k \equiv 1/\Delta$ intraday returns per day.

Garch::Compute_BV

Compute_BV(const mRet_table);

>mRet_table   in: $T \times k$ matrix with intraday returns

Return value

Returns a $T \times 1$ vector bi-power variation.

Description

Computes bi-power variation as defined in Equation (7.38). Note that each row of
mRet_table corresponds to one day. The first column corresponds to the first return of
the day. There are $k \equiv 1/\Delta$ intraday returns per day.

Garch::Compute_BVStag

```
Compute_BVStag(const mRet_table);
```
   mRet_table in: $T \times k$ matrix with intraday returns

Return value

Returns a $T \times 1$ vector containing staggered bi-power variation.

Description

Computes bi-power (staggered version) variation as defined in Equation (**??**). Note
that each row of mRet_table corresponds to one day. The first column corresponds to
the first return of the day. There are $k \equiv 1/\Delta$ intraday returns per day.

Garch::Compute_LeeMykJump

```
Compute_LeeMykJump(const mRet_table, const siglevel, const nodrift,
const K);
```
   mRet_table in: $T \times k$ matrix with intraday returns
   siglevel in: Significance level for the test (in percentage points)
   nodrift   in: $1 =$ no drift in the underlying process, 0 otherwise
   K   in: window length for the local volatility estimator

Return value

Returns a $T \times k$ indicator matrix with ones when a jump is detected at the significance level siglevel.

Description

Detects jumps using Lee-Mykland statistics. See Section 7.8 for more details.

Garch::Compute_TQ

```
Compute_TQ(const mRet_table);
```
   mRet_table in: $T \times k$ matrix with intraday returns

Return value

Returns a $T \times 1$ vector containing tri-power quarticity.

Description

Computes tri-power quarticity as defined in Equation (7.46). Note that each row of mRet_table corresponds to one day. The first column corresponds to the first return of the day. There are $k \equiv 1/\Delta$ intraday returns per day.

Garch::Compute_TQStag

```
Compute_TQStag(const mRet_table);
```
　　　　mRet_table　　in: $T \times k$ matrix with intraday returns

Return value

Returns a $T \times 1$ vector containing tri-power quarticity (staggered version).

Description

Computes tri-power quarticity (staggered version) as defined in Equation (**??**). Note that each row of mRet_table corresponds to one day. The first column corresponds to the first return of the day. There are $k \equiv 1/\Delta$ intraday returns per day.

Garch::Covar

```
virtual Covar();
```
No return value

Description

Computes the variance-covariance matrix and allocates it to the class member variable m_mCovar.

Garch::COVAR

```
COVAR(const p);
```
　　　　p　　　　　　　　in: integer, 1 to print the variance-covariance matrix of the estimated parameters, 0 otherwise

No return value

Description

If p is 1, the variance-covariance matrix of the estimated parameters is printed in the output.

Garch::CSTS

```
CSTS(const cstM, const cstV);
```
　　　　cstM　　　　　　in: integer, 1 to include a constant term in the mean equation
　　　　　　　　　　　　　　0 otherwise
　　　　cstV　　　　　　in: integer, 1 to include a constant term in the variance equation
　　　　　　　　　　　　　　0 otherwise

No return value

Description

By default, a constant is estimated both in the mean and the variance equation. However, it is possible to remove one of both of them by fixing the corresponding argument to 0.

Garch::DQT

```
DQT(const choice, const lags);
```

       `choice`   in: integer, 1 to apply the Dynamic Quantile Test of

                                Engle and Manganelli (1999), 0 otherwise

       `lags`   in: integer, number of lags (p) of the Hit variable to include

                                  in the OLS regression, 0 otherwise

No return value

Description

The Dynamic Quantile Test is launched when calling `Tests()`. The VaR levels are specified using function VaR_LEVELS.

Garch::DISTRI

```
DISTRI(const dist);
```

      `dist`   in: integer, 0, 1, 2 or 3 depending on the desired distribution

No return value

Description

Selects the distribution. If `dist` = 0, the Gaussian (Normal) distribution is selected ; if `dist` = 1, it is the Student-t distribution, ; if `dist` = 2, it is the Generalized Error distribution (GED) and if `dist` = 3, it is the skewed-Student-t.

Garch::DoEstimation, Garch::Estimate

```
DoEstimation();
```

```
Estimate();
```

Return value

Returns if 1 if the model is successfully estimated

Description

`DoEstimation` is launched from the "Console version" of the program while `Estimate` is launched from the "OxPack version". These procedures are the core procedures of the program. They successively launch others procedures to run the formulated model (estimation, forecasting, tests...).

Garch::E_abseps

```
E_abseps(const dist, const par);
```

dist   in: integer, 0 (Gaussian), 1 (Student), 2 (GED) or 3 (Skewed-Student), i.e. distribution of z_t

par   in: vector of dimension depending on the distribution choice par = <> when dist=0, $< \nu >$ if dist=1 or 2 and $< \log(\xi);\nu >$ if dist=3.

Return value

  $E(|z_t|)$

Garch::EstimateGPH

```
EstimateGPH(const mY, const iTrunc, const fPrint);
```

mY   in: $T x 1$ matrix, dependent variable observation in time domain

iTrunc   in: int, truncation parameter in the frequency domain
                number of low frequency periodogram points used in estimation

fPrint   in: int, TRUE: print results

Return value

Returns a 1×3 vector with $\hat{d}$, $SE(\hat{d})$, and the p-value for two-sided testing of $d = 0$.

Description

  Estimate d (long-memory parameter) using the log-periodogram method. See Section 9.3 for more details.

Garch::EstimateGPH

```
EstimateGPH(const mY, const iTrunc, const fPrint);
```

mY   in: $T x 1$ matrix, dependent variable observation in time domain

iTrunc   in: int, truncation parameter in the frequency domain
                number of low frequency periodogram points used in estimation

fPrint   in: int, TRUE: print results

Return value

Returns a 1×3 vector with $\hat{d}$, $SE(\hat{d})$, and the p-value for two-sided testing of $d = 0$.

Description

  Estimate d (long-memory parameter) using the Gaussian semi-parametric method. See Section 9.3 for more details.

Garch::FEM

```
FEM(const forc, const obs);
```

forc   in: m_cTforc x 2 matrix, forecasted mean $\sim$ forecasted variance

obs   in: m_cTforc x 2 matrix, observed series $\sim$ observed variance

                 (i.e. m_Yfor $\sim$ m_Hfor)

Return value

Returns 1 if the tests are successfully run

Description

Computes and prints 10 forecast error measures for the m_cTforc forecasts of the mean and of the variance: Mean Squared Error (MSE), Median Squared Error (MedSE), Mean Error (ME), Mean Absolute Error (MAE), Root Mean Squared Error (RMSE), Heteroskedastic Mean Squared Error (HMSE), Mean Absolute Percentage Error (MAPE), Adjusted Mean Absolute Percentage Error (AMAPE), Percentage Correct Sign (PCS), Theil Inequality Coefficient (THEIL) and Logarithmic Loss Function (LL). See Brooks, Burke, and Persand (1997) for more details about these measures.

Garch::FFF_filter

FFF_filter(const ret_table, const sigma_sq_daily, const J, const P, const X, const names_X);

ret_table   in: $T \times k$ matrix with intraday returns

sigma_sq..   in: $T \times 1$ vector of daily volatilities (GARCH, RV, etc.)

J   in: scalar, summation order of Equation (**??**), i.e. J

P   in: scalar, number of sin and cos terms in Equation (**??**), i.e. P

X   in: $Tk \times D$ matrix of variables. $I_k(t, n)$ terms in Equation (**??**)

names_X   in: array of dimension D containing the names of the variables in X

Return value

$T \times k$ matrix corresponding to the estimator of the intraday periodic component, i.e. $\hat{s}_{t,n}$ in Equation (**??**).

Description

Applies the FFF filter of Andersen and Bollerslev (1998b) as described in Section **??**.

Garch::FigLL

FigLL(const vP, const adFunc, const avScore, const aHessian);

vP   in: m_cP x 1 matrix, parameters to be estimated

                 out: estimated parameters

adFunc   in: address

	out: double, log-likelihood function value at vP
avScore	in: 0, or an address
	out: if not 0 on input, m_cP x 1 matrix with first derivatives at vP
aHessian	in: 0, as MaxBFGS and MaxSQPF do not require the Hessian

Return value

Returns 1 if successfully run

Description

This procedure is optimized by Ox with the MaxBFGS function for unconstrained models (that is, without bounds on the parameters). This function uses the Broyden, Fletcher, Goldfarb and Shanno (BFGS) quasi-Newton method (see Doornik, 2007 for further details). When using constrained parameters, FigLL is optimized with MaxSQPF, which enforces all iterates to be feasible, using the algorithm by Lawrence and Tits (2001). If a starting point is infeasible, MaxSQPF will try to minimize the squared constraint violations to find a feasible point.

Garch::FigLL2

FigLL2(const avF, const vP);

adFunc	in: address
	out: double, log-likelihood function value at vP
vP	in: m_cPar x 1 vector with unrestricted coefficients

Return value

Returns 1 if successfully run

Description

This procedure is used as first argument of NumJacobian, when computing the variance-covariance matrix. For more details about NumJacobian, see Doornik (2007b).

Garch::FixBounds

FixBounds();

Return value

Returns 1 if successfully run

Description

This fixes the upper and lower bounds for the m_cPar parameters and allocates them to the m_mBound variable. See Section 3.9 for more details on bounds.

Garch::FIXPARAM

FIXPARAM(const cfix, const fix);

cfix   in: integer, 1 to enable this option, 0 to disable it

fix   in: m_cPar x 1 matrix, binary vector (0: free parameter,
                    1: fixed parameter)

No return value

Description

When cfix = 1, this procedure fixes several of the m_cPar parameters to their starting values. For instance, in an simple ARCH(1) model there are by default 3 parameters to be estimated.[1] When using Initialization(<0.01;0.01;0.5>) to launch the estimation, the ARCH parameter is initialized at 0.5.[2] However, when setting FixParam(1, <0;0;1>), the ARCH parameter is not estimated but fixed at its initial value (i.e. 0.5 in this case). This option is quite flexible as it allows to estimate, say, an AR(2)-ARCH(1) model with the first AR lag fixed and the second one is free. There are five parameters to considered here: two constants, two AR parameters and the ARCH parameter. To do so, one has to select FixParam(1, <0;1;0;0;0>) for the AR(1) parameter to be fixed and for instance Initialization(<0.01;0;0.1;0.01;0.5>) to fix it to 0. For a description of the required order of the elements of the parameters' vector, see the GetPara function.

Garch::For_Aparch, Garch::For_Egarch, Garch::For_Figarch_BBM,
Garch::For_Fiaparch_BBM, Garch::For_Fiaparch_Chung, Garch::For_Fiegarch,
Garch::For_Figarch_Chung, Garch::For_Garch, Garch::For_GJR

```
For_Aparch(const e, const hh, const p, const q, const alpha, const
beta, const gamma, const delta, const level_forc, const Ki);
For_Egarch(const e, const hh, const p, const q, const alpha, const
beta, const theta1, const theta2, const level_forc, const Cst);
For_Fiaparch_BBM(const e, const hh, const p, const q, const
d, const alpha, const beta, const gamma, const delta, const
level_forc, const laglamb, const Ki);
For_Fiaparch_Chung(const e, const hh, const p, const q, const
d, const alpha, const beta, const gamma, const delta, const
level_forc, const Ki);
For_Fiegarch(const e, const hh, const p, const q, const d, const
alpha, const beta, const theta1, const theta2, const level_forc,
const dist, const laglamb);
```

---

[1] We assume here no AR(FI)MA effects in the mean, no regressors and a Gaussian distribution.
[2] Alternatively, one can use SetStartValue("m_valphav",<0.5>);.

For_Figarch_BBM(const e, const hh, const p, const q, const d,
const alpha, const beta, const HY, const level_forc, const laglamb);
For_Figarch_Chung(const e, const hh, const p, const q, const d,
const alpha, const beta, const level_forc);
For_Garch(const e, const hh, const p, const q, const alpha, const
beta, const level_forc);
For_GJR(const e, const hh, const p, const q, const alpha, const
beta, const leverage, const level_forc, const prob_neg);

e	in: m_cT x 1 matrix, in-sample residual values
hh	in: m_cT x 1 matrix, in-sample conditional variance
p	in: integer, GARCH order
q	in: integer, ARCH order
alpha	in: m_cQ x 1 matrix, ARCH coefficients
beta	in: m_cP x 1 matrix, GARCH coefficients
leverage	in: m_cQ x 1 matrix, asymmetry coefficients of the GJR, i.e. ω_i in Equation (4.8)
gamma	in: m_cQ x 1 matrix, asymmetry coefficients of the (FI)APARCH, i.e. γ_i in Equations (4.9) and (4.20) (or double if m_cQ = 1)
delta	in: double, standard deviation exponent of the (FI)APARCH, i.e. δ in Equations (4.9) and (4.20)
theta1	in: m_cQ x 1 matrix, sign effect of the (FI)EGARCH, i.e. θ_1 in Equations (4.4) and (4.19)
theta2	in: m_cQ x 1 matrix, magnitude effect of the (FI)EGARCH, i.e. θ_2 in Equations (4.4) and (4.19)
Cst	in: double, the expected value of the standardized residuals (i.e. $E\lvert z_t\rvert$)
Ki	in: m_cQ x 1 matrix, output of KiAparch(dist, q, par, delta, gamma)
prob_neg	in: double, probability that $\epsilon < 0$
dist	in: integer, selected distribution (0: Normal, 1: Student, 2: GED, 3: skewed-Student)
level_forc	in: (m_cT + m_cTforc) x 1 matrix with $\omega + \sum_{i=1}^{n_2} \omega_i x_{i,t}$, for $t = 1,\ldots, m\_cT + m\_cTforc$
HY	in: double, $\log(\alpha)$ if the HYGARCH is used, 0 otherwise.
laglamb	in: integer, truncation order (BBM method)

Return value

Returns a m_cTforc x 1 matrix with the forecasts of the conditional variance.

Description

These are the forecasting procedures. prob_neg equals 0.5 for the symmetric distributions and $1/(1 + \xi^2)$ for the skewed-Student-t.

Moreover level_forc is equivalent to $\omega_t = \omega + \sum_{i=1}^{n_2} \omega_i x_{i,t}$, for $t = 1, \ldots, m_{cT}$ in Equation (3.14). If there is no independent variables, level_forc is a m_cT x 1 vectors composed of the same value for each observations (i.e. ω).

See Sections 3.10 and 4.8 for further details.

Garch::For_Arma, Garch::For_Arfima

For_Arma(const y_1, const p, const q, const arma, const level_forc, const e);

For_Arfima(const y_1, const p, const q, const d, const arma, const level_forc, const e);

y_1	in: (m_cT x 1) matrix, with $y_l = y_t - \mu_t$
p	in: integer, AR order
q	in: integer, MA order
arma	in: (1 x (m_cAR + m_cMA)) matrix, AR coefficients followed by MA coefficients
level_forc	in: (m_cT+ m_cTforc x 1) matrix, μ_t, for $t = 1, \ldots, $m_cT+ m_cTforc
e	in: (m_cT x 1) matrix, residuals series (ε_t)
d	in: double, long memory coefficient (ζ)

Return value

Returns a m_cTForc x 1 matrix with the forecasts of the mean.

Description

These are the forecasting filters for the mean equation and compute forecasts for ARMA and ARFIMA specifications (without explanatory variables).

Garch::For_Graphs

For_Graphs(const plot, const pre, const type, const valcrit,...);

plot	in: integer, area wherein the first graph is plotted
pre	in: integer, number of pre-observations
type	in: integer, type of confidence intervals (0: none, 1: bands, 2: bars, 3: fans)

valcrit	in: double, critical value for the confidence interval (forecasts $\pm$ valcrit x standard errors)
	(Optional) in: integer, 1 to plot the sample average of the conditional variance

No return value

Description

Displays graphics of forecasts of the mean (with confidence intervals) and forecasts of the variance. Graphs are plotted in OxMetrics Desktop.

Garch::FORECAST

FORECAST(const i, const nbForc, const iprint);

i	in: integer, 1 to compute forecasts, 0 otherwise
nbForc	in: integer, number of forecasts
iprint	in: integer, 1 to print the forecasts, 0 otherwise

No return value

Description

If i is 1, one-step ahead forecasting will be executed. The number of forecasts is given by the value of nbForc. These forecasts will be printed as part of the output if iprint is 1.

Garch::Forecasting

Forecasting();

Return value

Returns a m_cTForc x 2 matrix containing the forecasts for the mean and for the variance (i.e. the class member variable m_mForc)

Description

This procedure executes the forecasts first for the mean, then for the variance by launching different filters (FOR_GARCH, FOR_APARCH...) depending on the specification of the model.

Garch::FOREGRAPHS

FOREGRAPHS(const d, const s, const file);

d	in: integer, 1 to draw forecasts graphics, 0 otherwise
s	in: integer, 1 to save forecasts graphics, 0 otherwise
file	in: string, name of the EPS file containing the saved graphics

No return value

Description

This function calls `FOR_GRAPHS` to draw forecasts graphics in OxMetrics Desktop when using the "Light" version. It also allows saving these graphs in a EPS (Encapsulated PostScript) file.

Garch::Garch

`Garch();`

No return value

Description

   Constructor.

Garch::~Garch

`Garch();`

No return value

Description

   Destructor.

Garch::GaussLik, Garch::GEDLik, Garch::StudentLik, Garch::SkStudentLik

```
GaussLik(const vE, const vSigma2);
GEDLik(const vE, const vSigma2, const a);
StudentLik(const vE, const vSigma2, const v);
SkStudentLik(const vE, const vSigma2, const s, const v);
```

vE	in: m_cT x 1 matrix, residuals
vSigma2	in: m_cT x 1 matrix, conditional variance
a	in: double, asymmetry coefficient υ in Equation (3.17)
s	in: double, asymmetry parameter, $\log(\xi)$ in Equation (3.18)
v	in: double, degree of freedom, υ in Equation (3.16)

Return value

Returns a m_cT x 1 with the individual log-likelihoods.

Description

Computes the log-likelihood function of the various available distributions.

Garch::Get_T1

`Get_T1();`

Return value m_iT1est

Description

Returns the value of m_iT1est (modelbase global variable)

Garch::Get_T2

Get_T2();

Return value m_iT2est

Description

Returns the value of m_iT2est (modelbase global variable)

Garch::GetcT

virtual GetcT();

Return value

Returns the number of observations.

Description

This returns the value of the class member variable that indicates the number of observations (i.e. m_cT).

Garch::GetDistri

GetDistri();

Return value

Returns the index of the selected distribution.

Description

Returns the class member variable that indicates the selected distribution (i.e. m_cDist): 0 for the Normal, 1 for the Student, 2 for the GED or 3 for the skewed-Student.

Garch::GetForcData, Garch::GetXBetaForc, Garch::GetZBetaForc

GetForcData(const iGroup, const cTforc);

GetXBetaForc(const cTforc);

GetZBetaForc(const cTforc);

iGroup	in: string, name of the variable group
cTforc	in: integer, the number of forecasts N_f

Return value

Returns a N_f x 1 matrix containing the realized values of the regressors (in the mean or in the variance).

Description

GetForcData collects the realized values matrix of all the regressor(s) for the forecasting period $[T + 1; T + N_f]$. GetXBetaForc and GetZBetaForc do the same for the regressor(s) in the mean and the regressor(s) in the variance, respectively.

Garch::GetModelName

GetModelName(const mod);

        mod   in: integer or string, index or name of the desired model

Return value

The name of the model (either in its string version or its numerical version).

Description

If mod is an integer, the returned value is the corresponding string (for instance, when using an APARCH model, mod = 4 and the returned value is "APARCH"). If mod is a string, the returned value is numerical (for instance, when using an APARCH model, mod = "APARCH" and the returned value is 4).

Garch::GetNbPar

GetNbPar();

Return value

Returns the number of estimated parameters in the specification.

Description

This function returns m_cPar, the class member variable that indicates the number of parameters (both free and fixed).

Garch::GetPara;

GetPara();

Return value

Returns 1 if successfully run.

Description

It constructs the vector of parameters based on individual class member variables and allocates it to m_vPar. The sequence of the parameters is the following:[3]

- constant in the mean (1 variable, μ)
- regressors in the conditional mean (m_cXM variables, δ_i)
- ARFIMA coefficient (1 variable, ζ)

---

[3] If a parameter is not relevant for the specified model, it is skipped.

- AR coefficients (`m_cAR` variables, ψ_i)
- MA coefficients (`m_cMA` variables, θ_i)
- constant in the conditional variance (1 variable, ω)
- regressors in the conditional variance (`m_cXV` variables, ω_i)
- Fractional integration coefficient in the variance (1 variable, d)
- ARCH coefficients (`m_cQ` variables, α_i)
- GARCH coefficients (`m_cP` variables, β_i)
- GJR coefficients (`m_cQ` variables, γ_i)
- EGARCH coefficients (`m_cQ` x 2 variables, γ_{1i} and γ_{2i})
- APARCH coefficients (`m_cQ` + 1 variables, γ_i and δ for the APARCH or 2 variables γ and δ for the FIAPARCH)
- skewness (asymmetry) coefficient (1 variable, $\log(\xi)$)
- degree of freedom (1 variable, υ)
- HYGARCH coefficient (1 variable, $\log(\alpha)$)
- In-mean effect coefficient (1 variable, ϑ)

For more details on these coefficients and the theory behind the models, see Chapter 3.

Garch::GetParEs

GetParEs();

Return value

A `m_cPar` x 3 matrix structured as `m_vPar` $\sim$ `m_vStdErrors` $\sim$ (`m_vPar` ./ `m_vStdErrors`)

Description

Returns a `m_cPar` x 3 matrix with the parameters estimates, their standard errors and their t-statistics. It is used together with `SAVEPAR` to store estimated parameters of a given model in an external file (Microsoft Excel spreadsheet).

Garch::GetParNames, Garch::GetXNames, Garch::GetYNames, Garch::GetZNames

GetParNames();

GetXNames();

GetYNames();

GetZNames();

Return value

Returns an array of strings with the names of the variables or parameters.

Description

These procedures collect the name of the dependent variable (GetYNames), the name of the estimated parameters (GetParNames), the name of the regressors in the mean equation (GetXNames) or the name of the regressors in the variance equation (GetZNames).

Garch::GetRes

GetRes(const y, const x);

   y   in: m_cT x 1 matrix, dependent variable

   x   in: m_cT x m_cX matrix, regressors in the variance

Return value

  Returns a m_cT x 1 matrix containing the residuals.

Description

  Computes $\varepsilon = y_t - \mu_t$ as illustrated in Equation (9.6).

Garch::GetSeries

GetSeries();

Return value

  Returns a m_cT x 3 matrix with the following format: m_mY $\sim$ m_vE $\sim$ m_vSigma2.

Description

  Returns three series: the dependent variable (i.e. the series being studied), the residuals and the conditional variance (m_mY, m_vE and m_vSigma2 respectively).

Garch::GetValue

GetValue(const name);

   name   in: string, name of a class member variable

Return value

  The value of the variable name (integer, double or matrix).

Description

  Returns the value of a class member variable. The argument name must be a string (thus between quotes) and correspond to the exact name of the variable (case-sensitive). For instance, GetValue("m_cDist") is correct while GetValue(m_cDist) or GetValue("m_cdist") is not. The list of global variables is available in the Garch.h file.

Garch::GetXB

GetXB(const x, const n);

x	in: m_cT x m_cXM matrix, the explanatory variables in the mean
n	in: integer, number of observations

Return value

Returns a m_cT x 1 matrix with the following format: m_clevel + m_vbetam' * x.

Description

Returns the mean, prior to any AR(FI)MA specification, see Equation (9.6).

Garch::GetZB

GetZB(const x, const n);

x	in: m_cT x m_cXV matrix, the explanatory variables in the variance.
n	in: integer, number of observations

Return value

Returns a m_cT x 1 matrix with the following format: m_calpha0 + m_vpsyv' * x.

Description

Returns the conditional variance, prior to any GARCH specification, see Equation (3.14).

Garch::GRAPHS

GRAPHS(const d, const s, const file);

d	in: integer, 1 to draw graphics of the estimation, 0 otherwise
s	in: integer, 1 to save graphics of the estimation, 0 otherwise
file	in: string, name of the EPS file with the saved graphics

No return value

Description

This function calls Test_Graphic_Analysis to draw various graphics resulting from the estimation. These graphs are displayed in OxMetrics Desktop. GRAPHS also allows saving these graphs in a EPS (Encapsulated PostScript) file.

Garch::HourNames

HourNames(const opentime, const closetime, const freq);

opentime	in: integer, first interval of the day (format hhmm). The first figure of hhmm must not be zero, except for midnight which is written 0. For example, 9.25 am is written 925, 5 past midnight is written 5, and 1.15 pm is written 1315).

closetime   in: integer, last interval of the day (same convention as opentime).

freq   in: integer, intradaily frequency in minutes

(for example 5 if you use five minute returns).

Return value

Returns an array of string containing the hour names.

Description

Convenient to give names that correspond to intra-day hour. Returns an array of string containing the names. For example, if opentime=925, closetime=1600, and freq=5, it will return "925","930","935",....,"1600".

Garch::ICriterion

ICriterion(const LogL, const n, const q);

LogL   in: double, the value of the log-likelihood function

n   in: integer, number of observations

q   in: integer, number of parameters

Return value

1 if the test is successfully run, 0 otherwise.

Description

Computes and prints four information criteria (divided by the sample size): the Akaike, Schwarz, Shibata and Hannan-Quinn tests. See Section 9.3 for more details about this test.

Garch::INFO_CRITERIA

INFO_CRITERIA(const choice);

choice   in: integer, 1 to print the information criteria

0 otherwise

No return value

Description

The information criteria are computed in function **ICriterion**.

Garch::InitGlobals

InitGlobals();

Return value

Returns 1 if successfully run

Description

Initializes the class member variables when constructing the object. The default model is a GARCH(1,1) model with a constant in the conditional mean and in the conditional variance, a Normal distribution, no bounds on the parameters, no post-estimation tests and no forecasts.

The GarchEstim_Modified.ox example illustrates the simplest case: no specification is made and the default model is launched on returns of the French CAC40 index.

```
                                           GarchEstim_Modified.ox

#import <packages/Garch42/garch>

main()
{
    decl garchobj;

    garchobj = new Garch();

    garchobj.Load("/data/cac40.in7");
    garchobj.Select(Y_VAR, {"CAC40",0,0} );
    garchobj.SetSelSample(-1, 1, -1, 1);

    garchobj.Initialization(<>) ;
    garchobj.DoEstimation(<>) ;
    garchobj.Output() ;

    delete garchobj;
}
```

Garch::InitData

InitData();

Return value

Returns 1 if successfully run

Description

Initializes the model by allocating to relevant class member variables the Y series (m_vY) and the regressors (m_mXM and m_mXV) , computing the number of observations of the sample and the number of parameters to be estimated.

Garch::Initialization

Initialization(const vStart);

        vStart   in: a m_cPar x 1 vector, the starting values of the parameters to be estimated

No return value

Description

Launches the InitData() and InitStartValues() procedures. If vStart = <>, then the default starting values will be used.

Garch::InitStartValues

`InitStartValues(const init_par, const init_bounds);`

> `init_par`   in: integer, 1 to fix default starting values, 0 otherwise

> `init_bounds` in: integer, 1 to fix default bounds, 0 otherwise

No return value

Description

Initializes the starting values when the user do not enter any specific starting values. These values are:

- Constant in the conditional mean: 0.05
- Regressors in the conditional mean: 0.01
- ARFIMA(p,d,q): $p_1 = 0.2$, $p_{>1} = 0.05$, $d = 0.1$, $q_1 = 0.15$, $q_{>1} = 0.02$
- Constant term in the conditional variance equation: 0.01
- Regressors in the conditional variance : 0
- GARCH: $\beta_1 = 0.7$ (if GARCH) or 0.45 (if FIGARCH), $\beta_{>1} = 0.1$.
- ARCH: $\alpha_i = 0.1$
- FIGARCH: $d = 0.5$
- GJR: $\omega_i = 0.01$
- EGARCH: $\phi_1 = -0.1$ and $\phi_2 = 0.2$
- APARCH: $\delta = 1.2$, $\gamma_1 = 0.15$, $\gamma_{>1} = 0.05$
- skewed-Student distribution: $\log(\xi) = 0.01$
- Student distribution: $\upsilon = 6.0$
- GED distribution: $\upsilon = 2.0$
- HYGARCH : $\log(\alpha) = 0.0$
- In-Mean : $\vartheta = 0.0$

The user can change these initial values by using the `SetStartValue` function. An example is provided in `GarchEstim.ox`. Note that if `init_bounds = 1`, `FixBound` is launched at the end of the procedure.

Garch::InterpolateMissingValues

`InterpolateMissingValues(const amPrice);`

> `amPrice`   in: address, matrix with prices (including path).
>   The data must be organized as follows:
>   rows must correspond to days and columns must
>   be intra-day periods.
>   The first column must be the date vector with format yyyymmdd.

> Missing points must be zero.
>
> out: matrix, same matrix with prices where missing points are linearly interpolated.

No return value

Description

This function checks whether the first and the last element of the raw price table are zero. If yes, they are replaced by the nearest point. Then, a linear interpolation is performed to replace missing values. Missing values must be zeros.

Garch::INVCDFGED, Garch::INVCDFTA

```
INVCDFGED (const p, const nu);
INVCDFTA (const p, const logxi, const nu);
```

p	in: double, probability
logxi	in: double, logarithm of the skewness parameter
nu	in: double, degree of freedom

Return value

Returns the solution of the integral equation $p = F(x|.)$ (double).

Description

Computes the inverse CDF of the GED (INVCDFGED) and the skewed-Student (INVCDFTA).

Garch::ITER

```
ITER(const i);
```

i	in: integer, number of iterations between intermediary prints

No return value

Description

With G@RCH, it is possible to print intermediary results of the estimation. This function allows the user to select the number of iterations between printed results. For instance, if i = 10, intermediary values of the parameters and the log-likelihood function will be printed every 10 iterations. When i = 0, no intermediary result is printed. Notice that this code line can be removed from GarchEstim.ox (G@RCH will then consider i = 0).

Garch::KPSS

```
KPSS(const series, const names, const lags, const option);
```

series	in: m_cT x k matrix, series to be tested

names   in: array of dimension k with the name of the series to be tested

lags   in: integer, number of lags in the KPSS test

option   in: integer, 1 for KPSS test without trend,

                        2 for KPSS test with a trend.

Return value

Description

Computes the KPSS unit root test. See Section 9.3 for more details about this test.

Garch::KUPIEC_TEST

KUPIEC_TEST(const choice);

       choice   in: integer, 1 to apply the Kupiec LRT of Kupiec (1995)

                        0 otherwise

No return value

Description

The Kupiec Test is launched when calling Tests(). The VaR levels are specified using function VaR_LEVELS.

Garch::MatrixToString

MatrixToString(const name_matrix, const val, const format);

       name_matrix in: string, name of the matrix to transform

       val   in: m x n matrix, value of this matrix

       format   in: integer, 0, 1 or 2.

Return value

Returns 1 if successfully run

Description

Transforms any type of matrix (scalar, vector, matrix) in a string and prints an Ox code line that is to be used in connection with SetStartValue (i.e. to modify starting values of parameters). Note that format = 0 for a scalar, format = 1 for a column vector and format = 2 for a k x k matrix. For instance, let mx be a 2x2 matrix of ones, MatrixToString("mx", mx, 2) will result in the printing of "object.SetStartValue("mx",<1,1;1,1>)".

Garch::Maxsa

Maxsa(const maxsa, const dT,const dRt, const iNS, const iNT, const vC, const vM);

       maxsa   in: integer, 1 to use the MaxSA algorithm, 0 otherwise

dT	in: double, initial temperature
dRt	in: double, temperature reduction factor
iNS	in: integer, number of cycles
iNT	in: integer, number of iterations before temperature reduction
vC	in: double, step length adjustment
vM	in: double, step length vector used in initial step

No return value

Description

In G@RCH, simulated annealing can be used as an alternative optimization algorithm (the default method is MaxBFGS for unbounded parameters and MaxSQPF when bounds are used). See Section 3.6.2 for a description of this technique. If maxsa=1, the optimization process will use a simulated annealing algorithm. If you do not want to use this optimization technique, MaxSA can be removed (this function being optional). Please note that our implementation is based on the code of Charles Bos[4], that replicates the approach described in Goffe, Ferrier, and Rogers (1994).

Garch::MLE

```
MLE(const method);
```
       method   in: integer, method selection

No return value

Description

Selection of the estimation method. If method = 0, Maximum Likelihood Estimation (MLE), with standard errors based on second derivatives. If method = 1, Maximum Likelihood Estimation (MLE), with standard errors based on numerical OPG matrix. If it is equal to 2, robust standard errors (QMLE) are computed (irrespectively of the density choice).

Garch::MLEMeth

```
MLEMeth(const par, const parnames, const title, const nbpar);
```
      par   in: m_cPar x 1 matrix, estimated parameters
      parnames   in: array of m_cPar strings, names of the estimated parameters
      title   in: string, name of the selected method
      nbpar   in: integer, number of parameters (m_cPar)

No return value

Description

---

[4]The code is available at http://www.tinbergen.nl/~cbos/software/maxsa.html.

Prints the estimated parameters, their standard deviations, t-tests and p-values with their names. Depending on user's choice, Maximum Likelihood estimates with second derivatives, Maximum Likelihood estimates with the numerical Outer Product Gradient (OPG) matrix or Quasi-Maximum Likelihood estimates will be printed.

Garch::MODEL

```
MODEL(const mod);
```

        mod   in: integer, index of the GARCH model

                                  OR string, name of the GARCH specification wanted.

No return value

Description

When mod is an integer, it corresponds to the ARCH model index (i.e. included in the $[1; 11]$ range):

0: RiskMetrics^{TM}	6: FIGARCH (BBM)
1: GARCH	7: FIGARCH (Chung)
2: EGARCH	8: FIEGARCH
3: GJR	9: FIAPARCH (BBM)
4: APARCH	10:FIAPARCH (Chung)
5: IGARCH	11:HYGARCH

If mod is a string, its value should be one of the following:

``RISKMETRICS''	``FIGARCH-BBM''
``GARCH''	``FIGARCH-CHUNG''
``EGARCH''	``FIEGARCH''
``GJR''	``FIAPARCH-BBM''
``APARCH''	``FIAPARCH-CHUNG''
``IGARCH''	``HYGARCH''

Remember to use the exact format of these strings, including the quotes and the upper case.

Garch::mom_trst

```
mom_trst(const mu, const k);
```

        mu   in: double, degree of freedom of the Student distribution

        k   in: integer, k-th moment

Return value

Returns a double that corresponds to the non-centered k-th moment of the standardized Student distribution.

Description

Computes the non-centered k-th moment of the standardized Student distribution truncated to positive values. See Lambert and Laurent (2001) for details.

Garch::MZ

```
MZ(const HFor, const For, const nbFor);
```
HFor	in: m_cFor x 1 vector, the forecasts of the conditional variance
For	in: m_cFor x 1 vector, the observed volatility
nbFor	in: integer, number of forecasts

Return value

Returns 1 if the tests are successfully run.

Description

Computes and prints the Mincer-Zarnowitz regression on the forecasted volatility. See Section 9.3 for more details about this regression.

Garch::Normality

```
Normality(const e);
```
e	in: m_cT x 1 matrix, series to be tested

Return value

Returns 1 if successfully run.

Description

Computes and prints skewness, excess kurtosis and Jarque-Bera normality test with the associated adjusted t-statistics and p-values. See Section 9.3 for more details about this test.

Garch::NORMALITY_TEST

```
NORMALITY_TEST(const choice);
```
choice	in: integer, 1 to apply the normality tests
	0 otherwise

No return value

Description

The normality tests are computed in function **Normality**.

Garch::NYBLOM

```
NYBLOM(const i);
```
i	in: integer, 1 to compute the Nyblom test, 0 otherwise

No return value

Description

If i is 1, the parameters stability test of Nyblom (1989) will be computed after the estimation.

Garch::Nyblom

Nyblom(const eh, const grad);

> eh   in: m_cT x 1 matrix, parameters to be tested
>
> grad   in: m_cT x m_cPar matrix, gradients

Return value

Returns 1 if the test is successfully run.

Description

Computes and prints the Nyblom test to check constancy of the parameters over time. See Nyblom (1989) and Lee and Hansen (1994) for more details.

Garch::Output

Output();

No return value

Description

Prints the output of the model: the specification of the formulated model, the estimated parameters and their standard errors.

Garch::PEARSON

PEARSON(const lags);

> lags   in: l x 1 matrix, vector containing the l desired lags for the test

No return value

Description

Fixes the lags wanted when computing the adjusted Pearson goodness-of-fit test (see Section 9.3 for more details). The required format of lags is $< lag_1; lag_2; ...; lag_l >$ and its default value is $< 40;50;60 >$. If lags is $<>$, the test will not be reported (this code line can also be removed as it is optional).

Garch::PearsonTest

PearsonTest(const cd, const ng, const np);

> cd   in: m_cT x 1 matrix, values of the cumulative distribution function
>
> ng   in: integer, number of classification groups
>
> np   in: integer, number of estimated parameters

Return value

Returns 1 if the test is successfully run.

Description

Computes and prints adjusted Pearson χ^2 goodness-of-fit test (Vlaar and Palm, 1993). See Section 9.3 for more detail about this test.

Garch::PrintBounds

```
PrintBounds(const p);
```

      p   in: integer, 0, 1 or 2

Return value

Returns 1 if successfully run.

Description

Prints the bounds fixed to the estimated parameters. If p = 0, nothing is printed. Here is an example of output given by this procedure, using respectively p = 1 and 2:

```
Bounds (p = 1)
======

Parameter           Lower Bound Upper Bound
Cst(M)              -100.000000  100.000000
d-Arfima              -1.000000    1.000000
Cst(V)                 0.000000  100.000000
ARCH(Alpha1)           0.000000    1.000000
GARCH(Beta1)           0.500000    1.000000
Student(DF)            2.000000  100.000000
-------------------------------------
Bounds (p = 2)
======
object.SetBounds("m_clevel", -100, 100);
object.SetBounds("m_dARFI", -1, 1);
object.SetBounds("m_calpha0", 0, 100);
object.SetBounds("m_valphav", 0, 1);
object.SetBounds("m_vbetav", 0, 1);
object.SetBounds("m_cV", 2, 100);
```

Notice that bounded estimation should be activated (i.e. by fixing the argument of BOUNDS to 1, BOUNDS(1) for PrintBounds to be taken into account. Moreover PrintBounds is not a mandatory expression in GarchEstim.ox and can thus be removed.

Garch::PrintStartValues

```
PrintStartValues(const p);
```

      p   in: integer, 0, 1, 2 or 3

Return value

1 if successful.

Description

Prints the starting values of the estimated parameters. If $p = 0$, nothing is printed. Here is an example of output given by this procedure, using respectively $p = 1, 2$ and 3.

```
Starting Values (p = 1)
===============
Parameter              Value

Cst(M)                 0.066000
d-Arfima               0.100000
Cst(V)                 0.050000
GARCH(Beta1)           0.800000
ARCH(Alpha1)           0.150000
Student(DF)            6.000000
-------------------------------------
Starting Values (p = 2)
===============
m_clevel    : 0.066
m_dARFI     : 0.1
m_calpha0   : 0.05
m_vbetav    : 0.80000
m_valphav   : 0.15000
m_cV        : 6
-------------------------------------
Starting Values (p = 3)
===============
object.SetStartValue("m_clevel",0.066);
object.SetStartValue("m_dARFI",0.1);
object.SetStartValue("m_calpha0",0.05);
object.SetStartValue("m_vbetav",<0.8>);
object.SetStartValue("m_valphav",<0.15>);
object.SetStartValue("m_cV",6);
```

Notice that `PrintStartValue` is not a mandatory expression in `GarchEstim.ox` and can thus be removed.

Garch::RBD

`RBD(const lags);`

> `lags`   in: l x 1 matrix, vector containing the l desired lags for the test

No return value

Description

Fixes the lags wanted when computing the Residual-Based Diagnostic test (see Section 9.3 for more details about this test). The required format of `lags` is $< lag_1; lag_2; ...; lag_l >$ and its default value is $< 10;15;20 >$. If `lags` is `<>`, the test will not be reported (this code line can also be removed as it is optional).

Garch::RBD_Test

`RBD_Test(const e, const M);`

> `e`   in: `m_cT` x 1 matrix, standardized residuals
>
> `M`   in: k x 1 matrix, number(s) of lagged squared standardized residuals in the OLS regression.

Return value

Returns 1 if successfully run.

Description

Computes the Residual-Based Diagnostic for Conditional Heteroskedasticity of Tse (2002).

Garch::ReleaseBounds

ReleaseBounds(const i);

        i   in: integer, 0 or 1

No return value

Description

If i = 1, the bounds are set to $< -\infty; \infty >$ for all parameters. This removes thus any bounds previously specified.

Garch::RISKMETRICS

RISKMETRICS(const choice);

      choice   in: double, RiskMetrics *lambda* parameter

                          0 otherwise

No return value

Description

This function allows to change the value of λ. By default $\lambda = 0.94$.

Garch::RS_test

RS_test(const R, q, const print_output);

      R   in: m_cT x 1 matrix, series to be tested

      q   in: q parameter of the $(R/S)_{Lo}$ statistics

      print_output in: 1 to print the output, 0 otherwise

Return value

Returns a 1×2 vector with respectively the $(R/S)_{Man}$ and $(R/S)_{Lo}$ statistics

Description

Computes and prints the Rescaled Range tests of Mandelbrot (1972) and Lo (1991). See Section 3.12.3 for more details about the tests.

Garch::Runs_test

Runs_test(const y, const print_output);

      y   in: m_cT x 1 matrix, series to be tested

      print_output in: 1 to print the output, 0 otherwise

Return value

Returns a 1×2 vector with respectively the Runs statistics and its associated p-value

Description

Computes and prints the Runs statistics of a three-valued data sequence ($< 0; 0; > 0$). See Section 3.12.2 for more details about the test.

Garch::SAVEPAR

```
SAVEPAR(const i, const file);
```

i	in: 0: stores nothing, 1: stores parameters estimates, 2: stores parameters estimates and standard errors, 3: stores estimates, std.errors and t-statistics
file	in: string, name of the Excel file wherein the values will be stored

Return value

Returns 1 if successful run.

Description

Allows to store optimized parameter estimates, their standard errors and the robust standard errors in a *.xls* file (Excel spreadsheet) for further analysis.

Garch::SBT

```
SBT(const i);
```

i	in: integer, 1 to run the SBD test, 0 otherwise

Return value

1 if the test is successfully run, 0 otherwise.

Description

When i=1, the Sign Bias Test, the negative Size Bias Test, the positive Size Bias Test and the joint Test for the three effects will be computed and reported after the estimation.

Garch::SCHMIDT-PHILLIPS

```
SCHMIDT-PHILLIPS(const series, const names, const lags, const option);
```

series	in: m_cT x k matrix, series to be tested
names	in: array of dimension k with the name of the series to be tested
lags	in: integer, number of lags in the SCHMIDT-PHILLIPS test
option	in: integer, 1 for Z(rho) statistics and 2 for Z(tau)

Return value

Description

Computes the SCHMIDT-PHILLIPS unit root test. See Section 9.3 for more details about this test.

Garch::SetBounds

```
SetBounds(const name, const lbound, const ubound);
```

       `name`   in: string, class member variable corresponding to the parameter of interest

       `lbound`   in: different types (double, matrix, ...), wanted lower bound of this class member variable

       `ubound`   in: different types (double, matrix, ...), wanted upper bound of this class member variable

Return value

    Returns 1 if `lbound` and `ubound` have a correct dimension.

Description

    This procedure allows the user to set for a given parameter different bounds than the default ones. As an example, `GarchEstim.ox` uses a newly created function named `StartValues` to call `SetBounds` and therefore modify the bounds of the parameters. The following example bounds the value of `m_vbetav` (which is the variable corresponding to β in the various equations of Section 3.5) between 0.5 and 1:

```
...
StartValues(const object)
{
object.SetBounds("m_vbetav", 0.5, 1);

object.GetPara();
object.Initialization(object.GetValue("m_vPar"));
}
...
main()
{
...
garchobj = new Garch();
...
StartValues(garchobj);
...
}
```

    Hint: call the function `garchobj.PrintBounds(2);` (with an exit code `exit(0);`) before changing the bounds. Doing so, you know exactly the name of the relevant class member variables and you can copy-paste the output of this procedure in the `StartValues(const object)` function.

Garch::SetStartValue

```
SetStartValue(const name, const stval);
```

       `name`   in: string, class member variable corresponding to the parameter of interest

       `stval`   in: different types (double, matrix, ...), wanted value of this class member variable

Return value

1 if stval has a correct dimension.

Description

This procedure allows the user to set for a given parameter a different starting value than the default one. As an example, GarchEstim.ox uses a newly created function named StartValues to call SetStartValues and therefore modify the initial starting values of the parameters. The following example changes the initial value of m_clevel (which is the variable corresponding to the constant in the mean, μ, in Section 3.4) to 0.066:

```
... StartValues(const object)
{
object.SetStartValue("m_clevel",0.066);

object.GetPara();
object.Initialization(object.GetValue("m_vPar"));
}
...
main()
{
...
garchobj = new Garch();
...
StartValues(garchobj);
...
}
```

Hint: call the function garchobj.PrintStartValues(3); (with an exit code exit(0);) before changing the starting values. Doing so, you know exactly the name of the relevant class member variables and you can copy-paste the output of this procedure in the StartValues(const object) function.

Garch::SignBiasTest

Sign_Bias_Test(const res, const cvar);

      res   in: m_cT x 1 matrix, residuals

      cvar   in: m_cT x 1 matrix, conditional variance

Return value

1 if the test is successfully run, 0 otherwise.

Description

Computes and prints the Sign Bias Test, the negative Size Bias Test, the positive Size Bias Test and the joint Test for the three effects described in Engle and Ng (1993). See Section 9.3 for more details about this test.

Garch::SigJumpZTestStat

```
SigJumpZTestStat(const vRV, const vBV, const vTQ, const cPer);
```

vRV	in: vector, T× 1 vector containing realized volatility
vBV	in: vector, T× 1 vector containing bi-power variation
vTQ	in: vector, T× 1 vector containing tri-power quarticity
cPer	in: integer, count of intra-day periods

Return value

Returns a T× 1 vector containing Z test stat for significant jumps as defined in equation **??**

Description

Compute a test statistic to assess statistical significance of jumps.

Garch::SigJumpZTestStat2

```
SigJumpZTestStat2(const vRV, const vBV, const vTQ, const cPer);
```

vRV	in: vector, T× 1 vector containing realized volatility
vBV	in: vector, T× 1 vector containing bi-power variation
vTQ	in: vector, T× 1 vector containing tri-power quarticity
cPer	in: integer, count of intra-day periods

Return value

Returns a T× 1 vector containing Z test stat for significant jumps as defined in equation **??**

Description

Compute a test statistic to assess statistical significance of jumps.

Garch::Simul_Wiener_process

```
Simul_Wiener_process(const m, const deltat);
```

m	in: scalar, number of simulated points
deltat	in: scalar, length of the simulated Wiener process (i.e. Δt)

Return value

$m \times 1$ vector of simulated Wiener processes

Description

Simulates a univariate Wiener process as described in Section 7.1.

Garch::Simul_Continuous_GARCH

Simul_Continuous_GARCH(const p_0, const s2_0, const m, const Delta, const theta, const omega, const lambda, const p, const s2);

p_0	in: scalar, initial log price
s2_0	in: scalar, initial spot volatility
m	in: scalar, number of simulated observations
Delta	in: scalar, Δ
theta	in: scalar, θ
omega	in: scalar, ω
lambda	in: scalar, λ
p	in: address
	out: $m \times 1$ vector of simulated log prices
s2	in: address
	out: $m \times 1$ vector of simulated spot volatilities

No Return value

Description

Simulates a continuous-time GARCH process a described in Section 7.2.

Garch::Simul_Continuous_GARCH_JUMPS

Simul_Continuous_GARCH_JUMPS(const p_0, const s2_0, const m, const Delta, const theta, const omega, const lambda, const dLambda, const sigma_k, const p, const s2, const k, const q);

p_0	in: scalar, initial log price
s2_0	in: scalar, initial spot volatility
m	in: scalar, number of simulated observations
Delta	in: scalar, Δ
theta	in: scalar, θ
omega	in: scalar, ω
lambda	in: scalar, λ
dLambda	in: scalar, parameter of the Poisson distribution, i.e. l
sigma_k	in: scalar, standard deviation of the jump process, i.e. σ_k
p	in: address
	out: $m \times 1$ vector of simulated log prices
s2	in: address

out: $m \times 1$ vector of simulated spot volatilities

k   in: address

out: $m \times 1$ vector with the simulated $\kappa(t) \sim N(0, \sigma_k^2)$

q   in: address

out: $m \times 1$ vector with the simulated $dq(t) \sim Poisson(l)$

No Return value

Description

Simulates a continuous-time GARCH process with jumps a described in Section 7.4.

Garch::SplitDate

`SplitDate(const vDate);`

vDate   in: vector, dates (format yyyymmdd)

Return value

returns yyyy, mm, and dd in three different variables.

Description

Splits dates with format yyyymmdd into yyyy, mm, and dd separately.

Garch::SplitPara

`SplitPara(vP);`

vP   in: m_cPar x 1 matrix, parameters vector

Return value

Returns 1 if successfully run

Description

Splits the parameters vector and allocates each one to the corresponding class member variables. See the `GetPara` function for more details.

Garch::STORE

`STORE(const res, const res2, const condv, const mfor, const vfor, const name, const file);`

res	in: integer, 1 to store the residuals, 0 otherwise
res2	in: integer, 1 to store the squared residuals, 0 otherwise
condv	in: integer, 1 to store the conditional variance, 0 otherwise

mfor	in: integer, 1 to store the mean forecasts, 0 otherwise
vfor	in: integer, 1 to store the variance forecasts, 0 otherwise
name	in: string, suffix added to "Res_", "SqRes_", "CondV_", "MeanFor_" or "VarFor_" to name the saved series
file	in: if 0, saves as a new *.xls* file. If 1, saves as a new *.in7* file

No return value

Description

Allows the storage of the residuals, the squared residuals or the conditional variance of the estimated models, but also the forecasted mean and variance. Argument 6 provides a default suffix ("01") that can be modified. If argument 7 equals 0 (default value), the series will be stored in a new *.xls* file (Microsoft Excel spreadsheet). If it is equal to 1, the series will be stored in a new *.in7* file (OxMetrics database).

Garch::Tests

Tests();

No return value

Description

Launches successively the various selected tests.

Garch::TESTS

TESTS(const p, const a);

p	in: 0 or 1
a	in: 0 or 1

No return value

Description

Runs selected tests either for the raw series, PRIOR to any estimation ($p = 1$) or for the estimated series, AFTER the optimization ($a = 1$). This function is optional and can be removed from GarchEstim.ox.

Garch::TestGraphicAnalysis

TestGraphicAnalysis(const ser, const res, const sqres, const stdres, const mean, const h, const hist, const plot);

ser	in: 1 or 0; 1 if raw series graph wanted
res	in: 1 or 0; 1 if residuals graph wanted
sqres	in: 1 or 0; 1 if squared residuals graph wanted
stdres	in: 1 or 0; 1 if standardized residuals graph wanted

mean	in: 1 or 0; 1 if cond.mean graph wanted
h	in: 1 or 0; 1 if cond.variance graph wanted
hist	in: 1 or 0; 1 if histogram of standardized residuals wanted
plot	in: integer, area wherein the first graph is plotted

No return value

Description

Displays graphics of the series and/or the residuals and/or the squared residuals and/or the conditional mean and variance in the OxMetrics front-end.

Garch::TRUNC

TRUNC(const t);

trunc	in: integer, truncation order (this argument is only used with BBM's approach)

No return value

Description

This function is related to the fractionally integrated (FI) model selection. If the estimation method follows BBM's (1996) specification, the value of trunc will be used as the truncation order.

Garch::VaR_DynQuan

VaR_DynQuan(const Y, const emp_quan_pos, const emp_quan_neg, const th_quan, const p, const X, const print_ols) ;

Y	in: T x 1 vector, the observations
emp_quan_pos	in: T x 1 vector, empirical quantiles for short positions
emp_quan_neg	in: T x 1 vector, empirical quantiles for long positions
th_quan	in: k x 1 vector, theoretical quantiles
p	in: integer, number of lagged Hit to be included in the regression
X	in: T x m matrix, additional explanatory variables in the regression
print_ols	in: integer, 1 to print OLS estimates, 0 otherwise

Return value

Returns a 1 x 2 matrix: test statistic $\sim$ p-value of the test.

Description

Computes the Dynamic Quantile Test of Engle and Manganelli (1999). This test statistic follows a $\chi^2(g)$ where $g = p + m + 1$.

Garch::VaR_LEVELS

VaR_LEVELS(const choice);

choice	in: K x 1 vector, VaR levels
	0 otherwise

No return value

Description

This function function sets the VaR levels to be used in the KUPIEC and Dynamic Quantile tests.

Garch::VARIANCE_TARGETING

VARIANCE_TARGETING(const choice);

choice	in: int, 1 to apply variance targeting
	0 otherwise

No return value

Description

Variance targeting is supported for the following models: GARCH, GJR, EGARCH, APARCH and FIGARCH-CHUNG.

Garch::VaR_Test

VaR_Test(const Y, const emp_quan_pos, const emp_quan_neg, const th_quan);

Y	in: T x 1 vector, the observations
emp_quan_pos	in: T x 1 vector, empirical quantiles for short positions
emp_quan_neg	in: T x 1 vector, empirical quantiles for long positions
th_quan	in: k x 1 vector, theoretical quantiles

Return value

Returns 1 if successfully run.

Description

Computes and prints the Kupiec LR test. In the output, ESF1 is the expected shortfall defined as the average size of the loss when the quantile is exceeded and ESF2 is the average size of the (loss/predicted loss) when the quantile is exceeded. See Section 6 for more details.

Garch::VR_test

VR_test(const R, N, const print_output);

       R   in: m_cT x 1 matrix, series to be tested

       N   in: Number of lags

      print_output in: 1 to print the output, 0 otherwise

Return value

    Returns a 1×3 vector with respectively the $VR = \frac{V(N)}{NV(1)}$, the statistics z_N and the associated p-value

Description

    Computes and prints the Variance-ratio test of Lo and MacKinlay (1988). See Section 3.12.1 for more details about the tests.

10.4 MGarch **Member Functions List**

Here is the list of the MGarch member functions and a brief description for each of them.

Constructor

MGarch   Constructor

Model Formulation (used in the "Console Version")

CSTS	Specifies if constants are wanted in the mean and in the variance
DISTRI	Specifies the desired distribution
ARMA_ORDERS	Specifies the AR and MA orders in the mean
GARCH_ORDERS	Specifies the p and q orders of the MGARCH(p, q) or the UGARCH$(p, q$
MODEL	Specifies the MGARCH-type of models in the conditional variance
VARIANCE_TARGETING	Allows to set the unconditional variance equal to the sample variance
ITER	Specifies the number of iterations between prints of intermediary results
TSE_LAGS	Set the order m to calculate the correlation matrix Ψ of the DCC model of Tse and Tsui (2002)
MLE	Specifies the estimation method of the standard errors
PrintOutput	Prints the model specification and launches other post-estimation procedures
UGARCH_MODELS	Specifies the UGARCH-type of models in the conditional variance (for CCC/DCC and (G)OGARCH models only)

GARCH_TRUNC	Truncation order for the F.I. models using the method of Baillie, Bollerslev, and Mikkelsen (1996) (for CCC/DCC and (G)OGARCH models only)
GARCH_ARFIMA	Specifies if ARFIMA is wanted in the mean (for CCC/DCC and (G)OGARCH models only)
GARCH_PrintOutput	Allows to print the output of the univariate GARCH models
et_UGARCH_MODELS	Returns the index (or string version) of the UGARCH model used
GARCH_VARIANCE_TARGETING	
	Allows to apply variance targeting on the univariate GARCH models.
NE_STEP	Allows to estimate CCC and DCC models with a 1-step ML approach

Model Information and Parameters Management

ppend_in	Appends new variables to the database (starting at obs m_iT1est)
ppend_out	Appends new variables to the database (starting at obs m_iT2est +1)
et_T1	Returns the value of m_iT1est (modelbase global variable)
et_T2	Returns the value of m_iT2est (modelbase global variable)
nitGlobals	Initializes the class member variables
etDistri	Gets the index of the selected distribution (0: Normal, 1: Student)
etcT	Gets the number of observations
etZParNames	Gets the names of the parameters in the variance equation
etZNames	Gets the names of the regressors in the variance equation
etPara	Constructs the parameters vector
plitPara	Allocates the value of each element of the parameters vector to the correct variable
etParNames	Gets the names of the parameters in the parameters vector
rintStartValues	Prints the starting values of the parameters to estimate
etRes	Filters the data from a constant and X regressors
etXNames	Gets the names of the regressors in the mean equation
etXBetaForc	Gets the data (regressors) used in the forecast
aram_ARMA	Builds a vector with the ARMA coefficients
skMetrics_lambda	Sets the parameter m_clambda (modelbase global variable)

Initialization

| itialization | Initializes the model and the associated parameters |

| InitStartValues | Initializes the starting values of the parameters to estimate |
| OGARCH_M | Sets the value of m_cM (number of factors in the OGARCH model) |

Estimation Process

DoEstimation	Estimates the model
Covar	Computes and stores the variance-covariance matrix of the
PC	Principal component analysis
S_B	NLS objective function of the GOGARCH model.

Filters

Create_MARMA	Filters data from ARMA(p,q) components
BEKK_H	Filters the variance equation for the BEKK type models
CCC_filter	Filters the variance equation for the CCC model
DCCE_filter	Filters the variance equation for the DCC model by Engle (2002)
DCC_TSE_filter	Filters the variance equation for the DCC model by Tse and Tsui (2002)
DECO_DCCE_filter	Filters the variance equation for the DECO model by Engle and Kelly (200

Distributions

| logmnpdf | Computes the log-likelihood for the multivariate Gaussian distribution |
| logmtpdf | Computes the log-likelihood for the multivariate Student-t distribution |

Forecasting

FORECAST	Specify if forecasts are wanted and the number of observations to forecast
FORECASTING	Launches the forecasting procedure
GetForcData	Gets the data used for the forecast
For_Arma	Forecasts from an ARMA(p,q) model
Forecast_BEKK	Forecasts from the BEKK type models
Forecast_RiskMetrics	Forecasts from the Riskmetrics model
Forecast_ccc_dcc	Forecasts from the CCC-DCC type models
O_GARCH_Forecast	Forecasts from the (G)OGARCH model

Tests

| RUNTESTS | Allows to specify that the selected tests have to be applied after the estimation |
| Tests | Launches the selected tests and prints their results |

MC_test	Launches the LMC statistics of TSE (2000)
Criteria	Computes the Akaike, Schwarz, Shibata and Hannan-Quinn Tests
NFO_CRITERIA	Launches the Akaike, Schwarz, Shibata and Hannan-Quinn Tests
ORMALITY_TEST	Computes the skewness, kurtosis and Jarque and Bera (1987) test, with associated t-test and p-values
TEST	Set parameters for the Box-Pierce Q-statistics on $\hat{z}_t$
2_TEST	Set parameters for the Box-Pierce Q-statistics on $\hat{z}_t^2$
NORMALITY_TEST	Set parameters for the Multivariate normality test
OSKING_TEST	Set parameters for the Hosking's Multivariate Portmanteau Statistics on $\hat{z}_t$
OSKING2_TEST	Set parameters for the Hosking's Multivariate Portmanteau Statistics on $\hat{z}_t^2$
_MCLEOD_TEST	Set parameters for the Li and McLeod's Multivariate Portmanteau Statistics on $\hat{z}_t$
_MCLEOD2_TEST	Set parameters for the Li and McLeod's Multivariate Portmanteau Statistics $\hat{z}_t^2$
MC_TEST	Set parameters for the LMC statistics of TSE (2000)
GLE_SHEPPARD_TEST	Set parameters for the LM test of Constant Correlation of Engle and Sheppard
ormality	Computes the Individual Normality Test
xPQ	Computes the Box-Pierce Q-statistics
MC	Computes the LMC statistics of TSE (2000)
st_CC_Engle_Sheppard	Computes the LM test of Constant Correlation of Engle and Sheppard
sking	Computes the Hosking's Multivariate Portmanteau Statistics
_McLeod	Computes the Li and McLeod's Multivariate Portmanteau Statistics

mulation Procedures

mul_BEKK	Simulates a BEKK model
mul_CCC	Simulates a CCC model
mul_DCCE	Simulates a DCC model of Engle (2002)
nul_DCCTSE	Simulates a DCC model of Tse and Tsui (2002)

nctions related to matrices

tract_cor	Stacks the correlations of a correlation matrix (except the 1's) into a vector
eate_cor	Construct from a stacked vector of correlationts the corresponding

correlation matrix

Distance metrics

GetVarianceCovariances

> Transforms an array of variance matrices into a matrix
> which holds in each row the $vech(H_t)$

GetForecastedVarianceCovariances

> Transforms an array of forecasted variance matrices into a matrix
> which holds in each row $vech(H_{t+h})$

EigenvalueMetric　　　　Calculates the average distance between two matrices based on the eigenvalue norm

ForstnerMetric　　　　Calculates the average distance between two matrices based on the Forstner and Moonen norm

CosMassMetric　　　　Calculates the average distance between two matrices based on the cosinus mass norm

10.5 MGarch Members Functions

MGarch::ARMA_ORDERS, Garch::GARCH_ORDERS

ARMA_ORDERS(const cAR, const cMA);

GARCH_ORDERS(const cP, const cQ);

cAR	in: integer, AR order
cMA	in: integer, MA order
cP	in: integer, GARCH order
cQ	in: integer, ARCH order

Return value

> No return value

Description

> Fixes the ARMA and GARCH orders.

Garch::Append_in

Append_in(const variable, const name);

variable	in: $T \times k$ matrix with the new variables
name	in: array with k variable names of the new variables

Jo return value

Description

Appends new variables to the database (starting at obs m_iT1est)

Garch::Append_out

```
ppend_in(const variable, const name);
```

variable	in: $T \times k$ matrix with the new variables
name	in: array with k variable names of the new variables

Jo return value

Description

Appends new variables to the database (starting at obs m_iT2est + 1)

1Garch::BEKK_H

```
EKK_H(const eps, const mC, const cXV, const mXV, const mD, const
A, const aG, const p, const q, const varsamp, const res2, const
ogdet, const eta, const Ht, const acor, const dH);
```

eps	in: m_cT x m_cN matrix, residuals from the ARMA(p,q) model
mC	in: m_cN x m_cN matrix, lower triangular matrix of constants
cXV	in: int, number of regressors in variance
mXV	in: m_cT x m_cXV matrix, regressors in variance
mD	in: m_cN x m_cN matrix, coefficients of the regressors in variance
aA	in: q x (m_cN x m_cN) array, ARCH coefficients
aG	in: p x (m_cN x m_cN) array, GARCH coefficients
p	in: int, GARCH order
q	in: int, ARCH order
varsamp	in: int, 1: variance targeting, 0: estimates the constant
res2	out: m_cT x m_cN matrix, squared standardized residuals
logdet	out: m_cT x 1 matrix, $log\,|H_t|$
eta	out: m_cT x m_cN matrix, standardized residuals
Ht	out: m_cT x (m_cN x m_cN) array, conditional variance matrices
acor	out: m_cT x (m_cN x m_cN) array, conditional correlation matrices
dH	out: m_cT x (m_cN x m_cN) array, diagonal of the conditional variance matrices

turn value

  No return value

Description

This is the filter for the BEKK family of MGARCH models which includes the full, diagonal and scalar versions.

MGarch::BoxPQ

BoxPQ(const z, const ncor, const adj, const names);

z	in: data matrix
ncor	in: vector of lags
adj	in: int, number of degrees of freedom
names	in: array of strings containing the names of the variables in z

Return value

1 if the function is successfully evaluated

Description

Computes Box-Pierce Q-statistics on standardized residuals and squared standardized residuals

MGarch::CCC_filter

CCC_filter(const vE, const dH, const vcorr, const res2, const logD, const zt, const aHt, const cor);

vE	in: m_cT x m_cN matrix, residuals from the ARMA(p,q) model
dH	in: m_cT x m_cN matrix, univariate conditional variances
vcorr	in: $m\_cN(m\_cN-1)/2$ x 1, parameters for the conditional correlation matrix
res2	in: m_cT x m_cN matrix, squared standardized residuals
logD	in: m_cT x 1 matrix, $log\,|H\_t|$
zt	out: m_cT x m_cN matrix, standardized residuals
aHt	out: m_cT x (m_cN x m_cN) array, conditional variance matrices
corr	out: (m_cN x m_cN) matrix, conditional correlation matrix

Return value

No return value

Description

This is the filter for conditional variance of the CCC model. It calculates the (constant) conditional correlation matrix starting from m_cN sequences of variances from univariate GARCH models.

MGarch::Covar

```
Covar(const Loglik1, const Loglik2, const para);
```

        Loglik1   in: the function LLOptim

        Loglik2   in: the function LLOptim2

Return value

   No return value

Description

   Calculate the standard errors for the parameters as well as the robust (Quasi Maximum Likelihood Estimation) standard errors.

MGarch::Create_MARMA

```
Create_MARMA(const cAR, const cMA, const mAR_MA, Etemp, const vE);
```

    cAR   in: intreger, Autoregressive order

    cMA   in: integer, Moving average order

    mAR_MA   in: m_cAR+m_cMA x 1 vector, parameter values

    Etemp   in: m_cT x m_cN matrix, dependent variable (pre filtered for the constant and regressors)

    vE   out: m_cT x m_cN matrix, residuals from the ARMA(p,q) model

Return value

   No return value

Description

   This is the filter for the ARMA(p,q) model for the mean.

MGarch::CSTS

```
CSTS(const cstM, const cstV);
```

    cstM   in: int, 1 to include and estimate a constant in the mean equation, 0 otherwise

    cstV   in: int, 1 to include a constant in the variance equation 0 otherwise

Return value

   No return value

Description

   Allows to include a constant in the mean and the variance equations. By default, a constant is estimated both in the mean and the variance equations.

MGarch::DCCE_filter

DCCE_filter(const vE, const dH, const vcorr, const vtheta_q, const vtheta_p, const res2, const logD, const zt, const Ht, const cor, const aQ);

vE	in: m_cT x m_cN matrix, residuals from the ARMA(p,q) model
dH	in: m_cT x m_cN matrix, univariate conditional variances
vcorr	in: m_cN(m_cN-1)/2 x 1, parameters for the conditional correlation matrix
vtheta_q	in: rows(vtheta_q) x 1 vector, parameter of the DCC model
vtheta_p	in: rows(vtheta_p) x 1 vector, parameter of the DCC model
res2	in: m_cT x m_cN matrix, squared standardized residuals
logD	in: m_cT x 1 matrix, $log\,|H_t|$
zt	in: address, out: m_cT x m_cN matrix, standardized residuals
aHt	in: address, out: m_cT x (m_cN x m_cN) array, conditional variance matrices
corr	in: address, out: m_cT x (m_cN x m_cN) array, conditional correlation matrices
aQ	in: address, out: m_cT x (m_cN x m_cN) array, Q_t

Return value

   No return value

Description

   Computes the conditional correlation following Engle (2002).

MGarch::DCC_TSE_filter

DCC_TSE_filter(const vE, const dH, const lags_TSE, const vcorr, const vtheta_q, const vtheta_p, const res2, const logD, const zt, const Ht, const cor);

vE	in: m_cT x m_cN matrix, residuals from the ARMA(p,q) model
dH	in: m_cT x m_cN matrix, univariate conditional variances
lag_TSE	in: int, the order m to calculate the correlation matrix psi
vcorr	in: m_cN(m_cN-1)/2 x 1, parameters for the conditional correlation matrix
vtheta_q	in: rows(vtheta_q) x 1 vector, parameter of the DCC model
vtheta_p	in: rows(vtheta_p) x 1 vector, parameter of the DCC model
res2	in: m_cT x m_cN matrix, squared standardized residuals
logD	in: m_cT x 1 matrix, $log\,|H_t|$
zt	out: m_cT x m_cN matrix, standardized residuals
Ht	out: m_cT x (m_cN x m_cN) array, conditional variance matrices
cor	out: m_cT x (m_cN x m_cN) array, conditional correlation matrices

Return value

   No return value

Description

   Computes the conditional correlation following Tse and Tsui (2002).

MGarch::DECO_DCCE_filter

```
DECO_DCCE_filter(const vE, const dH, const vcorr, const vtheta_q,
const vtheta_p, const res2, const logD, const rhot);
```

vE	in: m_cT x m_cN matrix, residuals from the ARMA(p,q) model
dH	in: m_cT x m_cN matrix, univariate conditional variances
vcorr	in: m_cN(m_cN-1)/2 x 1, parameters for the conditional correlation matrix
vtheta_q	in: rows(vtheta_q) x 1 vector, parameter of the DCC model
vtheta_p	in: rows(vtheta_p) x 1 vector, parameter of the DCC model
res2	in: m_cT x m_cN matrix, squared standardized residuals
logD	in: m_cT x 1 matrix, $log\,|H_t|$
rhot	in: address, out: m_cT x 1 matrix, dynamic equicorrelation

Return value

   No return value

Description

   Computes the conditional correlation following Engle and Kelly (2007).

MGarch::DISTRI

```
DISTRI(const dist);
```

        dist   in: int, 0 for the gaussian distribution, 1 for the Student-t distribution

Return value

   No return value

Description

   Selects the distribution.

MGarch::DoEstimation

```
DoEstimation();
```

Return value

   1 if the models is succesfully estimated

Description

   Launches the estimation procedure.

MGarch::extract_cor, MGarch::create_cor

```
extract_cor(const cor)
create_cor(const cor, const n)
```

        cor   in: m_cN x m_cN correlation matrix for extract_cor,

                           $m\_cN(m\_cN-1)/2$ x 1 vector of stacked correlations for create_cor

        n   in: int, number of variables

Return value

   Vector of dimension $m\_cN*(m\_cN-1)/2$ containing the stacked correlations for extract_cor, correlation matrix for create_cor

Description

   The first function stacks the correlations of a correlation matrix (except the 1's) while the second constructs a correlation matrix from the vector of stacked correlations.

MGarch::For_Arma

```
For_Arma(const y_1, const p, const q, const arma, const level_forc,
const e);
```

y_1	in: m_cT x 1 vector, data pre-filtered for the constant and regressors in the mean, $y_t - \mu_t$
p	in: int, AR order
q	in: int, MA order
arma	in: 1 x p+q vector, AR coefficients followed by MA coefficients
level_forc	in: m_cT+m_cStep x 1 vector, fixed component of the mean (constant plus regressors) followed by its forecasts
e	in: m_cT x 1 vector, residuals from the ARMA(p,q) model

Return value

m_cStep x 1 vector containing forecasts of y_t

Description

Computes the forecasts of the conditional mean equation.

MGarch::FORECAST

FORECAST(const forecast, const steps);

forecast	in: 1 to compute forecasts, 0 no forecast
steps	in: int, number of forecasts

Return value

No return value

Description

This function reads the inputs into global variables m_cForecast and m_cStep.

MGarch::Forecast_BEKK   Forecast_BEKK(const step, const eps, const mC, const aA, const aG, const cP, const cQ, const varsamp, const aHt, const cXV, const mD, const data_Z, const aaFHt);

step	in: int, number of forecasts
eps	in: m_cT x m_cN matrix, residuals from the ARMA(p,q) model
mC	in: m_cN x m_cN matrix, lower triangular matrix of constants
aA	in: q x (m_cN x m_cN) array, ARCH coefficients
aG	in: p x (m_cN x m_cN) array, GARCH coefficients

cP	in: int, GARCH order
cQ	in: int, ARCH order
varsamp	in: int, 1: variance targeting, 0: estimates the constant
aHt	in: m_cT x (m_cN x m_cN) array, conditional variance matrices
cXV	in: int, number of regressors in the variance
mD	in: m_cN x m_cXV matrix, coefficients of the regressors in the variance
data_Z	in: m_cT x m_cXV matrix, regressors in variance
aaFHt	in: address, out: step x (m_cN x m_cN) array, v-c forecasts

Return value

   No return value

Description

   This procedure computes the forecasts for the BEKK models.

MGarch::Forecast_ccc_dcc

Forecast_ccc_dcc(const step, const vE, const dH, const dH_forecast, const vcorr, const vtheta_q, const vtheta_p, const lags_TSE, const aQ, const aFHt);

step	in: int, number of observations to forecsts
vE	in: m_cT x m_cN matrix, residuals from the ARMA(p,q) model
dH	in: m_cT x m_cN matrix, univariate conditional variances
dH	in: m_cT x m_cN matrix, univariate conditional variances forecasts
vcorr	in: m_cN(m_cN-1)/2 x 1, parameters for the conditional correlation matri
vtheta_q	in: rows(vtheta_q) x 1 vector, parameter of the DCC model
vtheta_p	in: rows(vtheta_p) x 1 vector, parameter of the DCC model
lag_TSE	in: int, the order m to calculate the correlation matrix Ψ
aQ	in: m_cT x (m_cN x m_cN) array, Q_t
aFHt	in: address, out: m_cT x (m_cN x m_cN) array, v-c forecasts

Return value

   No return value

Description

   This procedure computes the forecasts for the CCC-DCC models.

MGarch::Forecast_RiskMetrics

Forecast_RiskMetrics(const step, const eps, const aA, const aG,
const aHt, const cXV, const mD, const data_Z, const aaFHt);

step	in: int, number of forecasts
eps	in: m_cT x m_cN matrix, residuals from the ARMA(p,q) model
aA	in: double, ARCH coefficients
aG	in: double, GARCH coefficients
aHt	out: m_cT x (m_cN x m_cN) array, conditional variance matrices
cXV	in: int, number of regressors in the variance
mD	in: m_cN x m_cXV matrix, coefficients of the regressors in the variance
data_Z	in: m_cT x m_cXV matrix, regressors in variance
aaFHt	in: address, out: step x (m_cN x m_cN) array, v-c forecasts

Return value

No return value

Description

This procedure computes the forecasts for the RiskMetrics model.

MGarch::FORECASTING

FORECASTING();

Return value

No return value

Description

This function launchs the forecasting procedure.

MGarch::EigenvalueMetric, MGarch::ForstnerMetric, MGarch::CosMassMetric

EigenvalueMetric(const mM, const mBM)

ForstnerMetric(const cor, const n)

CosMassMetric(const mM, const mBM)

mM	in: array of matrices
mBM	in: array of matrices

Return value

Double, the average distance computed with a given loss function

Description

Calculates the average distance between two matrices based on eigenvalue (spectral norm), Forstner and Moonen norm and cosinus mass norm respectively.

MGarch::GetDistri

`GetDistri();`

Return value

String containing the name of the selected distribution

Description

Returns the string corresponding to the value of `m_cDist` (modelbase global variable)

MGarch::GetForcData

`GetForcData(const iGroup, const cTforc);`

`iGroup`	in: int, variables group index
`cTforc`	in: int, forecasts time horizon

Return value

matrix containing data from `iGroup` used in the forecast

Description

Selects a partition of the data matrix from the specified group (`iGroup`) of size length `cTforc`

MGarch::GetPara

`GetPara();`

Return value

`m_vPar`

Description

Returns a vector containing the values of the parameter of the model. The partitions of this vector are organized in the following way (if a parameter is not estimated then it is skipped):

- vector m_cN x 1 of constants in the mean
- m_cN*m_cXM x 1 coefficients of the regressors in the conditional mean
- sumc(m_cAR) x1 AR coefficients
- sumc(m_cMA) x1 MA coefficients
- diagonal-BEKK: vech(m_mC), diagonal(m_abetav), diagonal(m_aalphav)
- scalar-BEKK: vech(m_mC), m_abetav, m_aalphav
- CCC: beta_ugarch, m_vcorr, m_cN(m_cN-1)/2 strictly lower diagonal elements of the correlation matrix
- DCC: beta_ugarch, m_vcorr, m_dtheta1, m_dtheta2
- m_cN*m_cXV x 1 coefficients of the regressors in the variance (only for BEKK type and Riskmetrics models)
- degree of freedom of the Student-t distribution

MGarch::GetParNames, MGarch::GetXNames

MGarch::GetZParNames, MGarch::GetZNames

```
GetParNames();
GetXNames();
GetZParNames();
GetZNames();
```

Return value

array of strings containing the names of variables or parameters

Description

The procedure collects the names of the parameters of the model (GetParNames()), those of the regressors in the mean equation (GetXNames()), in variance equation (GetZNames();) and the names of the parameters on the variance (GetZParNames())

MGarch::GetRes

```
GetRes(const y);
```

y   in: m_cT x m_cN matrix containing the data

Return value

m_cT x m_cN matrix containing the filtered data

Description

Filters the data from a constant and X regressors in mean

MGarch::GetcT

```
GetcT();
```

Return value

integer, the number of observations

Description

Returns the value of m_cT (modelbase global variable)

MGarch::Get_T1

```
Get_T1();
```

Return value

m_iT1est

Description

Returns the value of m_iT1est (modelbase global variable)

MGarch::Get_T2

```
Get_T2();
```

Return value

m_iT2est

Description

Returns the value of m_iT2est (modelbase global variable)

MGarch::GetVarianceCovariances, MGarch::GetForecastedVarianceCovariances

```
GetVarianceCovariances()
```
```
GetForecastedVarianceCovariances()
```

Return value

m_cT x m_cN*(m_cN+1)/2 and m_cStep x m_cN*(m_cN+1)/2 matrices containing respectively the estimated and forecasted variances and covariances

Description

Transforms an array of variance matrices estimated or forecasted in a matrix which holds in each row the $vech(H_t)$.

MGarch::GetXBetaForc

```
GetXBetaForc(const cTforc);
```

      `cTforc`   in: int, forecasts time horizon

Return value

    m_mXM_f, matrix containing the regressors in mean used in the forecast

Description

    Stacks the portion of the egressor in the Mean matrix used for the forecast

MGarch::Hosking

```
Hosking(const mY, const m, const p_q, const print_output);
```

      `mY`   in: m_cT x m_cN matrix of row data

      `m`   in: k x 1 vector, lags of the multivariate Portmanteau tests

      `p_q`   in: int, m_cAR+m_cMA, for the test on $\hat{z}_t$, m_cP+m_cQ for the test on $\hat{z}_t^2$

      `print_output`   in: int, 1 to print the output

Return value

    k x 3 matrix containing lags, statistics and p-values of the test

Description

    Computes Hosking's Multivariate Portmanteau Statistics.

MGarch::ICriteria

```
ICriteria(const LogL, const n, const q);
```

      `LogL`   in: int, Loglikehood value

      `n`   in: int, number of observations

      `q`   in: int, number of parameters

Return value

    1 if the function is successfully evaluated

Description

    Computes the Akaike, Schwarz, Shibata and Hannan-Quinn Tests.

MGarch::INFO_CRITERIA, MGarch::LMC_TEST,

MGarch::M_NORMALITY_TEST, MGarch::NORMALITY_TEST,

MGarch::Q_TEST, MGarch::Q2_TEST,

MGarch::HOSKING_TEST, MGarch::HOSKING2_TEST,

MGarch::LI_MCLEOD_TEST, MGarch::LI_MCLEOD2_TEST,

MGarch::ENGLE_SHEPPARD_TEST

```
INFO_CRITERIA(const i);
LMC_TEST(const i);
M_NORMALITY_TEST(const i);
NORMALITY_TEST(const i);
Q_TEST(const i,...);
Q2_TEST(const i,...);
HOSKING_TEST(const i,...);
HOSKING2_TEST(const i,...);
LI_MCLEOD_TEST(const i,...);
LI_MCLEOD2_TEST(const i,...);
ENGLE_SHEPPARD_TEST(const i,const lags);
```

i	in: int, 1 to select the specified test, 0 otherwise
lags	in: int, set the lags for the LM test of Constant Correlation of Engle and Sheppard

Return value

   No return value

Description

   Once a test is selected, the statistic is evaluated and the result printed by calling the function `Tests()`

MGarch::InitGlobals

```
InitGlobals();
```

Return value

   No return value

Description

   Initializes the class member variables when constructing the object. The default model initialized here is a scalar-BEKK(1,1) with constant in mean and variance and a Gaussian distribution.

MGarch::Initialization

```
Initialization(const vStart);
```

> vStart   in: m_cPar x 1 vector of starting parameters

Return value

   No return value

Description

   Launches the procedures `InitData()` and `InitStartValues()` which initializes and check the dataset and starting values respectively

MGarch::InitStartValues

```
InitStartValues();
```

Return value

   No return value

Description

   Provides a vector of default starting values to start up the maximization procedure.

MGarch::ITER

```
ITER(const i);
```

> i   in: int, number of iterations between intermediary prints

Return value

   No return value

Description

   Prints intermediary results during the numerical optimization process. This function allows the user to select the number of iterations between printed results. For instance, if $i = 10$, intermediary values of the parameters and the log-likelihood function will be printed every 10 iterations. When $i = 0$, no intermediary result is printed.

MGarch::Li_McLeod

```
Li_McLeod(const mY, const m, const p_q, const print_output);
```

mY	in: m_cT x m_cN matrix of row data
m	in: k x 1 vector, lags of the multivariate Portmanteau tests
p_q	in: m_cAR+m_cMA, for the test on $\hat{z}_t$, m_cP+m_cQ for the test on $\hat{z}_t^2$
print_output	in: int, 1 to print the output

Return value

k x 3 matrix containing lags, statistics and p-values of the test

Description

Computes the Li and McLeod's Multivariate Portmanteau Statistics.

MGarch::LLOptim

LLOptim(const vP, const adFunc, const avScore, const amHessian);

vP	in: m_cPar x 1 vector of strting parameters
adFunc	in: address, out: double, log-likelihood function value at vP
avScore	in: 0 or address, out: if address in input, m_cPar x 1 vector of numerical first derivatives
amHessian	in: 0, as MaxBFGS and MaxSQPF do not require the Hessian

Return value

1 if the function is successfully evaluated

Description

Log-liklihood function. LLOptim is optimized with MaxSQPF, which enforces all iterates to be feasible, using the algorithm by Lawrence and Tits (2001). If a starting point is infeasible, MaxSQPF will try to minimize the squared constraint violations to find a feasible point.

MGarch::LLOptim2

LLOptim2(const avF, const vP);

| adFunc | in: address, out: double, log-likelihood function value at vP |
| vP | in: m_cPar x 1 vector with unrestricted coefficients |

Return value

Returns 1 if the function is successfully evaluated

Description

This procedure is used as first argument of NumJacobian, when computing the variance-covariance matrix. For more details about NumJacobian, see Doornik (2007b).

MGarch::LMC

```
LMC(const gradients_ugarch_CCC, const eps, const res, const rho);
```

> gradients_ugarch_CCC
>
> > m_cT x m_cPar matrix, gradients from the CCC model
>
> eps   in: m_cT x m_cN matrix, standardized residuals
>
> res   in: m_cT x m_cN matrix, residuals
>
> rho   in: m_cN x m_cN matrix, correlation implied by the CCC model

Return value

1 if the function is successfully evaluated

Description

Computes the LM test of constant correlation of TSE (2000).

MGarch::LMC_test

```
LMC_test();
```

Return value

   No return value

Description

Launches the LM test of constant correlation of TSE (2000).

MGarch::logmnpdf, MGarch::logmtpdf

```
logmnpdf(const res2, const ldet_vc, const N);
logmtpdf(const res2, const ldet_vc, const N, const df);
```

> res2   in: m_cT x 1 vector
>
> ldet_vc   in: m_cT x 1 vector
>
> N   in: int, number of series, m_cN
>
> df   in: double, degrees of freedom (Student-t only)

Return value

m_cT x 1 vector with the loglikelihood contribution of each observation

Description

Defines the multivariate gaussian and the Student-t(df) loglikelihood contribution of each observation. $\texttt{res2} = \varepsilon_t H_t^{-1} \varepsilon_t'$ and $\texttt{ldet\_vc} = log\,|H_t|$.

MGarch::MLE

```
MLE(const method);
```

```
method        in: int, 0, 1 or 2
```

Return value

   No return value

Description

Specifies the estimation method of the standard errors, that is: 0 based on the Hessian, 1 outer product of the score, 2 sandwich formula.

MGarch::MODEL

```
MODEL(const mod);
```

```
      mod           in: integer, index of the MGARCH model or string with the name
                    of the MGARCH model to estimate
```

Return value

   1 if the function is successfully evaluated

Description

   Selects the MGARCH model. The index and the corresponding string are:

0: SCALAR_BEKK	5: DCC_TSE
1: DIAG_BEKK	6: OGARCH
2: RiskMetrics	7: GOGARCH_ML
3: CCC	8: GOGARCH_NLS
4: DCC	

Remember to use the exact format of these strings, including the upper case.

MGarch::Normality

```
Normality(const z, const names);
```

```
      z             in: data matrix
      names         in: array of strings containing the names of the variables in z
```

Return value

   1 if the function is successfully evaluated

Description

   Computes individual skewness, excess kurtosis, Jarque-Bera tests, associated adjusted t-statistics and p-values

MGarch::O_GARCH_Forecast

O_GARCH_Forecast(); *Return value*

  No return value

Description

This procedure computes the forecasts for the (G)OGARCH model. Note that the global variables m_cForecast and m_cStep must be previously set, for example by calling the procedure FORECAST(const forecast, const steps).

MGarch::OGARCH_M

OGARCH_M(const choice);

choice	in: int, sets the value of the global variable m_cM, i.e. number of factors in the OGARCH model

Return value

  No return value

Description

Sets the value of m_cM

MGarch::ONE_STEP

ONE_STEP(const choice);

choice	in: int, 1 to estimate the CCC or DCC model with a 1-step ML procedure, 0 for 2-step

Return value

  No return value

Description

Allows to estimate the CCC and DCC with a 1-step ML procedure. By defaut these models are estimated with the 2-step procedure described in Section 9.6.2.

MGarch::PC

PC(const x, const stand, const nPC, ...);

x	in: residuals matrix
stand	in: 1 standardizes the data matrix
nPC	in: int, number of principal components to be evaluated

Return value

Returns 1 if the function is successfully evaluated

Description

This procedure allows to select nPC principal components evaluated on the row or standardized residuals and evaluates the correlation between the PC and the variables.

MGarch::PrintOutput

```
PrintOutput(const printoutput);
```

   printoutput in: int, 1 to print results, 0 otherwise

Return value

 No return value

Description

Option to print the model specification and output.

MGarch::PrintStartValues

```
PrintStartValues(const p);
```

    p   in: int, p = 0, 1, 2 or 3

Return value

 No return value

Description

Prints the satrting values of the estimated parameters. if $p = 0$ no output is printed, $p = 1, 2, 3$ represent three different formats

MGarch::RiskMetrics_lambda

```
RiskMetrics_lambda(const lambda);
```

   lambda in: double, λ coefficient of the RiskMetrics model

Return value

 No return value

Description

Sets the value of the parameter λ. The value is set to 0.94 by default.

MGarch::RUNTESTS

```
RUNTESTS(const i);
```

     i   in: int, 1 to run the selected tests, 0 otherwise

Return value

    No return value

Description

MGarch::S_B

```
S_B(const vX, const avF, const avScore, const amHessian);
```

vP	in: m_cPar x 1 vector of strting parameters
adFunc	in: address, out: double, log-likelihood function value at vP
avScore	in: 0 or address, out: if address in input, m_cPar x 1 vector of numerical first derivatives
amHessian	in: 0, as MaxBFGS and MaxSQPF do not require the Hessian

Return value

Description

    Function to be optimized by NLS in the GOGARCH model/

MGarch::Simul_BEKK

```
Simul_BEKK(const mC, const abetav, const aalphav, const mv);
```

mC	in: m_cN x m_cN matrix, lower triangular matrix of constants
abetav	in: array of dimension p of m_cN x m_cN matrices, GARCH coefficients
aaphav	in: array of dimension q of m_cN x m_cN matrices, ARCH coefficients
mv	in: m_cT x m_cN matrix of iid random variables
discard	in: int, number of observations to be discarded (to initialise the process)
y	in: address, out: m_cT x m_cN matrix of simulated returns
Ht	in: address, out: m_cT x (m_cN x m_cN) array of variance-

Return value

    m_cT x m_cN matrix of simulated data following the required BEKK(p, q) model.

Description

    This procedure allows to simulate a BEKK(p, q) model (including a full BEKK).

MGarch::Simul_CCC, MGarch::Simul_DCCE, MGarch::Simul_DCCTSE

Simul_CCC(const Model, const omega, const alpha, const beta, const rho, const gamma, const delta, const theta, const z, const discard, const y, const sigma2);

Simul_DCCE(const Model, const omega, const alpha, const beta, const rho, const vtheta_q, const vtheta_p, const gamma, const delta, const theta, const z, const discard, const y, const sigma2);

Simul_DCCTSE(const Model, const omega, const alpha, const beta, const rho, const vtheta_q, const vtheta_p, const lags_TSE, const gamma, const delta, const theta, const z, const discard, const y, const sigma2);

Model	in: array of dimension m_cN specifying the univariate GARCH models Choices: GARCH (or 0), GJR (or 1), APARCH (or 2) and EGARCH (or 3), e.g. {GARCH,GJR}.
omega	in: m_cN x1, constants of the univariate GARCH models
alpha	in: m_cN x (q x 1), ARCH coefficients of the univariate GARCH models
beta	in: m_cN x (p x 1), GARCH coefficients of the univariate GARCH models
rho	in: m_cN x m_cN matrix: constant term in the DCC models
vtheta_q	in: double, α parameter of the DCC models
vtheta_p	in: double, β parameter of the DCC models
lag_TSE	in: int, the order m to calculate the correlation matrix Ψ for DCC of Tse and Tsui (2002)
gamma	in: m_cN x (q x 1) vector, asymmetry coefficient in GJR and APARCH models
delta	in: m_cN x 1 vector, power parameters of the APARCH model
theta	in: m_cN x (2 x 1) array, coefficients for EGARCH models
z	in: m_cT x m_cN matrix of *iid* random variables
discard	in: int, number of observations to be discarded (to initialise the process)
y	in: address, out: m_cT x m_cN matrix of simulated returns
Ht	in: address, out: m_cT x (m_cN x m_cN) array of variance-covariance matrices

Return value

Description

This procedure allows to simulate a CCC or DCC model. Note that the GARCH orders must be tha same for all series ($p_i = p_j$ and $q_i = q_j$ $\forall i, j = 1, ...m\_cN$).

See example file `Simul_CCC_DCC.ox` for an illustration.

MGarch::SplitPara

`SplitPara(const vp);`

  vP   in: vector of parameters

Return value

 No return value

Description

 Extracts the elements from a vector of parameters and allocates them to the corresponding global variables.

MGarch::Tests

`Tests();`

Return value

 No return value

Description

 Launches the selected tests and prints their results.

MGarch::Test_CC_Engle_Sheppard

`Test_CC_Engle_Sheppard(const eps, const M);`

  eps   in: m_cT x m_cN matrix, standardized residuals

  M   in: k x 1 number(s) of lagged squared standardized residuals
         in the OLS regression

Return value

 1 if the function is successfully evaluated

Description

 Computes the test of constant correlation of Engle and Sheppard.

MGarch::TSE_LAGS

`TSE_LAGS(const lags);`

  lags   in: int, number of lags used to compute the empirical correlation matrix in the DCC model of Tse and Tsui (2002)

Return value

    No return value

Description

    Set the order m to calculate the correlation matrix Ψ in DCC model of Tse and Tsui (2002).

MGarch::UGARCH_ARFIMA

UGARCH_ARFIMA(const cARFI);

        cARFI   in: int, 1 to add fractionally integrated coefficients to the univariate model 0 othewise

Return value

    1 if the function is successfully evaluated

Description

    Allows to include a fractional integrated term in the conditional mean equation of the univariate GARCH. For CCC, DCC and (G)OGARCH models only.

MGarch::UGARCH_PrintOutput

UGARCH_PrintOutput(const choice);

        choice   in: int, 1 or 2 to print the output of the univatiate GARCH models, 0 otherwise

Return value

    No return value

Description

    Allows to print the output of the univariate GARCH estimation.

MGarch::UGARCH_TRUNC

UGARCH_TRUNC(const t);

        t   in: int, number of lags for the truncation

Return value

1 if the function is successfully evaluated

Description

Truncation order of the FIGARCH-type models.

MGarch::VARIANCE_TARGETING, MGarch::UGARCH_VARIANCE_TARGETING

```
VARIANCE_TARGETING(const varsamp);  UGARCH_VARIANCE_TARGETING(const
choice);
```

varsamp	in: int, 1 to target the variance of a MGARCH model
	0 otherwise
choice	in: int, 1 to target the variance of a GARCH model
	0 otherwise

Return value

1 if the function is successfully evaluated

Description

Allows to apply variance targeting to the MGARCH and GARCH models respectively.

10.6 `Realized` **Member Functions List**

Here is the list of the `Realized` member functions and a brief description for each of them.

Constructor and Destructor

`Realized`	Constructor
`~Realized`	Destructor

Model Class

`SetModelClass`	Choice between MC_RV (for univariate RV),
	MC_LM (for L&M test) and MC_RCOV (for multivariate COV)

Options for MC_RV

`IV`	Choice between BV (1) and ROWVar (2), 0 otherwise

`OPTIONS_ROWVAR`	Options for ROWVar (i.e. HR/SR weight function, β and $f_{t,i}$)
`OPTIONS_JUMPS_TEST_BV`	Options for the 'daily' jumps test based on BV
`OPTIONS_JUMPS_TEST_ROWVAR`	Options for the 'daily' jumps test based on ROWVar
`Graphs_RV`	Options for graphics on RV and extensions
`RV`	1 to compute RV, 0 otherwise

Options for MC_LM

`Graphs_LM`	Options for graphics on L&M test
`OPTIONS_JUMPS_TEST_LM`	Options for the 'intraday' jumps test based on the L&M statistic
`STORE_LM`	Store some relevant variables related to the L&M test

Options for MC_RCOV

`ICOV`	Choice between RBPCOV (1) and ROWQCOV (2), 0 otherwise
`Graphs_RCOV`	Options for graphics on RCOV and extensions
`RCOV`	1 to compute RCOV, 0 otherwise

Procedures for MC_RV

`Compute_BV`	Computes bi-power variation
`Compute_ROWQuarticity`	Computes ROWQuarticity as in Equation 7.48
`Compute_RR`	Computes realized returns
`Compute_RV`	Computes realized volatility
`Compute_ROWVAR`	Computes ROWVar
`Compute_TQ`	Computes tri-power quarticity
`Compute_QQ`	Computes quad-power quarticity
`Get_ctd_ROWVAR`	Returns c_w, θ and d_w as in Table 7.4
`Hard_Rejection`	Hard rejection weight function (see Equation (7.41))
`Soft_Rejection`	Soft rejection weight function (see Equation (7.42))
`Z_STAT`	Computes the Z statistic in Equation (7.45)
`Z_STAT_log`	Computes the $logZ_t$ statistic in Equation (7.49)
`Z_STAT_max_log`	Computes the $maxlogZ_t$ statistic in Equation (7.50)

Procedures for MC_LM

`Compute_LeeMykJump`	Computes Lee-Mykland statistic for jump detection
`Get_Gumbel_critical_value`	Returns the Gumbel critical value

Procedures for MC_RCOV

`Compute_MCD`	Computes the Fast MCD scale estimator as in Equation (7.62)
`Compute_RRCOV`	Computes realized returns for the N series (on common sample)
`Compute_RCOV`	Computes RCov
`Compute_RBPCOV`	Computes RBPCov
`Compute_ROWQCOV`	Computes ROWQCov
`Get_cw_ROWQCOV`	Returns the correction factor c_w for ROWQCov as in Table

Procedures for intraday periodicity

`madc, madr`	Computes the MAD scale estimator as in Equation (7.21)
`ShortH_scalec`	Computes the Shortest Half scale estimator as in Equation (7.23)
`TaylorXu`	Computes Taylor and Xu (1997)'s periodicity filter as in Equation (7.20)
`Robust_periodicity`	Computes the three periodicity filters $\hat{f}_{t,i}^{MAD}$, $\hat{f}_{t,i}^{ShortH}$ and $\hat{f}_{t,i}^{WSD}$

10.7 Realized Members Functions

Realized::Compute_BV

`Compute_BV(const mRet_table);`

      `mRet_table`   in: $T \times M$ matrix with intraday returns

Return value

    Returns a $T \times 1$ vector with BV_t

Description

    Computes bi-power variation as defined in Equation (7.38). Note that each row of mRet_table corresponds to one day. The first column corresponds to the first return of the day. There are $M \equiv 1/\Delta$ intraday returns per day.

Realized::Compute_LeeMykJump

`Compute_LeeMykJump(const mRet_table, const mS_table, const Siglevel, const n, const TLeeMyk, const Sign_jumps, const c_v);`

`mRet_table`	in:	$T \times M$ matrix with intraday returns
`mS_table`	in:	0 or $T \times M$ matrix with filtered intraday returns $r_{t,i}/\hat{f}_{t,i}$
`Siglevel`	in:	Significance level for the test (in percentage points)
`n`	in:	int n. Typical values are $n = 1$, $n = M$ or $n = M \times T$
`TLeeMyk`	out:	$T \times M$ matrix with $J_{t,i}$. See Equations (7.53) and (7.54)
`Sign_jumps`	out:	$T \times M$ matrix with $I(J_{t,i} > G^{-1}(1-\alpha)S_n + C_n)$
`c_v`	out:	double, $G^{-1}(1-\alpha)S_n + C_n$

Return value

No return value

Description

L&M test. See Section 7.8 for more details.

Realized::Compute_MCD

Compute_MCD(const data, const bdp, const nres, const ncsteps,
const rewMCDcov);

data	in: $T \times N$ matrix
bdp	in: double, breakdownpoint (e.g. 0.5 for 50%)
nres	in: int, number of initial choices of halfsamples
ncsteps	in: int, number of times the observations in the halfsample with highest outlyingness are replaced by those with lowest outlyingness
rewMCDcov	out: $N \times N$ matrix with MCD scale estimator

Return value

No return value

Description

Computes the Fast MCD scale estimator of Rousseeuw, P.J. and Van Driessen, K. (1999), "A Fast Algorithm for the Minimum Covariance Determinant Estimator," Technometrics, 41, pp. 212-223.

Realized::Compute_QQ

Compute_QQ(const mRet_table);

mRet_table	in: $T \times M$ matrix with intraday returns

Return value

Returns a $T \times 1$ vector containing quad-power quarticity.

Description

Computes quad-power quarticity as defined in Equation (7.47). Note that each row of mRet_table corresponds to one day. The first column corresponds to the first return of the day. There are $M \equiv 1/\Delta$ intraday returns per day.

Realized::Compute_RCOV

Compute_RCOV(const common_dates, const a_dates, const a_ret);

common_dates in: $T \times 1$ vector with the common dates of the N series

a_dates   in: array of N elements containing the dates of each series

a_ret   in: array of N elements containing $T_i \times M$ matrices with intraday returns, $i = 1, \ldots, M$

Return value

Returns an array of T elements with $N \times N$ realized covariance matrices

Description

Computes $RCov_t$ as in Equation (7.57).

Realized::Compute_RBPCOV

Compute_RBPCOV(const common_dates, const a_dates, const a_ret);

common_dates in: $T \times 1$ vector with the common dates of the N series

a_dates   in: array of N elements containing the dates of each series

a_ret   in: array of N elements containing $T_i \times M$ matrices with intraday returns, $i = 1, \ldots, M$

Return value

Returns an array of T elements with $N \times N$ (pairwise) realized bi-power covariance matrices

Description

Computes $RBPCov_t$ as in Equation (7.59).

Realized::Compute_RR

Compute_RR(const mRet_table);

mRet_table   in: $T \times M$ matrix with intraday returns

Return value

Returns a $T \times 1$ vector with $\sum_{i=1}^{M} r_{t,i}$

Description

Computes daily returns.

Realized::Compute_RRCOV

Compute_RRCOV(const common_dates, const a_dates, const a_ret);

common_dates in: $T \times 1$ vector with the common dates of the N series

a_dates   in: array of N elements containing the dates of each series

a_ret   in: array of N elements containing $T_i \times M$ matrices with intraday returns, $i = 1, \ldots, M$

Return value

Returns a $T \times M$ matrix with daily returns

Description

Computes realized returns for the N series (on common sample).

Realized::Compute_ROWQCOV

```
Compute_ROWQCOV(const common_dates, const a_dates, const a_ret);
```
    common_dates in: $T \times 1$ vector with the common dates of the N series

    a_dates   in: array of N elements containing the dates of each series

    a_ret   in: array of N elements containing $T_i \times M$ matrices with
                 intraday returns, $i = 1, \ldots, M$

Return value

Returns an array of T elements with $N \times N$ realized outlyingness weighted quadratic covariation matrices

Description

Computes $ROWQCov_t$ as in Equation (7.62).

Realized::Compute_ROWQuarticity

```
Compute _ROWQuarticity(const mRet_table, const beta, const HR_SR,
const di);
```
    mRet_table in: $T \times M$ matrix with intraday returns

    beta   in: double, $\beta = 1, 0.99, 0.975, 0.95, 0.925, 0.90, 0.85$ or 0.80

    HR_SR   in: int, 1 for soft rejection weight function, 0 for hard rejection.

    di   in: $T \times 1$ vector holding the outlyingness measure $d_{t,i}$

Return value

Returns a $T \times 1$ vector containing $ROWQuarticity_t$.

Description

Computes the Realized Outlyigness Weighted Quarticity as defined in Equation (7.48). Note that each row of mRet_table corresponds to one day. The first column corresponds to the first return of the day. There are $M \equiv 1/\Delta$ intraday returns per day.

Realized::Compute_ROWVAR

```
Compute_ROWVAR(const mRet_table, const beta, const HR_SR, const
periodicity, const day_week, const di, const wi);
```

mRet_table   in: $T \times M$ matrix with intraday returns

beta   in: double, $\beta = 1, 0.99, 0.975, 0.95, 0.925, 0.90, 0.85$ or 0.80

HR_SR   in: int, 1 for soft rejection weight function, 0 for hard rejection.

periodicity in: int, 0 to compute $d_{t,i}$ on $r_{t,i}$, 1, 2 or 3 to compute it on
$r_{t,i}/\hat{f}_{t,i}^{MAD}$ $r_{t,i}/\hat{f}_{t,i}^{ShortH}$ and $r_{t,i}/\hat{f}_{t,i}^{WSD}$ respectively

day_week   in: $T \times 1$ vector containing the day-of-the-week
(e.g. Monday=1, etc.).

di   out: $T \times 1$ vector holding the outlyingness measure $d_{t,i}$

wi   out: $T \times 1$ vector with $w(d_{t,i})$

Return value

Returns a $T \times 1$ vector with $ROWVar_t$.

Description

Computes ROWVar as defined in Equation (7.43). Note that each row of mRet_table corresponds to one day. The first column corresponds to the first return of the day. There are $M \equiv 1/\Delta$ intraday returns per day. When $periodicity \neq 0$, $d_{t,i}$ is computed on filtered returns, i.e. $r_{t,i}/\hat{f}_{t,i}$. If day_week contains integer values corresponding to the day-of-the-week, the length of the periodicity filter is equal to $max(\text{day\_week}) - min(\text{day\_week}) + 1$ (i.e. 5 in most cases). To impose the same periodicity filter for all the days-of-the-week, set day_week to ones(T,1).

Realized::Compute_RV

```
Compute_RV(const mRet_table);
```
     mRet_table   in: $T \times M$ matrix with intraday returns

Return value

Returns a $T \times 1$ vector with realized volatility.

Description

Computes realized volatility as defined in Equation (7.12). Note that each row of mRet_table corresponds to one day. The first column corresponds to the first return of the day. There are $M \equiv 1/\Delta$ intraday returns per day.

Realized::Compute_TQ

```
Compute_TQ(const mRet_table);
```
     mRet_table   in: $T \times M$ matrix with intraday returns

Return value

Returns a $T \times 1$ vector containing tri-power quarticity.

Description

Computes tri-power quarticity as defined in Equation (7.46). Note that each row of mRet_table corresponds to one day. The first column corresponds to the first return of the day. There are $M \equiv 1/\Delta$ intraday returns per day.

Realized::Get_ctd_ROWVAR

Get_ctd_ROWVAR(const beta, const HR_SR);

      beta   in: double, $\beta = 1, 0.99, 0.975, 0.95, 0.925, 0.90, 0.85$ or 0.80

      HR_SR   in: int, 1 for soft rejection weight function, 0 for hard rejection.

Return value

    3×1 vector with c_w, θ, d_w. *Description*

    Returns c_w, θ, d_w for several critical levels (β) and for the hard and soft rejection weight functions. See Table 7.4 for more details.

Realized::Get_cw_ROWQCOV

Get_cw_ROWQCOV(const beta, const HR_SR, const N);

      beta   in: double, $\beta = 1, 0.99, 0.975, 0.95, 0.925, 0.90, 0.85$ or 0.80

      HR_SR   in: int, 1 for soft rejection weight function, 0 for hard rejection.

      N   in: int, number of series.

Return value

    c_w

Description

    Returns the correction factor c_w for ROWQCov as in Table 7.5. Recall that for the HR weight function defined in (7.41) with threshold $k = \chi_N^2(1 - \alpha)$, $c_w = (1 - \alpha)/F_{\chi_{N+2}^2}(\chi_N^2(1 - \alpha))$, where $F_{\chi_{N+2}^2}(\cdot)$ is the χ_{N+2}^2 distribution function.

Realized::Get_Gumbel_critical_value

Get_Gumbel_critical_value(const Siglevel, const n);

      Siglevel   in: Significance level for the test (in percentage points)

      n   in: int n. Typical values are $n = 1$, $n = M$ or $n = M \times T$

Return value

    double, $G^{-1}(1 - \alpha)S_n + C_n$

Description

    Critical value of the L&M test. See Section Equation (7.54).

Realized::Graphs_LM

Graphs_LM(const Histo, const S);

  Histo   in: int, 1 to plot the number of detected jumps per period of time

  S   in: int, 1 to plot the estimated periodicity factor $\hat{f}_{t,i}$

Return value

  No return value

Description

  Displays some graphics on the L&M test in the OxMetrics front-end.

Realized::Graphs_RCOV

Graphs_RCOV(sel, const plot_RVCOV, const plot_RCOV, const plot_RCORCOV, const plot_IV, const plot_IVCOV, const plot_IVCORR);

  sel   in: int, -1 to plot the selected graphs for all the series
                 or $k \times 1$ vector (with $k \leq N$) with the numbers of the series to be
                 plotted (e.g. <0,2> to plot the first and third)

  plot_RVCOV   in: int, 1 to plot the realized variance(s)

  plot_RCOV   in: int, 1 to plot the realized covariance(s)

  plot_RCORR   in: int, 1 to plot the realized correlation(s)

  plot_IV   in: int, 1 to plot the robust estimates of the integrated variance(s)

  plot_IVCOV   in: int, 1 to plot the robust estimates of the integrated covariance(s)

  plot_IVCORR in: int, 1 to plot the robust estimates of the integrated correlation(s)

Return value

  No return value

Description

  Displays graphics of the above time series in the OxMetrics front-end. Note that robust estimates of the integrated covariance matrix are either RBPCov or ROWQCov depending on the option chosen by the user in ICOV().

Realized::Graphs_RV

Graphs_RV(const RR, const RV, const BV, const ROWVAR, const SR_RV, const SR_BV, const SR_ROWVAR, const RJ, const Level, const Acf, const Density, const lag_acf, const jump_stat);

  RR   in: int, 1 to plot realized returns r_t, 0 otherwise

  RV   in: int, 1 to plot realized variance, 0 otherwise

  BV   in: int, 1 to plot bi-power variation

ROWVAR	in: int, 1 to plot ROWVar, 0 otherwise
SR_RV	in: int, 1 to plot standardized returns $r_t/\sqrt{RV_t}$, 0 otherwise
SR_BV	in: int, 1 to plot standardized returns $r_t/\sqrt{BV_t}$, 0 otherwise
SR_ROWVAR	in: int, 1 to plot standardized returns $r_t/\sqrt{ROWVar_t}$, 0 otherwise
RJ	in: int, 1 to plot realized jumps, 0 otherwise
Level	in: int, 1 to plot the above selected times series in level, 0 otherwise
ACF	in: int, 1 to plot the ACF of the above selected times series, 0 otherwise
Density	in: int, 1 to plot the above unconditional density of the above selected times series, 0 otherwise
lag_acf	in: int, lag-length of the ACF
jump_stat	in: int, 1 to plot the jumps statistics (in log) $\max\limits_{i=1,\dots,M}\sqrt{d_{t,i}}$, Z_t, $\log Z_t$ or $maxlog Z_t$ together with the (log of the) critical value.

Return value

No return value

Description

Displays graphics of the above time series in the OxMetrics front-end. Note that as explained in Section 7.7 realized jumps are the significant ones at the $\alpha\%$ critical level, i.e.

$$J_{t,\alpha}(\Delta) = I_{t,\alpha}(\Delta) \cdot [RV_t(\Delta) - I\hat{V}_t(\Delta)]$$

and the bi-power variation and ROWVar are computed as follows:

$$C_{t,\alpha}(\Delta) = [1 - I_{t,\alpha}(\Delta)] \cdot I\hat{V}_t(\Delta) + I_{t,\alpha}(\Delta) \cdot I\hat{V}_t(\Delta).$$

Realized::Hard_Rejection

Hard_Rejection(const z, const k);

| z | in: $m \times 1$ vector |
| k | in: int, tuning parameter. |

Return value

$m \times 1$ vector with $w_{\text{HR}}(z)$

Description

Hard rejection weight function (see Equation (7.41)).

Realized::ICOV

```
ICOV(const choice,...);
```
      `choice`   in: integer, 0, 1 or 2

      `periodicity` (when $choice = 2$) in: int, 0 to compute $d_{t,i}$ on $r_{t,i}$, 1, 2 or 3
                   to compute it on $r_{t,i}/\hat{f}_{t,i}^{MAD}$ $r_{t,i}/\hat{f}_{t,i}^{ShortH}$ and $r_{t,i}/\hat{f}_{t,i}^{WSD}$ respectively.

      `local_cov`   (when $choice = 2$) in: integer, 0 for MCD, 1 for pairwise BPCov

Return value

    No return value

Description

BPCov is computed when $choice = 1$ while ROWQCov is computed when $choice = 2$. When $choice = 0$, no robust to jumps measure of ICov is computed. `periodicity` allows to compute the outlyingness measure $d_{t,i}$ on filtered returns. Note that the N periodicity filters are estimated separately. `local_cov` concerns the choice of the local covariance matrix S in Equation (7.61). When `local_cov` is set to 0, the MCD is used while when `local_cov` is set to 1, pairwise BPCov is used.

Realized::IV

```
IV(const choice);
```
      `choice`   in: integer, 0, 1 or 2

Return value

    No return value

Description

BV is computed when $choice = 1$ while ROWVar is computed when $choice = 2$. When $choice = 0$, no robust to jumps measure of IVar is computed. Note that $C_{t,\alpha}(\Delta) = [1 - I_{t,\alpha}(\Delta)] \cdot RV_t(\Delta) + I_{t,\alpha}(\Delta) \cdot I\hat{V}_t(\Delta)$ (see Equation (7.52)) is stored in the global variable `m_vIV`.

Realized::madc, madr

```
madc(const data);
madr(const data);
```
      `data`   in: $T \times M$ matrix

Return value

    madc returns a $1 \times M$ vector holding the MAD of each column of `data`

    madr returns a $T \times 1$ vector holding the MAD of each rows of `data`

Description

    Computes the MAD scale estimator as in Equation (7.21).

Realized::OPTIONS_ROWVAR

OPTIONS_ROWVAR(const HR_SR, const beta, const periodicity);

      HR_SR   in: int, 1 for soft rejection weight function, 0 for hard rejection.

      beta   in: double, $\beta = 1, 0.99, 0.975, 0.95, 0.925, 0.90, 0.85$ or 0.80

      periodicity in: int, 0 to compute $d_{t,i}$ on $r_{t,i}$, 1, 2 or 3 to compute it on
$r_{t,i}/\hat{f}_{t,i}^{MAD}$ $r_{t,i}/\hat{f}_{t,i}^{ShortH}$ and $r_{t,i}/\hat{f}_{t,i}^{WSD}$ respectively

Return value

    No return value

Description

    Options for ROWVar. When $periodicity \neq 0$, $d_{t,i}$ is computed on filtered returns, i.e. $r_{t,i}/\hat{f}_{t,i}$. The second option (beta) concerns the outlyingness threshold k. Recall that both rejection functions contain a tuning parameter k equal to the $\beta = 1 - \alpha$ quantile of the χ_1^2 distribution function. This option allows the chose β. Usually, β is set to 0.95 which corresponds to the 95% quantile of the χ_1^2 distribution function.

Realized::OPTIONS_JUMPS_TEST_BV

OPTIONS_JUMPS_TEST_BV(const choice, const IQ, const Z, const alpha);

      choice   in: int, 1 to compute the Z test for daily jump detection presented in Section 7.7, 0 otherwise

      IQ   in: int, 0 to base the test on $\hat{IQ}_t = TQ_t(\Delta)$ and 1 for $\hat{IQ}_t = QQ_t(\Delta)$. See Equations (7.46) and (7.47)

      Z   in: int, 0 for Z_t statistic (7.45), 1 for $logZ_t$ (7.49) and 2 for $maxlogZ_t$ (7.50).

      alpha   in: double, critical level α of the test, e.g. 0.9999

Return value

    No return value

Description

    Options for the daily jump tests based on $RV_t(\Delta) - \hat{BV}_t(\Delta)$. See Section 7.7 for more details.

Realized::OPTIONS_JUMPS_TEST_LM

OPTIONS_JUMPS_TEST_LM(const beta, const n, const periodicity);

      beta   in: double, critical level β of the test, e.g. 0.9999 periodicity in: int, 1 for $\hat{f}_{t,i}^{MAD}$, 2 for $\hat{f}_{t,i}^{ShortH}$, 3 for $\hat{f}_{t,i}^{WSD}$ and 0 otherwise

n   in: int, value n for the Gumbel critical value.

Return value

No return value

Description

Options for the L&M test for intraday jumps detection. Recall that $J_{t,i} = \frac{|r_{t,i}|}{\hat{\sigma}_{t,i}}$. When $periodicity = 0$, $\hat{\sigma}_{t,i}$ is replaced by $\hat{s}_{t,i} = \sqrt{\frac{1}{M-1} \times BV_t}$. When $periodicity > 0$ $\hat{\sigma}_{t,i}$ is replaced by $\hat{s}_{t,i}\hat{f}_{t,i}$, with $\hat{f}_{t,i} = \hat{f}_{t,i}^{MAD}, \hat{f}_{t,i}^{ShortH}$ and $\hat{f}_{t,i}^{WSD}$ when $periodicity = 1, 2$ and 3 respectively. Note that typical values for n are $n = 1$, $n = M$ and $n = M \times T$. Recall that in this case, the expected number of spurious detected jumps respectively equals $\alpha \times T \times M$, $\alpha \times T$ and α (i.e. ≈ 0).

Realized::OPTIONS_JUMPS_TEST_ROWVAR

```
OPTIONS_JUMPS_TEST_ROWVAR(const choice, const n, const choice_test,
const alpha);
```

choice   in: int, 1 to compute the test for daily jump detection presented in Section 7.7, 0 otherwise

n   in: int, value n for the test based on $\max_{i=1,\dots,M} \sqrt{d_{t,i}}$.

choice_test in: int, 0 to select the test based on $\max_{i=1,\dots,M} \sqrt{d_{t,i}}$, 1 for Z_t (7.45), 2 for $log Z_t$ (7.49) and 3 for $maxlog Z_t$ (7.50).

alpha   in: double, critical level α of the test, e.g. 0.9999

Return value

No return value

Description

Options for the daily jump tests based on $RV_t(\Delta) - R\hat{OW}Var_t(\Delta)$. See Section 7.7 for more details. Typical values for n are $n = M$ and $n = M \times T$. Recall that when $n = M$ or $n = M \times T$, the expected number of spurious (daily) detected jumps respectively equals $\alpha \times T$ and α (i.e. ≈ 0).

Realized::RCOV

```
RCOV(const choice);
```

choice   in: integer, 0 or 1

Return value

No return value

Description

RCov is computed when *choice* $= 1$, 0 otherwise. $RCov_t$ is stored in the global variable (array) a_RCOV.

Other important global variables:

m_RV_COV $= T \times M$ matrix containing the realized volatilities.

a_CORR = array with the realized correlations

m_vechCORR $= T \times N(N-1)/2$ matrix with the vech of the realized correlation

m_vechCOV $= T \times N(N-1)/2$ matrix with the vech of the realized covariance

Realized::Robust_periodicity

```
Robust_periodicity(const day_week, const data, const si, const
no_zero_ret, const s, const s_all, const filtered, const method);
```

day_week	in: $T \times 1$ vector containing the day-of-the-week (e.g. Monday=1, etc.)	
data	in: $T \times M$ matrix with intraday returns	
si	in: $T \times 1$ vector $\hat{s}_t$, e.g. $\sqrt{\frac{1}{M-1}} \times BV_t$	
no_zero_ret	in: int, 1 to compute the filter on non-zero returns, 0 otherwise	
s	out: $k \times 1$ vector with the estimated periodicity filter	
s_all	in: if method=2, $T \times M$ matrix with $\hat{f}_{t,i}^{\mathrm{MAD}}$ or $\hat{f}_{t,i}^{\mathrm{ShortH}}$ out: $T \times M$ matrix with the estimated periodicity filter	
filtered	out: $T \times M$ matrix with filtered intraday returns	
method	in: int, 0 for MAD, 1 for ShortH and 2 for WSD	

Return value

No return value

Description

Computes Boudt, Croux, and Laurent (2008b)'s robust periodicity filters $\hat{f}_{t,i}^{\mathrm{MAD}}, \hat{f}_{t,i}^{\mathrm{ShortH}}$ and $\hat{f}_{t,i}^{\mathrm{WSD}}$. If day_week contains integer values corresponding to the day-of-the-week, the length of the periodicity filter is equal to $k = max(\texttt{day\_week}) - min(\texttt{day\_week}) + 1$ (i.e. 5 in most cases). To impose the same periodicity filter for all the days-of-the-week, set day_week to ones(T,1).

Realized::RV

```
RV(const choice);
```

choice	in: integer, 0 or 1

Return value

No return value

Description

RV is computed when $choice = 1$, 0 otherwise. RV_t is stored in the global variable m_vRV.

Realized::SetModelClass

```
SetModelClass(const choice);
```
       choice   in: integer, MC_RV (0), MC_LM (1) or MC_RCOV(2)

Return value

   No return value

Description

Choice between three model classes: MC_RV (for univariate RV), MC_LM (for L&M test) and MC_RCOV (for multivariate COV)

Realized::ShortH_scalec

```
ShortH_scalec(const data);
```
       data   in: $T \times M$ matrix

Return value

   Returns a $1 \times M$ vector holding the Shortest Half scale estimator of each column of data

Description

   Computes the Shortest Half scale estimator as in Equation (7.23).

Realized::Soft_Rejection

```
Soft_Rejection(const z, const k);
```
       z   in: $m \times 1$ vector
       k   in: int, tuning parameter.

Return value

   $m \times 1$ vector with $w_{\text{SR}}(z)$

Description

   Soft Rejection weight function (see Equation (7.42)).

Realized::Store_LM

```
Store_LM(const table, const title, const path);
```
       table   in: $T \times M$ matrix
       title   in: string, prefix of the name of the M columns

path   in: string, filename (with extension). Supported are: .csv, .dat, .dht, .in7, .xls.

Return value

No return value

Description

Saves table in an external file.

Realized::TaylorXu

TaylorXu(const day_week, const data, const si, const no_zero_ret, const s, const s_all, const filtered);

day_week	in: $T \times 1$ vector containing the day-of-the-week (e.g. Monday=1, etc.)
data	in: $T \times M$ matrix with intraday returns
si	in: $T \times 1$ vector $\hat{s}_t$, e.g. $\sqrt{\frac{1}{M-1}} \times BV_t$
no_zero_ret	in: int, 1 to compute the filter on non-zero returns, 0 otherwise
s	out: $k \times 1$ vector with the estimated periodicity filter
s_all	out: $T \times M$ matrix with the estimated periodicity filter
filtered	out: $T \times M$ matrix with filtered intraday returns

Return value

No return value

Description

Computes Taylor and Xu (1997)'s periodicity filter. If day_week contains integer values corresponding to the day-of-the-week, the length of the periodicity filter is equal to $k = max(\text{day\_week}) - min(\text{day\_week}) + 1$ (i.e. 5 in most cases). To impose the same periodicity filter for all the days-of-the-week, set day_week to ones(T,1).

Realized::Z_STAT

Z_STAT(const vRV, const vhatIV, const vhatIQ, const ctheta, const cPer);

vRV	in: $T \times 1$ vector containing realized volatility
vhatIV	in: $T \times 1$ vector containing estimates of IVar
vhatIQ	in: $T \times 1$ vector containing estimates of IQ
ctheta	in: double, θ
cPer	in: integer, count of intra-day periods

Return value

Returns a T× 1 vector containing Z_t

Description

Computes the Z_t statistic as in Equation (7.45)

Realized::Z_STAT_log

```
Z_STAT_log(const vRV, const vhatIV, const vhatIQ, const ctheta,
const cPer);
```

vRV	in: T× 1 vector containing realized volatility
vhatIV	in: T× 1 vector containing estimates of IVar
vhatIQ	in: T× 1 vector containing estimates of IQ
ctheta	in: double, θ
cPer	in: integer, count of intra-day periods

Return value

Returns a T× 1 vector containing Z_t

Description

Computes the $log Z_t$ statistic as in Equation (7.49)

Realized::Z_STAT_max_log

```
Z_STAT_max_log(const vRV, const vhatIV, const vhatIQ, const
ctheta, const cPer);
```

vRV	in: T× 1 vector containing realized volatility
vhatIV	in: T× 1 vector containing estimates of IVar
vhatIQ	in: T× 1 vector containing estimates of IQ
ctheta	in: double, θ
cPer	in: integer, count of intra-day periods

Return value

Returns a T× 1 vector containing Z_t

Description

Computes the $maxlog Z_t$ statistic as in Equation (7.50)

Bibliography

ALEXANDER, C. (2001.): *Market Models*. Wiley, New York.

ALEXANDER, C., and A. CHIBUMBA (1997): "Multivariate Orthogonal Factor GARCH," University of Sussex, Mimeo.

ANDERSEN, T., T. BOLLERSLEV, P. CHRISTOFFERSEN, and F. DIEBOLD (2006): "Volatility and Correlation Forecasting," in *Handbook of Economic Forecasting*, ed. by G. Elliott, C. Granger, and A. Timmermann, pp. 778–878. North-Holland, Amsterdam.

ANDERSEN, T., T. BOLLERSLEV, and F. DIEBOLD (2007): "Roughing it up: including jump components in the measurement, modelling and forecasting of return volatility," *The Review of Economics and Statistics*, 89(4), 701–720.

ANDERSEN, T., T. BOLLERSLEV, F. DIEBOLD, and P. LABYS (2003): "Modeling and Forecasting Realized Volatility," *Econometrica*, 71, 579–625.

ANDERSEN, T., T. BOLLERSLEV, and D. DOBREV (2007): "No-arbitrage Semi-martingale Restrictions for Continous-time Volatility Models Subject to Leverage Effects, Jumps and i.i.d. noise: Theory and Testable Distributional Implications," *Journal of Econometrics*, 138, 125–180.

ANDERSEN, T. G., and T. BOLLERSLEV (1997): "Intraday Periodicity and Volatility Persistence in Financial Markets," *Journal of Empirical Finance*, 4, 115–158.

——— (1998a): "Answering the Skeptics: Yes, Standard Volatility Models do Provide Accurate Forecasts," *International Economic Review*, 39, 885–905.

——— (1998b): "DM-Dollar volatility: intraday activity patterns, macroeconomic announcements and longer run dependencies," *The Journal of Finance*, 53, 219–265.

ARTZNER, P., F. DELBAEN, J.-M. EBER, and D. HEATH (1999): "Coherent measures of risk," *Mathematical Finance*, 9, 203–228.

BAILLIE, R. T. (1996): "Long Memory Processes and Fractional Integration in Econometrics," *Journal of Econometrics*, 73, 5–59.

BAILLIE, R. T., and T. BOLLERSLEV (1989): "The Message in Daily Exchange Rates: A Conditional-Variance Tale," *Journal of Business and Economic Statistics*, 7, 297–305.

BAILLIE, R. T., T. BOLLERSLEV, and H. O. MIKKELSEN (1996): "Fractionally Integrated Generalized Autoregressive Conditional Heteroskedasticity," *Journal of Econometrics*, 74, 3–30.

BAILLIE, R. T., C. F. CHUNG, and M. A. TIESLAU (1996): "Analyzing Inflation by the Fractionally Integrated ARFIMA-GARCH Model," *Journal of Applied Econometrics*, 11, 23–40.

BARNDORFF-NIELSEN, O., and N. SHEPHARD (2004a): "Measuring the impact of jumps in multivariate price processes using bipower covariation," *Discussion paper, Nuffield College, Oxford University*.

——— (2004b): "Power and bipower variation with stochastic volatility and jumps (with discussion)," *Journal of Financial Econometrics*, 2, 1–48.

——— (2006): "Econometrics of testing for jumps in financial economics using bipower variation," *Journal of Financial Econometrics*, 4, 1–30.

BAUWENS, L., P. GIOT, J. GRAMMIG, and D. VEREDAS (2000): "A Comparison of Financial Duration Models Via Density Forecasts," CORE DP 2060.

BAUWENS, L., and S. LAURENT (2005): "A New Class of Multivariate Skew Densities, with Application to GARCH Models," *Journal of Business and Economic Statistics*, 23, 346–354.

BAUWENS, L., S. LAURENT, and J. ROMBOUTS (2006): "A review of Multivariate GARCH Models with Applications to Financial Data," *Journal of Applied Econometrics*, 21.

BEINE, M., S. LAURENT, and C. LECOURT (2002): "Accounting for Conditional Leptokurtosis and Closing Days Effects in FIGARCH Models of Daily Exchange Rates," *Applied Financial Economics*, 12, 589–600.

BERA, A. K., and M. L. HIGGINS (1993): "ARCH Models: Properties, Estimation and Testing," *Journal of Economic Surveys*, 7, 305–362.

BLACK, F. (1976): "Studies of Stock Market Volatility Changes," *Proceedings of the American Statistical Association, Business and Economic Statistics Section*, pp. 177–181.

BOLLERSLEV, T. (1986): "Generalized Autoregressive Conditional Heteroskedasticity," *Journal of Econometrics*, 31, 307–327.

——— (1987): "A Conditionally Heteroskedastic Time Series Model for Speculative Prices and Rates of Return," *Review of Economics and Statistics*, 69, 542–547.

——— (1990): "Modeling the Coherence in Short-run Nominal Exchange Rates: A Multivariate Generalized ARCH model," *Review of Economics and Statistics*, 72,

498–505.

BOLLERSLEV, T., R. Y. CHOU, and K. F. KRONER (1992): "ARCH Modeling in Finance: A Review of the Theory and Empirical Evidence," *Journal of Econometrics*, 52, 5–59.

BOLLERSLEV, T., R. F. ENGLE, and J. M. WOOLDRIDGE (1988): "A Capital Asset Pricing Model with Time Varying Covariances," *Journal of Political Economy*, 96, 116–131.

BOLLERSLEV, T., and E. GHYSELS (1996): "Periodic Autoregressive Conditional Heteroskedasticity," *Journal of Business and Economics Statistics*, 14, 139–152.

BOLLERSLEV, T., and H. O. MIKKELSEN (1996): "Modeling and Pricing Long-Memory in Stock Market Volatility," *Journal of Econometrics*, 73, 151–184.

BOLLERSLEV, T., and J. M. WOOLDRIDGE (1992): "Quasi-maximum Likelihood Estimation and Inference in Dynamic Models with Time-varying Covariances," *Econometric Reviews*, 11, 143–172.

BOSWIJK, H., and R. VAN DER WEIDE (2006): "Wake me up before you GO-GARCH," UvA-Econometrics Discussion Paper 2006/03.

BOUDT, K., C. CROUX, and S. LAURENT (2008a): "Outlyingness weighted quadratic covariation," Mimeo.

——— (2008b): "Robust estimation of intraweek periodicity in volatility and jump detection," Mimeo.

BROOKS, C., S. P. BURKE, and G. PERSAND (1997): "Linear and Non-Linear (Non-)Forecastability of High-Frequency Exchange Rates," *Journal of Forecasting*, 16, 125–145.

——— (2001): "Benchmarks and the Accuracy of GARCH Model Estimation," *International Journal of Forecasting*, 17, 45–56.

BROWNLEES, C., and G. GALLO (2006): "Financial Econometric Analysis at Ultra-high Frequency: Data Handling Concerns," *Computational Statistics & Data Analysis*, 51, 2232–2245.

BRUNETTI, C., and C. GILBERT (2000): "Bivariate FIGARCH and Fractional Cointegration," *Journal of Empirical Finance*, 7, 509–530.

CHUNG, C.-F. (1999): "Estimating the Fractionally Integrated GARCH Model," National Taïwan University working paper.

COMTE, F., and O. LIEBERMAN (2003): "Asymptotic Theory for Multivariate GARCH Processes," *Journal of Multivariate Analysis*, 84, 61–84.

CONRAD, C. (2007): "Non-negativity conditions for the hyperbolic GARCH model,"

KOF Working Papers No. 162, ETH Zrich.

CONRAD, C., and B. HAAG (2006): "Inequality constraints in the fractionally integrated GARCH model," *Journal of Financial Econometrics*, 4, 413–449.

CRIBARI-NETO, F., and S. ZARKOS (2003): "Econometric and Statistical Computing Using Ox," *Computational Economics*, 21, 277–295.

CROUX, C., and G. HAESBROECK (1999): "Influence function and efficiency of the minimum covariance determinant scatter matrix estimator," *Journal of Multivariate Analysis*, 71(2), 161–190.

DAVIDSON, J. (2001): "Moment and Memory Properties of Linear Conditional Heteroscedasticity Models," Manuscript, Cardiff University.

——— (2004): "Moment and memory properties of linear conditional heteroscedasticity models, and a new model," *Journal of Business and Economics Statistics*, 22, 16–29.

DICKEY, D., and W. FULLER (1981): "Likelihood Ratio Statistics for Autoregressive Time Series with a Unit Root," *Econometrica*, 49, 1057–1072.

DIEBOLD, F. X., T. A. GUNTHER, and A. S. TAY (1998): "Evaluating Density Forecasts, with Applications to Financial Risk Management," *International Economic Review*, 39, 863–883.

DIEBOLD, F. X., J. HAHN, and A. S. TAY (1999): "Multivariate Density Forecast Evaluation and Calibration in Financial Risk Management: High-Frequency Returns on Foreign Exchange," *Review of Economics and Statistics*, 81, 863–883.

DING, Z., C. W. J. GRANGER, and R. F. ENGLE (1993): "A Long Memory Property of Stock Market Returns and a New Model," *Journal of Empirical Finance*, 1, 83–106.

DOORNIK, J. A. (2007a): *An Introduction to OxMetrics 5 - A Software System for Data Analysis and Forecasting*. Timberlake Consultant Ltd., first edn.

——— (2007b): *Ox 5.0 - An Object-oriented Matrix Programming Language*. Timberlake Consultant Ltd., first edn.

——— (2009): *An Introduction to OxMetrics 6 - A Software System for Data Analysis and Forecasting*. Timberlake Consultant Ltd., first edn.

DOORNIK, J. A., and M. OOMS (1999): "A Package for Estimating, Forecasting and Simulating Arfima Models: Arfima package 1.0 for Ox," Discussion paper, Econometric Institute, Erasmus University Rotterdam.

DUFOUR, J.-M., L. KHALAF, and M.-C. BEAULIEU (2003): "Finite-sample Diagnostics for Multivariate Regression with Applications to Linear Asset Pricing Models," Working Paper No. 06-2003, CIREQ.

ENGLE, R. (2002): "Dynamic Conditional Correlation - a Simple Class of Multivariate GARCH Models," *Journal of Business and Economic Statistics*, 20, 339–350.

ENGLE, R., and B. KELLY (2007): "Dynamic Equicorrelation," Mimeo, The Stern School, New York University.

ENGLE, R., and F. K. KRONER (1995): "Multivariate Simultaneous Generalized ARCH," *Econometric Theory*, 11, 122–150.

ENGLE, R., and S. MANGANELLI (1999): "CAViaR: conditional autoregressive Value at Risk by regression quantiles," Mimeo, San Diego, Department of Economics.

ENGLE, R., and J. MEZRICH (1996): "GARCH for Groups," *RISK*, 9, 36–40.

ENGLE, R. F. (1982): "Autoregressive Conditional Heteroscedasticity with Estimates of the Variance of United Kingdom Inflation," *Econometrica*, 50, 987–1007.

ENGLE, R. F., and T. BOLLERSLEV (1986): "Modeling the Persistence of Conditional Variances," *Econometric Reviews*, 5, 1–50.

ENGLE, R. F., and G. GONZÁLEZ-RIVERA (1991): "Semiparametric ARCH Model," *Journal of Business and Economic Statistics*, 9, 345–360.

ENGLE, R. F., and B. T. KELLY (2008): "Dynamic Equicorrelation," Mimeo, Stern School of Business.

ENGLE, R. F., D. M. LILIEN, and R. P. ROBBINS (1987): "Estimating Time Varying Risk Premia in the Term Structure: The ARCH-M Model," *Econometrica*, 55, 391–407.

ENGLE, R. F., and V. K. NG (1993): "Measuring and Testing the Impact of News on Volatility," *Journal of Finance*, 48, 1749–1778.

ENGLE, R. F., and K. SHEPPARD (2001): "Theorical and Empirical properties of Dynamic Conditional Correlation Multivariate GARCH," Mimeo, UCSD.

FAMA, E. F. (1965): "The Behaviour of Stock Market Prices," *Journal of Business*, 38, 34–105.

FERNÁNDEZ, C., and M. F. J. STEEL (1998): "On Bayesian Modelling of Fat Tails and Skewness," *Journal of the American Statistical Association*, 93, 359–371.

FIORENTINI, G., G. CALZOLARI, and L. PANATTONI (1996): "Analytic Derivatives and the Computation of GARCH Estimates," *Journal of Applied Econometrics*, 11, 399–417.

FIORENTINI, G., E. SENTANA, and G. CALZOLARI (2003): "Maximum Likelihood Estimation and Inference in Multivariate Conditionally Heteroskedastic Dynamic Regression Models with Student t Innovations," *Journal of Business and Economic Statistics*, 21, 532–546.

FRANSES, P. H., and D. VAN DIJK (2000): *Non-Linear Series Models in Empirical Finance*. Cambridge University Press, Cambridge.

GEWEKE, J. (1986): "Modeling the Persistence of Conditional Variances: A Comment," *Econometric Reviews*, 5, 57–61.

GEWEKE, J., and S. PORTER-HUDAK (1983): "The Estimation and Application of Long Memory Time Series Models," *Journal of Time Series Analysis*, 4, 221–238.

GIOT, P., and S. LAURENT (2003): "Valut-at-Risk for Long and Short Positions," *Journal of Applied Econometrics*, 18, 641–664.

GLOSTEN, L. R., R. JAGANNATHAN, and D. E. RUNKLE (1993): "On the Relation Between Expected Value and the Volatility of the Nominal Excess Return on Stocks," *Journal of Finance*, 48, 1779–1801.

GOFFE, W. L., G. D. FERRIER, and J. ROGERS (1994): "Global Optimization of Statistical Functions with Simulated Annealing," *Journal of Econometrics*, 60, 65–100.

GOURIEROUX, C. (1997): *ARCH Models and Financial Applications*. Springer Verlag, Berlin.

GRANGER, C. W. J. (1980): "Long Memory Relationships and the Aggregation of Dynamic Models," *Journal of Econometrics*, 14, 227–238.

GRANGER, C. W. J., and R. JOYEUX (1980): "An Introduction to Long-Memory Time Series Models and Fractional Differencing," *Journal of Time Series Analysis*, 1, 15–29.

HANSEN, B. E. (1994): "Autoregressive Conditional Density Estimation," *International Economic Review*, 35, 705–730.

HARVEY, A., E. RUIZ, and N. SHEPHARD (1992): "Unobservable Component Time Series Models with ARCH Disturbances," *Journal of Econometrics*, 52, 129–158.

HE, C., and TERÄSVIRTA (2002): "An Application of the Analogy Between Vector ARCH and Vector Random Coefficient Autoregressive Models," SSE/EFI Working Paper series in Economics and Finance No. 516, Stockholm School of Economics.

HE, C., and T. TERÄSVIRTA (1999): "Higher-order Dependence in the General Power ARCH Process and a Special Case," Stockholm School of Economics, Working Paper Series in Economics and Finance, No. 315.

HENDRICKS, D. (1996): "Evaluation of Value-at-Risk Models using Historical Data," *Federal Reserve Bank of New York Economic Policy Review, April 1996.*

HIGGINS, M. L., and A. K. BERA (1992): "A Class of Nonlinear ARCH Models," *International Economic Review*, 33, 137–158.

HOSKING, J. (1980): "The Multivariate Portmanteau Statistic," *Journal of American Statistical Association*, 75, 602–608.

HSIEH, D. A. (1989): "Modeling Heteroskedasticity in Daily Foreign Exchange Rates," *Journal of Business and Economic Statistics*, 7, 307–317.

HURST, H. (1951): "Long-term storage capacity of reservoirs," *Transactions of the American Society of Civil Engineers*, 116, 770–799.

JARQUE, C., and A. BERA (1987): "A Test for Normality of Observations and Regression Residuals," *International Statistical Review*, 55, 163–172.

JEANTHEAU, T. (1998): "Strong Consistency of Estimators for Multivariate ARCH models," *Econometric Theory*, 14, 70–86.

JORION, P. (1996): "Risk and Turnover in the Foreign Exchange Market," in *The Microstructure of Foreign Exchange Markets*, ed. by J. Frankel, G. Galli, and A. Giovanni. The University of Chicago Press, Chicago.

———— (2000): *Value-at-Risk: The New Benchmark for Managing Financial Risk*. McGraw-Hill, New York.

J.P.MORGAN (1996): *Riskmetrics Technical Document, 4th ed.* J.P.Morgan, New York.

KARIYA, T. (1988): "MTV Model and its Application to the Prediction of Stock Prices," in *Proceedings of the Second International Tampere Conference in Statistics*, ed. by T. Pullila, and S. Puntanen, Finland. University of Tampere.

KAROLYI, G. (1995): "A Multivariate GARCH Model of International Transmission of Stock Returns and Volatility: The Case of the United States and Canada," *Journal of Business and Economic Statistics*, 13, 11–25.

KEARNEY, C., and A. PATTON (2000): "Multivariate GARCH Modelling of Exchange Rate Volatility Transmission in the European Monetary System," *Financial Review*, 41, 29–48.

KÖNIG, H., and W. GAAB (1982): *The Advanced Theory of Statistics*, vol. 2 of *Inference and Relationships*. Haffner, New York.

KOOPMAN, S. J., N. SHEPARD, and J. A. DOORNIK (1998): "Statistical Algorithms for Models in State Space using SsfPack 2.2," *Econometrics Journal*, 1, 1–55.

KRONER, F. K., and V. K. NG (1998): "Modelling Asymmetric Comovements of Asset Returns," *The Review of Financial Studies*, 11, 817–844.

KUPIEC, P. (1995): "Techniques for Verifying the Accuracy of Risk Measurement Models," *Journal of Derivatives*, 2, 173–84.

KWIATKOWSKI, D., P. C. PHILLIPS, P. SCHMIDT, and Y. SHIN (1992): "Testing the Null of Stationarity Against the Alternative of a Unit Root: How Sure Are we that the

Economic Time Series Have a Unit Root?," *Journal of Econometrics*, 54, 159–178.

LAMBERT, P., and S. LAURENT (2000): "Modelling Skewness Dynamics in Series of Financial Data," Discussion Paper, Institut de Statistique, Louvain-la-Neuve.

———— (2001): "Modelling Financial Time Series Using GARCH-Type Models and a Skewed Student Density," Mimeo, Université de Liège.

LAURENT, S., and J.-P. PETERS (2002): "G@RCH 2.2 : An Ox Package for Estimating and Forecasting Various ARCH Models," *Journal of Economic Surveys*, 16, 447–485.

LAURENT, S., and J.-P. URBAIN (2003): "Bridging the Gap between Gauss and Ox using OXGAUSS," Forthcoming in *Journal of Applied Econometrics*.

LAWRENCE, C. T., and A. L. TITS (2001): "A Computationally Efficient Feasible Sequential Quadratic Programming Algorithm," *SIAM Journal of Optimization*, 11, 1092–1118.

LECOURT, C. (2000): "Dépendance de Court et Long Terme des Rendements de Taux de Change," *Economie et Prévision*, 5, 127–137.

LEE, S. S., and P. A. MYKLAND (2008): "Jumps in Financial Markets: A New Non-parametric Test and Jump Dynamics," *Review of Financial Studies*, 21, 2535–2563.

LEE, S. W., and B. E. HANSEN (1994): "Asymptotic Properties of the Maximum Likelihood Estimator and Test of the Stability of Parameters of the GARCH and IGARCH Models," *Econometric Theory*, 10, 29–52.

LI, W., and A. MCLEOD (1981): "Distribution of the residual autocorrelation in multivariate ARMA time series models," *Journal of the Royal Statistical Society B*, 43, 231–239.

LIEN, D., and Y. TSE (2002): "Some Recent Developments in Futures Hedging," *Journal of Economic Surveys*, 16, 357–396.

LING, S., and M. MCALEER (2002): "Stationarity and the Existence of Moments of a Family of GARCH Processes," *Journal of Econometrics*, 106, 109–117.

———— (2003): "Asymptotic Theory for a Vector ARMA-GARCH Model," *Econometric Theory*, 19, 280–310.

LO, A. (1991): "Long-term memory in stock market prices," *Econometrica*, 59, 1279–1313.

LO, A. W., and C. MACKINLAY (1988): "Stock Market Prices Do Not Follow Random Walks: Evidence from a Simple Specification Test," *Review of Financial Studies*, 1, 41–66.

LOMBARDI, M. J., and G. M. GALLO (2001): "Analytic Hessian Matrices and the Computation of FIGARCH Estimates," Manuscript, Università degli studi di Firenze.

LONGIN, F., and B. SOLNIK (1995): "Is the Correlation in International Equity Returns Constant: 1960-1990?," *Journal of International Money and Finance*, 14, 3–26.

LUMSDAINE, R. L. (1996): "Asymptotic Properties of the Quasi Maximum Likelihood Estimator in GARCH(1,1) and IGARCH(1,1) Models," *Econometrica*, 64, 575–596.

MACKINNON, J. G. (1991): *Critical Values for Cointegration Tests*in Long-Run Economic Relationships. Readings in Cointegration, Engle, R.F. and Granger, C.W.J. (Edts), pp. 267-276. Oxford (Oxford University Press).

MANDELBROT, B. (1972): "A Statistical Methodology for Non-periodic Cycles: From the Covariance to R/S Analysis," *Annals of Economic and Social Measurement*, 1, 259–290.

MARAZZI, A., and V. J. YOHAI (2004): "Adaptively truncated maximum likelihood regression with asymmetric errors," *Journal of Statistical Planning and Inference*, 122, 271–291.

MARONNA, R. A., D. R. MARTIN, and V. J. YOHAI (2006): *Robust Statistics: Theory and Methods*. Wiley.

MARTENS, M., Y.-C. CHANG, and S. J. TAYLOR (2002): "A comparison of seasonal adjustment methods when forecasting intraday volatility," *Journal of Financial Research*, 25, 283–299.

MCCULLOUGH, B. D., and H. D. VINOD (1999): "The Numerical Reliability of Econometric Software," *Journal of Economic Literature*, 37, 633–665.

MCLEOD, A. I., and W. K. LI (1983): "Diagnostic Checking ARMA Time Series Models Using Squared Residuals Autocorrelations," *Journal of Time Series Analysis*, 4, 269–273.

MINCER, J., and V. ZARNOWITZ (1969): *The Evaluation of Economic Forecasts*Economic Forecasts and Expectations. in J.Mincer, New York: National Bureau of Economic Research.

NELSON, D. B. (1991): "Conditional Heteroskedasticity in Asset Returns: a New Approach," *Econometrica*, 59, 349–370.

NELSON, D. B., and C. Q. CAO (1992): "Inequality Constraints in the Univariate GARCH Model," *Journal of Business and Economic Statistics*, 10, 229–235.

NEWEY, W. K., and D. S. STEIGERWALD (1997): "Asymptotic Bias for Quasi Maximum Likelihood Estimators in Conditional Heteroskedasticity Models," *Econometrica*, 3, 587–599.

NOCEDAL, J., and S. J. WRIGHT (1999): *Numerical Optimization*. Springer-Verlag, New York.

NYBLOM, J. (1989): "Testing for the Constancy of Parameters Over Time," *Journal of the American Statistical Association*, 84, 223–230.

PAGAN, A. (1996): "The Econometrics of Financial Markets," *Journal of Empirical Finance*, 3, 15–102.

PALM, F. C. (1996): "GARCH Models of Volatility," in *Handbook of Statistics*, ed. by G. Maddala, and C. Rao, pp. 209–240. Elsevier Science, Amsterdam.

PALM, F. C., and P. J. G. VLAAR (1997): "Simple Diagnostics Procedures for Modelling Financial Time Series," *Allgemeines Statistisches Archiv*, 81, 85–101.

PAOLELLA, M. S. (1997): "Using Flexible GARCH Models with Asymmetric Distributions," Working paper, Institute of Statistics and Econometrics Christian Albrechts University at Kiel.

PENTULA, S. G. (1986): "Modeling the Persistence of Conditional Variances: A Comment," *Econometric Reviews*, 5, 71–74.

ROBINSON, P. M., and M. HENRY (1998): "Long and Short Memory Conditional Heteroscedasticity in Estimating the Memory Parameter of Levels," Discussion paper STIDERC Econometrics EM/98/357, London School of Economics and Political Science.

ROUSSEEUW, P., and K. V. DRIESSEN (1999): "A Fast Algorithm for the Minimum Covariance Determinant Estimator," *Technometrics*, 41, 212–223.

ROUSSEEUW, P., and A. LEROY (1988): "A robust scale estimator based on the shortest half," *Statistica Neerlandica*, 42, 103–116.

SCAILLET, O. (2000): "Nonparametric Estimation and Sensitivity Analysis of Expected Shortfall," Mimeo, Université Catholique de Louvain, IRES.

SCHMIDT, P., and P. C. PHILLIPS (1992): "LM tests for a unit root in the presence of deterministic trends," *Oxford Bulletin of Economics and Statistics*, 54, 257–287.

SCHWERT, W. (1990): "Stock volatility and the crash of '87," *Review of financial Studies*, 3, 77–102.

TAYLOR, S. J. (1986): *Modelling Financial Time Series*. J. Wiley & Sons, New York.

——— (1995): *Asset Price Dynamics, Volatility, and Prediction*. Princeton University Press, Princeton.

TAYLOR, S. J., and X. XU (1997): "The incremental volatility information in one million foreign exchange quotations," *Journal of Empirical Finance*, 4, 317–340.

TEYSSIÈRE, G. (1997): "Double Long-Memory Financial Time Series," Paper presented at the ESEM, Toulouse.

TIMMERMANN, A. (2000): "Density Forecasting in Economics and Finance," *Journal of Forecasting*, 19, 120–123.

TSAY, R. S. (2002): *Analysis of Financial Time Series*. Wiley-Interscience.

TSCHERNIG, R. (1995): "Long Memory in Foreign Exchange Rates Revisited," *Journal of International Financial Markets, Institutions and Money*, 5, 53–78.

TSE, Y. (2000): "A Test for Constant Correlations in a Multivariate GARCH Model," *Journal of Econometrics*, 98, 107–127.

TSE, Y., and A. TSUI (1999): "A Note on Diagnosing Multivariate Conditional Heteroscedasticity Models," *Journal of Time Series Anaysis*, 20, 679–691.

——— (2002): "A Multivariate GARCH Model with Time-Varying Correlations," *Journal of Business and Economic Statistics*, 20, 351–362.

TSE, Y. K. (1998): "The Conditional Heteroscedasticity of the Yen-Dollar Exchange Rate," *Journal of Applied Econometrics*, 193, 49–55.

——— (2002): "Residual-based Diagnostics for Conditional Heteroscedasticity Models," *Econometrics Journal*, 5, 358–373.

VAN DER WEIDE, R. (2002): "GO-GARCH: A Multivariate Generalized Orthogonal GARCH Model," *Journal of Applied Econometrics*, 17, 549–564.

VLAAR, P. J. G., and F. C. PALM (1993): "The Message in Weekly Exchange Rates in the European Monetary System: Mean Reversion, Conditional Heteroskedasticity and Jumps," *Journal of Business and Economic Statistics*, 11, 351–360.

WEISS, A. A. (1986): "Asymptotic Theory for ARCH Models: Estimation and Testing," *Econometric Theory*, 2, 107–131.

ZAKOIAN, J.-M. (1994): "Threshold Heteroskedasticity Models," *Journal of Economic Dynamics and Control*, 15, 931–955.

Subject Index